BODY TRADE

The following essays are in honour of Gananath Obeyesekere

BODY
TRADE

Captivity, Cannibalism and Colonialism in the Pacific

Edited by
BARBARA CREED
and
JEANETTE HOORN

First published in 2001 by
Routledge in association with
Pluto Press Australia Pty Ltd

Routledge
29 West 35th St, New York, NY 1001, USA
www.routledge.ny.com

Publshed in Australia by
Pluto Press Australia Pty Ltd
Locked Bag 199, Annandale, NSW 2038, Australia

Publshed in New Zealand by
University of Otago Press
56 Union Street, Dunnedin, New Zealand

Cover design by Nada Backovic and Justin Archer
Cover painting: *Portrait of Three People from Palau,* © British Museum, Oil on Canvas,
unsigned and undated. From the collection of The Department
of Ethnography, The British Museum, London

Copyedited by Lucy Sussex

Index by Neale Towart

Typeset by Chapter 8 Pty Ltd

Printed and bound by McPherson's Printing Group

Australian Cataloguing-in-Publication Data

   Body trade: captivity, cannibalism and colonialism the Pacific

   Bibliography.
   Includes index.
   Routledge ISBN 0 415 93842 2
   Pluto Press Australia ISBN 1 86403 184 0
   University of Otago Press ISBN 1 877276 12 X

   1. Body, Human — social aspects — Australia.
   2. Body, Human — social aspects — Pacific Area.
   3. Indigenous peoples — Australia.
   4. Indigenous peoples — Pacific Area.
   5. Cannibalism. 6. Australia — Colonization.
   7. Pacific Area – Colonization.
   I. Creed, Barbara. II. Hoorn, Jeanette.

306.4

Contents

Acknowledgments

THERE ARE MANY people who provided help in the research and writing of this book who the editors and authors wish to thank. The National Library of Australia provided a Harold White Fellowship and the University of Melbourne a MacGeorge Fellowship which enabled Gananath Obeyesekere to travel to Australia to undertake research on Peter Dillon. The Ian Potter Foundation, the Faculty of Arts, the Australian Centre, University of Melbourne, and James Cook University gave generous support for the running of the Captivity Narratives and the Body Symposium (1997) at which many of the chapters in this volume were delivered as papers.

The editors wish to thank the following for permission to reproduce materials in their collections: the Australian Film Institute; the Baillieu Library, Melbourne University; the British Film Institute; Marlon Fuentes; Film Stills Archive, the Museum of Modern Art, New York; HarperCollins; the La Trobe Collection, State Library of Victoria; the Mitchell Library and Dixson Galleries, State Library of New South Wales; the National Library, Canberra; the National Museum of Australia, Canberra; the Library of the Northern Territory; the John Oxley Library, Brisbane; Screen Sound Australia; the University of Wollongong Archives, University of Wollongong.

Individuals to whom special thanks are due include: Patrick Wolfe; Mrs Honore Forster; Mr Graeme Powell of the National Library of Australia; Sandra Burt, Australian Manuscripts Librarian, National Library of Australia; Amiria Salmond of the Gisborne Museum, New Zealand; Sylviane Jacquemin and Isabelle Guy of the Musée National des arts d'Afrique et d'Océanie, Paris; Marie-Claire Bataille Benguigui of the Musée de l'Homme, Paris; and Harry Persaud, Department of Ethnography, British Museum.

Special thanks are due to the team who worked on putting the manuscript together: our editor Lucy Sussex for her wonderfully trained 'eye' and excellent suggestions; and our research assistant Fiona Villella for her expertise and tireless support. Their enthusiasm and labour made the book a much better one than it would otherwise have been. We are particularly grateful to Tony Moore and Kate Florance at Pluto Press who supported the project from the beginning.

We wish to thank the following individuals for their help in many different ways: Theo Hoorn; Laleen Jayamanne; Mark Nicholls; Ranjini Obeyesekere; Alan Oldfield; Nikos Papastergiardis; Ian Sheil; Deborah Thomas; Michele Velik; Stuart McIntyre. A special thanks is due to Kay Hoorn, who identified the Mozart piano sonata from which Jedda plays in Chauvel's film of the same name.

A different version of Sue Martin's chapter (first delivered at the Captivity Narratives and the Body Symposium) appears in the forthcoming book, *Captive and Free: Colonial Incarceration,* edited by G. E. Harper, Cassell, 2001, by mutual permission. Paul Lyons' chapter was first published in *Inside/Out,* a collection of essays edited by Rob Wilson and Vilsoni Hereniko (Rowan & Littlefield 1998). The editors wish to thank Rowan & Littlefield for permission to republish the essay. Some material in Julie Carr's chapter (first delivered at the Captivity Narratives and the Body Symposium) also appears in her book, *The Captive White Woman of Gippsland: In Pursuit of the Legend*, Melourne University Press, Carlton, 2001.

We are indebted to the Australian Research Council for a grant which made our research possible.

Foreword

SINCE I WAS disappointed not to be able to attend the symposium for Gananath Obeyesekere on which this book is based, it's a particular honour to be asked to become the book's first reader and to offer the first comments on its contents. The editors' Introduction will explain the book's structure and describe its chapters in some detail: as a foretaste of their more substantial account, I'll merely offer a very personal indication of some of the pleasure and instruction that readers can expect to find.

I certainly don't write as an expert on the Pacific materials which form the subject matter of *Body Trade*, but it may be appropriate enough for somebody who works on the Caribbean to write about a book which features so prominently the topic of cannibalism — a word etymologically cognate with 'Caribbean'. In addition, several years ago I organised a symposium at the University of Essex at which Obeyesekere gave the second of his detailed deconstructions of cannibal stories, the third of which takes centre stage in *Body Trade*.[1] Obeyesekere's long-running dispute with Marshall Sahlins about the interpretation of the events leading up to the death of Captain Cook at the hands of Hawaiians in 1779 has become one of the set pieces of post-colonial studies. Arguably, however, his incredibly detailed readings of cannibal stories (also often against the grain of Sahlins's deployment of them in his historical anthropology) are even more emblematic of that important strain of post-colonial work which brings together literary analysis, historical contextualisation, and anthropological understanding in truly interdisciplinary fashion to unpick a set of colonial 'truths'. What marks all three of Obeyesekere's cannibal pieces is an alertness to the social dynamics of the various cultural encounters that produced the cannibal 'evidence': he knows just how to read what Paul Lyons calls 'the poetics of "witness"'.[2] Obeyesekere's essay in this book is especially impressive for its development of the connection between the cannibal story and the 'narrative of the self' — that autobiographical strategy which tends to seduce the reader through 'the power of eye-witness narrative couched in the language of verisimilitude'.[3]

Peter Dillon, the subject of Obeyesekere's paper, claimed to have been born in Martinique, previously a stronghold of the Carib people whose name became synonymous with cannibalism, although Martinique seems to feature in his story as a link to the Franco-Irish aristocratic family resident there, who were connected through marriage to the Empress Josephine.[4] Dillon's possibly imaginative trajectory from the Caribbean to Ireland to the Pacific to the Indian subcontinent is one small example of the truly global relationships that began to develop after European settlement of Australia and the Pacific islands in the second half of the eighteenth century: the careers of individual soldiers and scientists and administrators could subsequently expect to unfold all around the world. Even more noticeably, relative improvements in transportation meant that commodities, including people, could now be moved more easily around the globe. The vast and tragic saga of indigenous people brought forcibly to Europe and the U.S. between Columbus's kidnapping of Caribs in 1493 and the last colonial expositions of the 1950s continues to be pieced together, and to form the subject of reflections such as Marlon Fuentes's *Bontoc Eulogy*, a piece of auto-ethnographic film-making which tells of his unsuccessful attempt to find traces of his grandfather, a Filipino Igorot taken to St Louis to form part of the Louisiana Purchase Exposition of 1904 (St Louis World Fair). Jeanette Hoorn's chapter about *Bontoc Eulogy* blends discussion of the Fair with a subtle placing of the film in relation to more mainstream films with colonial themes, such as *Out of Africa* and *The Scent of Green Papaya*.

As Hoorn points out, *Bontoc Eulogy* is about what we have to call a 'reverse' captivity narrative — in recognition that the phrase 'captivity narrative' has long been captured to designate the distinctly minority experience of whites, usually white women, held captive by non-Europeans. Much of the discussion of captivity narratives has focused on American examples, but the Australian ones are just as resonant, especially the phantasmagoric 'White Woman of Gipps Land', who appears in two chapters of *Body Trade*. The Tasmanian romance, *Younâh!*, the subject of Susan Martin's chapter, demonstrates how useful the captivity theme is for fictional explorations of cross-cultural issues, even though the chapter's final revelation places this theme as firmly subordinate to the developing touristic impulse.

A comment in one of Paul Turnbull's earlier essays had already alerted me to the fact that the trade in indigenous skulls formed a particular link between the Pacific and the Caribbean: if the *Bounty* had completed its voyage as planned, it would have carried Australian Aboriginal skulls along with the breadfruit plants from Tahiti to the island of St Vincent. After unloading the breadfruit, it would have had added to its cargo the skull of a Carib chief dug up at dead of night from a sacred burial place by Alexander Anderson, the Scottish botanist who ran the botanical garden in St Vincent and who had as his patron Sir Joseph Banks.[5] In *Body Trade* Turnbull continues his intriguing history of early Australian science, this time arguing the need to understand the kind of hold that phrenology had on scientific thinking in the early nineteenth century. Like Chris Healy's essay on breastplates, which follows, Turnbull manages to find a sensitive voice in which to discuss a pressing contemporary issue at the same time as emphasising the need for a better historical understanding of outmoded ideas, which are all too easy to dismiss as pseudo-science.

All I've had the opportunity to do here is to comment on the first essays in each of *Body Trade*'s four sections: all four set the tone for the equally fine essays that follow them. Taken as a whole, *Body Trade* offers an example of some of the best current work in postcolonial studies, work which is now beginning to combine imaginative textual reading with careful archival study. This combination often produces the spark of original phrases, the kind that readers want to take away and ponder and make use of in their own work, phrases like 'native theatricality' or 'reauthenticate the environment'.[6] These are just small tokens of what can be drawn from this exciting collection.

Peter Hulme
Professor of Literature
University of Essex

Introduction

I N A CORNER of the Student's Reading Room of the Department of Ethnography (formerly the Museum of Mankind) in the British Museum hangs a painting of three people from the Pacific. Represented loosely within the convention of the Three Graces, the trio is striking and unique. The central figure is sexually ambiguous. Unlike the accompanying figures, s/he is naked. A suggestion of hermaphroditism is achieved through an ambiguity of signifiers — a feminine face, phallic spear, penis, small breasts. The painting disturbs because it seems to undermine the classical image of the Three Graces as one of consolidated femininity while asserting a difference, one grounded in a play of generic familiarity and racial and sexual otherness. As in the classical tradition of the Three Graces, the identity of the black three graces is unknown. The British Museum has very little information about the picture, which is thought to have been painted by the Chinese painter known as Spoilum.[1] This artist painted in Macau in the late eighteenth century; he was one of the first Chinese artists to paint in a western style. The subject of the painting is thought to be three people from the Palau Islands who were taken captive by a Russian sea captain and landed in Macau. Further research into the painting has revealed almost nothing.

As with so many texts about captivity, this image is marked by anonymity, ambiguity and loss. Who were these people? Why is one painted as a hermaphrodite? Where were they going? What was their fate? Why did the trade in bodies produce such enigmatic texts? We have chosen this image for the cover of *Body Trade* because it raises all of these questions. Like the hermaphroditic body in the painting, the body of the black captive fascinated its white captors because it signified otherness as a mystery — something to be conquered and captured, its 'primitiveness' transformed into a more civilised, known, identifiable form. Captive peoples who resisted such changes were frequently put on display in circuses and fairs, living testimonials to what was thought to be their immutable difference and hence inferiority. *Body Trade* explores the image of the captive body in a variety of contexts in order to re-examine myths about captivity, cannibalism and colonialism in a range of texts and practices in Australia and the Pacific. The central site for this exploration is the body itself.

In theoretical debates of the past two decades, much has been written about the body — the gendered body, the decorated body, the desiring body, the abject body, and the politicised body. These discussions have proven central to debates in psychoanalysis, feminism, queer theory, post-colonial writings, the cinema, literature and the visual arts. In many of these discourses the notion of the subjugated, captive body has emerged as a central construct in relation to debates about the body. For instance, in feminist theory, the captive female body is related to concepts of patriarchal power, female disenfranchisement and sexual slavery; in post-colonial theory, slavery assumes a central theoretical place in terms of the history of the colonised indigenous other; in psychoanalytic writings the master/slave relationship is aligned to notions of sadism and masochism; in writings on spectatorship, the look has been conceptualised as a 'controlling gaze'; and in theories of narrativity, the spectator/reader has been posited as 'captive' of the text. Notions of captivity and imprisonment are also fundamental to Foucault's writings about the nature of power and the ambiguous way in which it is exercised by and between individuals caught up in relations of power and powerlessness.

Drawing on contemporary theories about the body, this book uses the concept of 'body trade' as a means of re-reading traditionally racist, sexist and Eurocentric views about race relations in the Pacific from the time of early European contact to the present. A further aim is to demonstrate the relevance of feminist and psychoanalytic theory for post-colonial theory, which, with the exception of the writings of scholars such as Homi Bhabha and Michael Taussig, often ignores the crucial areas of desire and the unconscious. *Body Trade* is also indebted to Henry Reynolds, whose pioneering work on the history of race relations in Australia has inspired a number of the chapters.

This book uses the concept of body trade to bring together the many inter-related ways in which the indigenous body has been marked and exploited by colonial practices. The various chapters address issues of racism, sexism and post-coloniality in relation to a range of Pacific nations such as Australia, New Guinea, New Zealand, Fiji, the Marquesas Islands, New Caledonia, the Philippines, Indonesia and Korea. *Body Trade* is the first book to theorise the body in relation to the colonial histories of Australia and the Pacific. Its themes include: cannibalism and the nineteenth-century trade in heads in the Pacific; the holding of indigenous women by white colonisers; mythic tales of the real/imaginary capture of white women by black others; the touring and display of native peoples in circuses throughout Europe and America; and the representation of the colonised/captive body in literature, photography, painting and film. The conventionally understood captivity narrative, namely stories about the holding of white women captive by indigenous people in a frontier context, is revisited and the definition of the term broadened to include a range of circumstances involving the captivity of indigenous people. The essays also explore, in more detail than has been possible in the past, the politics of contact in the Pacific during the period 1770–2000, through such themes as friendship and betrayal, disavowal and ambivalence and the making of the exotic/erotic body.

The essays are divided into four sections. The first, 'Circus, Trade & Spectacle', deals with the trade in human heads in the Pacific; the 'gift' of breastplates by white colonisers to Australian Aborigines; the exhibition of Polynesian 'cannibals' in France; and a series of paintings depicting members of the Australian Native Mounted Police. All of the chapters in this section examine different ways in which the bodies of indigenous subjects (through trade, display, the wearing of colonial artefacts) are used by colonial cultures to advance their discourse about the superiority of white civilisation while simultaneously attempting to supplant indigenous culture with its own.

The early circulation of heads, their arrival in centres of learning and the development of craniology and other pseudo-sciences in nineteenth-century England and Europe was an important tool in the circulation and consolidation of imperial power. From the first visit of Captain Cook to New Zealand the officers and crew were interested in the collection of artefacts and these included Maori heads. On his second visit (1772–1775) the effects of these demands were already being felt among the native population. Reinhold Foster reports that because 'artefacts' were scarce in the area, native people raided other tribes in order to 'possess themselves of those things which are so coveted by the Europeans'. Interest in the construction of the Pacific as a site of unspeakable horrors led to the emergence of cannibalism as a trope in travel writing and fiction. The pseudo-scientific and literary representation of so-called abject primitive practices, however, reveals more about the culture that produced written texts about the 'other' than it does about the cultures themselves.

Paul Turnbull's opening chapter examines the scientific interest in the bones of Aboriginal peoples and demonstrates how this interest led to widespread desecration of traditional burial places and in some instances to the illegal procurement of remains. By the 1860s, many European museums and universities had become the site of scientific work focused on re-interpreting the nature of human origins in the light of evolutionary theories. A consequence of this interest in mapping the course of human prehistory was that the bodies of Australian Aboriginal people took on different meanings and value. The morphological peculiarities of Australian skulls and skeletons were viewed as a crucial source of information about the relation of modern Europeans to what were thought to be very ancient and primitive forms of humanity.

In the hands of European anatomists, the remains of Aboriginal people were, as Turnbull argues, made to perform acts of ventriloquism in so far as they were used by anthropologists to justify their belief in the primitive nature of Aboriginal ways and — as a consequence — the inevitability of the expropriation of their traditional lands by so-called superior peoples. Often the testimony generated through a study of Aboriginal remains made explicit the violent entanglement between science and colonialism in nineteenth-century Australia. Turnbull's chapter documents the surviving utterances of collectors, revealing how they were caught up in a system of exploitation and were forced to resolve as best they could the conflicting claims of morality, ambition and the needs of science.

Chris Healy's chapter 'Chained to their signs: remembering breastplates' examines the political and cultural uses of photographs of Aboriginal people wearing breastplates conferred upon them by the colonial invaders. The first appearance of breastplates in Australia is officially recorded in 1815. These were granted by Governor Lachlan Macquarie to Aboriginal people 'willing to abide by a proclamation which had outlawed armed individuals or groups of six or more from coming within a mile of any town, village or farm occupied by British subjects'. As Healy recounts, Aboriginal men who contravened this law could be shot. Macquarie decreed that their bodies should be hung 'on the highest trees and in the clearest parts of the forest'. Aboriginal men who obeyed the ruling were granted a 'passport' that offered some protection. The practice of conferring breastplates persisted in all states in Australia except Tasmania and South Australia until the 1930s. Healy's argument that the breastplates also acted as a signifier of a genocide-to-come brings his piece to a powerful conclusion.

Yves Le Fur, in the third chapter, examines the arrival of the first Polynesian peoples into France. How can one be Oceanian? This question embodies the responses of Europeans who for the first time came face to face with 'the physical reality of exotic bodies' coming from the South Pacific. Le Fur argues that the case of the first Polynesians arriving in Europe is important because they were presented more or less as 'consenting guests'. Their tattooed bodies inspired engravings, drawings and paintings and exerted a profound influence on the evolution of contemporary thought, which ranged from wonderment to repulsion.

A journalist and author of several publications about New Caledonia described his visit to the village of Kanak in the Colonial Exhibition of 1931. Frightened to approach the 'eaters of men', his fear turned to surprise when he recognised some Kanaks, whom he knew to be educated men working in such French trades as printing. The presence of fake cannibals in the form of shop mannequins in the Musée de L'Artillerie, and in the Trocadero in Paris, enhanced the general impression that it was possible to observe, in a leisurely way, dangerous bodies supposedly capable of swallowing the spectator. Le Fur's chapter draws attention not only to the practice of exhibiting the so-called 'primitive' body but also to the voyeurism of the so-called civilised European spectator whose curiosity involved a different but equally central form of racism based on codes of looking.

In the final chapter of the first section, Mary Mackay examines a perverse aspect of the history of black and white relations in nineteenth-century Australia, that of the Native Mounted Police Corps and their representation in the paintings, postcards and drawings of the period. In embracing and operating under a power system that was remote in every sense from tribal values and rules, the native police upset the stereotype of 'primitive' or 'savage' constructed by the white settlers and entered a space where their cultural identity was rendered ambivalent. Frequent hostile confrontations with members of warring clans contributed to their difficult position as black troopers enforcing white rule. The result of these encounters often left members of the Corps in a political no-man's-land where they were scorned by blacks as turncoats and criticised by the whites as taking on the trappings of a cultural code in conflict with their own. Their interaction with European-based society and their zeal in exerting authority in situations of wrongdoing was often misinterpreted by white offenders, and contributed further to the perversity of their situation. In taking on the trappings of whiteness, their new 'white' identity was expressed through a form of mimicry. Mackay, however, argues that despite the public statements issued by the colonial culture about assimilation — the Native Police offering an instance of this — a close study of the representations (paintings, photographs, drawing) of the period reveals that the police were more captive than captors and that the colonial intentions underlying their creation were racist.

The second section, 'Manufacturing the "Cannibal" Body', examines the different ways in which Europeans constructed — consciously or otherwise — the myth of the 'cannibal' through journals, literature and other forms of story-telling in order to represent indigenous people as primitive savages. The authors in this section also draw attention to the voyeuristic nature of European interest in cannibalism. The opening chapter is central to the project of this book. It is written by Gananath Obeyesekere, whose groundbreaking research, which has led to a reconceptualisation of the origins, meaning and — in some instances — the very existence of cannibalism, is fundamental to the theoretical approaches which inform *Body Trade*. Obeyesekere wrote his chapter, 'Narratives of the self: Chevalier Peter Dillon's Fijian cannibal adventures', while in Australia where he was able to access a range of key primary sources. His work has provided the impetus and inspiration for this collection of chapters which all — in different degrees — seek to re-read the past and the processes of myth-making to which indigenous peoples have been subjected by the colonising powers of the western world. Many of these chapters were first presented as papers in a symposium held on Magnetic Island in September 1997 in his honour.

Obeyesekere's chapter re-examines the writings of, and about, Peter Dillon, who was the first seaman to describe in detail a 'cannibal feast', which he claimed to have witnessed in Fiji in 1813. The chapter interrogates the way in which Dillon created himself as the hero of an adventure story in which he does battle with a horde of terrifying cannibals who capture, cook and devour his companions. Starting from the position that the act of cannibalism itself is a mythic construct, Obeyesekere subjects the texts of a number of authors, who lauded Dillon as a hero of the high seas, to meticulous scrutiny. His essay is a carefully woven piece of detective work replete with logic, suspense and wit revealing that the verisimilitude of eyewitness accounts — particularly of ritual events such as a cannibal feast — is an 'ethnographic deception'. He writes that 'perfect verisimilitude is only possible in invented accounts or fiction'. Obeyesekere demonstrates how the fabrication of a narrative and the invention of the self are inextricably linked. This concept, of course, can be extended to include the fabrication and/or distortion of events and the invention of the nation, specifically the colonising nations of the western world. In the act of invention — whether of self or nation — the 'other' is invariably stereotyped as an abject being, a threat to the so-called superior values and moral standards of the colonising power.

In the second chapter in this section, Robert Dixon examines cannibal references in the writings of Ion L. Idriess. Between 1933 and 1950 Idriess wrote four exceedingly popular books about white people captured by headhunters in the Torres Strait — *Drums of Mer* (1933), *Headhunters of the Coral Sea* (1940), *Isles of Despair* (1947) and *The Wild White Man of Badu* (1950). He drew his information partly from Islander informants, partly from A. C. Haddon's *Reports of the Cambridge Anthropological Expedition to Torres Straits* (1904–35). These in turn, as Dixon points out, were based on interviews and transcripts supplied to Haddon by his Islander informants in the 1880s. This network of appropriations is revealing about the nature of colonial textuality. Idriess', books about cannibalism are themselves cannibalised from a variety of other textual material, much of it stolen from Islander sources. Dixon's chapter provides a new way of looking at fiction which draws on the colonial arena by focusing attention on the importance of language and original source material tracing the genealogies of myth.

Paul Lyons examines Herman Melville's *Typee*, demonstrating ways in which, in shifting the focus from cannibals to his own fear of being devoured, Melville critiques the discourse of cannibalism that he saw circulating through early texts of Pacific exploration and exchange. At several points during *Typee*, Melville refers to the central character, Tommo, as having been 'consumed' by 'fearful apprehensions'. As Lyons argues, 'the pun on "consume" makes literal the link between cannibalism and fear', but Melville is trapped by his own critique, even as he attempts to expose the ways in which the Euro-American gaze of this period seems almost unavoidably held by a series of potentially phantasmal perceptions. Melville manages as well to suggest some of the relays from the cultural to the political, from Robinson Crusoe's imagined massacres of cannibals to the actual loathing and massacre of cannibals in Wilkes's narrative of the American expedition. Lyons' chapter offers a powerful analysis of the ways in which an author's own anxieties, in this instance, anxieties surrounding cannibalism, can subtly influence the creative activities of observation and writing.

The third section, entitled 'Captive White Bodies & the Colonial Imaginary in "Terra Australis"', examines the emergence of captivity narratives in Australia in newspaper reports, documentary accounts and fiction. Susan K. Martin explores Mrs W. I. Thrower's *Younâh!: A Tasmanian Aboriginal Romance of the Cataract Gorge* (1894), an obscure novel which tells the story of a white heiress kidnapped and raised by Tasmanian Aboriginal people. In *Younâh* a narrative ostensibly sympathetic to the situation of Aboriginal people ultimately works to replace them with 'better' versions of themselves in a reconfigured landscape. The novel's elegaic treatment of Tasmanian peoples comfortably post-dates the period when they were regarded as supposedly 'extinct' and by reinforcing this in its pseudo-historical narrative, *Younâh*, for all its well-meaning rhetoric, is also complicit in the ongoing dispossession and disavowal of Aborigines.

Julie Carr's chapter examines the popular stories surrounding the White Woman of Gippsland. In December 1840, pioneering settler Angus McMillan's sighting of a white female 'captive' among the Kurnai in Gippsland appeared in the *Sydney Morning Herald*. Rumors of the 'captive' woman continued to surface periodically over the next few years and in 1846 a public meeting was held in Melbourne and a publicly-funded expedition was sent in quest of her. The imagined plight of a genteel, Christian, white woman held in thrall by 'savages' provided the colonists of Port Phillip with salacious reading, an opportunity for point-scoring against the government and a pretext for heroic endeavour. Carr investigates how anxieties about possession of the female body, cannibalism and miscegenation, projected onto the Kurnai, fed racist views which validated the expropriation of Kurnai land by European settlers and speculators. Her discussion of the way in which racist discourses intersect with those of gender offers a powerful way of re-reading the narrative of the White Woman of Gipps Land.

Kate Darian-Smith's chapter examines the role of material culture in stories about captivity. The history of the White Woman of Gipps Land — the most fully documented captivity narrative of colonial Australia — can be traced through expedition journals, official papers, newspapers, fictional accounts and folklore. It can also be told through objects: the items of personal property listed in the *Sydney Morning Herald* letter; the mirrors and handkerchiefs bearing messages for the white woman distributed throughout Gippsland; and the wooden ship's figurehead of Britannia which was eventually located by one of the search parties. This chapter explores the meanings of both European and Aboriginal material culture in circumscribing the white captivity experience in Australia through examining the use of objects and signs in the White Woman of Gippsland narrative and comparing it to a different set of objects associated with the death of Mary Watson in colonial Queensland forty years later. Darian-Smith's chapter examines the details of material culture — signs too frequently overlooked in critical discourse — to offer a complex and fascinating study of the popular colonial narrative of captive women.

The final section, 'Film, Desire & the Colonised Body', explores the representation of colonial subjects in both documentary and fiction films. Jeanette Hoorn examines Marlon Fuentes' documentary, *Bontoc Eulogy*, in which the director, through the strategies of auto-ethnography, presents a narrative of his life as a Filipino living in America. This present-day narrative is produced in relationship to the taking of his grandfather Marcod from the Philippines and his display in the Filipino pavilion of the St Louis World Fair, along with more than one thousand other Filipino people. Representatives from a range of ethnicities were exhibited according to a kind of evolutionary ladder, from what was perceived to be the most primitive to the most civilised. The film uses original footage from the period not only of the Filipino people on display but also the so-called civilised Americans strolling through the villages of the exposition subjecting the 'other' to a curious and superior gaze. Fuentes uses melancholia as a trope for his narrative, painfully enacting both his loss and that of the Philippines as an independent nation. Through a series of inversions of mainstream filmic structures, he interrogates the project of colonialism and its representation in popular culture as well as the culture of the museum.

In a re-reading of Charles Chauvel's *Jedda* (1955), Barbara Creed identifies the film as a stolen generations story told through and disguised by the trope of a reverse captivity narrative. Creed traces the film's interest in representing Jedda's captivity in the context of a morality tale — the pastoralist family's quest to rescue Jedda from her own people ('the dirty little monkeys') and transform her into a 'white' girl in line with the controversial assimilationist policies of the day. The second captivity story — a classic captivity narrative — is about Jedda's abduction by Marbuk, a renegade Aborigine. As Jedda matures into a young woman, she finds herself torn between two cultures. Her unspoken desire to return to her own people is brought into sharp focus when she encounters Marbuk, a 'rogue' male who is in trouble with his own people and with the police, for stealing women. Sexually attracted to Marbuk, who is represented in the film as an exotic black 'other', Jedda at first responds freely to his overtures but then finds herself taken captive and forced to flee with him into the bush. The film explores the theme of eroticism and sexual captivity in relation to Jedda's ambivalent response to Marbuk's appeal. The chapter argues that, although the ending of *Jedda* is problematic and open to a number of interpretations, it nonetheless draws on the classic captivity tale with its themes of sexuality and eroticism to cover over the story of Jedda's original captivity and suffering as one of the stolen generations.

The history and current plight of the Korean 'comfort women' as depicted in such film texts as *The Murmuring* is considered by Freda Freiberg in the final chapter. Freiberg documents the provision of comfort women for the Japanese military forces stationed in the Pacific and on the Asian mainland during World War II, involving the organisation and administration of an elaborate network of 'comfort stations' over a vast area. The problem of the staffing of these stations with adequate numbers of comfort women was solved by resorting to the abduction, rape, incarceration and forced labour of women of many different nationalities. This persuasively argued chapter explores the personal, political and aesthetic issues involved in the representation of this hitherto hidden history, after fifty years of silence, with particular reference to documentary productions made in China, Korea, the Philippines, Japan, New Guinea and Australia. The story of the comfort women is one of enduring shame — for their captors.

The Editors

Part I:
Circus, Trade
& Spectacle

Chapter 1

'Rare work amongst the professors': the capture of indigenous skulls within phrenological knowledge in early colonial Australia
Paul Turnbull

E ARLY IN April 1829, a satire appeared in the *Sydney Gazette*. It took the form of a letter, addressed to 'Jeremiah Bumpkin', supposedly a leading member of the settlement's new phrenological society. In the letter, a business proposition was put to Bumpkin by one 'Jack Sprat, Esquire, of Chuckabiddy Lane, London', wholesaler of fake tomahawks and adulterated gunpowder to traders of a mind to swindle Amerindian and Oceanic peoples.

Of the various stings in the satire, the most pointed was Sprat's portrayal of Sydney's phrenologists as dupes, or worse, men whose professed scientific interest in procuring and examining Australian indigenous skulls masked a ghoulish desire to generate and profit from a 'free trade in skulls, black and white, red and raw'. 'We have as much right', declared Sprat, 'to an honest penny by the outside of the skulls of heathens, as others by adorning the inside of the same', imploring Bumpkin to secure him as many of the skulls of the natives of New South Wales as he could. Sprat wrote:

> They are buried somewhere in the bush, and it will not be diffi-
> cult for a drop o' bool to find them out. I have been advised to
> send out some rum for distribution among the living, in which
> case some specimens might be obtained. But not to speak of the
> questionable morality of the act, I find it will be too expensive.[1]

Expropriation of land, social anomie, alcoholism and violence made it a ripe time for traffic in skulls. 'For depend on it', urged Sprat, 'in this science, there is nothing like a skull well heightened and hal-lowed, and as every blow of the waddie must deepen some depression, or flatten some organ, we shall have rare work amongst the professors'.

This was not the first time phrenology had been ridiculed in the colonial press. Over the decade prior to 1829 a number of satires by metropolitan critics of the science had been recycled in Sydney and Hobart newspapers. Yet, what distinguished the letter to Jeremiah Bumpkin was its targeting of phrenological interest in disclosing the cerebral origins of what champions of the science assumed were the intellectual and cultural peculiarities of the indigenous peoples of Australia.

Bumpkin and Sprat were fictional persona, but by the end of the 1820s a small number of colonial phrenologists had plundered indigenous burial places for skulls — 'rare work' which critics could exploit through the pages of the conservative *Gazette*.

From the early 1820s until well into the 1840s, the premium placed on Australian indigenous skulls in phrenological investigations of racial difference was the principal cause of deliberate desecration of burial places. Even so, archives of museums and anatomy schools reveal that prior to the 1840s only a small number of collectors tracked down skulls, and then were concerned to justify the morality of their opening of Aboriginal burial places. In the information they supplied together with the skulls, no collector mirrored Sprat's callousness. He had no regard for the disruption of life-ways and ill-health that so often followed the expropriation of indigenous country. Further, in their heyday, Britain's largest phrenological collections were those assembled by James Deville, a London-based dealer in phrenological casts, and George Mackenzie, curator of the museum of the Edinburgh Phrenological Society. Neither Deville nor the Edinburgh society could boast more than half a dozen indigenous Australian remains. By the early 1850s, Britain's largest collection of non-European skeletal material lay in the Royal College of Surgeons, a centre of anti-phrenological opinion. It contained only five Australian skeletons, some twenty-three skulls and skull fragments, and nine Palawa (Tasmanian) skulls.

Around the time of the Bumpkin-Sprat satire there were rumours that phrenologists were beneficiaries of frontier violence. In October 1827, some fifteen months before the establishment of the Sydney Phrenological Society, the *Australian* newspaper reported — though not without registering disbelief — that the following commentary had appeared in an English newspaper:

> The Sydney papers notice a new export from the Colony, a great phrenologist having sent to England twenty heads of the Aborigines, who had lately fallen in a skirmish with the settlers in the interior.[2]

The Reverend Lancelot Threlkeld, who for many years minis-
tered to the Awabakal people at Lake Macquarie, made similar accu-
sations, in reminiscences written for the Sydney *Christian Herald*
between 1852–1858. He claimed to have been told by a magistrate
at Bathurst that, during the conflict between local settlers and
Wiradjuri in the mid-1820s, some forty people had been driven
into a billabong and shot, and their heads boiled down for phrenological specimens.[3]

Yet, there is no evidence that such relatively large numbers of
skulls were systematically procured in the aftermath of frontier violence. The value of such collections in the eyes of phrenologists
would have ensured the survival of catalogues and comment. News
of skulls changing owners rarely figure in the surviving private correspondence of leading phrenological collectors. Australian and
Tasmanian skulls appear very infrequently in the catalogues regularly printed by the many natural history dealers and auctioneers in
the first half of the nineteenth century whose business extended to
catering for metropolitan and colonial phrenological communities.

My aim in this chapter, however, is not to tally the number of
skulls that found their way into collections. Even if in recent times
the magnitude of the outrage against the indigenous dead has been
exaggerated, this in no way excuses us for neglecting the significance of what was done with those remains, which became entangled within phrenological discourse.[4] Indeed, as I show in this chapter, in New South Wales between 1815 and 1830 the knowledge
produced through phrenological examination of what, by comparison with post-Darwinian interest in indigenous remains, were a
small number of crania, was a significant determinant of how the
nature, origins and destiny of indigenous peoples were viewed
amongst the colonial elite.

Historians interested in the play of racial thought in shaping
indigenous settler relations in nineteenth-century Australia have
found it hard to take phrenology seriously. Despite its popularity, and
the fact that it enjoyed the support of leading figures within contemporary British scientific circles, phrenology has been explained light-
ly and none too well as a seductive species of quackery, a pseudo-science, or perhaps even a form of secular religiosity. Its core theoretical
assumptions about the correspondences between mental qualities and
head shape have been treated as an embarrassing cultural anachro-
nism, or mentioned in passing in studies of nineteenth-century racial
thought as a tragic example of how forcefully colonial ambition overpowered and biased observation of the human condition.

However, as Roger Cooter has persuasively argued,[5] the intellectual products and practices of phrenology were far more influential, subtle and pervasive within British culture during the course of the nineteenth century than we have hitherto appreciated. Cooter has shown how, in various ways, phrenology captured the imagination because it was understood to be grounded in the same modes of knowing and experimental procedures as those privileged and replicated within contemporary communities of physical, natural and social scientists. Moreover, it was seen by many as a science that, through the concerted application of its core truths, would bring a new degree of scientific accuracy to both the natural and civil history of humanity.

For historians of racial thought in colonial Australia there is much to be learnt by exploring how phrenological knowledge informed metropolitan and colonial perceptions of Australian indigenous peoples. The period between about 1815 and the early 1830s saw the emergence and popularity of phrenological mapping of non-western skulls in British metropolitan centres and various spheres of colonial ambition. Examinations of indigenous crania were undertaken with implicit faith in phrenology's core tenet that the mind was the sum of discrete mental faculties produced by specific cerebral 'organs'; but these investigations differed significantly in terms of what investigators believed they had established.

In no respect did the conclusions phrenologists drew differ more widely than in their assessments of the capacity or otherwise of indigenous peoples to embrace civilisation. Phrenological examination, to some, proved that the capacity of Australia's indigenous peoples for civilisation was much decayed, but still capable of resuscitation through education and paternal guidance.[6] For others, the shape of the Aboriginal head confirmed the impossibility of ever bringing about their inclusion within settler society. In short, the history of the uses of indigenous skulls in phrenological hands serves to illustrate that the new cerebral science was the product of its culture.

What follows is a contextualised study of what three men active in early colonial intellectual circles made of indigenous cranial morphology. I first examine the skull-collecting activities of Alexander Berry, a leading colonial entrepreneur and pastoralist. I draw attention to Berry's involvement in the short-lived Australasian Philosophical Society — traditionally seen as New South Wales's first formally constituted scientific society — before examining the phrenologically inspired ethnographic musings of another member of the Society, Barron Field, a colonial jurist, poet and would-be natural historian of humanity. I suggest that Berry and Field's interest in indigenous skulls needs to be seen in the context of contemporary British antiquarianism. They were concerned to bring antiquarian practices to bear on the study of the origins of indigenous societies. At the same time, they sought to make antiquarianism truly scientific by grounding it in the core truths of phrenology. Finally, I show how this desire to re-fashion antiquarian practice informed the exhumation of indigenous graves by John Oxley, Colonial Surveyor and explorer, who was also a member of the Australasian Philosophical Society.

At various points in this exploration, I will illuminate the historically situated complexities, and differences, in how these men viewed Australian ancestral remains. Yet, at the same time, I want to show how the knowledge they generated through examination of the indigenous dead was nonetheless a product of their belief that phrenology would resolve a colonial question of the late 1820s: what, ultimately, was the destiny of indigenous Australians in relation to the expansion of settler society?

Alexander Berry: 'laird of the Shoalhaven and phrenologist'

By the early 1820s, phrenology had captured the imagination of many newly graduated surgeons and physicians employed on naval, convict and trading vessels, or holding military or civilian posts in New South Wales. Probably the most influential early colonial champion of the science was Alexander Berry (1781–1873). Berry was a former East India Company surgeon who by the early 1820s had established himself as a leading New South Wales merchant and landholder. His involvement in the procurement of indigenous remains can be traced to 1819, although it was his 1827 desecration of the grave of Arawarra, an elder of the Wadi Wadi people, that provides the best starting point from which to understand Berry's phrenological ambitions.

Some time in 1824–5 Arawarra returned to die in his ancestral country on the lower Shoalhaven River, beneath the mountain he and his people called Cooloomgatta. The frail old man found his country in the possession of the white men Alexander Berry and his business partner Edward Wollstonecraft, who had established in 1822 a thriving timber business in the densely forested Shoalhaven, and cleared with convict labour several hundred acres of Wadi Wadi land for cereal crops, cattle and pigs.

Arawarra died within two days of returning and was buried in accordance with Wadi Wadi tradition deep in sand dunes near the mouth of the Shoalhaven. Yet his re-incorporation within the land lasted at most a mere three years. In August 1827, Berry wrote, from the homestead he had built in the shadow of the mountain, and named Cooloomgatta, to Michael Goodsir, a Royal Naval surgeon attached to the colonial medical department:

> I have the pleasure of sending you a craniological specimen being the skull of a former chief of the neighbourhood, valuable on account of a part of the History of the personage to whom it originally belonged being known. He was of the rank of a German Prince, or the chief of a Highland clan, and renowned for many dark deeds of Blood.
>
> Many years before Shoal Haven was settled by Berry and Wollstonecraft it was resorted to by parties of Cedar cutters, in course of time these were either all destroyed or driven away by the natives. Arawarra the owner of the present specimen attacked and destroyed a Party of these sawyers who were employed at Black Head seven miles to the North of Shoal Haven River and utterly destroyed them, and if report speaks true, afterwards feasted on their flesh.
>
> He has left a numerous Progeny behind him, and notwithstanding the bloody deeds of his youth lived to an extreme old age and died in time. On our arrival here he was tottering on the verge of human life.
>
> About 2 or 3 three years ago I met Charlie his youngest son, a peaceable well disposed native like another Pious Orcus carrying this once formidable warrior upon his shoulders. The venerable old gentleman [who had] merely come to take a last look of Cooloomgatta now occupied by strangers, died two days after & was buried in the neighbourhood. He was buried in the sand to the depth of ten feet, laying on his face with his head pointing to south. Thus although this man of blood escaped punishment and died in peace, yet mark eternal Justice his bones have not been allowed to rest in their grave & it is to be hoped that his skull will throw such light on science as may sufficiently expiate the crimes he committed.[7]

It seems at first glance hard to credit that Berry, a hard-headed entrepreneur who over many years courted key figures in the colonial establishment, investing much of his precious capital to secure the first leases in the Shoalhaven district, would jeopardise his success by alienating the Wadi Wadi and their neighbours, the Gurandaga people. Yet he was prepared to transgress indigenous religion and customary law by supervising the opening of their elder's grave and the removal of his skull.

Berry's letter allows us to go some way towards explaining what led him to risk procuring Arawarra's skull. It shows how his desire to promote phrenological knowledge was complexly related, and shaped in response, to contemporary perceptions of the challenges confronting civilisation on the Australian frontier, the ends of medical professionalism and the nature of justice.

As with the naming of his homestead Cooloomgatta — a mountain with profound significance within the Wadi Wadi cosmology — Berry's ironic styling of Arawarra's youngest son as Orcus, the Roman lord of the underworld, was meant to impress upon his metropolitan correspondent that he had successfully gained dominion over the wilderness of Shoalhaven and brought civilisation amongst its savage peoples. British eighteenth-century literati and savants found in Greek and Roman authors rich resources for the creation of burlesques and mock-epics, in which truths relating to people or things could be overthrown by representing them through the medium of sarcastic or patently absurd allusions to antiquity. In common with many other Britons in the colonial sphere, Berry could easily avail himself of this satirical tradition to undercut the legitimacy of Wadi Wadi claims to hold and enjoy their land.

Berry's freedom with classical allusion comes as little surprise on examining what we know of his early life. He was a Scot of lowland bourgeois origin, born near Cupar, Fifeshire, in 1781. In common with most men of his age and class he gained an easy familiarity with Roman and some Greek writers through early schooling in Latin. After Cupar Grammar School, he attended the University of St Andrews, before settling on a career in medicine that led to extramural medical tuition and the study of medicine at Edinburgh.

We know very little about how Berry's thinking was influenced during his university years, except that he developed a strong interest in geology. However, it seems clear enough that his understanding of the world by the time he left Edinburgh in 1804 was fairly conventional, insofar as, like most of his university peers, he embraced the civic humanism and associated ideas of societal development articulated by William Robertson, Adam Ferguson and other philosophic Whig literati, who were associated with the moderate party of the Church of Scotland. 'The History of the Personage' of Arawarra we thus find implicitly located within a universal scheme of history characterised by the evolution of human societies through successive stages of development, starting from primordial states of savagery and culminating in commercial and polite society. The owner of the skull Berry had acquired was an archetypal savage chief, only distinguishable, perhaps, from the martial Germanic warrior kings depicted in Tacitus or the hereditary leaders of the Highland clans destroyed in the 1745 rebellion, by the darkness of his 'deeds of blood'.

Berry claimed to have justly made Arawarra atone in death for his alleged atrocities by removing his rights to burial in British and indigenous law, and transforming his skull into a 'craniological specimen'. In this regard Berry's letter draws our attention to what was an important intersection within the culture of the time between ideas of punishment and the aims and practices of anatomical science, and one that helps greatly to explain why early nineteenth-century procurers of skulls appear to have been little troubled by desecrating the resting places and remains of the indigenous dead.

In the century or so before Berry completed his medical training, the social distinctions existing between learned physicians and 'empiric' practitioners of surgery had progressively collapsed. During the course of the eighteenth century, new markets for medical services emerged within Britain's expanding urban and colonial spheres. In the process the traditional sway of university professors over the course and content of medical teaching came to be challenged by prominent surgeons holding posts within the growing number of hospitals established in urban centres, and by an increasing number of independent teachers of anatomy and surgery. These men communally re-fashioned surgery into a science, and profession, worthy of high social esteem. They offered practical instruction in treating the kinds of injury and disease students were most likely to encounter as healers, but importantly this pragmatic outlook was far removed from the simple empiricism of earlier generations of 'barber-surgeons'. It was informed by theories about the internal structure and workings of the body, largely produced through clinical dissection and close scrutiny of human corpses.

Logically enough, as the popularity of these new modes of medical training grew, so too did the demand for corpses suitable for dissection. The legal privileges secured by the Colleges of Surgeons during the eighteenth century extended to inheriting the rights enjoyed by the old barber-surgeon guilds to 'anatomise and dissect' publicly a small number of convicted felons. Even after dissection was made a mandatory element of the capital sentence for murder by Parliament in 1752, the number of bodies that could be legitimately secured by medical teachers met only a fraction of the demand. Surgeons' agents were left to procure the corpses of people convicted for murder direct from the place of execution, with the result that they were often foiled in their quest by the deceased's family and friends, or barred from approaching the gallows by outraged spectators. Consequently, until the passage of the Anatomy Act in 1832, a brisk but secretive trade in corpses illegally exhumed from graveyards or stolen from workhouse infirmaries characterised the British medical economy.[8]

Even the 'resurrection business', as this trafficking in the dead was cynically known, fell far short of supplying the needs of a burgeoning market in medical education. For no small number of students between 1789 and 1793, the solution was to cross the channel to Paris, where the revolution had brought about the unification of the various branches of the medical profession and led to the restructuring of the city's charitable hospitals as teaching institutions. The attraction of the French capital moreover was not simply that it offered cheap and plentiful work with cadavers, but exposure to what, as many British medical authorities conceded, were the revolutionary advances achieved by French investigators through clinically investigating the body. It appeared that the revolution in politics had its aftermath in the production of a body of knowledge that refined and relocated received wisdom amongst physicians and surgeons within a new theoretical framework, which was given the name of pathology.

By the time Berry arrived at Edinburgh, the politics and intellectual life of the Scots capital had been galvanised into conservatism by the war with revolutionary France. While the hostilities continued they proved profitable for Edinburgh's medical teachers, by stifling the flow of students to Paris while increasing employment opportunities for their pupils as naval and military surgeons. In reminiscences he composed in old age, Berry was to recall that: 'Delighted with the accounts of the naval victories of Nelson, Duncan, and others, I determined to enter the navy, therefore only passed for a surgeon'.[9] Only the opposition of his father and the Peace of Amiens, he wrote, led him to change his mind. We know little more about Berry's time at Edinburgh, but it seems clear that, in common with his fellow students, he wholeheartedly endorsed the use of the bodies of condemned murderers for medical instruction, and was quite probably conscious that the shortage of bodies had severely impeded his gaining knowledge of human anatomy.

It is further worth noting an earlier, well-publicised, colonial instance of punishment by post-mortem dissection: that of Alexander Pearce, by James Scott, colonial surgeon and comptroller of medical services at Hobart.[10] A graduate of Edinburgh University, Scott was intrigued by phrenology. After taking up his post in 1820, he regularly dissected convict corpses from the settlement's hospital and gallows, with a view to refining the connections phrenology assumed to exist between brain, cranial form and criminal behaviour. In the wake of deepening conflict between settlers and Tasmanian peoples during the 1820s, Scott extended his researches to indigenous crania, procuring skulls and securing casts from the heads and faces of Tasmanian men tried for murder and executed at Hobart.

However, his best-known investigation was his dissection of Pearce, the original of Marcus Clarke's fictional cannibal convict in *For the Term of His Natural Life*.[11] In early 1825 the semi-official *Hobart Town Gazette* justified the dissection by surgeons Scott and Crockett of Pearce as follows:

> We trust these awful and ignominious results of disobedience to law and humanity will act as a powerful caution; for blood must expiate blood! And the welfare of society imperatively requires, that all whose crimes are so confirmed, and systematic, as *not* to be redeemed by lenity, shall be pursued in vengeance and extirpated with *death*![12]

These sentiments bear a remarkable similarity to those voiced by Berry some two-and-a-half years later when announcing the procurement of Arawarra's skull.

Like many of his professional contemporaries, Berry gave up medicine for colonial trade and pastoralism. Even so, he laid great store in his medical credentials, and readily drew upon the social authority they bestowed. For Berry, indigenous skulls appear to have been a tangible sign of that authority. When he cleaned the moist sand from the cranial cavities of the elder's skull, the pleasure he derived arguably stemmed not only from being able to provide his British correspondent with Arawarra's skull, but from being able to continue exercising the intellectual monopoly over post-mortems that his surgical qualifications licensed.

Berry's involvement in the procurement of indigenous remains can be traced back as far as 1819. In that year he enlisted the help of the Reverend Robert Knopwood, chaplain to the convict settlement at Hobart, to get Tasmanian Aboriginal crania for Thomas Hobbes Scott, then visiting the colony of New South Wales as secretary to his brother-in-law, Commissioner Bigge. Scott was keen to acquire skulls for various metropolitan scientific societies, including the celebrated Hunterian Museum at the Royal College of Surgeons of England, by this time Europe's largest collection of comparative anatomy. When broaching the subject of crania with Knopwood, whom he knew to have a long-standing interest in the culture and physical peculiarities of the indigenous peoples of the Derwent, Berry playfully let drop:

> ...that Mr. Scott is a craniologist. This is generally not suspected here, still I know it to be the case. Therefore you will oblige me by procuring him if possible a native cranium, but it may be as well if you advise such of your friends as have any reason to be doubtful of their own heads to allow him to feel their bumbs [sic] lest he should discover what is inside.[13]

Knopwood found it hard to oblige Berry, not least because the Tasmanian peoples' mortuary ceremonies involved treating the body in ways that rendered the skull scientifically useless. Nonetheless after some months he sent a 'very fine native skull', and ominously advised Berry that he had been promised more from the interior of the island.

Berry's manner of requesting Knopwood's help suggests that at this time he was reticent to divulge his true views on phrenology for fear he alienate the cleric and his powerful friends within the colonial establishment. One of the strongest arguments against phrenology was that emanating from churchmen, who argued that the science was a thinly disguised form of materialism. Even so, Berry probably knew from colonial surgeons that Knopwood's interest in Tasmanian peoples extended to regarding as scientifically important the procurement and examination of human remains, and that he could use his own medical authority to prevail upon Knopwood. When Scott returned to England in 1821, he was able to present the College of Surgeon's Hunterian Museum with a preserved Maori head and two Tasmanian skulls, the latter probably secured thanks to Knopwood. On being thanked by the College Council, Scott wrote:

> ...I receive these thanks from so illustrious a Body with the highest gratification, and deference: attributing much more to their kindness and encouragement of Science than to any merit of my own; and I much regret this small Collection...[14]

It was probably through Berry that Scott was also able to donate natural history specimens to the Newcastle Literary and

Philosophical Society, and the anatomy school at Oxford, his old university. He included amongst his gifts to the latter the '...skull of a Black Male, not woolly headed, of New South Wales, and a Maori head...the skin curiously tattooed'.[15]

Berry differed from Scott in having, by virtue of his success in colonial trade, little need to cultivate the patronage of leading metropolitan scientific figures such as the conservative medical grandees who sat on the council of the College of Surgeons. During the 1820s he made generous donations of geological and natural history specimens to his old universities of St Andrews and Edinburgh. But he focused his intellectual energies on the production of scientific knowledge within, and primarily for the benefit of, settler society.

In late 1821 Berry gained election to the short-lived Australasian Philosophical Society, founded the previous June by seven figures prominent in the administration and business life of New South Wales. As historian Michael Hoare has shown, Berry and his co-founders modelled the Society on similarly select metropolitan clubs of philosophically minded gentlemen, adopting much the same rules politely circumscribing discussion of potentially controversial religious and political questions.[16] Even so, they sought to capitalise on the Society's geographical location by sponsoring production and dissemination of accurate knowledge of the '...natural state, capabilities, productions, and resources of Australasia and the adjacent regions'. In this, they aimed for a measure of intellectual independence from scientific grandees, like Joseph Banks, who had long conceptualised the colonial sphere as a source of raw knowledge for processing by metropolitan intellectual communities.

Much like the Royal Society under Banks, the scope of the Philosophical Society was ambitiously envisaged as promoting investigations across the spectrum of 'natural history...the various branches of physical sciences' and 'the history and character of man, together with his language'.

Indigenous origins: the musings of Barron Field

The refashioning of the natural history of humanity in the light of phrenological discoveries was a project in which Berry was joined by another of the Society's prime movers, Barron Field, poet, antiquarian and New South Wales' first Supreme Court Judge.

In early 1822 Field gave the Society a lengthy discourse 'on the Aborigines of New Holland and Van Diemen's Land', a version of which he subsequently included in *Geographical Memoirs on New South Wales*, a collection of papers read before the Society that he edited and persuaded John Murray, at this time Britain's leading publisher of exploration and scientific travel narratives, to add to his lists for 1825.

Field's essay attracted little comment in years immediately following its publication beyond the scorn of one colonial critic, who dismissed it as '…a mere tissue of random hypotheses' made worse by the author's clumsy attempts at wit.[17] His rediscovery by modern historians has resulted in a series of brief assessments, which generally speaking have done little more than endorse John Mulvaney's appraisal of Field in his groundbreaking survey of ethnographic representation of Aboriginal peoples, published in the late 1950s.

Mulvaney identified Field's essay as one of the earliest articulations of belief in the physiological incapacity of Aboriginal people for civilisation and the inevitability of their extinction as a distinct people. Astutely, he also noted that the witticisms of Field served to underscore these conclusions, his '…condemnation of [Aboriginal peoples'] social status', for example, being a clear allusion to the 'very scriptural text [they know not their nakedness] which Cook had quoted in order to praise them'.[18] However, in Bob Reece's 1974 study of Aboriginal people and colonial society in New South Wales during the 1830s and 1840s, he was struck by the language used by Field to describe the symptoms of this physiological incapacity.[19] At one point Field had argued that, of the Aboriginal people settlers had so far encountered, 'they have quick conceptions, and ready powers of imitation; but have no reflection, judgment or foresight.'

Here, Field clearly employs the nomenclature of phrenology, and as such was one of the earliest colonial writers to theorise indigenous resistance to Christian civilisation and the inevitability of their extinction in phrenological terms. But there is arguably more to be learnt from re-reading Field's essay in the light of the contemporary circulation of phrenological knowledge. For all that his love of rhetorical figures and poetic ornament irritates the modern reader, Field clearly sought to address concerns shared within different but overlapping contemporary metropolitan intellectual communities of antiquarians, natural historians and anatomists. Above all, he aimed to make a significant contribution to what by the mid-1820s had become an important question within these communities in respect of the origins and extent of human difference.

Irrespective of whether racial difference was believed to result from environmental modification, separate creation, or gradual transmutation, there was broad agreement that the extent and origins of human difference were explicable only so far as careful observation of the current state, or recent history, of the earth's peoples allowed the establishment of indisputable fact. For environmentalists such as Field there was a need to establish the lines of distinction between various national groups, to substantiate beyond question the differences which had come to exist, and then seek to reconstruct as best reliable evidence allowed the history and pace of change through which the natural history of man had become a story of gradual diversity.

In this regard Field employs phrenological examination of indigenous Australian people as a means of producing new and conclusive evidence to correct the extremely influential taxonomy of national difference devised by Blumenbach. As I have discussed elsewhere, the celebrated Göttingen anatomist considered humanity as one race that over time had become providentially divided into five distinct varieties. Most mainland Aboriginal peoples he classed as members of the Malay variety, while Tasmanians and peoples on the northwest coast of Australia he saw as belonging to the Papuan variety.[20]

Field, however, argues that comparative examination of 'New Hollander' and 'Van Diemen's-Lander' cranial morphology, skin colour and life-ways reveal differences so slight as to overturn received opinion that they belonged respectively to the Malay and Papuan varieties of humanity. Rather, they are all Papuans. The investigations he had been able to pursue suggest, moreover, that the Papuan variety of mankind is in fact an offshoot of the Ethiopian variety. 'The skull, the genius, the habits, of the Australians', Field writes, 'have, in all of them, the degenerate Ethiopian character, like that of the Andamaners, and the negro races of the Indian Islands.'

Phrenological knowledge from the colonial sphere is not only presented as a powerful corrective to the taxonomic ambitions of metropolitan ethnography, but also offered as the basis for the evolution of effective strategies for the governance of indigenous Australians. The clear inference to be drawn from international comparison of skull shapes, correlated with observations of mental characteristics, is that indigenous Australian peoples will never be civilised. The burden of the colonist, as Field outlines poetically by way of closing his essay, is to recognise the biological impossibility of incorporating the native within settler society, and to ease humanely their natural recession into history:

Still let him prompt the lib'ral colonist
To tender offices and pensive thoughts.
Then let him pass, — a blessing on his head!
And, long as he can wander, let him breathe
The freshness of the woods.
May never we pretend to civilize,
And make him only captive!
Let him be free of mountain solitudes;
And let him, where and when he will, sit down
Beneath the trees, and with his faithful dog
Share his chance-gather'd meal; and, finally,
As in the eye of Nature he has lived,
So in the eye of Nature let him die![21]

By encouraging researches such as Field's into the 'history and character of man', the Australasian Philosophical Society can be seen as an attempt — albeit short-lived — to give institutional form and phrenological underpinnings to the study of indigenous Australian antiquities.

The colonial re-fashioning of antiquarianism

By Berry and Field's day, British antiquarianism had a lengthy history, with substantial origins in the religious and governmental reforms of the Tudor monarchy during the sixteenth century. Amongst wealthy landholders, reformism in church and state was inextricably connected with the evolution of new perceptions of national identity and purpose, which found expression, among other ways, in sponsoring the collection of information relating to historically important figures, ancient buildings, artefacts and customs. In patronising such researches, landholders, more or less, self-consciously presented themselves as restoring a knowledge of things past to the lands over which they ruled and often exercised ancient rights and privileges by virtue of the Crown. By the late eighteenth century, antiquarianism was well established as an important feature of the cultural life of the British elite, characterised by aristocratic and genteel patronage of a wide-ranging network of scholars, collectors and publishers. Within this intellectual economy, institutions such the Royal Society and the Societies of Antiquaries of England and Scotland served as important cultural nodes for the sponsorship and dissemination of antiquarian knowledge.

By the last third of the eighteenth century the antiquarian interests of these societies ranged well beyond the history and antiquities
of the British Isles, to encompass what to the modern eye seems a
bewildering array of heterogeneous inquiries. Members of the
English Society of Antiquaries heard learned discourses on subjects as
diverse in terms of time and cultural space as examination of Egyptian
mummified cats and English medieval minstrelsy. Some contemporaries found the diversity too much to bear. In the early 1770s Horace
Walpole, influential arbiter of taste and long-standing member of the
above Society, was exasperated to the point of complaining: 'It seems
all is fish that comes into the net of the Society. Mercy on us! What
a cartload of bricks and rubbish and Roman ruins they have piled
together!'[22] However, as John Gascoigne has recently suggested, when
tracing the antiquarian interests of Joseph Banks, the universal scope
of these researches was in fact indicative of a growing desire in
Enlightenment antiquarian circles to accumulate evidence of human
custom and habits, confident that this wealth of information could be
ordered as systematically as natural historians had arranged different
plant and animal forms using the taxonomic schema evolved by
Linneaus, the great Swedish botanist.[23]

Antiquarianism never remotely came to resemble the orderly
patterning of Enlightenment botanical and zoological researches.
But by the turn of the nineteenth century, a number of prominent
antiquarians had been drawn to excavate barrow burials and the
foundations of prehistoric megaliths. This research, moreover, was
systematic insofar as it involved the adaptation of techniques
evolved by contemporary geological researchers, such as the cutting
of clear sections through earthworks and the recording of strati-
graphic contexts in which bones and artefacts were discovered.[24]
Methodical approaches to excavation were well in evidence by the
late 1780s, and the political turbulence of the 1790s appears to have
furthered the trend. Antiquarians responded to the combination of
national emergency, patriotic rhetoric and denial of safe access to
continental Europe and the Mediterranean by concentrating their
energies on recovering their own national past.[25] So confined, excavation became a more structured science in terms of technique and
the assessment of discoveries.

By the early nineteenth century, the resting places of Britain's
prehistoric dead had come to be understood as sites giving antiquarianism empirical strengths it had hitherto lacked. 'We speak
from facts, not theory', declared Sir Richard Colt Hoare, in the
preface to his 1810–21 *Ancient History of Wiltshire*. In this lavish

work, methodically detailing several hundred barrow excavations he had sponsored, Hoare offered his fellow antiquarians what he called a 'plain unvarnished tale', inviting them to 'draw from it such conclusions as shall appear not only reasonable, but even uncontradictable'. While not wanting to discount the evidential worth of Roman and medieval authors, or the work of earlier antiquarian scholars, Hoare and other leading participants in this new culture of excavation saw themselves as relocating the study of the ancient British past firmly outside the 'fanciful regions of romance' into which many earlier antiquarians had strayed. They also saw themselves as producing a reliable intellectual matrix within which to assess and order evidence illustrative of the general course of human prehistory located within different but often interrelated contemporary discourses of conjectural history, linguistics, human anatomy, and exploratory voyaging.

Earlier antiquaries, for example, had considered exploratory voyaging as an important source of knowledge, though without specifying its likely significance. In 1772 Jeremiah Milless, the then president of the English Society of Antiquaries, took pleasure in reading from the chair a letter from Johann Reinhard Forster, then about to depart on Cook's second voyage, in which Forster assured '...the Society, that he shall be most happy to execute, as far as lies in his power, any commands the Gentlemen of the Council may have for him, or those of any Member of this honourable Society...'[26]

Early nineteenth-century excavators drew focused comparisons, especially between the mortuary practices of ancient Britons, the treatment of the dead as recorded in the Old Testament and Greco-Roman texts, and accounts of funerary traditions recorded by travellers in America, the contemporary Middle East and Asia.[27] Importantly, they also compared the forms and uses of artefacts from Britain's distant past with those produced within the cultures encountered in its new Oceanic possessions. In 1801 Charles Joseph Harford spoke before the English Society of Antiquaries about stone axe heads, unearthed in the Quantock Hills, suggesting that, in reconstructing their uses, '...probably we may obtain a Clue respecting the latter from a Consideration of similar Instruments, which have within these few years, been brought into this Country from the South Sea Islands...'[28] Harford readily extended his comparison to conclude that, 'Our Forefathers doubtless attached the Celt by thongs to the handle, in the same manner as modern savages do, and like them formed a most useful Implement'.

For all that early nineteenth-century excavators like Hoare claimed to eschew romantic interpretations of the past, they too were seduced by the pleasures of the imagination. During one excavation on the Wiltshire Downs, a sudden fierce storm forced a party of antiquarian gentlemen led by Hoare to take shelter within the opened barrow, near a skeleton of large proportions buried with jet ornaments and a 'brazen dagger'. When, amidst the lightning and torrential rain, the cutting through which they had entered the barrow threatened to collapse, they had no choice but to scramble out and 'abide the pelting of the pitiless storm upon the bleak down'. The following day one of the party, one Reverend William Lisle Bowles, sent what struck Hoare as a 'beautiful and spirited poem...truly descriptive of the awful scene we had lately witnessed'. The poem began with the voice of the 'British hero' they had discovered protesting:

Let me, let me sleep again;
Thus, methought, in feeble strain,
Plain'd from its disturbed bed
The spirit of the mighty dead.[29]

For all his concern to present his researches 'unvarnished', Hoare incorporated the complete poem in his *Ancient Wiltshire*, so that it formed a conclusion to his account of this particular barrow's structure and contents.

Hoare was himself tempted to draw imaginative parallels between Britons' ancient forebears and the 'savage' peoples their settler descendants had encountered in America. The discovery of the remains of a dog and a man in one barrow chamber, along with flint arrowheads and a tangle of stags' horns prompted him to exclaim: 'Can the language of history or poetry speak more forcibly to our feelings, than these mute and inanimate memorials of the British hunter'. He went on to adapt Pope's depiction in the *Essay on Man* of the Amerindian to represent the ancient Briton, 'whose untutor'd mind' had been equally disposed to pantheism and who likewise believed that in his final journey into the realm of spirit, 'His faithful DOG shall bear him company'.[30]

Yet, as is clear from the poetry Reverend Bowles was inspired to write in the aftermath of his encounter with the ancient British dead, the intellectual premium antiquarians placed on opening burial places was inflected with doubt as to the morality of their inquiries. Antiquarians who dared take advantage of renovations within the consecrated fabric of ancient churches to examine remains in crypts and transit tombs were publicly condemned and satirised as being on a par with anatomists. The latter's needs for cadavers suitable for dissection led them to buy corpses secretly, rarely if ever questioning the legality of how they had been obtained. Excavators of what were unquestionably pagan burial sites also found themselves the target of moral censure. As Hoare felt obliged to stress, 'the true antiquary will ever respect…remains; and whilst he enters into their views by endeavouring to revive their memory, he will also, as far as possible, consult their wishes, in leaving to their bones their ancient place of sepulture'.[31]

Given the importance that excavation of ancient British burial places had come to assume within early nineteenth-century metropolitan antiquarian circles, we would do well to see the opening of indigenous Australian graves as motivated by similar intellectual aims. When exhuming Arawarra in 1827, Berry recorded evidence of indigenous mortuary ceremonies with as much care and precision as that taken by contemporary antiquaries in excavating ancient British barrows. Moreover, in their researches into the 'history and character of man', Berry and Field both sought to give antiquarianism more concrete scientific foundations through grounding their investigations of indigenous ancestral remains in the tenets of phrenology.

John Oxley, phrenological antiquarian

Alexander Berry and Barron Field were not the only members of the Australasian Philosophical Society concerned to shed light on the antiquities and customs of indigenous Australians. John Oxley, appointed Surveyor-General of New South Wales in 1812, was also a prominent member of the Society.

In 1817, Oxley had been given command by Governor Macquarie of an expedition through the still unknown country along the course of the Lachlan River. Macquarie's instructions in part charged Oxley and his party to describe 'such natives or aborigines' they might meet.

Returning up the Lachlan in July 1817, after the disappearance of the river into swamps made further progress westwards impossible, the expedition came across a 'raised mound of earth which had somewhat the appearance of a burial place'. Oxley had the convicts in the party open the mound, to reveal ashes so reduced as to be unidentifiable, although that it was a grave seemed clear enough to Oxley from a trench 'dug round one side of it, as if for seats for persons in attendance'. This was to be the first of several similar Wiradjuri burial sites the expedition encountered, a second being discovered close to camp the following afternoon, which Oxley again had opened to reveal remains decayed into 'unctuous clayey matter'.[32]

By the end of July the expedition had journeyed far enough upstream on the Lachlan for Oxley to conclude they had located its origins. Taking stock of the health of his party, the scarcity of fish and game, and what remained of their rations, he decided to establish a camp from which to ferry the expedition across the river, swollen by recent rains, then strike out to the north-east for the Macquarie River and follow it back to Bathurst. Again the expedition found they had camped near a burial place. In his journal, Oxley carefully described the site and its surrounds and had his deputy, George Evans, sketch the site. Delayed by rain, the convicts assigned to the expedition spent two miserable days digging the earth mound.

As they dug, Oxley recorded the progress of the excavation in his journal, carefully noting the state of the body found within, and the artefacts with which the Wiradjuri man had been buried, in a manner paralleling Hoare's descriptions of his investigations within ancient British barrows. In the edition of his journal published in 1820, Oxley included a full account of the excavation, accompanied by an engraved illustration of the site taken from Evan's sketch. He also took care to point how the 'whole outward form and appearance of the place was...totally different from that of any custom or ceremony in use by the natives on the eastern coast...'

The way in which the body of the Wiradjuri man had been arranged in the grave also struck Oxley as resembling the way the dead had generally been found positioned in ancient British graves, and which antiquarians had been at a loss to explain. So similar did they seem to Oxley that he was drawn to underscore the resemblance by quoting from Shakespeare's tragedy of ancient British life, *Cymbeline*: 'Nay Cadwal, we must lay his head to the east; my father has a reason for it'.[33]

Finally, in his published account of the expedition, Oxley took pains to assure his readers that he had opened the grave with no intention of violating native custom, or offending the moral sensibilities which Aboriginal people and Europeans shared alike:

> I hope I shall not be considered as either wantonly disturbing the remains of the dead, or needlessly violating the religious rites of a harmless people, in having caused the tomb to be opened...[34]

After having 'satisfied our curiosity', Oxley wrote that precious time and energy was spent on ensuring that '…the whole was carefully re-interred, and restored as near as possible to the situation in which it was found'. However, as Allan Cunningham, the colony's botanist and member of the expedition, recorded in his diary, '…this skull Mr Oxley intends to take with us, as a subject for the study of craniologists'.[35]

In this paper I have sought to tease out the circumstances in which indigenous remains were procured and phrenologically examined in New South Wales between 1815 and the late 1820s. In doing so, I have shown how the pursuit of phrenological knowledge was believed to justify the transgression of received morality in respect of the dead. In the eyes of Alexander Berry, those who resisted the taking of their ancestral country legitimately, risked being called upon by settler society to make amends beyond the grave. For Oxley, the claims of phrenology appear to have outweighed respect for the customs of others who had lived, and died, beyond the pale of European settlement. For Barron Field, cranial shape licensed pessimism about the destiny of indigenous people in the wake of colonialism.

These are strands in a larger, complex story of the relations between European sciences of humanity and colonial aspirations in nineteenth-century Australia. We would do well, for example, to consider the phrenological interests of Berry, Field and Oxley together with what survives by way of evidence of indigenous resistance to scientific trafficking in ancestral remains. Likewise, we need to take account of the subtle ways in which, though reduced to the cognitive status of specimens, ancestral remains continued to have an agency of sorts, which, on occasion, catalysed doubts about the legitimacy of colonial ambitions in respect of indigenous land and culture.[36] Here, however, I have been concerned to open a small historicist window to show how complex relations between phrenological science and colonial aspirations were in early New South Wales. What can be reconstructed of the captivity of indigenous skulls serves, much as in earlier meditative discourses, as a mirror within which the dead allow us to place the historically constituted hopes, ambitious and pretensions of the living in sharper focus.

Chapter 2
Chained to their signs: remembering breastplates
Chris Healy

For just as nature abhors a vacuum, so the vertiginous cultural interspace effected by the reflection makes many of us desperate to fill it with meaning, thereby defusing disconcertion. To resist this desperation is no easy task. After all, this is how cultural convention is maintained. But let us try. Let us try to uncover the wish within such desperation and be a little more malleable, ready to entertain unexpected moves of mimesis and alterity across quivering terrain, even if they lead at the outermost horizon to an all-consuming nothingness.[1] — *Michael Taussig*

AT FIRST GLANCE, breastplates might appear to be just another device in the technology of colonial capture in Australia. Take the photograph of Bilin Bilin wearing a plate inscribed 'Jackey Jackey — King of the Logan and Pimpama' (see Illustration 1). The plate, the chain and the conventions of photography produce a Yugambeh elder as a shackled criminal on display — he is both a primitive in tableau and one of 'the usual suspects'. The image seems to both document captivity and evoke those 'frontier photographs' of Aboriginal prisoners in the desert bound together with heavy chains attached to manacles around their necks.[2] This initial impression is right in that it recognises some of the ways in which colonial captivity is not only about actual imprisonment but equally about how captivity is understood, represented, interpreted and made historical. Still, in this chapter I want to persuade you that breastplates and photographs of breastplates performed other roles: as cross-cultural objects and signs. In particular I want to emphasise two processes: first, the ways in which the exchange of breastplates encapsulates some of the ambivalences of colonial encounters; and second, the fact that the processes involved in post-colonial remembrance of breastplates have been more horrific than their colonial interchange. My argument works against the tendency to regard the relatively distant colonial past as *the* time of injustice towards indigenous peoples which should, therefore, be judged as a history of human and moral failure. Such gestures are both true and too glib in attempting to separate past from present. My suggestion is that the remembrance of breastplates is an example of a colonialism that constitutes our present, a remembrance that belongs not only to dead generations but also burdens the living.

The first use of breastplates in Australia is recorded in 1815. In that year Lachlan Macquarie, Governor of New South Wales, gave to Boongaree a plate engraved 'Boongaree — Chief of the Broken Bay Tribe 1815' and a regimental uniform. Both, it seems, were soon thrown away.[3] This minor setback did not deter Macquarie who, in the following year, distributed a number of plates at the first of what would be annual 'friendly gatherings' at Parramatta, held until 1835. Those upon whom Macquarie wished to confer 'chieftainship' were presented with engraved brass plates. The design of the plates derived from gorgets, military decorations worn by British regiments in the eighteenth century, which in turn derived from armour used to protect the throat — a piece of metal which stopped the wearer from getting it in the neck. Distributed until the 1930s, primarily along the East Coast but in all states of Australia except Tasmania and South Australia, the plates signified a number of different but inter-related narratives — ownership, political strategies, mis-recognition. They marked alterity and made familiar Aboriginal 'chiefs' into 'kings', 'queens' and 'princes'; they also recognised service and heroism.[4]

Breastplates, according to the substantial survey put together as a catalogue for the exhibition *Poignant Regalia*, were two sided. On the one hand, 'breastplates show…attempts on the part of the Aborigines to somehow come to terms with the needs of the Europeans'.[5] On the other hand, they were a means by which non-Aboriginal people conferred 'titles' on indigenous people. 'Collectively', writes Cleary, 'the inscriptions on the breastplates tell the story of European domination and subjugation through years of indiscriminate slaughter and martial law imposed on Aborigines'.[6] Let's begin with those two sides.

I. Whose plates are these anyway? 'Aboriginal breastplates'?

Are these 'Aboriginal breastplates' or should we think of these plates as made by and therefore speaking about non-Aboriginal people?

All of these objects were given to Aboriginal people, so in this sense they belonged to Aboriginal people. But for gifts to be owned they have to be accepted or avowed in the terms offered by the exchange. It's easy for an ungrateful recipient to become unworthy of a gift, and conversely a gift given without worthy intentions is one which can be rejected as worthless. Immediately, then, we confront two questions: in what ways did Aboriginal people understand, and how did they make use of these gifts?

In a very moving article, 'Bilin Bilin — King or Eagle?', Ysola (Yuke) Best, great-great-grand-daughter of Bilin Bilin, writes about the photograph of her ancestor wearing the plate:

> Look into the eyes of *Bilin Bilin*, yes, they tell a story of the burden he was forced to bear when these intruders failed to respect his family and land. The metal plate and chains are symbols of his burden.[7]

In this photograph Bilin Bilin is framed to perform a vision of primitiveness: his nakedness and the breastplate name him as an authentic lone indigene. Implicit in this solitude is the image's melancholia animated by the white myth of Aborigines as a 'vanishing people'. To judge by another photograph of Bilin Bilin at the Deebin Creek Industrial Mission, it would seem that he had considerable successes in ensuring the survival of many of his people, but at what cost? In this photograph too he is wearing the plate, stage right but somehow central, and surrounded by people who are respectably dressed, industrious in an industrial mission and most definitely surviving. Perhaps the breastplate here is, like the European garb, a burden to be borne as a sign of accommodation, or perhaps, as Phil Gordon suggests, the 'recipients may have been looked down upon because they were seen to be assisting the white man's never ending quest for land and control over the land and Aboriginal people'.[8]

In the absence of substantial documentation of Aboriginal interpretations of the plates it is hard to answer these questions about Bilin Bilin with any certainty. But we do not have to decide if the plates identified canny tacticians or collaborators — as if such labels could tell us a great deal. The few records of Aboriginal responses or reactions to breastplates are the product of white interpretations. In late nineteenth-century Queensland the German 'ethnographer among cannibals' Carl Lumholtz thought that, 'Every native is anxious to become "king", for the brass plate, which is considered a great ornament also secures the bearer many a meal'.[9] In 1835 a Reverend Handt writes that, when invited to join him at his fire, three Aboriginal men who possessed plates refused, saying they were gentlemen. Cleary interprets the account thus: 'The import of their reply was that it was a gentleman's privilege to give not take orders'.[10] This conclusion seems confused on at least two fronts. It is not clear what the relationship is between an invitation to join someone at a fire and taking 'orders'. Of course 'invitations' and 'status' can be deeply imbricated but we get little sense of how these complicated relationships were understood in this instance. Second, and this is a mistake widely shared among those non-indigenous people writing about the plates, there is a clear assumption that the white *intent* inscribed on the plates is transparently adopted by their Aboriginal wearers. In this case the intention is (assumed to be) that the wearers were being granted the status of European gentlemen and that their recipients adopted this European status as their own. Cleary relates another instance in which a similar, if even more transparent, understanding of the meaning of the plates is demonstrated. In this second case, from 1849:

> the Commandant at Brisbane had given a breastplate inscribed 'Moppy, King of the Upper Brisbane Tribe' to an influential Aborigine: 'The rest of the tribe could not, of course, read the inscription on the plate; but being shrewd enough to discover that it had meaning, they requested the supposed Boraltchou [a runaway convict assimilated into the tribe] to explain to them what it meant. And when told that it signified that Moppy was their master, and that they were all his servants, they got into a prodigious talking at his supposed usurpation of kingly authority over themselves, as free and independent natives of Australia, and insisted that Moppy should carry back the plate to the Commandant, under pain of death'.[11]

This story may have served some purpose for its narrator in terms of representing the egalitarian impulses of indigenous people or it may well tell us more about Boraltchou's role in his adopted community. Certainly the story alerts us to the ways in which non-indigenous people understood the political role of breastplates. But I think it's a white fantasy to imagine that breastplates functioned as a command for Aboriginal people — to believe that because the plate names Moppy as king of the tribe, that the plate had the effect of making him king of the tribe. Moppy might well have used the plate in order to promote his authority, but the plate itself may not have achieved the effect it named; white magic was simply not that strong.

So it is difficult to be sure about how Aboriginal people understood and used breastplates as semiotic objects deployed in the often
violent, baffling and unequal world of colonial exchange. Certainly,
the plates were understood as part of the power-play of signs and
exchange, they were both target and shield. There might be further
clues in the fact that, although a significant number of plates sur-
vive, there are relatively few photographs of Aboriginal people
wearing them. Maybe the plates were simply uncomfortable or
impractical; certainly one recipient is reported to have found her
plate was too heavy and she was rarely sighted wearing it. There
may have been moments of shared recognition and mutual regard
in their receipt, but for this to be more than wishful white thinking
we'd need to know more about the particularity of the exchanges,
about which there are precious few details. So, in the end, perhaps
the plates were felt to be demeaning or unattractive, perhaps they
were traded or perhaps other uses were found for them — uses
beyond the white semiotic intent engraved on their surfaces.

For indigenous people contemplating these plates today there
are further complicating factors beyond the instability of the
objects themselves — particularly the questions of how they were
collected, their current ownership and the emotional resonances of
the plates. Photographs of the plates being worn connote a world
(not an actual world) in which Aboriginal people are wandering
around as labelled exhibits in an open-air museum.[12] Disturbing
and shocking as this is, the story of the survival of these breastplates
may be even more sordid. The provenance of many extant plates is
vague. However there is enough ambiguity in the accounts of finding breastplates to indicate that some may have been found as a
result of deliberate and 'accidental' grave-robbing. Plates are
described as being 'unearthed at the old Aboriginal Reserve',[13] discovered on a property that included 'their burial ground' and
exposed after big floods 'unearthed his remains and swept them
away leaving the heavier metal plate'.[14] And another: 'Aborigines
generally buried their dead in an upright position…They did not
dig very deep graves so their heads would not be very deeply
buried. If Mulwaree Tommy's plate was hung around his neck in
death, this is perhaps how it came to be ploughed up'.[15] It is clear
that, for some collectors, bodily remains were just as collectable as
breastplates.[16] These associations are, inevitably and understandably,
painful for indigenous people and recall the implications of museums and their collections in such practices. Ysola Best is keenly
aware of these possibilities:

Bilin Bilin died c1901 and it has been alleged that he was buried seated in an upright position, in a high rocky shelter overlooking the Albert River in the nesting place of eagles. Has he been left in peace or has the sanctity of his burial place been invaded by scavengers seeking to gather human remains for scientific studies and brass plates for museum collections?[17]

So for some Aboriginal people at least it would seem that, although the plates might act as mnemonic objects which can invoke an ancestor or provide a more general link with the past, in the end breastplates are overdetermined by their origin as colonial objects deployed for colonialism's (worst) ends.

Phil Gordon, writing 'an Aboriginal point of view', offers a more heterogeneous perspective. He evokes the strongly conflicting emotions experienced in the face of the plates and their images: 'anger, hate and sorrow [and] pride...because they also symbolise not only past inequalities but the fact that Aboriginal people have survived and continue as a people against huge odds today'.[18] When I first read this sentence I was puzzled as to how Gordon could feel pride in staring at these ambivalent objects. The anger and the hate make sense to me, not only in terms of the past but equally through the ways in which breastplates articulate with other 'brandings' like the twentieth-century Queensland mission 'dog-tags'. A sense of sadness too seemed appropriate. Sorrow is, I believe, an emotion which can be shared when confronting some of the losses inaugurated by colonialism — despite Aboriginal resilience, the absence of all those peoples, all that knowledge and all those languages is a deeply sorry inheritance. But why pride? For Gordon breastplates can be regarded with, or inspire, pride because they are signs of colonialism's failure. Because breastplates are not 'monuments' to a successful genocide, Gordon's celebration is a simple but profound one: 'Aboriginal people have survived and continue as a people against huge odds today.' To understand how breastplates can mark that extraordinary achievement we have to dwell on their meanings for non-Aboriginal people.

II. Whose plates are these anyway? 'Degraded symbols of colonialism'?[19]

Because the history of colonial dispossession, violence and inhumanity hangs heavily over my sense of an Australian landscape, I view breastplates with a kind of pre-emptive foreboding. Being aware of the history of colonial encounters I assume that these objects, if not stained with blood, are at least marked by the injustice which enabled their production. And this impulse is right, I can prove it. Take this example of vicious satire in relation to royal titles from the *Australian*, 27 May 1844:

> Distinguished Foreigners. Among the distinguished visitors at the levee at Government House on the Queens Birthday, by some unlucky oversight (for which we humbly apologise to their sable Majesties) the names of King Bungaree and Queen Gooseberry, who were in attendance in full regal costume, were omitted. Her majesty was attired in a new pink robe of very curious workmanship, and a Dunstable straw bonnet, wearing the order of her tribe in the form of a crescent, suspended by a brass chain from her ebon neck, and a natural rose, in honor of her Royal Sister Victoria, on her forehead. The King — bless his sable Majesty! — appeared in a rusty cast-off suit, enveloped in a new blanket, which hung in graceful folds about his royal person, rendered irresistibly monarchical by a short pipe being thrust, transversely, through the cartilage of his royal nose.[20]

The 'joke' for the white writer, and no doubt for many of his readers, is in the first place simply mockery of the uncivilised, which is then doubled by the absurdity of a primitive claiming sovereign status. The witticism becomes a kind of torturer's amusement at the damage they've been able to inflict. But the joke is also directed at those whites so stupid as to believe that the granting of the status of royalty could be anything other than a bad joke. In other words the arrogance and hatred in these lines is about how plates were read and understood by those fools, both black and white, who believed in them as anything other than buffoonery. It is this aspect of the production of plates that is missed if we think of them as being about the conferring of 'fantasy titles'. It's certain that breastplates were in no sense adequate or mutually recognised signs of exchanges between equals. But what gestures, words and artefacts of cross-cultural interactions are? Mis-recognition and murder, captivity and exchange, disdain and wonder, and much else besides were all part of the invasion and occupation of Australia. We hide the variability of those processes when we employ the term 'colonialism' in an abstract way. Useful as the term is, particularly for its descriptive value, analytically it is important to hold onto the sense that colonialism consisted of differential processes. Thus if breastplates are not simply bad colonial objects, then the problem becomes one of articulating the specific historical use of breastplates in colonial performances. If we accept that, as a general proposition, the colonisation of Australia did not require the use of breastplates, and if we accept that there were (many) whites, like the writer in the *Australian*, who saw no use in breastplates, then we need to ask what kinds of purposes the plates served for some non-indigenous peoples.

In the first place, the breastplates were a state initiative. The earliest Australian breastplates were, you will recall, conferred by the representative of royalty in the colony. They were, as Cleary writes, 'a token of recognition from one "chief" to another'.[21] Macquarie's rule, more than that of any other colonial governor, exemplifies the contradictions of autocracy, 'liberalism', violence, dispossession, incorporation and acceptance with which Aboriginal people had to deal. At the same time as he was holding his picnics for Aboriginal people, Macquarie had issued proclamations that outlawed armed Aboriginal people or unarmed groups of six or more from coming within a mile of any town, village or farm occupied by British subjects. Aboriginal men in breach of this proclamation could be shot by landowners or convict servants, in which case Macquarie instructed that their bodies be hung 'on the highest trees and in the clearest parts of the forest'.[22] Those men who abided by the proclamation were offered a '"passport" or certificate, bearing his signature, that would permit them to move across their land and protect them from being injured or molested'.[23] In this context, breastplates were an attempt at domination, of a different order from systematic shooting. Macquarie regarded Aboriginal people as his (i.e. the Crown's) subjects. Unfortunately for him, they were subjects who had yet to consent to that status. So Macquarie's seemingly ambiguous actions — shoot some Aboriginal people and 'reward' others — makes sense as a repertoire designed to establish the conditions of governance. The plates were an element in that repertoire.

Even before Macquarie returned to the Northern Hemisphere his monopoly over the distribution of plates became a matter of some concern for other colonists. However, with Macquarie's replacement by Sir Thomas Brisbane, the distribution of settler-bestowed breastplates throughout New South Wales proliferated significantly between 1830 and 1850, as the land under colonial control expanded. This led to the use of lead and other metals in the breastplates, stylistic variation and major inscription changes. Cleary interprets this 'privatisation' of breastplate distribution as leading to their debasement; they became a 'medal' bestowed independently of the Crown's representative for any number of reasons.

This is certainly evident in inscriptions such as 'Mr Verge's King Charlie' and 'Mr Verge's King Michie' granted in the Macleay River district, where conflict was severe. But equally I'm struck by two more productive aspects of this privatisation. First, it makes transparent the fact that the colonisation of Australia (and hence our contemporary sense of who might take responsibility for those processes) depended on both state initiatives and those of relatively autonomous settlers. The complex process of 'contact' — the literal dispossession of indigenous people, episodes of negotiation, intimidation, accommodation, subordination and so on — was performed as much by individuals as by state functionaries. Secondly, and this is particularly noticeable in the variety of breastplate inscriptions, the non-governmental distribution of breastplates highlights some of the more intimate and personal aspects of colonial relationships. Compare, for example, the impersonal act of Macquarie conferring the generic title of 'king' with a much later inscription: 'Paddy/For Saving Life'. Would it be too much to imagine some shared respect in the use of the honorific in the inscription 'Mr Briney of Pialliway', or some mutual gratitude or even common warmth in the plate inscribed 'Presented to Baraban by Sheperd Laidley/In remembrance of 9th Decr 1867' that features an engraved scene of a drowning child being rescued. My point is a simple one: breastplates are varied, and in their forms and inscriptions, and in written accounts, it seems that they served a number of non-Aboriginal goals. Breastplates are neither exclusively Aboriginal nor non-Aboriginal, but transactional objects produced in various modes of colonial exchange, besides those of capture. However, the post-colonial remembrance of breastplates is a different matter.

III. Remembering genocide

For non-Aboriginal people, I think breastplates can shock because the cold brass is so clean and yet so encrusted with a patina of colonial relationships we would rather forget. Remember the double nature of Macquarie's first breastplates: they were insignia given to people who could be shot, and they were tokens of recognition — target and shield. This doubleness was repeated 165 years later when, in the early 1980s, a breastplate sold at auction in Sydney for $6,500. A report of the sale noted: 'Farmers in the Narrandera district used to nail them to trees for potshot practice. Keen bidders at a recent Sydney auction treated them with much more respect'.[24] From target to brand-name — the association of breastplates with the right to shoot Aboriginal people is displaced onto the use of the plates for target practice and displaced again onto collectors' benign bidding which, while respectful of the market value of the plates, should not be taken as indicative of respect for indigenous people. These displacements enable one of those characteristically modern historiographic conceits: a separation of past from present which enables the here and now to be a place which is always so much better ('Keen bidders at a recent Sydney auction treated them with much more respect'). In this sense breastplates are objects which represent the distance between a violent past and a respectful present. However, in this final section I want to suggest that it's worth regarding breastplates (and photographs of Aboriginal people wearing breastplates) as proleptic objects, i.e. objects directed towards, or involving, a calculation about the future. Rather than, or perhaps in addition to, thinking about breastplates as representations that fix meaning, I want to consider them as attempts to remember for the future, objects which anticipate successful genocide. Let me unpack this somewhat convoluted proposition.

Some breastplates are historical in the sense of commemorating an event. This is particularly the case with plates distributed as 'rewards' or in recognition of service bearing inscriptions such as 'Woondu/of/Amity Point/Rewarded by the Governor,/for the assistance he afforded with five of his countrymen,/to the survivors of the wreck of the Steamer "Sovereign"...', or 'A reward for merit to/Charley/of Tullungunnully'. These plates record, acknowledge or memorialise existing relationships and thus can be said to be already archival in their production. But the vast majority of plates in using 'fantasy titles' are future-oriented: in naming and identifying a king or a queen they do not account for the past but seek to put in place relationships which will be of use in the future. The plates would enable non-indigenous people to recognise those with whom they might bargain. The hope of those who conferred them was that their recipients would magically become what the inscriptions proclaimed them to be. The inscribed titles are thus less 'fantasy' and more attempts at magic by white people. Perhaps the best example of this mimetic magic, and an example that takes us to the post-colonial remembrance of breastplates, is the plate given to Coomee Nullanga in the first decade of the twentieth century:

> A nice brass shield, suitably inscribed, has been sent to old 'Coomie' (Maria) who is the only survivor of the old

Murramarang Aboriginal tribe. It has been given to her by Mr Milne, Railway Inspector of Orange, who was in Milton a short time back on holiday. Mr Milne takes a deep interest in the Aboriginal races and is supposed to have the best collection of Aboriginal weapons in New South Wales. The stipulation is that 'Coomie' must not part with her shield til death.[25]

The breastplate given to Coomee Nullanga is inscribed, 'Coomee/Last of her Tribe/Murramarang'. This inscription is, if not unique, certainly rare. Very few of the breastplates recorded in the catalogue of *Poignant Regalia* and the book *Kingplates* are in fact 'plates given…to the last living member of a tribe'. Most existing and recorded brass plates refer, as I've already noted, to titles or recognise the provision of a service. Paradoxically, it is precisely breastplates as marking 'the last' which feature in remembrances of them. For example, in 1952 Fred McCarthy, a Curator of Anthropology at the Australian Museum, wrote:

> A tragic aspect of the contact between the whites and the natives in Australia is revealed by the plates given, as many of them were, to the last living member of a tribe — thus they represent the final act in the struggle of our native tribes in those localities.[26]

McCarthy is not alone. There are also literary and historical references to the plates being give to 'the last'. Why are the plates remembered as things they were not? What does McCarthy mean when he writes that the plates 'represent the final act'?

Coomee was, predictably enough, not the 'last of her tribe' as her breastplate (pro)claimed. Even as Coomee was 'passing', in Daisy Bates's ambiguous term, or 'fading' as the 1990 local history imagined the matter,[27] nearby the Bomaderry Infants Home was being established for a predominantly indigenous 'clientele' by Miss Thompson, 'a missionary to the Aborigines'. Today we would describe Miss Thompson's 'mission' as an institution involved in the systematic removal of Aboriginal children from their families in order that they be raised white and, it was hoped, thus be assimilated. So, if the inscription on Coomee's breastplate was not a statement of fact, what was it? It was mimetic and proleptic.[28] The plate was inscribed not only with the words I've already quoted but with three parallel lines on either side of the inscription about which the accession notes comment, 'The three parallel gashes with raised edges either side of the breastplate inscription are similar to the initiation scars described by Milne on Coomee's shoulders'.[29] In other words these marks on the plate literally reproduced what are said to be Coomee's bodily scars while the inscription names her status — the last. These two features also make sense of the plate as proleptic because the plate was, I think, intended to stand in for Coomee once she was dead. The photograph of Coomee wearing the plates is obscene because the photograph actually performs what the breastplates are remembered as recording; it is a photograph of a woman who is of value because she is dead. This image and the other photographs are shocking in that they anticipate the death of the person photographed, both pre-empting and performing the prophesy of the death of 'the last'. The plates announce that event before its occurrence, and are, in the absence of bodies, the recorded proof of a successful extermination. The camera operates as the hands of a clock moving forwards in time, so that we see the imagined future. The photographs, like the breastplates themselves, are not representations but evidential artefacts of *methexis* — the performance of a seemingly successful genocide which could then be melancholically recalled.

I think of the light which emanates from the breastplates, as Barthes would have it, like an umbilical cord linking the body and the gaze. I think of the wax cylinder recordings of Fanny Corcoran Smith, once believed to be the last person able to sing Aboriginal songs in Tasmania. Seated across the table from her as she was about to be recorded were men who spoke about how wonderful it would be to study these songs after Fanny had died. Even before her last breath expired, they were looking forward to studying the physical reproduction of her bodily voice. I think of the body-casts made of Khoisan in South Africa, another people imagined as dying whose body traces were collected in anticipation. A vacuum opened up before the colonisers, in their erasure of alterity, which they were desperate to fill, to replace bodily absences with body traces which could be studied: sounds, casts and signs on plates. One last colonial performance, that of dying for the record, just had to be recorded. And so the post-colonial remembrance of breastplates began by calling them headstones of 'the last living member of a tribe'. This mis-remembering of colonial history left no place for post-colonial Aborigines. It sought to erase the 'unexpected moves of mimesis and alterity across quivering terrain' both historical and present.

Chapter 3
How can one be Oceanian?
The display of Polynesian
'cannibals' in France
Yves Le Fur

Skins as images

'HOW CAN ONE be Oceanian?' This question, in the manner of *The Persian Letters* of Montesquieu, introduces the reactions of Europeans confronted for the first time by the physical reality of exotic bodies from 'Terra Australis'. At this time of discoveries and cabinets of curiosities, a live body could be seen as the ultimate acquisition.

The cases of the first Polynesians to arrive in Europe are interesting to recall, because these people were often more or less willing participants in their own dislocation, and because their tattoos presented a strange image of the body. They became 'a la mode', inspiring representations which also captured the body of the 'other', making it a fictional site and displacing the reality of the encounters.

Centuries later, during the Colonial Exhibition of 1931 in Paris, the violence of the colonial gaze produced voyeuristic exhibitions where Kanaks from New Caledonia were exhibited in zoos in France and in Germany. Between the eighteenth and the twentieth century it seems that the theatrical production of the exotic body moved from one of wonder to one of denigration and repulsion.

There were also cases of Europeans captured by Oceanic people at the beginning of the nineteenth century. As they were integrated into the social life of their adopted tribe and marked with tattoos, what kind of curiosity did they inspire and what image of the myth of the Noble Savage did they reflect when they returned home? Their double dislocation throws some light on the different levels of the notion of captivity, and on its complexity.

Ahutoru (1737?–1771), the first Tahitian to visit Paris, did not imagine that the voyage would take so long. He thought that France was merely a little further than the Îles sous le vent, the limits of his world. Bougainville, the French navigator, had taken him on board as a translator and informer, wanting above all to present in France a living example of the inhabitants of 'New Citheria'. Ahutoru was the son of a Tahitian chief and a woman captured from an enemy tribe. According to Bougainville, he was not captured, but rather came with him to France of his own accord: 'the zeal of this insular [sic] to follow us was not ambiguous', wrote the navigator.

As the first Tahitian in Paris, he was presented at Court in 1769 and to the community of scholars such as Buffon, D'Alembert, Dr Brosses, and other Enlightenment philosophers. As a guest in Bougainville's home, he became friends with the Duchess of Choiseul and his 'gestures and capers' were admired by Madame de Deffand. Willing or unwilling, Ahutoru filled the role of Noble Savage, nourishing the local fashion for Tahitian exotica. As the Austrian diplomat Baron Godefroy van Swieten noted:

> The savage that M. de Bougainville has brought from the island he discovered has a dusky skin, and is quite gentle and sad. He wears on his buttocks marks of nobility that one prints in those countries with a hot iron as we do with horses in our climate. It was difficult to persuade him to wear clothes, precisely because this would hide his distinguished extraction and because he thought people would have less consideration for him.[1]

Thus, on the one hand, Ahutoru was an object of European curiosity. On the other, we can note the curiosity that the subject, Ahutoru, had for European culture. 'The only one of our spectacles that he attended was the Opera, because he passionately loves the dancing', wrote Bougainville. 'He knew the exact dates of all the open days, went alone, paid at the door like everyone else, and his favourite place was in the corridors' — these being the little balconies on each side of the stage where one could observe the changing of the scenery. The Tahitian's attention to the back of the stage seems to be significant. It also could indicate an interest in the mechanisms of representation and illusion which were integral rituals of social intercourse in this eighteenth-century society, as Diderot noted in Parodoxe sur le comédien. Ahutoru stayed in France until 1771. He died on Bourbon island (now Reunion island) while travelling back to Tahiti, his voyage funded by Bougainville. The criticism surrounding Bougainville's achievements and his promotion of the myth of a Pacific utopia was also articulated in Diderot's comments about Ahutoru in his *Supplément au voyage de Bougainville*. This polemic was less intense in the case of the famous Omai, the Tahitian man brought to Europe by Cook in 1774. Cook had previously attempted to bring Tupaia, a Tahitian chief and priest, but he had died in Batavia during the voyage.

Omai, 'although lowborn and regarded by Cook as dark, ugly and a downright blackguard',[2] was idealised in the paintings of Webber, Hodges and Reynolds. His presence contributed to the philosophical discussion, the literature and the myth of a Pacific paradise. He quickly adopted the conventions of 'civilised' behaviour, slipping neatly into the skin of the Noble Savage. His tattoos fascinated London society and 'his appearance sparked a tattooing vogue among the English aristocracy'.[3]

Eight years after his return to Tahiti, his name was used in the title of a pantomime by John O'Keeffe — *Omai, or, a trip around the world* — inspired by the journal of Cook. It was performed at Covent Garden in December 1785. This play blended Turkish imagery with romanticism and naturalism. Some of Jacques de Loutherbourg's costumes were based on information from Webber. The performance was enhanced by sensational machinery which produced thunder, clouds, waves and a shipwreck. The success of this show was followed in 1788 by that of *The Death of Captain Cook*, at the Theatre de l'Ambigue Comique in Paris. Here the emphatic representation of the exotic scene was, however, combined with images of death and savagery.

The case of the French sailor Joseph Kabris (1779?-1822) is less well known and reveals another side of the European fascination with the exotic. His adventures are narrated in a booklet of about fifteen pages, *Précis historique et véritable du séjour de Jh. Kabris, natif de Bordeaux, dans les îles de Mendoca, situées dans l'Ocean Pacifique*. The misfortunes of Kabris began at the age of fifteen, when he was shipwrecked off the coast of France. Taken prisoner by the English, he was held in a prison hulk at Portsmouth for fifteen months. In May 1795 he embarked on a whaleboat, and was shipwrecked for a second time near Santa Cristina (Tahuata) in the Marquesas Islands. He was a strong swimmer, and managed to save himself as well as an English companion named Robarts, who would later become his *frère ennemi* or 'brother enemy'. The pair was found by a group of Marquesans who took them to Nuka Hiva, where they were condemned to death. They escaped the death sentence thanks to the daughter of the chief, with whom Kabris married and had children.

As son-in-law he received his first tattoo, a blackening of the skin around his left eye, a design called *mata epo* or 'shitty eye'.[4] This tattoo is represented in Langsdorf's portrait of Kabris. The next markings he received were suns on the upper and lower eyelids of the right eye, 'that the people call *mehama* and which give me the title of judge'.[5] In one version of his account Kabris specifies that it was the chief himself who executed the first markings, the designs then being completed by a tattoo artist. In another version of the text he writes that they were not welcomed by the people until they had met the chief. He took them as friends, and after four months organised a tattooing ceremony, after which they could marry.

Having been integrated into the Marquesan tribe, Kabris fought for them in their battles with other groups. In one skirmish, he skilfully wounded an enemy chief with his sling and thereafter received a tattoo on his breast, becoming, according to his own account, 'Chief of the guard and viceroy of the tribe'. He wrote that he lived happily in his royal family, enjoying the friendship of everyone. Kabris never mentioned Robarts. He was also tattooed, but lived on the opposite side of the island, in Tiahoe Bay.

On the 7 May 1804 a Russian ship arrived in Tiahoe Bay. Robarts offered his services to von Krusenstern, the captain of the vessel, and told him that he had been abandoned on the island by his former crew members for refusing to participate in a plot. He added that the French should not be trusted. The hatred evident between Kabris and Robarts, two Europeans so far from home, drove von Krusenstern to reflect upon the hostility of nations towards one another. The captain then met Kabris, whose good relations with the Marquesans proved useful. Langsdorf, a member of the crew, remarked that the Frenchman had a better knowledge of the island than his English cohabitant. The evening before the ship's departure, Kabris was invited on board for dinner alone. Drunk on the liquor served to him by the captain, he fell asleep, and later awoke to find that the ship had set sail, and was now in the middle of the ocean. Whether it was to rid Robarts of his enemy, or because, as von Krusenstern later claimed, a sudden wind obliged him to leave, Kabris found himself removed from his adopted homeland. 'The captain employed all the ways to quiet me', he wrote, 'he told me that I was kidnapped to be presented to the Tsar Alexander as valuable object to stimulate his curiosity and to prove to him he had visited the people of remote islands'.[6]

Kabris disembarked at Kamchatka at the end of 1804 (although this is not mentioned by von Krusenstern in his account) and travelled to St Petersburg to be presented at the Court of the Tzar. Alexander admired his tattoos and compensated him for the 'inconvenience' he had suffered. Although Kabris expressed a desire to visit his parents in Bordeaux, he was still in Russia in 1817, employed as a swimming instructor in the Naval School at Kronshtadt. In the same year he was received at the court of the French king Louis XVIII, who gave him some money intended to pay for a return voyage to the Marquesas.

The royal gift was insufficient, however, and Kabris began to exhibit his tattoos in the Cabinet of Illusions in Bordeaux and in other fairs around France in order to earn money for his passage. As an accompaniment to his exhibition, he sold a booklet printed in Paris and Rouen of which only four known examples survived. Three are in the National Library in Paris, and one in Geneva (there may be a further copy in Grenoble, but research in the two libraries of this town failed to uncover it). In addition, portraits of Kabris exist with his tattoos rendered in more or less exact detail. According to Picot-Mallet, who annotated the Geneva booklet, he was 'a good sized man, very well built, with an agreeable physiognomy, a bit blackened by the climate, who intelligently answers any question which one asks him'.[7] Kabris died on 23 September 1822 in Valenciennes, after a rapid decline into sickness and misery. Aimé Leroy, a local journalist who interviewed him just before his death, wrote: 'This member of a royal family, whose misfortunes and strange fate were not well known, attracted few people, while the crowd flocked to the menagerie to see the 400 pound girl and the three-headed calf'.[8] Leroy also recounts that when Kabris died an amateur collector of curiosities attempted to obtain his skin in order to stuff and mount it for display. His corpse was buried between two old men to protect it from such attentions. Leroy wrote: 'This information could become very interesting if the illustrious descendants of Kabris one day demanded the return of his ashes to Europe'.[9]

The narrative of the skin-man merits some remarks. If his sad and romantic story can inspire a novel or a film, we can also see it as the intricate layering of different levels of captivity, symptoms of the occidental approach to the exotic body. Tattooed skin, engravings and narrative form an image in which illusion, theatre and power over the foreign body of an other are revealed.

Ahutoru and Omai were taken as strange bodies, bodies 'wrapped in images' (in reference to Alfred Gell). With unintelligible signs inscribed upon their skin, the image of their bodies was easily manipulated, enabling the creation of a 'mediatic' illusion, useful to a representation, to a fashion of tattooing (the word 'tattoo' originated from this time). The fascination Europeans had for tattoos could be read as symptomatic of the medium of the tattoo itself. Juliet Fleming says:

> Caused by the introduction of a foreign body under the skin, the
> tattoo marks the self as foreign. It consequently stands as a ready
> figure for the border skirmishing that defines conceptual relations
> not only between the inside and the outside of the body, but also
> between the inside and the outside of social groups.[10]

Kabris was a sailor, travelling the oceans for a living. He did not leave France in search of an exotic dream. When he returned to Europe his Marquesan identity was a novelty in Russia, which had only recently ventured into the Pacific, a fact which may explain the motive for his capture. When he arrived in France, however, the myth of the Noble Savage had ceased to fire the imagination — it was later revived by the painter Gauguin. Kabris turned the myth inside out. Unlike the Tahitians, he could not be seen as an incarnation of the myth and, paradoxically, his tattooed skin laid it bare. In contrast to Reynold's portrait of Omai, in which the Tahitian is pictured in antique draperies, Kabris, a Marquesan, appears as not more than a veneer of wonder and delight. His tattoos define him as somewhere between the low-class disreputable sailor and the savage. In Bordeaux's Cabinet of Illusions and in the fairs, he was a protagonist with and without costume, incongruous.

To be captive is to forfeit one's power. Kabris claimed that he was a member of the Marquesan nobility, as indicated in the engravings. His use of titles should be considered in the context of France at the time of the Restoration. Unfortunately all his powers were compromised. The armour of his tattoos stripped him of his authority. The imprimatur of his Marquesan identity marked him as a stranger, his biographical trophies relegated to the status of a stuffed trophy for an amateur collector of the bizarre. He was covered and trapped by his own skin, by unreadable patterns. His honourable disfigurement was the mark only of the high status of a Marquesan chief. He had become a monster in his own society and ended up with the monsters in a menagerie of anatomical and morbid curiosities.

It seems that the only power available to him lay in his own narrative. Inspired by the myth of a Pacific paradise, he modestly describes his experience as a life of happiness, also recounting tales of cannibalism (a practice in which, he makes clear, he did not participate). In addition, his narrative includes interesting descriptions of Marquesan art and life. Even if the facts of his departure from Nuka Hiva conflict in the different versions of his story, it caused a literary stir. A sentimental poem, 'Le départ de Joseph Kabris de l'Île de Nouka Hiva', signed M. C., is attached to the copy of his booklet in the Geneva library. Aimé Leroy described the capture thus:

> One day, while he was sleeping in the forest and dreaming of delicious things, Krusenstern, a Russian captain who was exploring this country and researching curiosities, saw him, took him prisoner, and conducted him to his ship, whipping him along the way and sent him to Saint Petersburg. The daughter of the king wrung her hands, and cried for so long that she is perhaps still crying.[11]

The life of Kabris was not unique. One can find a number of examples of Europeans who lived — willingly or unwillingly — among different oceanic peoples during the early contact period, such as that of William Mariner in Tonga, and Barnet Burns in New Zealand.

The story of William Mariner, as told by John Martin, was published in 1817. Mariner, the well-educated son of a London trader, was fascinated by travel stories. In 1805 he joined the crew of a corsair, the *Port au Prince*, which sailed from England on 12 February. After various adventures and battles, damage to the ship forced them to stop in Tonga for repairs. Here a disagreement between the crew and the captain led to the invasion of the ship by the Tongans and the massacre of all except five of the Europeans. While waiting for death, Mariner became King Finow I's friend and adviser, and was given the name of the king's dead son, as well as an adopted mother and a plantation. At one stage he attempted to construct a boat in order to travel to New Holland, but this endeavour failed. The Europeans had to obey the orders of King Finow I, but Mariner could sometimes refuse. They accompanied the King on numerous expeditions and battles throughout Tonga. When Finow died, Mariner continued his good relations with the royal family, now with the King's son, Finow II, as his patron. One day, some years later, he saw a European ship passing by the islands, and managed to get on board after killing one of the men in a canoe. Finow II then visited the ship, and was enchanted by all the things that he saw on board. Mariner and the ship's captain found it difficult to dissuade the King from his firm intention to accompany them back to Europe. Finally he made Mariner promise to return with a boat and to take him to visit his country.

There was no mention in William Mariner's narrative of tattoos. Barnet Burns, however, a sailor and trader who lived with Maori tribes in New Zealand, was covered in tattoos from head to foot. The experience of Burns can be seen as even more ambiguous than that of Kabris.

Burns, then known as George White, came to New Zealand in about 1830 in order to trade for flax. He stayed for eight months, becoming fluent in the Maori language. He then left the country, and later returned to New Zealand in February in 1831 as the agent of a Sydney merchant, installing himself as the first European trader on the Mahia Peninsula, on the east coast. He lived under the protection of a Maori chief of the Ngati Kahungunu tribe, whose daughter he married. After eleven months a vessel arrived from Australia with an order to close his trading station. White, or 'Hori Waiti' as he was known in Maori, refused to leave his pregnant wife. Threatened and attacked on several occasions for his goods, he was eventually captured by a rival group who killed members of his wife's tribe. He saved his own life by agreeing to fight for his captors, and to be tattooed. He then escaped before the tattoos were finished and found his way back to his family, with whom he moved to Uawa, from where he exported flax to Sydney. His tattoos were finished, giving him *mana,* and he became, according to his narrative, the chief of a tribe of 600 people. He has many descendants.

In October 1834 he sailed for Sydney to carry out some business and ended up sailing with the ship to England in February 1835. He adopted the name of Barnet Burns (perhaps in order to attract attention to his tattoos, which he described as a disfigurement). His face and thighs were inscribed with Maori tattoos, while the rest of his body was decorated with the tattoos of a sailor. Dressed in Maori costume, he exhibited his tattoos, along with the head of a hostile Maori chief, while narrating the story of his battles and adventures.

The booklet of his story was first published in 1835. The title of the version published in Belfast in 1844 is: *A Brief Narrative Of A New Zealand Chief Being The Remarkable History Of Barnet Burns An English Sailor With a Faithful Account Of The Way In Which He Became a Chief Of One Of The Tribes Of New Zealand, Together With a Few Remarks On The Manners And The Customs Of The People, And Other Interesting Matter — Written By Himself etc.*

In an attempt to attract sympathy, Burns writes in the introduction to his text of 'the severe hardships and great cruelties which the subject of this short history underwent during his ten years detention in New Zealand':

> We cannot refrain from indulging in the hope that the perusal of this pamphlet will act as a stimulus to Missionary exertion, and that the various societies who have long been engaged in sending persons to preach the Gospel to those who 'sit in darkness and the shadow of death' we trust that a holy emulation will arise among them, who shall do most to reclaim these savages who have inflicted these unheard of cruelties.[12]

He thus provides a justification for publishing his story: 'Since I find it impossible to walk the streets without exciting the curiosity of all who see me, from my remarkable appearance, and not always having an opportunity of satisfying them'.[13] Although he later attempted to return to New Zealand, Burns was never reunited with his Maori family. The last known reference to him is from 1859, and the date and place of his death are unknown.

What was said for Kabris could equally be applied to Burns — loss of power, dispossession of the self, living as a go-between at the border of social groups — in spite of the unique nature of their experiences. As displaced individuals, their bodies indelibly marking them as foreign, they can only win recognition in the illusional space of the theatre. But this theatre is no more than a space of voyeuristic exhibition, a kind of peep show. Kabris and Burns are merely strange refractions in the mirror of the colonial gaze.

This chapter began with the stories of two dislocated Oceanian people. I would like to close by briefly discussing the presence of a group of New Caledonian Kanaks at the Colonial Exhibition in Paris in 1931. An article on this topic was published in the New Caledonian journal *Mwà Véé* (No 13, 1996). The account demonstrates the importance of appreciating the complexity of captivity and the relations between the captive and the abductor.

New Caledonia, French territory since 1853, was represented in the Universal Exhibition of 1889 by a display that was small compared to that planned for the 1931 Colonial Exhibition, a group of ten bungalows drawn without 'pittoresque'. Visitors, expecting savage cannibals, felt that they had been deceived when confronted by this small group of quiet cultivators. For the Exhibition of 1931, in contrast, 111 Kanaks left Noumea for Paris, among them two albinos. They had been chosen by a Kanak chief from a different part of the island. Their travel arrangements, for the eight months they would spend in France, were made by the French Old Colonists' Federation (FFAC), which had promised a pleasant stay in the Exhibition, sightseeing around Paris, and a tour of France. Arriving in Marseilles five weeks before the opening in order to have time to acclimatise, they were instead taken directly to Paris. Instead of being installed in the Exhibition at the Bois de Vincennes, the Kanaks were exhibited at the Jardin d'Acclimatation in the Bois de Boulogne, on the other side of Paris, a park for exotic plants and animals! The FFAC, writes Jean-Pierre Velot, was connected to the company that operated the Jardin d'Acclimatation.[14] They justified this change of plan by pointing out the recreational advantages of the natural scenery. Newspapers ran stories about two sensational attractions with wild cannibals and a thousand crocodiles. Indeed the worst was yet to come.

The Jardin d'Acclimatation had arranged a temporary exchange with Hamburg Zoo of sixty Kanaks for a number of crocodiles. The Kanaks were exhibited in Berlin, Frankfurt, Hamburg, Leipzig and Munich as savage cannibals and polygamists, despite the fact that most of them were practising Catholics. From Hamburg, the Kanaks wrote to their Parisian acquaintances, and some of this correspondence survives. Auguste Badimoin, a Kanak school teacher from Canada, described the conditions in which they lived:

> I want to tell you that since our arrival in Hamburg we have had to dance from morning until night, without counting the other games: firing arrows, throwing spears, swimming, climbing up four high poles…after that we have to go immediately to carve three enormous trunks into canoes…Another order of the Director is that at the beginning of the show we have to go out naked, only with manou…Several of us are sick, as we have always to dance in cold rain…We sleep on the ground, without mats or straw as the Director says that the people must be made to believe that we are savage and that there are no Europeans in our country…[15]

They were forbidden to wear trousers or shoes, and were not allowed more than fifty metres from the camp. German people came to be pictured with these 'cannibals'. In some sense this activity can be seen as propaganda directed against France, suggesting that it was not able to present civilised people from its colonies.

Journalists, missionaries and the Chief Consul of New Caledonia expressed their concern at the treatment of the Kanaks. The minister Maurice Leenhardt voiced his indignation. Eventually the Kanaks returned to Noumea in November 1931. Seven of them decided to remain in France for several months or even years, and went on to work in a circus.

Nevertheless a number of the Kanaks made European acquaintances during their stay. The stories of some of these friendships have been recounted by people who participated in the exhibition and who are still alive today. A photographic record remains of the friendships between two little girls, Laura and Osla. When she grew up, Laura named her daughter Osla. Some of the Kanaks went on to correspond regularly with German friends, and for this reason were suspected of collaboration with the enemy during World War.II Marc Oiremoin and Essaou-Ido Tyuienon were children at this time. They consider that their parents succeeded in their mission to demonstrate to the French and German public the quality of Kanak dances, songs and their physical strength. 'For us it is a great pride to have parents who participated in the Colonial Exhibition of 1931. It was a great chief who chose them and asked them to accompany him.'[16] Gilbert Tyuienon, a senior civil servant whose grandfather participated in the exhibition, says:

> Before my grandmother told me about it I had a stereotyped judgement. My grandfather always said to her that he had a good, even a very good memory of it. For the first time in his life he met white men who considered him man to man as an equal, he said, and not as an inferior. This feeling of equality was strongest in Germany, and he recounted that he was regularly invited in the Hagenbeck family in Hamburg. Grandfather gave to his two daughters the name of his friend's daughters: Emily and Loti.[17]

Tyuienon further notes: 'The tendency is always to think, to act for the Kanak. It is this sense of colonial paternalism which is frustrating'.[18]

These different interpretations of the exhibition must be relativised. It might be considered, for example, that the family 'Hagenbeck' may have been the 'Hagenbergs'. They were in fact the entertainment promoters who had the exclusive contract to exhibit the Kanaks in Germany. The sentimental and apologetic address of memories should always be taken into account. This colonial episode, so bizarre in contemporary terms that it seems like an absurd comic masquerade, represents also a collection of individual experiences, both positive and negative. However, while for the Kanaks, it was in some ways an opportunity to forge relationships, it was still one of the worst examples of the voyeuristic theatre of the exotic ever mounted.

Chapter 4

Captors or captives? The Australian Native Mounted Police

Mary Mackay

A DIFFICULT but important area of race relations in nine-teenth-century Australia is the story of the Native Mounted Police. The role of the Aboriginal men who chose to become guardians of white law has created an agonistic space, replete with unresolved questions of cultural disjunction and racial tension. I will argue that although the Aboriginal men of the mounted force operated as enforcers of the law, apprehending offenders and bringing miscreants to justice, they were themselves captives of a regime which manipulated their minds and controlled their bodies. Membership of the force changed their way of think-ing and acting, and in turn their whole lifestyle, creating a situation which could only end in tragedy.

My intention is not to examine why some Aboriginal men enlisted in a corps whose main purpose became that of policing their own people. A number of reasons are possible: a belief that the work of the corps would lead to less loss of Aboriginal lives; or an acceptance of colonial values by some who had been brought up in mission schools. Rather, my purpose is to deconstruct the various representations — drawings, photographs and paintings — of the Native Mounted Police.

Historians have researched the various corps and learnt what can be discovered about the men themselves, yet there appears to be a dimension of the discourse that still requires analysis and theori-sation. When visual representation is included in an account, it is often passed over as simply 'illustrating' the history.[1] Instead, I will argue that the visual images of the Native Mounted Police should be viewed not as simple reflections of events within an established order, but rather as part of the construction of a racist discourse, its codes and its relationship with other cultural codes. Such images or representations are significant texts, and in some cases can be considered 'statements' in the Foucauldian sense of being crucial documents in the history of black and white relations.[2] I will relate this discussion to a number of colonial images of Aboriginal people produced in the early years of settlement, and compare them to a later group of sketches, paintings and photographs of members of the Native Mounted Police produced between the 1840s and the end of the nineteenth century.

The issue that most frequently emerges from histories of colonised lands is put best by Homi Bhabha in his article, 'The Other Question'. 'The objective of colonial rule', he writes, 'is to construe the colonised as a population of degenerate types on the basis of racial origin in order to justify conquest and to establish systems of administration and instruction'.[3] The overarching influence of imperialist British rule changed many spheres of the lives of the indigenes in post-settlement Australia, but none more so than those of the men who became members of the Native Mounted Police.[4]

The original corps, usually called the Native Mounted Police or the 'Black Police', was formed for a number of reasons — to help track bushrangers, to maintain the law in the countryside and to assist pacifying hostile blacks on the frontier, the outlying districts, known in colonial Australia as 'the border country'. The situation that prompted the idea of organising a special force was the number of serious skirmishes between 'blacks' and 'whites', often leading to death and inevitably producing grounds for further disturbances. Ostensibly, the job of the Native Mounted Police was pacification — to prevent battles over land — since it soon became clear that the spread of white settlement led to retaliation by the original owners and later general hostilities from tribes as hunting grounds were lost and sacred places desecrated. Occasionally local blacks put up immediate fierce resistance; more often they developed guerrilla warfare techniques in a continual struggle to regain the territories which were often the only source of their sustenance.[5]

Since the beginning of settlement, Aboriginal tribesmen had been employed as guides and trackers to apprehend runaway convicts, and as peacekeepers in their own clans. As early as 1825 it was recommended that native police be recruited to help control the bushranging menace. In 1837 Captain Alexander Maconochie, then secretary to Lieutenant-Governor Franklin in Hobart, advocated the creation of an organised regiment of Aboriginal constables and suggested that the model could follow the British example of the sepoys in India. He and others thought that a trained military-style force would help to 'civilise' the Aborigines.[6] The first native police units before the 1840s were not highly organised and did not last. Despite the designated role of the native police being suppression of conflict and peacekeeping, the great hope of the government was similar to that of Maconochie — that the benefits of employment and discipline would assist in the 'civilisation' of the young Aboriginal men. Civilisation of the Aboriginal people was a recurring theme in the plans of government but its implementation was visualised as emulation of white society rather than any proper investigation and course of action that might benefit a semi-nomadic race having to cope with the tragic consequences of foreign seizure and settlement of its land. Problems in the so-called civilising program began even before the men enlisted, as there were vocal critics of the idea that military-style training was the way to proceed. Many settlers opposed the plan and churchmen and others spoke against it. The Quaker James Backhouse came to the conclusion:

> It is gratifying to see the Government disposed to make efforts to benefit the people whose country they have usurped; but their effort in this case does not appear to us to be of a character such as Christians ought to make, being contrary to 'peace on earth, and good will toward men'.[7]

Maconochie had spoken of winning the loyalty of the native men and changing their attitudes from hostility to affection; the hope for this and similar gains overcame the doubts. It was eventually believed that a well-organised force could succeed, especially if white officers were used as mentors to teach the men and set an example.[8] In 1842 Captain Henry Dana was put in charge of the first permanent corps, a group of twenty from the Yarra tribe from the Port Phillip district, an area which extended into what is now New South Wales. Frederick Walker was an equally successful commander in the Middle District, northern New South Wales, a stretch of country that is now part of Queensland. Both commanders, Dana and Walker, achieved what was believed in some quarters to be impossible, the formation of a highly disciplined group. These were the main divisions but later a unit was assembled in Queensland and this corps continued to operate into the early years of the twentieth century.[9]

In embracing a set of knowledges and operating under a power system that was remote in every sense from tribal values and customs, these young men *undermined* the stereotype of 'primitive' or 'savage' established by the white settlers in the early days of the colonies. Bhabha suggests that 'the construction of the colonial subject in discourse and the exercise of colonial power through discourse, demands an articulation of forms of *difference* — racial and sexual'.[10] In nineteenth-century Australia, as in other colonised areas of the world, racial 'difference' was initially constructed through the *body* of the other: the colonisers first saw the naked state of the Aboriginal population as a sign that the 'wild men' they encountered were not only uncivilised, but at an early stage of human evolution. At a time when the discipline of anthropology was new, and the so-called 'science of the races' positioned the various peoples of the world on a hierarchical scale, it was easy to see the indigenes of this continent as low in the sequence of evolution and close to the 'wildness' of the country itself.

This stereotype was based on what was assumed to be historical evidence as well as local knowledge. Ancient and well-known traditions of the 'wild man' in biblical and other early records increased settlers' propensity to attach the less desirable characteristics of the wild man to the Aboriginal community. Hayden White speaks of a significant connection between early ideas of 'wilderness' and a general understanding of the type of people who dwell within it. He explains the interiorisation of the wild man in the western psyche as a projection of repressed desires and anxieties: desire for the freedom possessed by the wild man, countered by anxiety at what appears as inexplicable and threatening behaviour as well as the inability to communicate.[11] While specific thoughts of this nature were not necessarily entertained by colonisers in Australia, there are many colonial texts, including visual ones, that suggest the unconscious belief that to be wild is to be 'one whose physical attributes are in themselves evidence of one's evil nature'.[12] The visible physicality of unclothed Aborigines and their closeness to the land contributed to the colonisers' apprehension of wildness and savagery.

One of the first commentators on the coloniser/colonised relationship, Albert Memmi, argues that one of the ways the coloniser created his own superior image was to contrast his merits with the lesser virtues of the colonised:

> He will persist in degrading them, using the darkest colors to depict them. If need be, he will act to devalue them, annihilate them. But he can never escape this circle. The distance which colonisation places between him and the colonised must be accounted for, and, to justify himself, he increases this distance still

further by placing the two figures irretrievably in opposition: his glorious position and the despicable one of the colonised.[13]

The naked bodies of Aboriginal warriors advancing in combat, for example, were construed as objects outside known and accepted codes of interaction in warfare; their ability to attack and then disappear into the wildness of the bush made them seem treacherous and close to the cunning of beasts. Such actions were construed as devious conduct rather than appreciated as bush skills, while the comparisons with animals reduced the status of the men to physical bodies with instinctive impulses, bodies that did not have the advantage of intellectual thought. Referring to the western mind/body division that has persisted ever since the authoritative writings of Descartes, theorists such as Michel Foucault have questioned this dichotomy and argued for an indivisible relationship between the two. Foucault speaks of things that achieve expression in the body, events that happen outside the body, but also such things as desires, failings and errors, which he argues also have an impact on the body. His claims are centred on the historical inscription of the body by its own genealogy. 'The body', says Foucault, 'is the inscribed surface of events.'[14] This inscription takes various forms in a discourse that includes factors whose relationship to the body are, as it were, once removed: for example, clothing and other social discourses. Representation has the power to suggest common history and sentiments, yet in many cases it would appear that colonial artists projected the native person for visual consumption as pure 'body', in order to establish the European by contrast as intellect or 'mind'.

Paintings, sketches and later photographs of Aboriginal people in the early years of European settlement form a significant part of a discursive formation which constitutes the indigenous race as stereotypical figures — feral, fierce and untamed creatures, with barbaric customs and brutish actions. Artists sketching a fracas, for instance, made clear distinctions between the 'civilised' clothed bodies of the newcomers and the 'uncivilised' naked bodies of the indigenes. Thomas Baines' 1855 watercolour painting, *Meeting with Hostile Natives, Victoria River*, conveys a sense of uncontrolled passions in the advancing and threatening bodies of the naked 'other'.[15] Further evidence for this spurious belief in a lower form of humanity was gained from the corroboree dances, in which the imitation of animal behaviour appeared to provide proof of the untutored savages' attachment to acts and practices of a bestial nature. The colonisers ignored or were unaware of the ritual or spiritual significance of these activities, seeing them only as signs of an inferior and unsophisticated mentality. More importantly, the customs were not considered the products of cultural difference; instead the body of the other was fetishised. Abdul JanMohamed explains that this type of fetishisation operates by 'substituting natural or generic categories for those that are socially or ideologically determined'. The characteristics were thus seen to be *in* the race, an inherent 'natural' quality of the native person as opposed to being an acquired habit, part of the traditional activities of a particular culture. JanMohamed also speaks of the problematical nature of many western apprehensions of the indigene: 'In describing the attributes or actions of the native, issues such as intention, causality, extenuating circumstances, and so forth, are completely ignored; in the "imaginary" colonialist realm, to say "native" is automatically to say "evil" and to evoke immediately the economy of the Manichean allegory'.[16]

S.T. Gill's watercolour sketch of a corroboree is typical of many paintings by colonial artists which exhibit a powerful potential to portray the bands with this type of identification. Nearly all colonial paintings of the corroboree ceremony tend to stress the strangeness of the performance by enhancing the gloomy gothic quality of the night scene. A similar image by John Glover shows a mysterious clearing in the bush peopled with dancing and gesticulating figures whose painted bodies have turned to gruesome skeletons in the flickering firelight.[17] Even the daytime dances represented in David Collins' *Account of the Colony* and thought to be by the convict artist Thomas Watling, appear to have as subject matter dances in which the participants are imitating animal behaviour, thus suggesting to the reader that the bodies have a close affinity with both animality and animals. Thus 'difference' was sought out or deliberately constructed in certain types of imagery, in part to satisfy a demand for novelty and the public's interest in strange phenomena. Sometimes, however, it is clear that it was with an eye to demeaning the race for the reason outlined by Memmi: justification of the conquest.

Yet, as a mark of 'difference' the most noticeable characteristic of the corporeality of the black body was considered not its behaviour but the colour of the skin. Frantz Fanon's words resound through all subsequent writings on the other, for he equates a subaltern position with skin colour, black as a distinguishing mark of inferiority. Fanon's message is memorable: 'For not only must the man be black, he must be black in relation to the white man'.[18] In other words, the stigma of inferiority is produced in a most fundamental sense through opposition, and this diametrically opposed contrast with the 'white' is the key activating function in the construction of the other. Bhabha also makes the point that of all bodily characteristics it is skin that takes foremost place as 'natural' identity. 'Skin, as the key signifier of cultural and racial difference in the stereotype, is the most visible of fetishes', he claims, 'recognized as "common knowledge" in a range of cultural, political and historical discourses, and plays a public part in the racial drama that is enacted every day in colonial societies'.[19] Projecting the stereotype as fetish, in the affirmation of similarity — the anxiety or fear associated with the 'lack' or difference, the Aboriginal person's skin is not the same — the fetish represents the simultaneous play between metaphor as substitution and metonymy which registers the perceived lack.[20] Situated within an acknowledged scopic regime, the black skin of the Aborigine was equated with the belief, widely circulated in the late eighteenth and early nineteenth century, that the colour itself signified a less intelligent race. The various gradations of skin tones were remarked on not only in ethnographic documents but in many journals of Australian exploration, authors speculating that the darker the skin the more unlikely it was that the tribesman could be civilised. Attached then to a sphere of scopic evaluation were gradations of moral and ethnocentric classification based on approaches to skin colour.

When we remember that both caricature and the silhouette were established in the eighteenth century as popular art forms, it is not unexpected that several colonial artists took advantage of the black skin to portray the body in a style of what would now be called black and white art. The body was shown as black against a white background, as in T. Browne's watercolour sketch of a naked woman with dillybag, water-carrier and fishing line.[21] Indicated in the depiction is a suggestion of role reversal among a race already seen as different and strange. She appears as the provider of food for the family, but there is also a hint of ridicule and mockery in the pose. This same body of the indigene revealed not only black skin, but skin often monstrously mutilated with scarification. The cutting of the flesh in scarification or cicatrisation was viewed by the settlers much as the tattoo was viewed — acceptable for the lower ranks, such as in the navy where it was a very old tradition, but considered a barbarous custom elsewhere, unsuitable for any person of standing in society.[22] Men and women with tribal markings were often sought out by artists and later by photographers, in order to demonstrate in the images an excess of the singular, to accentuate the mark of difference in a body already seen under the gaze of the white coloniser as outrageously and dangerously different. The same naked body was known to be transformed for ceremonial occasions, daubed with clay or covered in feathers, all such 'primitive' customs being associated by the colonisers with the same low stage of the human evolutionary cycle.[23]

The painting by the artist known only as the 'Port Jackson Painter', of Colebee, a member of the Cadigal tribe, joins with similar portrayals to convey a strong message that the adornment of feathers on the upper part of his body was typical of the crude practices engaged in by his tribesmen.[24] That the occasion of the decoration was a funeral, with Colebee adorned in mourning raiment for his lost friend Balloderree, is not information made available to the viewer. Thus the image performs as part of a power system, discriminating by omission, through the lack of information offered. Projected with subtle overtones, such depictions form a discursive domain where ethnocentrism is the hidden metaphor forever fetishing the black body into a stereotypical alterity. The stereotype was continually re-enacted, as all stereotypes must be, in written and visual texts, and reinforced in everyday situations, proscribing the fate of the Aborigine to be forever seen as other, the natural opposite of the western. According to JanMohamed, 'genuine and thorough comprehension of "otherness" is possible only if the self can somehow negate or at least severely bracket the values, assumptions and ideology of his own culture'. In practice, however, this cannot happen, as the coloniser does not question his own society's formation, confidently assuming it is superior.[25]

Yet the myth of black inferiority and the fetishised body did not remain stable, but was invaded by incursions of doubt (the discontinuity that Foucault maintains is a feature of every discourse). Many settlers realised that in certain circumstances blacks could play out the role of 'other' and were able to outsmart the whites. Even as he was seen as inferior, most observers conceded that in the bush the black man was king. It was the acknowledged skill and experience of Aborigines as trackers in the bush that led to the idea of having a native police force.

With the organisation of the first permanent group of troopers in the 1840s, white society's popular image of 'primitive man' suffered a jolt and ethnographic assumptions had to be rethought. The men who entered the force soon undermined the stereotypical identity previously awarded to tribespeople. The metaphysical alterity created by colonial society shifted as the young police developed a new consciousness, one that appeared to fit easily into a settler society, and was apparent in their bodily actions and behaviour. One of Homi Bhabha's challenges is to insist that a rejection of difference is at the heart of the stereotype. In other words, its otherness and particularity is, in fact, fundamentally about similarity — about the impossibility of the other being fully assimilated. As suggested above, the body of the colonised other was not seen basically as simply different but constituted oppositionally by comparison with the body of the coloniser. When we come to consider the clansmen who relinquished living tribal lifestyles for the career, the clothes and the vicissitudes that accompanied the life of the trooper, such positioning of the stereotype offers a way of understanding the conflictual and hidden processes that concealed the construction of the Aboriginal males' new identity. Their position as police awarded them status as privileged members of a settler community which desperately needed their skills. And because the lives of the colonisers were ruled by a white protestant work ethic, that is, a belief in the virtue of 'self-help', white society approved the men's action in joining up: it was thought they would 'better' themselves.[26] The government's hope was that the Aboriginal population would become workmen and replace convict labour when transportation ceased. This was a classic situation of the government's double plan: a need to make use of the men for pacification but at the same time to take advantage of the situation and encourage the development of a labouring class.[27]

Whereas most Aborigines did not suffer easily the settlers' assumed dominance, the Aboriginal men of the NMP may have accepted the myth of equality held out to them, believing they might turn the situation to their advantage. Traditional tribal lifestyles were negated, by the horses the men rode, the new muskets they carried and the smart uniform that clothed their bodies. As the power they yielded was invested in these trappings, the men were encouraged to believe they constituted 'whiteness' despite the black skin. The uniform, the guns, the swords and even the horses inscribed their bodies and instigated changes in their conduct and in the identity they projected to others.

The large group of watercolours by the colonial artist, William Strutt, which was published in his album, *Victoria the Golden*, in 1857, even today convey white society's sense of surprise at the speed of the change in the men's lifestyle. Three of the images, titled *Black Troopers Quarters, Richmond Paddock. Vic.* (see Illustration 2); *Native Mounted Police, Black Trooper Sketched in the Quarters at Richmond Paddock,* and *Aboriginal Police Force, 1850 Details of Uniform* suggest the powerful shift from the body of the Aboriginal man inscribed with signifiers of his tribal habitas, to the 'new' body clothed in a uniform that was the visible sign of western law and order.[28] It is possible to read these images as more about that miraculous — ultimately impossible — metamorphosis, that sudden transformation from uncivilised to civilised, than about the very different realities of the lives of these men, who in the end were rejected by both black and white cultures.

Strutt's emphasis on the men's powerful black bodies constrained by a European military uniform works more to emphasise difference rather than sameness, thus giving physical form to Fanon's argument, mentioned earlier, that not only must the other be black but his blackness must be put into contradistinction with whiteness. Curbing the freedom of the body could also be seen as symbolic of the strictures that were imposed on the behaviour and the disposition of the men. Strutt did not appear consciously to denigrate the black troopers — quite the contrary, his drawings suggest he was impressed. In his journal, according to Geoffrey Dutton, 'he also exposed the tragedy of their lives, used by the white men for a while and then disbanded and left to wander back to their fellows, who murdered them, presumably for their activities in the police force'.[29]

The mentality that led Henry Dana to design a new outfit for the black troopers was part of a nineteenth-century English obsession with covering the body that was also a feature of mission stations. It was less a concern with decency than a power struggle, the desire to have the colonial subject conform to convention. The native police initially wore navy jackets, cast-offs from the police and military. Once Dana had them in smart green jackets and pants with red braid he exposed them to the public at every opportunity, proud of their appearance and their ability to take part in parades. Unkempt hair was cut short to accommodate a neat forage cap (a shako), and side-whiskers and a moustache gave them the appearance of mid-nineteenth-century 'gentlemen'. The moustache, worn by the NMP, had the effect of identifying the police, even when out of uniform, to both the settlers and the Aboriginal community. Yet it was an ambiguous signifier, functioning as a symbol of the new power enjoyed by the NMP, while also making it clear to all that such power was in effect without authority — it was conditional upon white sovereignty and hence deeply compromised.

Strutt's painting titled *Native Police on Horseback* emphasises the metamorphosis of black into white while, at the same time, demonstrating the artificiality of this change. The effect of the image is to say that the tribal black had mutated into a smart 'gentleman' rider in a long tradition of upper-class Englishmen who commissioned portraits of themselves on their horses. While not suggesting that the subjects realised the portent of their pose in the equine tradition, it is true that young Aboriginal men were aware of class distinctions. This is obvious from records that document their contempt for convicts turned bushrangers, and their emulation of the officers rather than the men of the ranks. To the white settler, however, this transformation was of a superficial nature. The squatter Henry Meyrick described the Aboriginal men who lived with him at his property on the Mornington Peninsula in Victoria as dressing like gentlemen, and calling themselves 'gentlemens'.[30] The doubling of the plural, the 's' on the end of the word, is a typical example of what Homi Bhabha is arguing in his classic phrase: 'Almost the same but not quite'. The rhyming of 'quite' with 'white' is not only a device to draw attention to the gap between the cultures but also to stress the impossibility of the black man's ability to bridge that space in the eyes of the white community. Bhabha explains the problem: 'The menace of mimicry is its double vision which in disclosing the ambivalence of colonial discourse also disrupts its authority'.[31] The colonised, despite their efforts, cannot leave behind their former lives.

The racist politics which lay at the heart of the institution of the NMP is also evidenced by the names conferred on individuals of the force by their white counterparts. Some were given the appellation 'gentleman' as in 'Gentleman Jemmy'. In taking on the trappings of a cultural code at variance with their own, members of the detachments were in a political no-man's-land where they mimicked the white but had few of the white's political privileges; this is most clearly evident in the refusal of the colonial powers to let them own land or vote. This factor alone clearly undermines the argument that the white society was genuinely attempting to 'civilise' the Aboriginal people and that the institution of the NMP was a forerunner in this endeavour. The native police were players in discourses constructed around imperialism's desire to make indigenous peoples appear Anglicised while denying them full English subjecthood. Homi Bhabha suggests that, in order to be effective, mimicry must 'continually produce its slippage, its excess, its difference'. He stresses what he calls the 'double vision' of mimicry, its ambivalence as problematic of colonial subjection.[32] While superficially the native police resembled their white colleagues, there were obviously conflictual identity effects which could not be broached with simple instruction. The resemblance they projected was a metonymic presence, new partial knowledge competing with entrenched tribal lore. Under the gaze of their fellow blacks their actions were inevitably viewed with anger but possibly also an anxiety that the power they yielded would be used to score against old enemies, and a concern for the imbalance their role created in the traditional structure of Aboriginal society. In being entrusted with many dangerous tasks — chasing bushrangers, apprehending offenders, carrying despatches, and acting as guards in the gold escorts[33] — they showed they were responsible and 'civilised', yet the ambivalence of their identity and their lack of real authority continued to manifest itself.

The attempted transformation took place under a regime whose power was vested in the metaphoric 'English book'.[34] Learned conduct, which in this case included not only the ability to mimic white behavioural patterns but a willingness to adopt the outward trappings, is one of the signs of knowledge being imparted, and that 'knowledge' is not simply an information process but a system by which the coloniser directs the thought process of the colonised: 'It displaces the colonised's original image of his own culture and identity and substitutes the values and beliefs of the coloniser'.[35] Even if the subject adopts a western mentality willingly and takes on a position as a 'mimic man', he cannot evade being torn between cultures, and turns hybrid, a synovial figure lost in a sea of ambivalence. The deliberate encouragement of such a falling was a significant strategy of imperialist power and domination, justified as assimilation, but not with any aim of equality.

In citing the position of one who might be considered as the ultimate example of mimic man, Marie Fels offers the case of the young Aboriginal Murrumwiller, who took the name Charles Never. He was educated at Merri Creek school, apprenticed to Mr Foreman, a tailor in Melbourne, and then joined the NMP as their tailor. When Charles Never saw the native police in their green uniforms with the red stripe, he said they were what he termed 'real black gentlemen'. He joined the force and made every endeavour to be a 'gentleman' himself, adopting the English language and refusing to speak pidgin. He sometimes wore elegant clothes, including a tall hat, a waistcoat, kid gloves and highly polished boots, and, to act out the complete integer, he carried a cane. In Strutt's 1851 painting, *Portrait of Charles Never*, he is depicted as a nineteenth-century gentleman suitably garbed, holding a military cap and sitting at ease (see Illustration 3). Never appears, in the context of colonialist values and manners, as dignified and respectable, a vindication of the rise of the intelligent and industrious black man. It is revealing that Strutt chose this formal pose, for new photography techniques had helped the formality of the eighteenth-century portrait stance give way to more informal postures. The effect of Strutt's drawing, which appears full of admiration for the sitter, may well have reinforced a conventional practice of the time — that of dressing indigenous peoples in European garb — in order to put them on display at special performances before European society. The image was reproduced in the *Illustrated Australian Magazine* in 1851 and was thus seen by a large section of settler society. The unfortunate ending to the story is that Charles/Murrumwiller was killed by fellow tribesmen who were angry at his obvious desire to mimic the white. Charles Never is like the model prisoner who tries to please his guards and is then 'lost' to the culture of both communities. The portrait no doubt would have found similar disfavour with the white community who could not accept this 'mimic man' who was 'not quite' white.

A representation, such as this one, which acts as cultural and social 'statement', contributes to the construction of identity — as difference — as seen through the eyes of the dominant group, especially when it is disseminated to a wide audience. It is also possible, however, that the excessiveness of Never's mimicry creates, for some spectators — particularly indigenous people — what Michael Taussig has described as a moment of 'mimetic excess', that is, a moment in which there is an 'understanding that artifice is natural, no less than nature is historicised'. 'Mimetic excess', he writes, 'provides access to understanding the unbearable truths of make-believe as foundation of an all-too-seriously serious reality, manipulated but also manipulatable'.[36]

William Strutt's celebrated images of the police were not only published in his own album, but several were turned into engravings for Thomas Ham's *Gold Diggers Portfolio* of 1854. This book had a wide distribution, and lithographs made from Strutt's original drawings were sold from the 1850s to the 1870s. Thus, despite Strutt's intentions, this body of imagery may be read as contributing to the construction of the image of the NMP in the consciousness of a public who may have publicly espoused the potential of the Aboriginal community for change, as well as the democratic ideal of equality for all races, but whose behaviour towards the Aboriginal people — the acts of dispossession, land seizure, violence, extermination — suggested the opposite.

Disciplined and regimented by the process of their training, the native police were viewed by the government primarily as useful agents of white expansion. Foucault tells us that a body becomes a useful force only 'if it is both a productive body and a subjected body'.[37] Part of the power they assumed had arrived from indoctrination into white military-style activities which gave them an ability to act efficiently in stressful situations. 'The great advantage of the force in future', wrote Commandant Walker to the Colonial Secretary, 'will be that they will accompany the settlers as they move out, and thus prevent those lamentable collisions between the settlers and the aboriginal natives which have invariably occurred when a new portion of this Colony has been at first occupied'.[38]

There were complaints about the constables' enthusiasm for guns, and for their taking the opportunity to retaliate against old enemies. Yet these were clearly exaggerated, as individuals had little power to act alone — all their actions were undertaken in conjunction with white superior officers. More important for white control of the countryside was an invisible micro-physics of power that operated without direct action on their part. Their existence constituted a form of surveillance over the tribal blacks, what Foucault calls 'an optics of power'; this came to mean that simply knowing the NMP were in a district put fear into the local clans, who had heard of their exploits, internalised the strength of their achievements, and wanted to avoid engaging with them.

Their presence in a district was often enough to avert incidents, so they gained some prestige in the eyes of the white settlers and were seen in some quarters as a successful experiment by the government. Bridges notes that 'the more colorful, but illicit exploits of the Corps were not enshrined for history in its official records'. There are references, for instance, to the mass killing of members of a Gippsland tribe during a search for a white woman believed to be held captive.[39] But since the commander in charge was Henry Dana, history can hardly allow the black troopers to assume too much of the blame. Under Commander Frederick Walker the Macintyre area was rescued from the continual depredations carried out by local tribesmen. Walker reported details of the incident to the Colonial Secretary:

An attempt made by the combined Fitzroy Downs, Dawson and Condamine blacks, about 150 in number, to repeat their attack on this station, brought on two collisions with the Native Police. On the first occasion the Fitzroy Down blacks, the same who had killed seven men of Mr. Macpherson's, and Mr. Blyth's shepherd, besides spearing himself, and also murdering two of Mr. Hughes's men, suffered so severely, that they returned to their own country, a distance of 80 miles.[40]

J. O'Sullivan makes the point that obviously the police have to be judged by the standards of their own times.[41] When they appear to have used unnecessary force, for instance, their tactics had probably averted worse massacres between settlers and local tribes.

Commanders Dana and Walker achieved what initially was believed to be impossible — the formation of a highly disciplined group who were expert riders, excellent shots with a gun, and courageous in carrying out their duties. Individual commanders in the force were responsible to the Colonial Secretary (Sir George Grey) and to Governor La Trobe in Port Phillip, and later in New South Wales to Governor Charles Fitzroy. Frederick Walker's letter to the Colonial Secretary includes the comment:

> I may observe, that in the different encounters with hostile blacks, the Native Police have frequently shewn great personal courage, and it is not easy to determine which is the best when all have behaved so well; but I do think that the two corporals are the pride of my little band; their cleanliness, obedience and steadiness, has been a good example to the remainder, and has done a great deal towards establishing the esprit de corps which now exists in the Native Police Force.

The esprit de corps was aided by the good relations between the commanders, the officers and the men, and by the admiration engendered on occasions when the corps were able to parade for official events. It did not follow, however, that because the colonisers approved of the absorption of the native police into white society through the former's adoption of a European mode of dress and behaviour that the colonisers believed that integration was ultimately possible or even desirable. The history of the native police accompanied by a close reading of their representation suggests otherwise — that the European colonisers believed that the 'primitive' Aborigine would always remain other.

William Strutt painted the line-ups at the opening ceremony of the Princes Bridge in Victoria and again when the NMP formed a guard of honour on each side of Government House. The *Melbourne Argus* of 29 December 1848 described a public ceremonial review of the corps by Superintendent (later Governor), La Trobe, at the Flagstaff in the presence of a large audience: 'The review lasted two hours and the police went through a variety of Cavalry evolutions'. The Governor complimented Sergeant Richard McLelland, who had originally been the troop sergeant in the 9th Lancers. Commandant Henry Dana mentions his efforts in a report from the camp at Narre Narre Warren, 14 January 1850: 'With regard to discipline, the men are in better order than usual, being much improved in their appearance and drill, owing to the constant attention of Sergeant McLelland'. Two external signifiers of entry into white conduct were foremost in McLelland's priorities, but to what extent the minds of the young police were equally conditioned is less clear.

When Dana lost most of his white officers to the goldrush and some of the native troopers also deserted, there was criticism that their loyalty had more to do with a consistent livelihood than a devotion to duty. The NMP were not only used in the gold escorts but also to check the licences of the diggers. In his journal, Strutt comments critically on this situation: 'It was an absurd mistake, however, employing them to collect or examine the diggers' licences. Of course their ignorance was then taken advantage of, as might have been anticipated. How could men unable to read, discriminate between one piece of printed paper and another?'[42] However, Strutt's assessment is challenged by Marie Fels, who claims that the men could certainly read as they had attended either government or mission schools.

Strutt's watercolour sketch, *Black troopers escorting a Prisoner from Ballarat to Melbourne 1851: A group I met on my way to the diggings* (see Illustration 4) is one of the most telling of the representations of the police — an image loaded with both the fear and admiration of the white culture. Role reversal is germane to the irony of the situation: the black men upholding white law and the miscreant in a position of shame. The demeanour of the young troopers suggests their task is nothing more than the line of duty, yet their position on horseback endows the two figures with power. Their power was often tested, with both white wrongdoers and black initially inclined to underestimate their considerable strengths and abilities. Yet, as originally argued, the knowledge they acquired was so far removed from their own tribal knowledge that the accompanying power was only of the negative kind. They were at the bottom of the scale of an extremely authoritative regime whose rules and regulations shaped their behaviour and taught them to be mimic men, captives themselves of the white society's fetishisation of superficiality, appearance and order. The authority under which they lived operated as a 'pastoral' regime, in contrast to policies based on force: yet their subtle indoctrination offered a much greater threat to their freedom than incarceration or banishment from tribal lands. They became conditioned in the ideological spheres, new dogmas and creeds replacing their earlier beliefs, or battling to cast out their tribal values.

Unable to sustain the pace of constant pressure to conform, many of the young men deserted, but one who remained with Dana when others returned to their own bands, or went off to the goldfields, was the extremely efficient constable Munite pictured in a portrait by Strutt. Munite was one of the boys recruited by the NMP from the school at Merri Creek. Fels suggests that the tribal men endeavoured to entice the boys away from the school and the corps in order to initiate them into traditional knowledge and tribal practices of growing into men.[43] If this is true, it might further complicate the ambivalence clouding the identity of the NMP: some may have been young boys coerced into training by the white authorities.

In contrast to Strutt's serious study of the two young police with an offender, discussed above, a watercolour sketch *Blacks on the way to Adelaide in Custody* by the engineer, surveyor and artist Edward Snell has a humorous slant, captured in the grinning face of the black trooper on the right escorting two prisoners. In the journal of his stay on the Yorke Peninsula, South Australia, Snell explained that the natives in custody in his watercolour were Balarra and Kerkeawilla, the first apprehended for stealing sheep at Rogue's Gully and the latter for spearing a shepherd named Bagnall. The drawing purports to be an honest record of the incident, giving an insight into the rough style of justice being meted out. However, the jocular, almost devilish, expression on the face of the native policeman as he glances back at the prisoners clearly suggests that this image was designed to represent the officer as a something of a 'black Sambo' figure of fun, enjoying the task. Representation here was clearly working against the interests of the indigenous people.

Snell records in a later entry of 17 June, 1850: 'The blacks were secured by being chained by the necks together, the middle of the chain being passed through a hole in a she oak tree — they were taken into the hut during the night and lamented very loudly in their way about being too cold'. A drawing of the little police station on Yorke Peninsula shows the men chained outside to the tree. Snell's diary entries continue: 'On June 22nd met the prisoners walking behind a cart and going to Adelaide in the "Frolic" (a boat) to be tried. A native police constable named Jem Crack, who appears to be the man on the right, gave evidence at the trial.' On 24 and 25 June, Snell has further entries: 'Painting the prisoners all day'. On 1 July 1850, he mentions 'McCoy and Coyte together with Jem Crack returned from Adelaide today, the prisoners being committed for trial'.[44] Snell's matter-of-fact account suggests a fair amount of interaction between the NMP and other people in the bush. Apparently Snell himself lived in close connection with the tribal communities on the peninsula, which suggests that his own position towards both cultures was grounded in a deep ambivalence. Bush dwellers like Snell had much to learn from the knowledge and skills of the Aboriginal groups. When the tribes were forced off the land and then returned to battle for areas that had been theirs for generations, trouble always followed.

The large number of tribespeople being apprehended in a watercolour drawing by William Cawthorne, *Natives Driven to Police Court by the Police for Trespassing,* suggests that the clan have been camping on what was possibly their own land, now seized by settlers. The irony is no doubt deliberate on Cawthorne's part, as he was an advocate of justice for the indigenes. He practised as a schoolteacher and also undertook freelance surveying, but his main interest was in studying and sketching the Aboriginal people of South Australia. *The Manners and Customs of the Natives* was a publication both written and illustrated by Cawthorne, and in December of 1852 he held an exhibition which included 200 sketches. Jean Tregenza, his biographer, notes that a review of the exhibition claimed that the 'greatest interest was excited by the department illustrative of the manners, habits and customs of the Aborigines of this country'.[45] Cawthorne's diary is extant but it does not enlighten us about the 'trespassing' image. He was known to champion the cause of payment for Aboriginal land, an unpopular cause in nineteenth-century Australia — as it is today.

Images of native police in postcards were very much part of the regime of racist representation at the time. One popular card depicted a constable of the NMP shooting at tribesmen who are retaliating with spears, with one of the group lying on the ground. The background is a painted scene of a peaceful lagoon or billabong. The image was one of a series on Aborigines put out as postcards by the studio of the commercial photographer Charles Kerry, and apparently a popular choice of collectors. Kerry employed travelling photographers who went around the countryside taking pictures for the postcard and view trade. The end-of-the-century public were enthusiastic collectors of cards and photographs, especially those sold in a series. The commercial studios encouraged collectors to fill out their albums and ensure they had every single image in the sequence. Another in the same series, *Aboriginals and Black Tracker, 1890s,* depicts a beach setting with a native policeman holding a carbine confronting Aborigines carrying spears, with one lying — presumably dead — on the sand.

We have no way of knowing if these images are accurate or what the Aboriginal people or the NMP made of them at the time. What we can ascertain is their political effect on the colonial viewer. Given the fact the NMP were used by white society as a weapon in the establishment of imperial power, it is clear that representations (photographs, paintings, postcards) of the police were also designed to reinforce that goal. With Kerry's posed photographs of the NMP, a degree of sensationalism was added, we presume to satisfy a market wanting drama and gore. The images of the police sensationalised the violence between native police and tribal Aboriginals at a time when controversy surrounded the NMP, and the only corps remaining was in Queensland. The postcard of the beach confrontation is even more questionable, because not only does the gaze of the viewer immediately construct the native policeman as killer of the tribal Aboriginal but another individual is about to succumb from a bullet just fired. The photograph reconstitutes these bodies and gives them a new cultural capital predicated on unresolved conflict.

By adopting the outward forms of colonial power and endeavouring to internalise imperialist codes and standards, the Native Mounted Police became captives of the coloniser's hollow promise of equality. They were 'Anglicised', but not English; given power but subjected to stern rules; free agents in exerting disciplinary power but captives of the police regime's creation of diaspora in their lives. They were the most mimetic of the nineteenth century's mimic men, their identity destroyed by an ethnocentric culture which urged but unconsciously feared the successful transformation from 'savage' to 'civilised'. The colonial gaze that created images of the civilised other was a double vision which, recognising the irony of the role reversal, portrayed them as a partial presence by disclosing the ambivalence of their identity and reproducing the slippage through representation. Despite the trappings of authority — the clothes, the guns, the horses — to the observer the captors remained the captives, victims of colonialism, figures of doubling, who were never almost the same but not quite.

Part II:
Manufacturing
the 'Cannibal' Body

Chapter 5

Narratives of the self: Chevalier Peter Dillon's Fijian cannibal adventures

Gananath Obeyesekere

Peter Dillon in Davidson's Biography

PETER DILLON, a well-known sea-captain, trader and self-designated explorer from Sydney, was perhaps the author of the earliest and most detailed account of a 'cannibal feast'. This graphic story is presented in Dillon's two-volume work on his search in Vonikoro in the Solomon Islands for the remains of La Perouse's two ships, *L'Astrolabe* and *La Boussole*, lost in the South Pacific in 1788.[1] The first chapter of this work gives his eyewitness description of the preparation, cooking and consumption of European and native enemies in a Fijian cannibal feast which, fortunately for him and us, excluded Dillon himself.[2] Why us? Because it can be shown that Dillon's description of cannibalism belongs to a specific genre of fiction which I call the 'narratives of the self' rather than a description of an empirically true event. And it is to Dillon's credit that he could persuade generations of historians and ethnographers the truth of his invented experience.

These kinds of cannibal narratives compel us to question the usefulness of the ethnographic category of 'cannibalism' itself. Peter Hulme and, more recently, Frank Lestringant have shown cannibalism's loaded pejorative meanings in the course of its association with the history of colonialism.[3] Consequently, I follow those who make the claim that the term cannibalism should properly be reserved for the fantasy found the world over, that the alien, the demon, the 'other' is going to eat us. This is not to say that multiple forms of anthropophagy, however rare, do not occur in the cross-cultural record; it only means that before we embark on an anthropology of anthropophagies we must be able to disentangle the multiple forms of cannibalism also found everywhere and everywhere confused with the former, that is, with anthropophagies. Very often this is because fictional narratives of the self and other cannibal stories have a tremendous persuasive power, tapping our own predilections for the fantastic through the various devices they employ, especially the power of eyewitness narrative couched in the language of verisimilitude which, I point out in this chapter, is a kind of 'deception'.

Furthermore, cannibal narratives often enough employ pieces of truth from such things as human sacrifices which do take place in some societies, including Polynesia, making it even more difficult to falsify them. But falsification must be done for the period of European expansion, because these narratives perpetuate derogatory colonial myths and ideologies of the other under the guise of truth. Hence the strategy of research ought not only to be 'deconstructive', as one undermines the truth value of the story, but also 'restorative' as one gives back the dignity that has been forcibly taken away from the other during the period of colonial expansion and conquest.

The title of Dillon's work informs us that he is not only concerned with the French wreck but also with the manners, customs, religion and the 'cannibal practices of the South Sea Islanders', self-consciously based on the journalistic example of 'the immortal Cook'.[4] Though the book was written in 1828–29, the cannibal feast itself occurred on 6 September 1813. I first read about this in the excellent 1975 biography of Dillon by J. W. Davidson.[5] Let me introduce the reader to the events leading up to the cannibal feast presented in chapter three of Davidson's biography of Dillon, entitled 'The Path to "Dillon's Rock".' We are in the period of the decline of the once profitable sandalwood trade (started around 1808) that in a few years virtually depleted the forests of Hawai'i and Fiji in order to perfume and aromatise temples, homes and bodies in China and India. In 1813 Captain Robson of the *Hunter*, based in Calcutta, asked Peter Dillon to join his ship as third mate in the quest for sandalwood. Dillon accepted because he was already familiar with Fiji, having been in Vanua Levu in 1809 for four months with Robson himself and perhaps also at other times.

Robson could not get enough sandalwood in Wailea village in 1809; two years later he returned to Fiji and entered into an alliance with Vonasa, the chief of Wailea in Naurore Bay in the northwest coast of Vanua Levu. Robson, Dillon claims, helped the Fijian chief to fight his neighbours, who had then been 'cut up, baked, and eaten in his presence'.[6] Robson returned in January 1813 from Norfolk Island in the *Hunter* and entered the Fijian Islands through the little-known southeast coast of Viti Levu, where the ship ran aground and lost her false keel. It did manage to get into Naurore Bay on 19 February and anchored in a creek near Wailea village. Robson's friend Vonasa informed him that there was little hope of collecting sandalwood because the people that Robson had helped to fight last time had revolted and joined with Dreketi, a village further east. The enemy would strike again if Vonasa's forces were to be deployed in gathering sandalwood; the chief urged Robson to help him once more to fight his enemies. Robson initially declined but, because the precious commodity was coming in too slowly for his comfort and purse, he finally agreed, on condition that he would be supplied with a cargo of sandalwood two months after the anticipated victory.

At the beginning of April 1813, Robson set out with three of his boats, twenty musketeers and forty-six Fijian canoes containing 1,000 warriors, while a larger native force travelled overland to Dreketi. This force reached the fortified island of Bekavu on the mouth of the Dreketi River. When the cannon mounted on one of the boats fired into the fortifications, the defenders fled while the attackers destroyed plantations and towns on the riverbank. Eleven Dreketi people were killed that day; one was sent to the Wailea folk at home to be consumed while the rest were prepared for the warriors. This is Dillon's first detailed account of the preparation for a cannibal feast and we will come back to it later.

If Robson helped forge an alliance with the chief of Wailea, another group of European beachcombers and deserters had already helped the local chiefs to make the tiny island of Bau a powerful kingdom to contend with, strategically located as it was on the coast of Viti Levu for capturing the emerging European and American trade. Among these outcasts was Charles Savage, a Swede, perhaps the oldest European resident in Fiji, having lived there since the time of the wreck of the brig *Eliza* in 1808.[7] With his knowledge of European warfare Savage became a terror to 'savage' others. Assisted by fellow beachcombers and outcasts he served Naulivou, the chief of Bau, and helped him to conquer Verata, a powerful neighbour of Bau. Savage was rewarded with chiefly titles and given two high-ranking women as wives. These Europeans also worked for sandalwood traders, including Robson, in order to supply themselves with European goods and alcohol.

Meanwhile the *Hunter* was joined by the cutter *Elizabeth*, also belonging to Robson. The *Hunter*, under the first officer Norman's command, stayed in Naurore Bay to collect the Wailea sandalwood. Because sandalwood was slow in coming, Robson decided to gather bêches-de-mer (sea slugs), which were in great demand in China and plentiful on the reefs at Kaba, a few miles south of Bau on the Viti Levu coast.[8] To ensure success, the *Elizabeth* dropped the Europeans and Fijian workers ashore under the command of Dillon while Robson left for trading elsewhere. Kaba was separated from Bau by a short strip of water and the workers were under the protection of Naulivou of Bau. According to Davidson (though Dillon himself does not make this point) Dillon cultivated the friendship of the chiefs of Bau during his three-month stay in Kaba; he had close relations with chief Naulivou and his brother.[9] This stint ended when Robson returned in the *Elizabeth* in late August. Apparently Robson had no trade goods to pay the workers but, presumably, such goods were available in the *Hunter,* which was waiting for the cargo of sandalwood.[10] Thus Robson and the Europeans 'travelled in the cutter to Naurore Bay, and a party of over 200 Fijians accompanied them in two canoes'.[11]

At the Wailea end where the *Hunter* was anchored, things were going badly and there were only 150 tons of sandalwood, a third of the expected cargo. Robson would not accept the chiefs' reasonable explanation that the forests were already depleted. He was furious and felt betrayed by his friends who, says Davidson, quoting Dillon, he 'helped to glut with the flesh of their enemies'.[12] But shortly afterwards they were told of the plentiful availability of sandalwood in Macuata Island, forty miles east. Robson, with Dillon, set out in the *Elizabeth* accompanied by several Wailean canoes to procure the wood but apparently only three boat loads were available.[13] About that time Charles Savage arrived from Bau with a message from Norman, the *Hunter's* first officer, that there was a Wailean conspiracy to seize the cutter. Robson therefore detained one Wailean in the canoe and sent seven or eight others, some of high rank, to the *Hunter* with a note saying they should be held as hostages. A couple of days later when the *Elizabeth* was returning to Naurore Bay she encountered several Wailean canoes with armed warriors. These were attacked on Robson's orders; ten were sunk and one native Fijian killed. That same evening Norman set fire to a part of Wailea village and killed several people.

Though trading with Waileans for sandalwood was over, it was not possible to sail out of Naurore Bay because both vessels had run aground. To repair them amidst hostile Waileans would be difficult. Therefore, following the advice of their Bauan allies, they thought it best to destroy the enemy canoes not yet sunk. To put this into effect on that fateful day of 6 September 1813, three officers — Norman, Cox and Dillon from the *Hunter* — along with the beach-combers and native Bauan warriors landed in three boats at Black Rock, after keeping their boats and canoes in deep water to prevent them from grounding. The assembled party found that the Wailean canoes could not be sunk: they were in shallow waters owing to the low tide. The party then broke into groups of three or four, with Norman and Dillon in one group. This group then moved down a level path and climbed a hill, where they were challenged by the Waileans. From there Norman led them into a hamlet, where they were challenged once again. In retaliation some of the Europeans fired their muskets, killing one native; then they burned over fifty houses to the ground.

They now heard enemy drums which, the Bauans told them, indicated that other members of the landing party had been killed. Dillon and Norman's group came down the hill where thousands of Waileans and their allies were gathering around the area between them and their boats. Soon they came upon the body of Terence Dunn, an Irishman living in Wailea, with his brains beaten out by a native club. Frightened, John Graham one of the whites living in Bau, ran into the bush, where he was also killed. Then Norman himself was struck by a spear which 'entered his back and passed out of his breast'.[14] Dillon killed the killer only to find another European named Parker dead. Dillon concluded that their best chance now lay in climbing a rock, known today as Dillon's Rock, 'on the seaward flank of Korolevu, a great flat-topped hill which dominates Naurore Bay...a commanding position readily defensible by a few men'.[15] Besides Dillon only five managed to get to the top of the hill, these being Charles Savage, Martin Buchert (a Prussian living in Bau with his Fijian wife), Luis the Chinese man (also from Bau), and William Wilson and Thomas Dafny from the *Hunter*. They were safe here; arrows were deflected by the wind, and spears and slingshots could not reach them.

Dillon, now in command, ordered that shots should be reserved for those enemies who dared to climb the rock. Several Fijians who attempted to do so were killed; meanwhile, down below preparations were being made for a cannibal feast. While this preparation was going on Dillon kept hoping that the Bau chiefs and Robson's crew would come to their rescue, even though he could see from his vantage point the former leaving for Bau in their canoes. Savage was planning to make a run for it but Dillon threatened to shoot the first deserter.

Dillon initiated discussions with the Fijians, reminding them that eight Waileans were still held prisoner in the *Hunter* but would be released if his group were permitted to go free. Eventually a priest came up and Dillon got Dafny, who was wounded, to take a message to the ship. According to Davidson's rendering of Dillon, the letter stated that four hostages should be released, and the others only when the men were safely aboard. Because Dafny went through unharmed, Savage also left thinking he could make it because he knew the Fijians and their language. Luis the Chinese man, who felt he could trust a chief whom he personally knew, stole away without Dillon's knowledge. Neither was successful. Says Davidson:

> Charles Savage was seized by the legs, and held in that state by six men, with his head placed in a well of fresh water until he was suffocated; whilst at the same instant a powerful savage got behind the Chinaman, and with his huge club knocked the upper part of his skull to pieces.[16]

They too were cut up and cooked in ovens.[17] Meanwhile Dillon and his two comrades on the Rock had virtually given up hope; they would rather shoot themselves than be tortured and killed in this gruesome manner.[18]

Davidson describes the situation of Dillon and his companions thus:

> By now the afternoon was well advanced, a time at which the off-shore wind usually falls away. The sun, sinking behind the shad-owed mountains of Yaqaga and Naivaka, illuminates a motionless landscape. This was the scene in which the three men on the hill-top awaited their fate against the background of exultant shouts from the Fijians feasting on human flesh below them.[19]

What was worse is that for some inexplicable reason Captain Robson, flouting Dillon's request, released all eight of the Wailea prisoners. Accompanied by the same priest who had been there ear-lier, they now came up to the Rock. They had obtained presents from Robson; they also claimed that they had instructions for Dillon to hand over their arms before being escorted to the boat. Dillon refused to part with his musket. Instead he pressed it to the priest's head and let him know that:

> I would shoot him dead if he attempted to run away, or if any of his countrymen offered to molest me or my companions. I then directed him to proceed before me to my boat, threatening him with instant death in case of non-compliance.[20]

The ruse worked and Dillon and his two companions safely arrived on board.

The deceptions of verisimilitude and the invention of the self

When I first read Davidson's rendering of the events of the Rock and the cannibal feast I was inclined to think it was a true event even though I had already deconstructed other eyewitness accounts of cannibal feasts — that of William Endicott and John Jackson (Cannibal Jack).[21] Yet when I read Dillon I was seduced, as I am sure Davidson was, by its stunning verisimilitude. Dillon is in the fore-front of the battle and the text: his 'We' and 'I' are everywhere. Gradually the 'We' becomes 'I' as the narrative develops and he starts constructing a heroic role for himself and posterity. He tries (futilely) to imitate the immortal Cook's journalistic style but unhappily he has very little to say about 'native customs and manners' in the places he visited. They have been better described by earlier navigators and in more detail. In Vanikoro itself he was too preoccupied with hunting and gathering pieces of the French wrecks to pay much attention to that country's ethnography. He pads the second volume of his journal with an eighty-page summary of Mariner's narrative of Tonga; and his first chapter deals with his cannibal adventures of 1813 even though they are only indirectly related to his theme. But that first chapter is the most vivid, well-written and absorbing part of the book: no wonder Davidson and I joined the ranks of the many readers who fell for it.

I will only examine parts of the text to illuminate Dillon's own self-valorisation as he re-presents his adventures in the first person. Let me begin with the natives of Wailea asking for Robson's aid in their wars with the Dreketi (known as Nanpacab in Dillon's text), which I have already summarised from Davidson:

> There were eleven of the Nanpacab people killed on this occasion, whose bodies were placed in the canoes of our party, excepting one, which was immediately despatched in a fast-sailing canoe to Vilear [Wailea], to be there devoured. After this short skirmish we proceeded fifteen miles up the river, and destroyed the towns and plantations on its banks. In the evening we returned to a landing-place, where the islanders began to cook their yams in a kind of oven which will be hereafter described. The dead bodies were placed on the grass and dissected by one of the priests. The feet were cut off at the ankles, and the legs from the knees; after-

wards the private parts; then the thighs at the hip joints; the hands
at the wrists, the arms at the elbows, the shoulders at the sockets;
and lastly, the head and neck were separated from the body. Each
of these divisions of the human frame formed one joint, which
was carefully tied up in green plantain leaves, and placed in the
ovens to be baked with the *tara* [taro] root.[22]

There is no way of disproving this account and I will not concern
myself with its truth or falsity. Instead, I want to deal with the
seductions of verisimilitude characteristic of the descriptions of
travel writers like Dillon, Endicott and Cannibal Jack. A strict
description of rapidly developing events, can, I believe, exist only in
a few limited ways. Though it appeals to our sense of reality, perfect
verisimilitude is only possible in invented accounts or fiction. In
ethnography, for example, it is the rare observer who can accurate-
ly describe performances he or she has witnessed, because such
activities are always complex and one must be especially lucky to
get a visually undisturbed vantage point. Hence any semblance of
verisimilitude in ethnography comes not from witnessing an event
but from more formal settings where one sits with a specialist and
gets idealised accounts of ritual procedures. In other words,
verisimilitude is an ethnographic deception because actions on the
ground rarely fit ideals. Dillon's description is rendered even more
suspicious because it is devoid of context, unlike his later account
of the consumption of his comrades. In contrast to the seeming
exactitude of the cutting up of the corpses is the vagueness of the
locale: 'in the evening we returned to a landing place, where the
islanders began to cook their yams in a kind of oven…'[23] This unex-
citing event surely did take place.[24]

Let me now give a few examples of the manner in which
Dillon further develops his heroised self in his continuing narrative:

> On landing, the Europeans began to disperse into straggling par-
> ties of two, three, and four in a group. I begged of Mr. Norman,
> our commander, to cause them to keep close together in an attack
> from the islanders; but no attention was paid to my remon-
> strance.[25]

Clearly if Norman had followed Dillon's advice many lives would
have been saved. There is a graphic description of Norman's death
when a native 'threw a lance at Mr. Norman, which entered his
back and passed out of his breast'. Dillon heroically shoots the killer.
As might be expected, when Dillon takes over the leadership, the 'I'

becomes more pronounced: 'I fired at this native'; 'I dashed along with all the speed that was possible'; 'I came across the dead body of William Parker...with his musket by him, which I took up and retreated with', but later 'I was obliged to throw Parker's musket away, as also a pistol which I had in my belt'.[26] 'In a moment after this I reached the foot of a small steep rock that stood on the plain. Finding it impossible to get to the boat through the pathway, I called out to my companions (some of whom were on my right), "take the hill! take the hill!".' Dillon is now the intrepid leader who takes over command as the narrative moves forward.

Let me now focus on the cooking scene, which Davidson quotes in full in his biography:

> Fires were prepared and ovens heated for the reception of the bodies of our ill-fated companions, who, as well as the Bau chiefs and their slaughtered men, were brought to the fires in the following manner. Two of the Vilear [Wailea] party placed a stick or limb of a tree on their shoulders, over which were thrown the body of their victims, with their legs hanging downwards on one side, and their heads on the other. They were thus placed on a sitting posture while the savages sung and danced for joy over their prizes, and fired several musket-balls through each of the corpses, all the muskets of the slain having fallen into their hands. No sooner was this ceremony over than the priests began to cut up and dissect those unfortunate men in our presence. Their flesh was immediately placed in the ovens to be baked and prepared as a repast for the victors.[27]

Once again the description is deceptive; it is quite unlikely that Dillon would have seen these activities taking place from where he was located. They were simply invented to show the savage cannibalism desired by his reading public, especially that of savages singing and dancing with joy over their prizes, firing musket balls through each of the corpses and the priests cutting up and dissecting these unfortunate people within sight of the Europeans on the hill. And Dillon himself is an eyewitness to this wondrous savagery. When the 'savage' Savage decides to leave with Luis, look what happened: 'he was seized by the legs, and held in that state by six men, with his head placed in a well of fresh water until he was suffocated; whilst at the same instant a powerful savage got behind the Chinaman, and with his huge club knocked the upper part of his skull to pieces'.[28] The deceptions of verisimilitude misled Davidson once again, for Dillon could not possibly have seen all of this with such complete clarity amidst the bustle and confusion of the fight. Here, as in our previous accounts of cannibalism, it is fiction that is stranger than truth; or a truth fictionalised because it is likely that Savage and Luis were in fact killed during this fray, though we will never know in what manner.

This fictionalisation of a truth is continued as the narration proceeds:

> We, the three defenders of the hill, were attacked on all sides by the cannibals, whom our muskets however kept in great dread, though the chiefs stimulated their men to ascend and bring us down, promising to confer the greatest honours on the man who should kill me, and frequently inquired of their people if they were afraid of three white men, when they had killed several that day. Thus encouraged they pressed close on us. Having four muskets between the three of us, two always remained loaded; for Wilson being a bad shot, we kept him loading the muskets, while Martin Bushart [Buchert] and I fired them off. Bushart had been a rifleman in his own country, and was an excellent marksman. He shot twenty-seven of the cannibals with twenty-eight discharges, only missing once.

But Dillon was no cold killer: 'I also killed and wounded a few of them in self-defence'.[29]

The narrative continues with its combination of the probable and the improbable.

> The human bodies being now prepared, they were withdrawn from the ovens, and shared out to the different tribes, who devoured them greedily. They frequently invited me to come down and be killed before it was dark, that they might have no trouble in dissecting and baking me in the night. I was bespoken joint by joint by the different chiefs, who exultingly brandished their weapons in the air, and boasted of the number of white men they had killed that day. In reply to all this I informed them, that if I was killed, their countrymen confined on board our vessel will get killed also, but that if I was saved they would be saved. The ruthless savages replied, 'Captain Robson may kill and eat our countrymen if he please; we will kill and eat you. When it is dark you cannot see to shoot at us, and you will have no more powder.'
>
> Myself and companions, seeing no hope of mercy on earth, turned our eyes towards heaven, and implored the Almighty Ruler of all things to have compassion on our wretched souls. We

had now not the most distant hope of ever escaping from the savages, and expected to be devoured as our companions were but a few minutes before. The only thing which prevented our surrendering quietly was the dread of being taken alive and put to the torture.

These people sometimes, but not very often, torture their prisoners in the following manner. They skin the soles of the feet and then torment their victims with firebrands, so as to make them jump about in that wretched state. At other times they cut off the prisoner's eye-lids and turn his face to the sun, at which he is obliged to look with his bare eyes: this is said to be a dreadful punishment. From the fingers of others they pull off the nails. By all accounts, however, these punishments are very rare, and only inflicted on persons who have given the greatest provocation; such as we had done this day, by shooting so many men in our own defence.

Having no more than sixteen or seventeen cartridges left, we determined, as soon as it was dark, to place the muzzles of our muskets to our hearts with the butts on the ground and discharge them into our breasts, thus to avoid the danger of falling alive into the hands of these cannibal monsters.[30]

We know the rest from Davidson's narrative. In it Captain Robson gets even worse press than first officer Norman. Why did he not keep four hostages as Dillon suggested? How come he released all eight and is it true that he had suggested to the chiefs that Dillon and his comrades give up their arms and trust the chiefs?

I expostulated with Captain Robson on his extraordinary conduct, in causing so many human beings to be unnecessarily sacrificed. He made use of some absurd apologies, and inquired if we were the only persons who had escaped: I replied, yes; but that if the natives could have made proper use of the muskets which fell into their hands on that occasion, we must all have been killed.[31]

In the La Perouse narrative he stands tall, this man Dillon — all of 'six feet four in height, heavily built, with a mop of red hair' as Davidson describes him.[32] Davidson is caught up in a not untypical biographer's dilemma. Dillon is a good character for a biography but biographers find it hard to escape admiring the creature they create. Consider the title of Davidson's book: *Peter Dillon of Vanikoro, Chevalier of the South Seas*. Certainly Dillon was knighted by the French for his discovery of La Perouse's two vessels but he was not titled 'Chevalier of the South Seas': that is Davidson's creation. But Chevalier is very French; how does one convert that into an English title? 'Peter Dillon of Vanikoro'? This title invokes the English aristocratic tradition, even though Dillon neither discovered Vanikoro nor did he settle there for any length of time. The actual French artefacts he collected were meagre, though they did come from La Perouse's ships. It is as if Davidson himself is creating what Dillon wanted to do all the time, identify with those Dillons who had aristocratic connections. The rock from which Dillon conducted his heroic defence is also mythologised by Davidson. It is impossible to locate it from Dillon's description but Davidson, with the help of Fijian historians and cartographers, located the place and labelled it 'Dillon's Rock'.

Though Dillon was 'physically impressive', what impressed Davidson:

> ...was his qualities of mind and spirit that principally distinguished him from the common run. He possessed both great courage and the instinct of command, was calm and effective in times of danger. He possessed intelligence and imagination that enabled him to gain a ready understanding of indigenous society. Above all, he possessed the capacity to appreciate pre-literate people in their own terms, unencumbered by a sense of cultural superiority. He judged them as individuals, not as types produced by a 'savage' culture.[33]

Admittedly, Dillon was a complex person; and he occasionally spoke with sympathy about Maoris and Tahitians. As an older man he wanted to write a history of Fiji, which he never did (and I think was incapable of doing). Again, in his later years, he championed the cause of natives and was strongly critical of missionary appropriation of indigenous lands in Polynesia, though he himself had elaborate plans for colonising New Zealand.[34] Nevertheless, one wonders how Davidson could read Dillon's account of the Fijians and still write about him as someone who understood native peoples — at least around the age of forty when he wrote about his cannibal experiences.[35]

The contemporary accounts: the Sydney Gazette and Dillon's deposition

Davidson's narration of Dillon's Fijian adventure is based on the various versions that Dillon himself gave during different times in his life. Instead of treating them as different stories, Davidson constructed a single coherent narrative, eliminating information that seemed flagrantly contradictory. For the fight with the Waileans and the retreat to Dillon's Rock, Davidson relied almost entirely on Dillon's La Perouse narrative of 1829. Yet this does not quite match with two contemporary accounts based on information supplied by Dillon himself. The first was published on 23 October 1813 in the *Sydney Gazette*, the day after Dillon landed in Sydney after his Fijian adventures. The second is his sworn deposition before a Sydney Justice of the Peace on 6 November of the same year.[36] While the two contemporary accounts contain in outline much of the Davidson-Dillon narrative sketched above, neither contains any reference whatever to natives engaged in a cannibal feast. Let me now explore this extraordinary finding in some detail.

The *Sydney Gazette* explicitly claims to have reported Dillon's own version. It agrees with the La Perouse account in depicting the sailors and their allies surrounded by upward of eight thousand hostile natives. In this deadly situation the newspaper simply says that 'the people in the vessels unconscious of their danger, were separated into straggling parties'. There is no question of Norman acting foolishly and flouting Dillon's wise instructions. In all versions Norman, the first officer, comes out as a despicable character; but only the La Perouse version says that he burnt a chief's house. In that account Dillon is focusing on Norman's ineptitude and his own circumspect and wise actions. Had Dillon been the leader none of this would have occurred. In the *Sydney Gazette* version Norman does not die in quite the graphic manner of the La Perouse story. It says that 'six of the Europeans, among whom were Mr. Norman, M'Cave, and Graham, confounded at the charge, threw down their muskets, and ran towards the boats but were intercepted, and massacred with spears and clubs'. Dillon and nine others made for a summit of a hill near the sea beyond the reach of spears and stones. The rest agrees with the La Perouse version except for some important details. The *Sydney Gazette* says that the priest came to see Dillon, and:

> …the business of his mission was to promise them security, provided they would release the eight natives who were prisoners in the vessels. *Gladly consenting to this proposition, one of the Europeans accompanied the priest…down to the boats; he went on board, and the eight natives were released accordingly.*[37]

By contrast, in the La Perouse version, Dillon asks Captain Robson to keep four of the natives as hostages; hence it is no wonder Robson appears there as a villain who released all eight hostages. Robson might well have been a scoundrel but the *Sydney Gazette* clearly indicates that he merely followed Dillon's own instructions. And third officer Dillon arrogantly 'expostulating' with his commander also does not appear in this contemporary account.

According to the *Sydney Gazette,* two Europeans, contrary to Dillon's orders, decided to go down; they were treated reasonably well; the natives urged Dillon also to come down and when he did not Dillon had the misfortune to see these two 'perish beneath the weight of innumerable weapons'. It is of course entirely possible that one of the Europeans was Charles Savage; but it is not likely that the Chinese man was called 'European' by Dillon. The priest then came back with the eight prisoners and urged Dillon and his comrades to come down, with the assurance that they would not be killed. But Dillon refused. While lacking the details of the La Perouse narrative, Dillon put a gun against the priest's back and they arrived safely on board the ship.

The names of Dillon's two companions who defended the hill are missing in the newspaper account. Nowhere is there any mention of preparing European bodies for a cannibal feast or of the feast itself. Instead, here is what happened the day after Dillon reached the ship:

> Next morning, the 7th, a party went on shore with a considerable property, to offer ransom for the bodies of their late ill-fated companions — but, alas! not one could be produced; and the wretched cannibals replied to the request, that they had been devoured the night before.

There is no reference to Dillon leading this party, though he might well have done so.

Two weeks later Dillon made his sworn statement. This contains a great deal more information on the activities of the ships' crew in collecting sandalwood and bêche-de-mer but the rest of it follows the *Sydney Gazette* account. The deposition repeats the account of priestly intervention:

> ...the deponent informed him [the priest] that if him and his party were saved that the eight Natives on board the ship Hunter should be restored to them, and deponent sent one of his Party with the Priest for that purpose.

Here also there is no indication whatever that Dillon urged Captain Robson to keep some of the prisoners as hostages. One can, I think, make a reasonable inference: Dillon believed that if the hostages were freed he and his comrades would be sent home unharmed. But something soon upset this expectation when Luis and Charles Savage (as in the La Perouse version but not the two Europeans of the *Sydney Gazette*) decided to go down, on the urging of several native chiefs. The natives 'suffered' them 'to Walk unmolested, entreating Deponent and the two others to go down also, and finding Deponent would not consent they killed those two who were down'.[38] Whether Dillon did the right thing or not one can never know, but Dillon's refusal to come down changed the equation and the two Europeans (or Savage and Luis) were killed. The changed situation obviously did not permit Dillon to come down peaceably. Instead Dillon made the bold move to put a gun against the priest's back. The two contemporary accounts therefore exonerate Robson from his completely irrational action reported in the La Perouse version. Robson was probably dead when Dillon published his later account in 1829 and there was no way that he could be contradicted. Finally, the deposition says that Dillon led the party to recover the bodies but was told, as the *Sydney Gazette* also states, that 'the Bodies had been eaten on the Evening before'.[39] Neither account even vaguely hints that Dillon witnessed the dressing of bodies and the consequent cannibal feast.

Bodies and bones

If the *Sydney Gazette* and the deposition do not mention the cannibal feast, do we know when the latter entered Dillon's narrative repertoire? This is a difficult question to answer but I can at least provide some insights into Dillon's inventive talents. Let me go back to the two earliest versions and their common agreement that after Dillon's escape either he (in the deposition account) or a party from the ship (in the *Sydney Gazette* account) tried to get the *bodies* of their dead comrades. Something anomalous stared at me: there was no way that Dillon could get hold of the bodies of his comrades, if one were to trust Dillon's La Perouse version, because the bodies of *all* of his comrades and the Bau chiefs had been dressed and cooked in full view of him.[40] If so, he should have known that only the bones and not the bodies were available for barter the next day.

When Dillon was in Calcutta in 1817, the *Sydney Gazette* article was reprinted in the *Calcutta Gazette* of 6 February, and again on Thursday 8 May, 1828, during a second visit to the city, when Dillon was now the famous discoverer of the French wrecks. Both accounts are faithful to the *Sydney Gazette* in affirming that it was their comrades' *bodies* that the Europeans sought the day after the adventure on the Rock. The second *Calcutta Gazette* article, however, has an addendum by the editor identifying William Wilson and Martin Buchert as the two companions on the Rock. It goes on to say that Dillon deposited Buchert and the lascar in Tikopia because, if they were left in Fiji, they too would eventually have been 'sacrificed'. This version, including the editor's addendum, is reprinted as an appendix to Dillon's two-volume work but with one important change: 'Next morning, the 7th, a party went on shore with a considerable property to offer a ransom for the *bones* of their late ill-fated companions...'[41] Dillon had noticed, as I did, that it was not possible to have the bodies recovered and astutely substituted 'bones' in the *Calcutta Gazette* reprint over which he had complete authorial control, thereby bringing it in line with the La Perouse account.[42] The latter neatly combines the *Sydney Gazette* and the deposition with Dillon's appendix when it says that Dillon was anxious to purchase the *bones* of a friend (Mr Cox) and the natives replied that:

> ...they had *neither the flesh nor bones* to spare, as they had all been devoured the night before. One of the savages held up the two thigh-bones of Mr. Norman (as he informed us), and inquired what I would give for them. I offered an axe. He exultingly laughed, and flourished the bones about, saying he would not sell them; they would make excellent sail-needles to repair his canoe sails.[43]

Many aspects of Fijian savage custom are brought together in the fabric that Dillon finally weaves into his book: Fijian cannibalism, their exultant brandishing of bones, and their prospective conversion of bones into tools.

The ethos of mutual suspicion: the Dillon-Tytler relationship

The thesis I want to develop in this essay is that the invention of the self and the 'fabrication' of a narrative — in this instance the tale of heroic resistance to cannibalism — are inextricably related. Dillon's life and character help us to interweave the person and his narration in the process of self-invention. Let me therefore deal with some aspects of Dillon's psychic make-up as he reveals himself in the continuing saga of his search for the wrecks of La Perouse's two ships.

I will refer the reader to Davidson for the details of this saga, except to state that when Dillon landed in the island of Tikopia in May 1826 en route from Valparaiso to Calcutta he found Walter Buchert, one of his comrades on the Rock, and a lascar who was also rescued from Fiji and, like Buchert, had taken refuge in Tikopia. Dillon was convinced that some artefacts in the lascar's possession were from La Perouse's two ships and further inquiries from Buchert and the Tikopeans added fuel to his conviction. Dillon was determined to search for the wrecks of the *L'Astrolabe* and *La Boussole*, partly motivated by the rewards promised by the French government. He proceeded to Calcutta and there persuaded the British representatives to furnish a ship, money, provisions and some personnel to supplement those from his own ship. This new ship, the *Research*, had a draughtsman, a representative of the French government, and a surgeon named Tytler whom Dillon himself recommended for the trip after an initial meeting. In his relationship with Doctor Tytler one gets a glimpse of Dillon's authoritarianism, suspiciousness, his propensity to violence and seeing the world through 'paranoid lenses'. By paranoid lenses I refer to a situation where someone looks at the outside world which then refracts back on him as part of his own inner world. I am not suggesting that Dillon was clinically paranoid; only that his characterological weaknesses surfaced in his confrontation with an equally difficult and self-centred character like Tytler and he began to see the world through paranoid lenses.

Let me begin with this difficult relationship, starting 11 January 1827 as Dillon describes it in his journal. After spending many weeks organising his expedition he spent a night taking leave of friends:

> Having been late up at a farewell party last night, on arriving at my lodgings this morning I directed my faithful Prussian servant to desire my sircar when he came, to have my boat ready for embarking, and intimated that during the interval I would repose on the couch.[44]

The Prussian servant is of course Buchert; we do not know Buchert's reaction to being relegated to servant status; 'my sircar' refers to his Bengali valet. Note the somewhat grandiose self-representation in this prose, the imagined imperious role of a ship's commander. Shortly afterwards Dillon was wakened from his 'repose' by his servant and his sircar; they informed him that Tytler had ransacked his room and read his papers while Dillon was asleep, then suddenly withdrew and 'inquired of the Prussian if I was very ill'. The latter denied this but, in response to Tytler's next question, agreed that Dillon slept with his firearms by his bedside. Tytler asked whether Dillon was addicted to alcohol but was told that he never drank for the whole duration of his voyages.[45] 'The Doctor then begged of the servant to prevail on me not to go to the ship that day, as I was, he said, exceedingly ill, and that he would call again'.[46]

The doctor's strange behaviour makes sense in relation to Dillon's own illness on 14 December, which Dillon thought was a cold but Tytler believed was an apoplectic fit. Davidson sums up the situation thus:

> He bled him, ordered his head to be shaved, and sought the opinion of two other government medical doctors. The former was unhappily conscious that some unexpected misfortune, such as a serious illness, might still prevent him from attaining his ambition; the latter, it seems, was becoming less enamoured of the prospect of serving under Dillon.[47]

However, it is hard to believe that Tytler simply ordered bleeding and head shaving if Dillon suffered from a common cold, rather than a more serious illness during which he was incoherent. The doctor did inquire from the Prussian whether Dillon was addicted to alcohol and, according to Dillon, he told Tytler that he never drank on board. This is simply not true. On 15 July 1826, when his ship was off the coast of Malaya en route to Calcutta, Dillon had drunk so much palm toddy that he had alcoholic hallucinations, according to Bayly, his third officer:'[He] fancied the Malays were attacking the Ship, so he jumped out of bed, seized his pistols which he always had under his pillow, loaded and fired them through the cabin windows'. He then went beserk firing his pistols in a 'dreadful rage' (fortunately hurting no one) and ended up abusing the second mate and striking him 'violently on the forehead' with his pistol till the 'blood streamed from the wound'.[48]

To go back to the bedroom incident, Dillon believed that the doctor had begun to misrepresent the state of his health to the Marine Board, and his suspicions were confirmed when Tytler arrived with another 'medical gentleman' at his door. 'He inquired in the most kind and affectionate manner how I found myself after *these violent attacks*, and if I thought the *state of my health* would allow me to go to sea'.[49] According to Dillon, Tytler feared that the ship was not seaworthy and in order to prevent it from sailing he was planning to inform the Maritime Board that Dillon was too sick to travel. In Tytler's defence one could say that his inquiry revealed a solicitous bedside manner; it is likely that he genuinely felt that Dillon was in no condition to command the ship.

Dillon wrote:

> The remainder of the day was spent in getting my baggage embarked in the boat, and waiting for the tide. During this interval, I was informed that the Doctor, ever plotting and restless, was busily engaged, endeavouring to obtain from Commander Hayes and others, documents to prove that the *Research* was not seaworthy, to enable him to present a protest against the ship to the Government, so as to put a stop to the expedition as now planned.[50]

Dillon went on board the ship on 12 January. On the next page the entry for 15 January reads:

> I also received private letters from town cautioning me to be on my guard when Doctor Tytler joined the ship, as it was his intention to get rid of the voyage by some artifice, and that if his other schemes failed in accomplishing his point, he would most likely endeavour to provoke me into a quarrel, which would afford him an excuse for carrying out his design of leaving the ship into execution.[51]

It is difficult to judge the truth of these statements. It is likely that Tytler was doing his best to get the expedition stopped; but Dillon's receiving anonymous letters reads like an invention to justify later occurrences.

The relationship developed for the worse on the 16th. The ship was still not given permission to leave. During breakfast the doctor insisted that his dresser should be provided with food from the captain's board. Dillon refused because that was not part of his victualling orders:

> He started up in a violent rage, and said, he could not sit there and hear me make use of such ungentlemanly language, in presence of the second officer, as to tell him he had no right to see my letters; and that he would immediately protest against my conduct, and not proceed an inch with the ship until the business was settled.[52]

Tytler's 'violent rage' seems quite uncharacteristic; Dillon's own representation of him as a 'schemer' seems more appropriate. On the other hand, Tytler is protesting against Dillon's use of ungentlemanly language: here we are on very safe ground because such language and the associated rage fit Dillon's character. It is likely that Tytler was very upset and angry at his language and forthwith sent a letter to the Marine Board (which he read to Dillon) requiring clarification of this issue. Dillon says that he 'resolved to preserve my coolness, and disregard his insolence as long as possible'.[53]

In spite of Dillon's counter-response to the Marine Board, the latter upheld Tytler, perhaps in the hope of preserving some measure of amity on board ship. This obviously could not occur, given the deep animosities of these two persons; indeed the first few days of the trip were full of petty squabbles.[54] The Maoris on board, taking Dillon's side of the conflict, were only too happy to eat Doctor Tytler when they got to New Zealand. Dillon generously told them not to molest the doctor, but one Maori aristocrat 'declared that it was positively his intention to have the poor Doctor grilled as an entertainment for his numerous wives and friends, the first opportunity that offered after his arrival in the river Thames in New Zealand'.[55] Dillon continues: 'I should not have mentioned this conversation, were it not that I wish to shew those in civilized life what the poor, ignorant, and uncultivated savages are capable of doing, and how susceptible they are of the sentiment of gratitude', even though, one is tempted to add, it was a rather strange way to set about it.[56]

The petty squabbling culminated in an event of the 29th when Dillon went into the second officer's cabin to open a clothes chest. There he saw an open book, which he read out of curiosity because he saw his name there. More likely he opened the second officer's log, which contained an unsettling report:

> That on the 24th instant, Doctor Tytler had said to the second officer that I (the Captain) was mad, and had all the symptoms of a madman; that he had observed me eating the carpenter's chips, which he said was a symptom of madness, and that I ought to be confined to my cabin, and lose a large quantity of blood.

I do not know what to make of this statement, particularly the idea of Dillon eating woodchips (though he might have done this during an alcoholic bout in Calcutta). Alternatively, this could be a ploy on Tytler's part to discredit Dillon. Dillon interpreted it to mean that the doctor was 'still plotting how to upset the expedition, place himself at the head of it', and make him a prisoner on the pretext of insanity.[57] Dillon's reaction was very revealing: 'I immediately loaded my pistols, and mentioned what I had observed to my faithful Prussian servant Martin Bushart'.[58] He urged Buchert to keep an eye on the doctor and on officers friendly to him and to be ready to assist Dillon: 'I deemed it an imperative duty to adopt every precaution to prevent mutiny and insubordination in the ship, and that as to permitting him to hold private consultations in his cabin, it was out of the question'.[59] In other words he was imagining that Tytler was planning a mutiny, an act for which there was little evidence. Not permitting Tytler to have private conversations in his own cabin with other officers must only have exacerbated Tytler's hatred and his suspicions of Dillon's sanity.

Dillon's actions the next day, 27 January, could not have helped matters: 'I wrote him a letter which hoped would make a favourable impression on his mind, and deter him from further prosecuting his mutinous schemes any further'. Dillon is here imitating Cook's style of journal writing. To add insult to injury he demeaned Tytler's geological samples as 'worthless rubbish' and then made horrendously gratuitous remarks about Tytler's sexual morality:

> He could not expect me to rest entirely satisfied of his sense of duty to me as his superior officer; especially when it was well known that he had not scrupled to violate one of the first and most sacred of human laws, in possessing himself of the wife of a person in whose house he resided; thus at once outraging the feelings of a husband, and profaning the sacred roof of hospitality; and, for the last fourteen years, he had been indulging in the fruits of this achievement with the wife of the person whose peace of mind he had destroyed for ever.[60]

He mentioned Tytler's propensity to quarrel with his superiors and then, once again in Cook's own imperious manner: 'concluded by warning him, that if he proceeded in such a course of action with me, he would find he had to deal with a person of some firmness and decision'.[61] Dillon is now seeing the world through paranoid lenses. Whatever Tytler's faults, he was at least faithful with his common-law wife, whereas the self-righteous Dillon was a flagrant womaniser and on this very trip he openly had sexual relations with at least one native woman whom he made pregnant while his wife was on board.[62]

Dillon's actions, I think, resulted in a kind of self-fulfilling prophecy when Tytler himself wrote a letter to the chief officer Blake (and showed it to several others) in which he expressed concern about Dillon's sanity. Dillon became aware of the contents of this letter only three months later during his trial at Hobart, Tasmania: 'I have not the smallest doubt, in my mind, as to his being in a state of mental aberration, which occasionally bursts forth into violent fits and frantic madness'.[63] In this letter Tytler looks at Dillon through his own paranoid lenses, as if the one was mimicking the other:

> My own life and that of my son I consider especially in danger, my being in the cabin next to him, and he having conveyed loaded fire-arms into his room for some purpose unknown. Captain Dillon ought now to be confined to his cabin, and take medicine, and be bled and purged, otherwise I fear his malady will increase and become permanent; and this I declare, before God, to be my solemn opinions communicated to you'.[64]

It is not surprising that the Tytler-Dillon tensions should have escalated in schismogenetic fashion. If Tytler's letter was meant for a few officers only, not so his public action:

> This day [27 January] at dinner the Doctor's conversation, as usual, was employed in ridiculing the ship to the lowest pitch, in the hearing of the officers, servants, and seamen at the wheel, and predicting her loss, apparently with the view of getting the crew to rise on me and force me to return.[65]

Tytler was at least getting his own back by denigrating the ship and the whole enterprise, and he was doing this repeatedly. I do not doubt that Tytler was so terrified of Dillon that he wanted the officers to confine Dillon to his cabin. But this was not an encouragement to mutiny. In fact Dillon himself may have rightly diagnosed one source of Tytler's anxiety: 'It would now appear that the Doctor himself left Calcutta under great apprehension of being lost in the ship; and, being of a weak and superstitious turn of mind, he used all means in his power to get clear of her'.[66] Tytler must also have worried about the safety of his son who was on board ship.

Dillon was unaware of Tytler's letter but he claims that the second officer warned him about a possible mutiny. This was all that Dillon needed. He now concluded that a mutiny was being hatched by Tytler and wanted to check its 'ringleader': 'I told him that there was a person on board trying to bring about a mutiny, and that it was time to arm and prevent it'.[67] Naturally Tytler was alarmed and told Dillon: 'Captain Dillon, there is not the least occasion for this trouble; I will do whatever you wish me.' This most reasonable attempt at reconciliation did not mollify Dillon. He continued to interpret Tytler's insulting remarks as attempts to foster mutiny: 'I would if necessity compelled me for the general safety, bring him to the capstan and have him flogged with five dozen, or put him in double irons'.[68] Naturally Tytler was 'alarmed about the consequences of his misconduct and promised to behave better in future'.[69] But Dillon was not appeased; he continued to believe in 'Doctor Tytler's mutinous conduct' and sent him a letter reminding him of 'his aspersions on the ship, and predictions of the dreadful disasters which are to befall her'. Dillon further informed Tytler that he might be 'put to the disagreeable necessity of close confining you, till an opportunity offers of handing you over to a military tribunal'.[70] A few days later, finding 'Doctor Tytler in close conversation with the man at the wheel, and taking his attention from his duty', he chastised both men.

Dillon was continuing to see the world through paranoid lenses, and the petty quarrels that occurred in the next few days did nothing to alleviate it. He did not budge from his original idea of a mutiny led by Tytler: there was 'corroborating evidence, and collateral circumstances, proving the existence of a settled plan to deprive me of the command of the ship, and throw me into confinement on the pretence of insanity'.[71] Remember that this was Dillon writing about this event long after it occurred and after he had access to the contents of Tytler's letter to Blake; it is justification after the fact. Dillon now 'resolved to adopt decisive measures' by placing Tytler under arrest. 'I walked up to him on the quarter-deck, and clapping my hand on his shoulder, said aloud, "I arrest you in his Brittanic Majesty's name".'[72] Afterwards on that day he said:

> I placed a sentry at my cabin-door to prevent the danger of immediate attack; and as there were some arms, the property of the Government, in the Doctor's cabin, I directed the chief officer to secure them, so as to preclude the Doctor and his adherents from making any resistance.[73]

And then: 'In the evening I distributed six or seven pairs of pistols amongst some old and trusty shipmates, with directions to be ready to use them when called for'.[74] He was obsessed with the mutinies that the great navigators of the past had to contend with, and saw one of his junior officers as a potential Fletcher Christian.[75]

I refer the reader to Davidson's account of Dillon's trial, conviction and fine. He was later freed on the intervention of several leading public figures in Hobart, Van Dieman's Land (Tasmania), owing to favourable public and press opinion in Hobart as well as in Sydney where he was well known. Davidson unhappily does not give Tytler a fair hearing. He believes that the Lieutenant Governor and the Supreme Court with its jury of military men were against Dillon, owing to their class and Calvinistic ethical prejudices. In spite of his opportunism and personal obnoxiousness, Tytler, for me, emerges as a much more reasonable person than appears in Davidson's portrait. The judges were no fools, and they certainly believed that the arrest was an illegal act, even if they did not accept Tytler's claim that Dillon: 'gave me a violent blow on the shoulder...and seizing me very forcibly by the arm, shoved me before him into my cabin, saying go in and consider yourself a prisoner'.[76]

Dillon's rage

It is hard to believe that Dillon behaved gently when he arrested Tytler. The propensity to violence is very much in Dillon's character, and Davidson himself noted that he 'was susceptible to sudden losses of self-control when he was capable of acting with disastrous violence'.[77] Dillon came to Calcutta after a previous trip to Valparaiso where George Bayly was his third officer in the *Calder*. Here is Bayly speaking:

> Captn D was the most passionate man I ever saw. His wife lived on board and he very frequently gave her a thrashing, very frequently striking her to the deck, and once broke his telescope to pieces about her head. A few days after I had joined the Brig he sent a boy on shore with 9 or 10 verbal messages to different people. When he returned on board with his answers he found he had forgotten to collect one of the houses he had been directed to, and Captn D was exasperated against him that he seized an axe that had laid beside him and hurled it after the boy, who foreseeing what was coming jumped behind the caboose the moment the axe came flying along the deck after him.[78]

The *Calder* foundered in Valparaiso and was later junked and sold in a very dubious Dillon deal.[79] Dillon bought another ship, the *St Patrick*, for his journey to Calcutta. Bayly noted that Dillon's sleeping birth was a veritable armoury. Therefore, the descriptions of his sleeping with guns around him and his arming people in the *Research* was nothing new: it simply reflected his extreme fear of violence from others, paralleling his own propensity to violence. I have already referred to Bayly's account of his alcoholic hallucinations. Bayly records an incident in Tikopia where Dillon in a rage tried to cut a native in two with an axe. It is not surprising that his subordinate officers stood in fear of him and his wrath. On 10 June

1826 Bayly mentioned an incident where Dillon challenged his fellow officer Captain Florence to a duel with pistols, and when the latter declined:

> Captain D. flew to his bedplace from which he took a stick, having a sort of dagger in the end of it (which jerked by a spring) he struck Captain F. with such violence just over his left eyebrow that the dagger laid it right open and the blood flowed in streams from the wound.

Captain Florence 'threatened to prosecute Captain D. as soon as the Ship arrived in India', just as Tytler threatened him with the Marine Board in Calcutta soon after.[80] Consequently, Tytler inquiring whether Dillon slept with his arms by his side might express the Doctor's malicious nature; on the other hand it also was a good piece of clinical investigation by an experienced, though no doubt difficult, physician.

Bayly, in a later account, (*Sea-Life Sixty Years Ago*) is much more sentimental about Dillon; yet even here he documents Dillon's sudden bursts of emotion leading to violence. It is likely that Tytler diagnosed these outbursts as apoplectic fits. Davidson's own research assistant scribbled a note to him about Dillon from her own perspective:

> He seems to me to have been a ruthless, mean-spirited, selfish, arrogant, double dealing [man] and a snob — and what's more he beat his wife. Maybe he treated Pacific Islanders well (by his standards) but on the other hand he beat his Bengalee steward with a cat o'nine tails…A thoroughly *nasty* man, if you ask me.[81]

The character of invention and the invention of character

Davidson has an interesting diagnosis of Dillon's character, though he does not fully appreciate its significance. 'The dangers he saw [from Tytler] was not chimerical; but, because he was a romantic, they assumed unreal proportions in his mind. He saw himself as the successor of Magellan and Mendana, of Drake and Dampier and Cook — and of lesser men as Bligh'.[82] 'Romantic' is hardly the word to describe him; but that dangers assumed unreal proportions in his mind is right on target. To express it differently, Dillon harboured delusions of grandeur in his identity with the great navigators of history. This self-delusion finds a parallel in his own personal life. During his trial, in a letter to Lieutenant Governor George Arthur, he wrote: 'I am the son of the late Peter Dillon Esquire, of Meath Ireland, Nephew of the late Sir William Dillon of the same place, and related in the next degree of affinity to the Countess Bertrand'.[83]

Little of this is true. He was born in Martinique in 1788, a son of an Irish immigrant named Peter Dillon, originally from County Meath. Owing to political troubles in Martinique he was taken home to Ireland around 1791 and later entered the Royal Navy and even claimed to have 'had the honour to serve at the battle of Trafalgar'.[84] His childhood could not have been pretty, if one infers that a man given to outbursts of violence, a sadistic wife-beater who whipped his servant mercilessly, could possibly have had a pleasant childhood. His early life, Davidson says, is full of obscurities. Davidson surmises that Dillon entered the navy as a servant of an officer or a petty officer and perhaps had to leave it around sixteen or seventeen owing to his propensity to violence. Be that as it may, he seemed to have gone to Calcutta afterwards and worked in ships that traversed Asian ports. No one knows when and why he came to the Pacific, and his writing and letters do not reveal much either. 'As an older man, when he devoted much of his time to writing, he was obsessed with gentility, so that the humble capacities in which he was obliged to seek work as a youth probably became matters that he deemed it needless, or even undesirable, to record', says Davidson.[85]

Contrary to Davidson, the letter to Arthur suggests a much earlier 'obsession with gentility'. There he claimed connections with aristocratic Dillons, such as Comte Arthur Dillon, the seventh Viscount Dillon, and with Arthur Dillon's elder brother who served in 1786 as Governor of Tobago (and was subsequently guillotined). Arthur Dillon's second wife was Marie Joseph de Girardin, cousin of the woman who later became Empress Josephine. The daughter of that union married Henri-Gratien Bertrand, companion to Napoleon in his last days in St Helena.[86] In my opinion Dillon naming one of his sons Joseph Napoleon was overdetermined by these imagined Napoleonic kinship connections and his idealisation of great figures, in this case combining the names of the Emperor and Empress.[87]

Davidson records many events in Dillon's life whose significance he does not fully appreciate. In May 1837 he was a witness at a trial in which he Frenchified his name into 'Chevalier de Dillon'. Davidson says:

> At this time, he seems to have been stressing his French connections, and he may himself have been using 'De Dillon'.

Throughout his later life he was very sensitive to the dignity of names and titles: Don Pedro Dillon, Count Dillon, the Chevalier Pierre Dillon, Chevalier Sir Peter Dillon, all appear at one time or another…it is also clear that he was disappointed at not receiving a British knighthood for the discovery of the fate of La Perouse.[88]

Davidson noted: 'The title chevalier had become so much a part of him that he could not forbear reference to it even when signing his name' as C. P. Dillon, 'C' standing for chevalier.[89] He claimed he was the French consul for the South Seas when he was not, though he tried very hard to get that position.[90] In January 1838 he was in Levuka (Ovalau, Fiji) and there he signed a memorandum in his imagined capacity as French consul 'and sealed it with a rough seal'.[91] The well-known French navigator Dumont d'Urville, who saw this document, sarcastically commented: 'Je souris en lisant cette piece de l'invention du Capitaine Dillon, et des titres qu'elle confère et a son possesseur et a son donateur…'[92]

Three years later, in a letter to the Duke of Bedford soliciting recognition (probably a knighthood), he inflates his own doings: 'At the risk of my own life I undertook to make peace [between natives and missionaries in New Zealand] and establish a mission there'.[93] Even minor actions reveal his wish to construct himself as a person of significance. In 1842, towards his life's end, he anonymously edited a book, *Conquest of Siberia and the History of the Transactions, Wars, Commerce, etc, etc, carried on between Russia and China from the Earliest Period*, which was, the title further indicated, 'Translated from the Russian of G. F. Muller…and of Peter Simon Pallas…' Dillon did not know Russian and Davidson says this book's content was 'actually taken from the English of William Coxe and anonymously edited by Dillon'.[94] But the next year a new edition appeared with Dillon's name squarely in front: *Conquest of Siberia, by the Chevalier Dillon, and the History…* One could put the matter thus: Dillon was trying to forget his past and his own personal and social inadequacies and, by identifying with the great navigators of history and especially his immortal Cook, was trying to invent himself by constructing a grandiose and imagined self wherever he could. The title 'Chevalier' granted by the French was surely something he deserved: thereby his delusions of grandeur could at last merge with reality but could hardly help resolve some of his fantasised imaginings, grandiose self-constructions and delusions as he went on covering up his past as a violent man, a wife-beater, and one born in obscurity. His obsession with gentility, I think, has deeper psychic roots in the infantile dilemma of the fantasised foundling who is in psychic reality the child prince found among the bullrushes.[95]

Fantasy and psychic reality in self-invention

It is time to move away from Dillon's obsession with mutiny — which threatened his narcissistic self-centredness, his authoritarianism, his vulnerability to real and imagined slights, and his grandiose self-imaginings — and return to his representation of the cannibal feast, the first on-the-spot description of an important event, even though it was an imagined one constructed from what he had heard or known of such repasts.

Initially, I had no methodological choice but to treat Dillon's deposition and the *Sydney Gazette* accounts as true in order to demonstrate the falsity of the claim of the cannibal feast in the later La Perouse account. Having accomplished that task it is now necessary to leave that methodological tangle, for even those earlier statements are after all self-representations and there is nothing to say that the Dillon who invented the one did not invent the other.

Let me begin with the frontispiece of his book entitled: 'Massacre at the Fejee Islands in September 1833: dreadful situation of Captn Dillon and the other Survivors'.[96] In this piece of self-aggrandisement we see a tall Dillon in his uniform, gun in hand, standing on the Rock that now bears his name with one person on his left, much smaller, and another, probably Buchert, the Prussian marksman, kneeling down and firing at the savages below. Further away on Dillon's left is a ship, the *Hunter* no doubt, while before him and Buchert are the hordes of savages whose physiques and gesticulations imitate (rather poorly) Webber's paradigm piece of savage violence, *The Death of Captain Cook*. One comrade is lying dead; the other is about to be killed, while in the distance a human body is cooked in an open fire (instead of the earth oven mentioned in the text).

This adventure is true, according to the La Perouse account, but that truth cannot be accepted uncritically. One can cast some doubts on the details: Buchert killing twenty-seven natives with twenty-eight shots is highly improbable given the kind of muskets available at that time, as is the claim that one could count enemies being killed during the difficult situation Dillon and his men were in. It is not even likely that Buchert retained his early marksman's skills during his stay in Fiji and Tikopia. Equally dubious are the versions of Dillon taking a priest hostage and going past the savage multitude without being killed by a musket or spear. And how does one know the truth of the multiple fates of Charles Savage and Luis, the Chinese man, except that they were killed by the Fijians? No one knows what happened to the other survivors when Dillon wrote his La Perouse narrative fifteen years later. I shall deal with the enigmatic Buchert later but will first consider Dafny (who went unmolested to the ship to procure the release of the Fijian hostages). He must have been a sight for sore Fijian eyes, according to Dillon's description of his bodily state immediately before ascending the Rock:

> He was wounded in several parts of the body, and he had four arrows stuck in his back: the point of the spear had pierced his shoulder, having entered from behind and came out in the fore part under the collar bone.[97]

Wilson, the second defender of the Rock, simply disappeared from the La Perouse scene. And Buchert? He could hardly speak English, according to Dillon; he did not even speak Tikopian, even though he had lived there for thirteen years.[98] There is little doubt that a 'massacre' of Europeans did take place that year, and it was in Dillon's character to act with courage and impetuosity. But Dillon's self-constructed role in all of his narratives is open to suspicion.

I now want to address a deeper and possibly unresolvable question: though the Fijian cannibal feast was an imagined one, did Dillon imagine it was an imagined one? Do imagined self-constructions *remain* imagined? Dillon's case compels me to explore this theme, albeit very tentatively, by getting back to the letter he wrote to the Duke of Bedford in 1841 where he mentions his Fijian experience: 'I miraculously escaped, after seeing several of my shipmates murdered, cut up, baked and devoured. On this occasion I saved my life, to be useful to the friends of humanity and science'.[99] Science and humanity aside, Dillon might well have come to believe the truth of his own story by this late stage in his life.

Let me start with a simple proposition: the prototypical condition where fantasy and reality meet is childhood. It is here that the boundary between the two is blurred. But, diverging from the classic Freudian position which argues that as the child grows older the reality principle supervenes and fantasy is pushed into the lower depths of the unconscious, I take the position that the boundary between reality and fantasy is being constantly blurred even through old age and death. To rephrase the issue in Todorov's terms, the fantastic permeates multiple sites, and in some instances fantasy is converted into reality through those complex processes that I have identified as 'the work of culture'.[100] In Freud's own time the Protestant work ethic was such that the role of fantasy in everyday life was often not given recognition. Yet even here one could act out one's sexual fantasies, for example, in special arenas such as brothels and bordellos. There was another realm where ordinary settlers, colonisers and seamen could act out their fantasies, in ships and islands, where their imaginations were peopled with noble or ignoble savages and, in terms of our present argument, with cannibals.

I am interested in the permeation of fantasy in our everyday lives, as we think of ourselves, as we recount or recollect our past, or begin to give our lives meaning and significance through narrative. Few can escape this 'fantasising in everyday life'; not as 'the psychopathology of everyday life' that Freud spoke of, but as everyday normal creativity (which is what Freud probably meant anyway). As I recount what happened to me when I did this or that, visited such and such a place or met so and so, I often embellish my account with splashes of invention, wittingly or unwittingly. Memory often helps by being selective in precisely this sense: the eliding or censoring of past occurrences and the harmless invention of events that never occurred get woven into one's story. Our lives are continual self-inventions of this sort. Once we begin to narrate our favourite experiences we might even begin to believe in them ourselves, till some occasion or other forces us to a recognition of the invented nature of our narratives of the self.

This everyday self-invention can easily merge with 'pathology', the extreme case being that of paranoid and other psychotic fantasies. But between the ordinary self-inventions of most of us and the extreme psychotic forms are those shadowed areas where individuals begin to invent and construct their selves under the governance of fantasy. We are familiar with them in fiction. In John Le Carre's *The Tailor of Panama*, Harry Pendel has a shop, 'PENDEL AND BRAITHWAITE, Panama and Saville Row Since 1932', which is patronised by the Panamanian elite. Pendel is heir to this dignified family business; his life revolves around this identity and not even his wife knows that he learned tailoring in an English prison until he is forced by a British agent to confront his invented life as a falsehood. But that life was not fiction to Pendel and for everyone who knew him. His invented identity is part of his being, inseparable from it, and Pendel's forced recognition of its empirical falsity produces the disastrous consequences that follow and eventually engulf him in his own death. Pendel is not a Dr Jekyll and Mr Hyde character leading two lives; he *is* his invented persona, even though he knows that it is an invented one. He is not a confidence trickster, either. The confidence trickster knows that his assumed identity is a false one; he sheds it when it is expedient; his play with a double identity is intrinsic to his persona. But even here the assumed identity sometimes becomes the dominant one, as with Thomas Mann's brilliant rogue Felix Krull, a trickster who revels in his invented identity, though the self-consciousness of his past, as with any confidence trickster, is necessary for his self-revelling. In other instances, such as that of Martin Guerre, the assumed identity might become more real that the other persona. At the O. J. Simpson trial Detective Furman, we are told, had invented himself as someone who had encountered adventure in Vietnam even though we know he never actually got off his ship in Saigon. I have known others who have invented Vietnam War experiences. One can weave into the phantasmagoria of war a new segment of the self because there is hardly any way of others knowing whether one's self-construction is a 'fabrication'. That Freudian touchstone of 'reality-testing' can have no sway over areas that are governed by the very absence of familiar life forms or the 'reality principle'. And war is one of those arenas where genuine heroism can be enacted, and also genuinely or disingenuously invented.

I became acquainted with this condition in Sri Lanka during a period which Sri Lankans themselves label as the 'time of dread' (*bhisana kalaya*). I will not theorise its ethos in this essay, except to say that the period produced not so much a 'culture of fear' but the very erosion of what one can reasonably call 'culture', when multiple and shifting forms of terror, intimidation and dread began to take hold over the spaces in which human beings construct their reality norms. Dreadful happenings, unbelievable in normal life, seemed to happen every day. In such a situation one does not know whether stories one hears are true or not. The ethoses of dread permit individuals not only to act out their fantasies and even create fleeting life forms out of them but they also permit persons to invent stories about themselves and others which can pass muster as real. Fabrication thrives in 'times of dread'. When my friend Wijedasa was captured by paramilitary thugs and 'disappeared', I could not believe the dreadful story of his disappearance; in fact to this day I can never prove it; I can only prove that many disappeared in similar fashion.[101] And there are plenty of invented stories of disappearances, and horror stories of such things as vampirism and cannibalism, even cannibal dances by paramilitary forces dressed in black, based on the dread actualities of that Sri Lankan time.

Invented stories sound true in the ethoses of that period because the fantastic as horror has also become real, fusing the real of everyday life with childhood's 'real'.

The 'time of dread' was roughly 1985–89, when ethnic Sinhala youth took over vast areas of the country and practised enormous atrocities; they were only eliminated by equally dreadful state terror. Both forms of coexisting terror resulted in the deaths of thousands of innocent non-combatants, as social, political and personal grudges began to be paid off. This period produced males who became addicted to torture and killing, which tapped their own unconscious fantasies, permitting them to act these out in the shifting ethoses of dread.

This youth rebellion had its precursor in 1971; here also dispossessed youth from rural areas controlled vast parts of the nation for about a month till they were quelled by massive government force, though not of the level of brutality unleashed during the dreaded second revolt. In 1971 I was teaching in the University of Sri Lanka at Peradeniya and I interviewed several students and activists on the run. One person I interviewed was an older man wanted by the police who came to see me in various guises, now dressed in this garb, now in that, now as an Anglican priest, now as a beggar. I was fascinated by his life as he gave me graphic accounts of his adventures. Those at home were nothing in comparison to his adventures in the British army during World War II in Burma, which were graphic, vivid, full of detail and verisimilitude. A white female diplomat was so seduced by his stories that she slept with the hero and protected him from the police. I was also seduced, as I later was by tall Dillon's tale; I fancied I could write a brilliant biography of a revolutionary. One day, as my friend was talking to me about his Burmese adventures, I was suddenly jolted from my own fantasy: my God, I thought, this is a plain invention, there were no Burma days and his adventures were just another of his many guises. It was not too difficult for me to verify that my friend joined the youth movement late and his work in blowing up bridges and his life in training camps were at best only peripherally true. He had lived in London for a long time and might even have been in Burma (though this was not clear) but his adventures there were totally invented. My informant-cum-friend and I were both caught up in a double fantasy. Both of us were bound, me by my youthful academic fantasy of writing a biography of a 'true revolutionary' and he by fantastic self-constructions in two ethoses, that of the Burma war and the youth rebellion, arenas or spaces especially well situated for inventions of the self. Many of his friends, myself included, could believe his stories because such stories seemed appropriate to the 'time of dread' in which we were living. I am convinced that my friend, like the tailor of Panama and Detective Fuhrman, came to believe (for most of the time) in his own fantastic self-inventions.

And so, I think, was it with Peter Dillon. Born a 'foundling' he wanted to be a prince; he achieved this when he was knighted by the French but that could not assuage his insatiable thirst for recognition. To be recognised he had to constantly invent himself. Dillon would have been pleased with the lordly title of Davidson's book. Yet let us be fair to Dillon. Not all his self-inventions were fictions; I am sure he fought natives in Fiji, perhaps bravely, and no doubt killed many, though perhaps not in the heroic manner he recounts in his several narratives. On the other hand he can be credited with the first published eyewitness account of savage cannibalism as Cook is read as being the first eyewitness of Polynesian human sacrifice. But Dillon was no Cook; a minor figure, he had to perforce invent his role as explorer-cum-ethnographer and simultaneously invent himself as hero, following the route of the great navigators of his imagined history. Let us now see how that history repeats itself as Dillon begins to repeat his history to other listeners and, I think, begins to believe in his own fiction of the Fijian adventure and the cannibal feast.

The context of narrative invention: the George Bayly version

I shall now discuss the first time that Dillon's cannibal adventures appear in the literary record, in two versions written by George Bayly. The first is an unpublished work entitled *Journal of Voyages*, written in 1831 in a straightforward journalistic style; and the second, a book based on the first but coloured by Bayly's sentimental reminiscences of 'sea-life sixty years ago', the title of his book published in 1885.[102] The latter has a vividness and immediacy lacking in the former; it is as if one can hear through Bayly's reporting Dillon's own voice recounting his adventures before an audience of shipmates.[103]

> Though naturally very excitable, and, when anything occurred to displease him, tyrannical in the extreme, he would frequently unbend, and would then entertain his brother-officers with such

graphic accounts of his adventures during voyages among the southern and eastern seas as made him *pro tem*, a very agreeable companion. From these he would sometimes diverge to tales of the 'ould counthry', and all unused to the melting mood, I have seen the big tear steal down his cheek as, in low murmuring tones, he would sing 'Savourneen Deelish', and other plaintive songs of his native land.[104]

Again: 'he had been spinning a long yarn about some adventure in those fairy lands, and he had an eager and attentive listener in myself'.[105] One might say that Bayly is inventing Dillon; but in so far as Bayly's invention is based on Dillon's own storytelling on board ship, one might reasonably argue that Dillon's invention of himself is re-presented by Bayly. We do not know whether Bayly had read Dillon's book when he wrote his first account in 1831: the two versions do not always tally, suggesting strongly that *Journal of Voyages* contains an earlier version of the Fijian adventure found in *La Perouse's Expedition*. The former anticipated the full-blown description of the cannibal feast in Dillon's book. However, Bayly's 'first narrative' is less interesting than his 'second narrative', which casts Dillon in the role of yarnster regaling his comrades with a feast of cannibal stories.

Let me begin an account of Bayly's second narrative, with Captain Robson's sense of betrayal by his Fijian friends for not bringing his full quota of sandalwood, and his determination to:

> possess himself by force of what he could not obtain by fair trad- ing…Having been informed that a considerable quantity of san- dal-wood was lying concealed in the native huts opposite the ship and having bargained with the Europeans on shore to side with the ship's crew, the captain sent a well-armed party on shore, under the command of Mr. Peter Dillon, with instructions to demand delivery of the sandal-wood.[106]

This narrative eliminates Norman, the first officer of the other accounts; Dillon is put in command and then he was joined by unnamed Europeans on shore. This does not fit with Bayly's first narrative, which says that Dillon 'was an Officer on board the ship Hunter' and also mentions the (unnamed) second officer as the one responsible for burning native huts.

The Fijian response was to summon their men for war by sounding their conches: 'A fight ensued, in which many of the poor creatures were shot, and the remainder, with the women and children, fled to the woods, whither Dillon did not deem it prudent to follow them'.[107] The raiding party took whatever sandalwood they could find, set fire to village huts, and loaded on board their booty together with eight natives they had captured. 'Under the impression that they would find another store of sandalwood at the neighboring village called Vilear [Wailea], on the following morning the officers asked permission of the captain to proceed there and get possession of it', fired by the success of the previous day.[108] The same party of thirty-seven:

> under the command of Peter Dillon and another officer, all well armed, left the ship with the determination of driving the natives out of Vilear and carrying the spoil...Mr. Dillon and his party landed on the beach in Vilear, formed in order, and marched up to the huts, much surprised that they had encountered no opposition...Suspecting that the natives were lying in ambush at no great distance, Dillon ordered his men to keep together, with the intention of retreating at once to the boats; but he had a lawless set to deal with in many of the men who had joined him. Deaf alike to his commands and warnings, and enraged at not finding any plunder, they separated into small parties, in order to set fire to the whole village at once, thus losing their only chance of getting back to the boats. Dillon only succeeded in retaining five to stand by him — Martin Buchert (a Prussian), two Englishmen, and a Chinamen, all of whom had been living with the natives, and William Wilson, a lad belonging to the ship. Each had a musket and pistols.
>
> Whilst Dillon was giving orders to these men as to what they should do in case of a sudden attack, the rest of them straggled about among the huts and commenced their work of destruction. Several huts were on fire, and with pirate-like recklessness the sailors were exulting in the fast-spreading desolation, as the towering flames rose up from the crackling bamboo huts, when suddenly, far above the shouts of the seamen and the noise of the blazing village, burst forth the war-cry of the savages and the boom of their war-conches, as with hideous yells they rushed from the woods where they had lain concealed.

The raiders put up a good fight but they were killed as they tried to reload their muskets. 'The savages then celebrated their victory by a fiendish dance over the prostrate corpses, while the air was rent by their horrid imprecations.'[109] The first narrative only gives the bare information; this is vividly elaborated in the second narrative.

However, both narratives say that the number of natives who confronted the group were about 1,000, not the 'several thousands' of the La Perouse version or the 8,000 or more of the *Sydney Gazette*.

To return to the second narrative. Dillon and his five comrades escaped the fate of their comrades as they climbed to a 'steep eminence'. While on the hill:

> ...the natives came rushing on, with the intention of serving them as they had served their late companions. Dillon allowed them to come within musket-range, when he and Buchert fired, and dropped the foremost of them; then, passing their muskets behind them, received the two loaded ones from William Wilson and the Chinaman. Meanwhile, the two Englishmen fired and killed two more; they also received the two re-loaded muskets. They took good aim, and every shot told. In this manner they kept the natives in check until they succeeded in taking up a position on the top of the rocky knoll. During this extraordinary retreat, Buchert killed twenty-seven men with twenty-eight shots, only wounding once, and this with the old Brown Bess since they had no rifles. Dillon and the other two also killed a great number.[110]

Buchert killing twenty-seven with twenty-eight shots is found in the first narrative also; one can assume this narrative element was invented by Dillon for the first time on board this trip.

The natives had by now surrounded the hill to cut them off and then:

> ...collected a quantity of wood, with which they made a number of large fires over the smouldering embers of their ruined village, and dragging along some of the bodies of the unfortunate seamen, cut them into pieces, and, with furious yells of triumph and demonaical dances and gestures, scorched and devoured them within sight and hearing of the unhappy remnant of the expedition.[111]

This account is more detailed than the first narrative, which says that the natives began to 'make a feast of Captain D's shipmates before his eyes'. In the La Perouse account Dillon has the victims placed in traditional earth ovens; yet the frontispiece painting of the adventures on the Rock depicts a victim being cooked in an open fire, more in keeping with the two Bayly narratives, strongly suggesting that this was the version Dillon had in mind when he authorised the painting.

Stimulated by their cannibal feast, they made the air resound with their war-shouts, uttering the most frantic expressions of hatred and revenge. The chiefs boasted of how many men they had killed, and called out to Dillon, 'Aromai no, Peter!' 'Come down, come down, and bring your men! If you don't come down now, we shall kill you and eat you as soon as it is dark; for then we'll rush up, and you won't see us'.[112]

But the savages had to contend with a 'master mind'; Dillon hurled back insults at them with his 'powerful lungs' telling them that the captain would probably kill the hostages. The natives did not seem to care: let the captain kill the prisoners, they will kill Peter and his comrades. Thereafter the natives went through the 'pantomime of cutting them up and roasting them'.[113] Both narratives refer to an interesting event missing in the La Perouse story: 'After they had remained some time on the hill Martin Buchert spied a man creeping up behind a hedge, he laid a musket on Captain D's shoulder and shot him in the act of throwing his spear which however wounded William Wilson one of their party severely'.[114] Quite appropriately it is Wilson who was sent with the priest in Bayly's first and second narratives, whereas it is William Dafny with native barbs sticking all over him who performs this task in Dillon's La Perouse version.

The two Englishmen (whose names are not mentioned) decided they could stand it no longer and risked going down because they had lived on friendly terms with the chief: 'The natives never stirred till the sailors reached the foot of the hill, when a number of them suddenly sprang up, and in an instant despatched them with their clubs. They cut up their bodies, and scorched the still quivering flesh in the fire.'[115] Now there were only four left, Luis grew desperate: 'Maski, mi go down'. He recognised a principal chief, his patron, down below. Dillon tried to dissuade him by warning him of the fate of the two Englishmen but heedlessly he left while the natives urged Peter Dillon to come down: 'Aromai no Peter!' 'Come down now, Peter; we will not hurt you'. But Dillon was too smart to trust them. Meanwhile Luis was led to a pool of water and 'one of the natives stooped down, seized the poor little fellow by the ankles, and tilted him over with his head in the water. The two held him in this position, amusing themselves with his convulsive struggles until life was extinct, when they cast him aside like a dead dog.'[116]

When Dillon was wondering whether it would not be better 'to fight their way through the mass of natives rather than endure such agonizing suspense', he saw a priest approach. 'They levelled their muskets at him; but he threw open his tappa (dress) to show that he was unarmed, shouting at the same time that he would take them past the natives and down to the shore.'[117] They allowed him to come near. He wanted Dillon to send word to the captain to give him a box of tools and cutlery and release the prisoners on board and he would guarantee that Dillon and his friends would come to no harm. Dillon however was smart. 'Inspired by a ray of hope' he tore a leaf from a notebook in his pocket and told the captain to give the priest whatever he wanted but 'on no account release the prisoners until they were rescued'.[118] But to his great disappointment he saw that *all* the prisoners come down from the ship's side:

> They now almost gave themselves up for lost; but Dillon instruct-
> ed his two followers how to proceed in the event of the priest
> coming back to them. Having secured his prize, he came direct-
> ly up the hill, and said he was ready to take them to the water-
> side. Dillon gave the preconcerted signal, and instantly one of the
> priest's arms was pinioned in his own iron grasp, whilst the other
> was seized by the almost equally powerful grasp of Martin
> Buchert; at the same moment, the lad Wilson brought a musket
> to bear on his back. Dillon assured him that if the natives attempt-
> ed to molest them in the least, Wilson would immediately shoot
> him.[119]

This ploy succeeded; the priest told his people that if they threw spears the 'pakehas' would shoot him and this will cause the sea to rise 'and swallow up the island'.[120]

Though the second narrative is couched in Bayly's words, Dillon's presence is unmistakable. At one point Bayly lets Dillon himself speak: 'Dillon, when relating the story in after years, used to remark with grim humour, "Auch! an' it's not iv'ry one that's had the j'ints of him bespoke for supper by the haythin cannibals"'.[121] Dillon belongs to a yarnster tradition of seafarers when he relates stories on board ship before an audience of mates, putting himself forward as hero in improbable adventures. And this the second narrative nicely captures. Norman, the first officer and 'our comman-der' of the La Perouse story is ignored in the second narrative; he is simply the second officer of the first narrative who wantonly killed natives, ignoring Dillon's advice. Norman's dramatic death obvious-ly cannot occur in this story. Dillon assumes command from begin-ning to end and has no part in the lawless acts of the Europeans who were 'deaf to his commands'. As in the La Perouse version, he stands firm on the Rock with five others. In the La Perouse version Savage, the Swede, decides to take a risk because he knows the Fijian language. He is unnamed in the Bayly version, but was probably one of the two Englishmen who decided to risk it because they knew a chief 'under whose protection they have been living' — a singular mistake for Savage to make (in this account and elsewhere) because his patrons happened to be the Bau chiefs, the very ones who were fighting the Wailea and were being consumed by them down below!

Because the *Sydney Gazette* also refers to two Europeans who went out and were killed, one must once again assume that this part of the story is Dillon's and not Bayly's invention. In the La Perouse version Dafny is hurt, hence one reason to send him to the ship with the priest and instructions to Robson. In the Bayly versions, Dillon fishes out his notebook and cunningly writes a letter to Captain Robson which he has the priest deliver. But Wilson the seaman, who was one of the three on the Rock, takes over Dafny's wound. In the Bayly version Luis the Chinaman does not scoot off unseen by Dillon; he drops his name as he goes to seek the protection of a principal chief only to be shoved into a pond and suffocated, a fate that overtook Charles Savage in the La Perouse version. In the Bayly retelling the two Englishmen get clubbed; in the La Perouse story the Chinese man suffers that fate. The latter did not even have the dubious honour of being eaten by the Fijians in the Bayly story: instead 'they cast him aside like a dead dog'. When the priest came to the Rock, the Dillon of Bayly's second narrative did not put the gun against his neck as he did in the La Perouse story; instead he pinioned one arm of the priest in his own iron grip; the other arm was in the equally ferrous grip of Buchert while Wilson 'brought a musket to bear on his back'. This wonderful bit of bravura is not in the first narrative, which has Buchert and Wilson walk 'each side of him, while he walked with their three muskets levelled at him [the priest]'.[122] The version in the second narrative is either Bayly's later invention or an alternative version narrated by Dillon and recollected by Bayly when he wrote his book.

In general one could say that Bayly's second narrative is for the most part an elaboration of his first one, which in turn was probably based on the information supplied by Dillon himself during the voyage from Valparaiso to Calcutta, perhaps after Dillon picked up Buchert in Ticopia. There is too much of Dillon here for us to say that these are Bayly's inventions. In my view Davidson engages in a completely futile task when he constructs a master historical account of what went on during that period from Dillon's multiple narratives. Dillon is a raconteur, but one who believes, partly or wholly, in the shifting truths of the stories of himself that he has woven.

The invention of Martin Buchert

In December 1827 a further account of Dillon's adventures appeared in the *Asiatic Journal*, published in Calcutta.[123] Dillon was now a famous man in that city, having returned with the French relics. This journal in turn refers to an account in one of the Sydney papers (whose name is not mentioned), purportedly by Dillon himself. While this unknown Sydney newspaper apparently follows pretty much the earlier accounts, there are some anomalies in it which the *Asiatic Journal* reports.[124] The major anomaly pertains to Dillon's 'omission of all mention of Martin Buchert, the Prussian sailor, who survived the massacre, and was his witness as to the story respecting Perouse…circumstances irreconcilable with the above account'. It adds: 'There appears to us to be a strange obscurity or mystery in this affair'.[125]

This obscurity is there in all the accounts of this affair up to 1827; it was clarified in the *Calcutta Gazette* of 8 May 1828, already referred to.

Captain Dillon's two remaining companions, who escaped with him, were William White [Wilson] and Martin Bushart [Buchert]. If Bushart and the Lascar, who also took refuge on board the *Hunter*, had returned to the island [Fiji], they certainly would have been sacrificed, and under this impression they besought Captain Robson to give them a passage to the first land he fell in with, in the prosecution of his voyage to Canton. Having finally left the Fejees on the 12th of September, the *Hunter* made land on the 20th, which proved to be the island of Tuccoppea…Here Bushart and a Lascar, with his wife a Fejee woman, requested to be put ashore, and they were accordingly left, and the ship pursued her voyage. In 1826, returning from Valparaiso, in the *St. Patrick*, Capt. Dillon came in sight of Tuccoppea, and curiosity prompted him to heave-to off the island, and ascertain whether the persons left there in 1813 were still alive. Both Martin Bushart and the Lascar appeared; when an old silver sword-guard, in possession of the latter, led to inquiries which terminated in the discovery of the relics obtained from the wreck of Perouse's vessels on the coral reefs which surround Manicolo. Thus it is to the circumstance of

Bushart and the Lascar having escaped the massacre at the Fejee Islands, and being accidentally landed at Tuccoppea, that we are indebted for the information industriously collected by Captain Dillon.[126]

One must assume that the addendum was suggested by Dillon himself, or by the editor of that journal on the basis of the many interviews given by Dillon in Calcutta before and after the discovery of the relics.

The 'strange obscurity' or 'mystery' of Martin Buchert is not difficult to resolve. Let me deal with Dillon's first interview, reported in the *Sydney Gazette* in 1813 and reprinted with or without variations in so many journals up to 1828. It gives a list of 'several Europeans and other strangers' who had lived in Bau and were now assisting in procuring the cargo: 'These persons were Charles Savage, John Graham, Michael M'Cave, Terence Dunn, Joseph Atkinson, William Williams, two Lascars, a Chinaman, and an Otaheitian'. It does not mention Martin Buchert who, according to Dillon's La Perouse account, was one of these European settlers. In its conclusion the *Sydney Gazette* states that all these ten people lost their lives in the affray along with the following persons from the ship: 'Mr. Norman and Mr. Cox, officers, Hugh Evans, seaman, and a lascar, named Jonno, belonging to the vessel, in all fourteen persons'. Let us see whether the details provided by Dillon confirms Dillon's number of fourteen dead.

During the first stage of the battle, six of the Europeans, including the officers Norman and M'Cave, 'threw down their muskets and ran towards the boats' and were killed. 'Nine others, among whom was Mr. Dillon (who reports this tragical event) collected themselves with a determination to resist as long as they were able' and climbed the summit of a hill. Only six managed to reach the top; the other three had to be left on the way, as they were either dead or dying. One of the Europeans (the man Dafny, according to the La Perouse account) went to the ship with the priest, leaving five on the Rock. Soon two Europeans (Charles Savage and Luis the Chinese man, according to the deposition and La Perouse) went down and were killed, leaving only three on the Rock. However, according to the foregoing description, the number of people killed in this encounter is eleven, not fourteen. To put it somewhat facetiously: if one were to take Dillon's count of fourteen seriously there was no one to defend the Rock — just Peter Dillon![127] But hold it: the elusive Mr Dillon himself seems to have soon realised his arithmetical inconsistencies; he therefore avoids or bypasses the number of the dead in the deposition given two weeks later. In the deposition Dillon only names one dead or dying person, a Bau resident, Terence Dunn, while the others are simply referred to indeterminately as 'the remainder'. Dunn's demise with unnamed others (the remainder) in the deposition now permits Dillon to defend the Rock with two others in the La Perouse account.[128] Nevertheless, whether or not the defence of the Rock took place as Dillon describes it, it is virtually certain that Buchert was not there.

But who was Buchert? There is little doubt that Buchert fled from Fiji and was taken to Tikopia with his wife and the lascar. Dillon met them again when he went to that island in May 1826 en route to Calcutta from Valparaiso. The lascar did not recognise him until Dillon told him that he 'was the captain of the cutter which brought him from the Beetee Islands and landed him with Martin Bushart'.[129] The lascar's forgetfulness was understandable because he was not a defender on the Rock. But Buchert? 'Having invited him on deck, I found that he also had lost all recollection of me; until I told him of our old acquaintance, and providential escape from Vilear'.[130] We can be certain that if Buchert was a Rock survivor he would have remembered Dillon. 'Mnemotechnics' is the word that Nietzsche used to designate occurrences that are 'burned into memory', and the adventure on the Rock was surely such an event. The deposition actually clinches the issue: not only is there no reference to Martin Buchert in both the *Sydney Gazette* and the deposition but the latter clearly provides a clue to his identity:

> Sayth that Deponent then proceeded to the Island of Topie [Tikopia] in Company with the Hunter, at which place a European Man and a Woman, belonging to the Feejee Islands, and a Lascar, who had long resided among those natives were by their own request Landed…[131]

Thus, it is virtually certain that Buchert was simply a passenger, who with his Fijian wife and the lascar left the island on the cutter during this time of troubles.

But why invent Buchert as a defender of the Rock? I think there is method to both Dillon's madness and his inventiveness. For Dillon the two volumes of his *La Perouse's Expedition* was his magnum opus written in the tradition of the immortal Cook. This work is introduced with Dillon's adventures in Fiji in 1813 and includes his description of the cannibal feast. In order to give his text a narrative unity he has to place this invented discovery alongside his discovery of the French relics in Tikopia followed by his search and discovery of the whereabouts of the shipwrecks. But there is no substantive connection between Dillon's Fijian adventures and his motivation to search for the site of the two French wrecks. How can the two narratives be linked? Through Buchert, of course. If Buchert is a defender of the Rock *and* the person whom Dillon dropped in Tikopia with his wife and the lascar *and* the person who, with the lascar, was connected to the relics that spurred Dillon in his search, then he is the figure that links the Fijian adventures with the main body of the text. He is the link that integrates the text; he must be invented as the defender of the Rock for the narrative to make sense. He was invented during the trip from Tikopia to Calcutta in the *St Patrick* in 1826. It is Bayly's account, I think, that gives the context in which that invention took place.

In this chapter I have identified a particular case of a more widespread genre of cannibal (and other kinds of) narrative in which the author, in inventing a story, also invents his imagined self and in that process comes perilously close to believing in his self-creation. Peter Dillon is a trickster, but one who plays a dirty game whose motive is to persuade us to believe in his invented story, quite unlike genuine cannibal tricksters of whom I have written earlier, like Cannibal Jack and William Endicott, who at least permit us to penetrate their trickery through ironic asides and the other kinds of veiled stylistic devises they employ.[132] In presenting Dillon's seemingly real account of Fijian man-eating, I have also dissected what many have taken as a true historical event that, along with others of similar genre, have provided fuel for the ethnographic understanding of savage anthropophagy. To show the fictional and invented nature of cannibalism entails a tremendous amount of research into archival sources and an imaginative reconstruction of how the various parts of the narrative have been invented and put together to form a story. It is therefore not surprising that my own narrative retelling of Dillon reads like a detective story, a genre to which I am somewhat addicted. Consequently it may seem to the reader that the ethnographer, in showing the invented nature of the cannibal myth, is himself in effect inventing another, more plausible, story, grounded though it be on the painstaking cultivation of 'evidence'. Yet it is this weaving of evidence, however opaque, into the body of the text that differentiates ordinary storytelling from ethnographic narratives.

Chapter 6
Cannibalising indigenous texts: headhunting and fantasy in Ion L. Idriess's Coral Sea adventures
Robert Dixon

IN 1996, at the Seymour Centre in Sydney, the Aboriginal Islander Dance Theatre (AIDT), in collaboration with Islander rock star Christine Anu, staged a production entitled *Drums of Mer*. The program notes explain that the production was a conscious attempt to develop a contemporary dance work from traditional legends of the Torres Strait Islands. In the course of his research, the company's artistic director, Raymond D. Blanco, consulted traditional custodians of the legends, but his immediate source of inspiration was Ion L. Idriess's 1933 novel *Drums of Mer*. The performance comprised eight episodes of dance and music, each illustrating an episode from Idriess's novel, which is quoted extensively in the program notes. It began, in a manner that must have been highly confronting for its Sydney audience, with a sensational episode of ritual decapitation and cannibalism, based upon the lurid opening chapter of Idriess's novel, 'The Dance of Death'.

Raymond Blanco's traditional consultants, Pinau Ghee and Dujon Niue, warned him that some matters relating to the 'Dance of Death' were still taboo, and so he found himself performing what he described as 'a tightrope walk between Tradition and western law'. But the niceties of 'western law' held a bitter irony for these Aboriginal and Islander performers. The AIDT found itself in the invidious position of having formally to acknowledge that Idriess's estate, now incorporated as Idriess Enterprises Pty Ltd, still held copyright in the published accounts of the legends, which Blanco's Islander consultants believed to be their own cultural heritage. Accordingly, the program included a legal notice of acknowledgment, though it was curiously inserted vertically in the margin:

The Aboriginal Islander Dance Theatre and Raymond D. Blanco gratefully acknowledge the generous agreement of Idriess Enterprises Pty Ltd. in its capacity as owner of copyright in the works of the late Ian [*sic*] L. Idriess, in allowing the use of material from the title of his book 'Drums of Mer' for the purpose of this production.[1]

Colonisation is indeed an ongoing process. To reclaim legendary material and make it speak to contemporary audiences, the AIDT was forced by Australian copyright law to acknowledge that legal ownership was vested in the estate of the white writer who had collected and used the material, largely without regard for Island custom, in the late 1920s.

Raymond Blanco's marginal acknowledgment of copyright law opens a window onto what is in fact a vortex of cultural appropriations. Between 1933 and 1950, Ion Idriess wrote four books about white people captured by head-hunters in Torres Strait: *Drums of Mer* (1933), *Headhunters of the Coral Sea* (1940), *Isles of Despair* (1947) and *The Wild White Man of Badu* (1950) (see Illustrations 5–6). Idriess drew his information partly from Islander informants and partly from A. C. Haddon's *Reports of the Cambridge Anthropological Expedition to Torres Straits* (1904–35). These, in turn, were based upon interviews and transcripts supplied to Haddon by his Islander informants in the 1880s. This network of appropriations is revealing about the nature of colonial textuality. The word 'text' derives from the Latin *textere*, or structure. The verb *texere* means to weave, or to compose (a work or letters). As Roland Barthes puts it, punning upon the Latin root, 'The text is a tissue of quotations drawn from the innumerable centres of culture'.[2] But the materials from which the colonial text is woven are not culturally discrete. Idriess's books about cannibalism are themselves cannibalised from a variety of other textual material, much of it ultimately taken from Islander sources. Colonial texts, then, are built up by plagiarism, whose Latin root, *plagiarius* or kidnapper, resonates with the history of indentured labour in Torres Strait. The plagiarism performed by colonial texts is a theft of cultural materials, another form of blackbirding, a kind of captivity.

In this paper I trace this network of appropriation from Haddon's *Reports*, through Idriess's novels, and then back to Raymond Blanco's production of *Drums of Mer*. In doing so, I examine two faces of colonial captivity — one textual, the other material. In the first place, I argue that colonial texts are a form of plagiarism, literally a 'kidnapping' of indigenous narrative materials, whose meanings are then altered to reflect the interests of their captors — Idriess's white, largely middle-class readers. Idriess's books constitute a systematic and sustained appropriation of legendary materials which white Australian readers reinvested with their own obsessions. I want particularly to link his use of decapitation as the definitive mark of savagery with anxieties about the moral decline of British and Australian culture during the inter-war period, a fear that liberal democracy in Britain and her Dominions might be weakened by the experience of total war.

But I will not confine my reading to the archive of colonial texts. I want also to make Idriess's stories about white captivity answerable to accounts of the real conditions under which Islanders lived at the time he did his research. Since 1897, the Islanders had enjoyed the protection of the *Aborigines Protection and Restriction of the Sale of Opium Act*, and would continue to be defined, officially, as 'inmates' until alterations were made to the Act in the mid-1930s. Being a 'captive' on a Torres Strait island in the late nineteenth century, or during the early decades of the twentieth century, was therefore an indeterminate state: its meaning depended on your point of view. The myth of savage captivity, of whites captured by Melanesians, was perhaps the dominant trope shaping white thinking about Torres Strait in the 1930s and 40s, the high water mark of 'White Australia'. Yet Idriess's historical romances about white captives amount to nothing less than a grotesque inversion of the truth about race relations in colonial Queensland, for they elided but simultaneously helped to justify a paternalistic administration. The real 'captives' were not the mythologised white castaways, but the descendants of their alleged captors, the Melanesian men and women whose lives were shaped so powerfully by the administrative presence of the State of Queensland on their island homes.

The cannibalistic complex

The work of Sri Lankan anthropologist Gananath Obeyesekere has helped us to understand why a fascination with head-hunting and cannibalism is a recurring, yet also unstable, feature of colonial discourse. In an important article titled, provocatively, 'British Cannibals', Obeyesekere argues that 'what is called cannibalism' in the eighteenth and nineteenth centuries was in fact a 'British discourse about the practice of cannibalism' that must be distinguished from 'the traditional sacrificial anthropophagy' of Polynesian and Melanesian peoples.[3] In traditional Islander society, warriors were admired for their fighting skills, and the taking of enemies' heads was a token of personal and clan prestige. The technique of removing an enemy's head was highly ritualised, and warriors carried a special bamboo knife and cane hoop to perform ritual decapitation. The severed heads were cooked, preserved, and made lifelike by the addition of beeswax noses and eyes of nautilus nacre, and then placed in a skull house, a sacred place. For the Islanders, these practices were an expression of their belief in life after death, of the spirit world interacting with the living. Through ritual anthropophagy, the *marki* or spirit of the dead might be imbibed by the living to enhance their potency. The skulls of departed relatives were preserved to enable direct communication with the *marki*, which might be consulted to increase the productivity of gardens or ensure a successful outcome for dugong hunts.[4]

These Islander beliefs and practices must be distinguished from the ideas that make up what Obeyesekere calls 'the cannibalistic complex' of Europeans: the obsession with head-hunting, cannibalism and captivity. The evidence now suggests that this was a British projection, bound up with the themes not only of late nineteenth-century anthropology, but also pseudo-sciences like phrenology and anthropometric measurement. While this cannibalistic complex was initiated by British ethnological inquiry, it was stimulated in turn by the demands of a reading public for whom travel literature, ethnography and adventure novels were often consumed indiscriminately. For example, Marianna Torgovnick has drawn attention to the importance of the severed heads that decorate Kurtz's hut in Conrad's novel *Heart of Darkness* (1902), where they function as an almost occulted statement about the white man's descent into the primitive. Comparing Kurtz's motives with accounts of ritualised head-hunting and cannibalism in anthropological texts, Torgovnick argues that Kurtz 'acted out a Western fantasy of savagery, with emotions different to those typically found among primitive peoples'.[5]

Following these suggestions, it can be argued that the network of colonial textuality carried away the meanings of ritual anthropophagy into the discourse on cannibalism, where they were perverted to western ends, performing a very different function for an entirely different audience — that is, as an index of western conceptions of the primitive. One shortcoming of Torgovnick's analysis, however, is her invocation of anthropology as an authoritative means of contrasting Kurtz's 'fantasy of savagery' with the apparently more accurate picture of 'savagery' found in anthropological texts. As Mary Louise Pratt has shown, the generic boundaries between anthropology and 'fantasy' are extremely porous.[6] Ethnographic texts — especially those of the early twentieth century — set themselves off from less 'legitimate' kinds of writing, such as adventure novels and travel books, while they actually share many literary conventions with these other forms. The first volume of Haddon's *Reports* was published in 1904, only two years after *Heart of Darkness*, and clearly illustrates the connections between the two forms of engagement with the primitive. The *Reports* are the first thread in the network of colonial texts with which I am here concerned, the first act of plagiarism.

Haddon's 'cannibal tours'

Alfred Cort Haddon spent eight months in Torres Strait in 1888–9. Ten years later, in 1898, he returned with colleagues W. H. R. Rivers, C. G. Seligman and Anthony Wilkin to spend a month on Mabuiag. Sensitive to how short a time he had spent in the field, Haddon acknowledged the fundamental contribution of his Islander informants: 'for the special work we had to do it was necessary to visit a people who were amenable and with whom communication was easy'.[7] Although edited and partly written by Haddon and his specialist colleagues, the *Reports of the Cambridge Anthropological Expedition to Torres Straits* (1904–1935) draw extensively on interviews with Islander informants, and on transcribed 'folk tales' written down by mission-educated Islanders.

Because it was not yet the kind of professional ethnography that would emerge in the 1920s after Malinowski,[8] the *Reports* is a heterogenous text which makes little attempt to submerge these other voices beneath an authoritative ethnographic discourse. A good example is the episode which opens volume five, an account of a trip by Haddon and Wilkin to a cave on the tiny island of Pulu near Mabuiag. The cave, called the Augudalkula, was associated with the legendary hero Kwoiam, whose decapitation of his enemies was re-enacted in the so-called 'dance of death'. Haddon's account of the legend and its associated rituals is partly comprised of his own ethnographic reporting and description, illustrated by Anthony Wilkin's photographs, but the material is heavily derived from Haddon's Islander informants, including Waria, the chief of Mabuiag in the 1890s, and his predecessor Nomoa. Haddon explains that the 'folk tales' have been taken down 'as told to me [or written down] in broken English'.[9] This same material was later drawn on repeatedly and in detail by Idriess, providing the bulk of information about ritual decapitation that informs both *Drums of Mer* and *The Wild White Man of Badu*.

Haddon's account of his visit to Pulu is motivated by a transparent fascination with head-hunting as the defining trope of the primitive. Although the writing purports to reconstruct what happened in traditional times, it is also an account of Haddon's own fascination with the site, his pilgrimage to the heart of darkness, which becomes a kind of adventure story. It is the discrepancy between these two modes that prevents Haddon from giving a suitably disinterested account of traditional society that is untainted by his own presence. One photograph, for example, shows the small bay where canoes landed from Mabuiag carrying the warriors who were to take part in the dance of death. Despite the text's attempt to recreate traditional times, we are struck by the presence in the photograph of Haddon's own sailing boat and one of the Cambridge team standing beneath Kwoiam's rock.

Ethnography's capacity to capture or subdue the 'other' for its own purposes is caught poignantly in a photograph of one of Haddon's informants posing, at his insistence, as the dying Kwoiam. Haddon remarks that 'when we visited Kwoiam's cairn I wished a man to be photographed in the attitude of the dying Kwoiam, there were no women about, but it was with the greatest difficulty we could get a man to strip, and then he behaved in a ridiculously prudish manner, but we were able to get the photograph'.[10] Despite its ethnographic intentions, Haddon's *Reports* began the process of kidnapping Islander legends from the sphere of ritual to the unstable realm of textuality, where ritual meanings were easily displaced by readers' fantasies about the primitive. In the 1930s, that process of transformation was completed in the books of Ion Idriess.

Idriess Enterprises, Pty Ltd

Idriess went to Thursday Island in January 1927 and used it as a base until early 1930, when he moved to Sydney. For three years, he worked as a labourer on the Thursday Island docks, and on ships which took him around the Islands. He also formed a lifelong friendship with William MacFarlane, Mission Priest of Torres Strait and Administrator of the Diocese of Carpentaria. MacFarlane was something of an amateur anthropologist who had systematically interviewed Islanders about their traditional culture. In the foreword he wrote for *Drums of Mer*, MacFarlane spoke of the 'rich store' of 'records and documents placed at [Idriess's] disposal'.[11] Idriess drew not only on MacFarlane's research, but made cruises with him around the Islands, where he spoke directly with MacFarlane's informants. Idriess explains in his Author's Note to *Drums of Mer* that:

> ...it was only after years of sympathetic friendship that [MacFarlane] gained the inner confidence of the old keepers of secrets...These at last...told much of their secret history to MacFarlane just about the time I came along and reaped the benefit of it.[12]

Idriess's field work was later supplemented by extensive archival research. His principal published source was Haddon's *Reports*, but he also read most of the other books then available on the history of Torres Strait, including Joseph Beete Jukes's *Narrative of the Surveying Voyage of H. M. S. Fly* (1847), J. MacGillivray's *Narrative of the Voyage of H. M. S. Rattlesnake* (1852), and R. L. (Logan) Jack's *Northernmost Australia* (1921). In addition to copying, often verbatim, large slabs of material from these works, Idriess's books were copiously illustrated with photographs lifted from numerous sources, including Haddon's *Reports* and the files of Australian photographers working in Torres Strait, including Colin Simpson and Frank Hurley.

There can be no doubt that in writing about Torres Strait, Idriess felt a sympathy for Islander people that was unusual, perhaps even remarkable, for the time, nor can we doubt that he believed in the legitimacy of his research from a historical and ethnographic point of view. But it is equally true that travel and travel writing were big business in the 1930s. *Walkabout*, the magazine of the National Travel Association, was expressly concerned with promoting travel as a means of fostering economic development, and Idriess was a regular, paid contributor. Idriess's writing was part of this conscious marketing of exotic locations. In conjunction with Walter Cousins, his editor at Angus & Robertson, he developed innovative marketing strategies for his books. He placed extracts from forthcoming books in the popular dailies to whet his public's appetite, used a radio program on Sydney's 2KY to market his material, and approached prominent figures to write endorsements for his dust covers. There were even plans to make a feature film of *Drums of Mer*, though negotiations proved fruitless.[13] However much Idriess may have boasted of their historical and ethnographic accuracy, his books were therefore written with at least one eye on the market for popular fiction. As one of his readers noted in a fan letter in February 1940, 'to me [your books] are ethnological studies; and in the writing of them I note that you have made them also narratives of adventure'.[14]

In his books about Torres Strait, Idriess was obsessed with decapitation and cannibalism as defining features of a 'vanishing' and 'primitive' society. They are copiously illustrated with photographs of skulls and their symbolic substitute, masks, and with illustrations of the instruments used for ritual decapitation. The experience of reading *Drums of Mer* begins with its striking frontispiece, 'Masks of the Great Au-Gud'. Idriess took the photographs from Haddon's *Reports*. Commenting on the use of photographs in anthropological texts, Elizabeth Edwards notes that photographs have no inherent meaning, but are substantially defined by context: 'material created with ethnographic intent…can be repositioned and reinterpreted outside the anthropological frame'.[15] Idriess's books exemplify this capture of meaning. In the context of Haddon's *Reports* the photographs at least have some degree of anthropological 'legitimacy' as illustrations of material culture. In *Drums of Mer*, they are removed from the space of anthropology into the space of adventure and romance, where they are fetishised even further as signs of the primitive.

The first chapter of *Drums of Mer* describes in a lurid manner the dance of death, with which Haddon had also begun volume five of the *Reports*. Its immediate literary ancestor, however, is Sir Henry Curtis's decapitation of the native Chief Twala in *King Solomon's Mines*. Idriess's descriptive set piece is accompanied by detailed drawings showing the instruments of decapitation and the display of a skull on the *sarokag* pole:

> Grasping the *singai* handle, Beizam jerked up the head so that the throat strained…One quick slash of the knife cut through the neck to the joint of the spinal cord. With a flick of the wrist the head was jerked sideways, so that the back muscles tautened, and the knife without a jar completed the circle. With the left hand stretching the *singai* and right twisting the head, Beizam pulled strongly but evenly upwards. There was a pronounced 'click' and sob, the head parted, and, as Beizam raised it on high, a tapering streak of marrow was drawn out with it.[16]

The point of this episode is to demonstrate that Idriess's protagonist, the white captive Jakara, who watches the ritual, can be immersed in a primitive culture without participating in its defining act. Although he has become a warrior of Mer, Jakara is known as 'Jakara the Strange' because he resists both ritual cannibalism and the love of native women. Despite twelve years' captivity, Jakara has 'done well — preserved his life, his intelligence, and a clean white heart'.[17]

'Lawful killing'

In her discussion of Conrad's use of head-hunting in *Heart of Darkness*, Marianna Torgovnick suggests that 'Africa and the Africans became Kurtz's grand fantasy-theatre for playing out his culture's notions of...power through the controlled, borrowed rituals attributed to certain groups within Africa, perverted to Western ends'.[18] Following her image of a fantasy theatre, I want now to ask: in what ways did Idriess's novels use 'borrowed rituals' attributed to Melanesians for playing out his culture's own preoccupations?

When he wrote *Drums of Mer* in the early 1930s, Idriess had only just finished the manuscript of his book *The Desert Column* (1932), a graphic account of his experiences as a member of the Light Horse at Gallipoli. There, at much the same time as he was writing the decapitation scenes for *Drums of Mer*, he described his experience fighting the Turks:

> ...the queer psychology of lawful killing...you saw a Turk's head, you saw his moustache and his eye glaring along his rifle sight; you fired too, with your breath in your belly, then rushed forward, screaming, to bayonet him, to club him, to fall on him and tear his throat out...and he met you with a replica of the berserk, frightened demon that was yourself.[19]

Perhaps the most extraordinary thing about the passage is its powerful interpolation of the reader as 'you', the AIF soldier, only to transfer the interpolation at the end suddenly but ambivalently on to the Turk who is 'yourself'. This structure of interpolation poses a fundamentally deconstructive question about the relation between the self and the other, between the idea of the civilised and the primitive. Idriess's battle scenes express not so much racist supremacy, as an acute anxiety about the legitimacy of civilisation. And it is no accident that he chose a pseudo-ethnographic style of writing in which to express it. For in British and Australian anthropology between the wars, there was an implicit connection between the decline of so-called primitive cultures and the potential decline of the West.

One of the most influential books on this theme was *The Clash of Culture and the Contact of Races* (1927) by the English anthropologist George Henry Lane-Fox Pitt-Rivers. In the preface, Pitt-Rivers explains that his field work among the 'primitive communities' of the south-west Pacific, which began soon after the war in 1920, led him to formulate the 'problem' of native depopulation. The frontispiece shows a native of Aua Island in British New Guinea. The figure in the foreground is in shadow, and the caption reads, 'Where the Sun Sets on a Vanishing Race'. In the preface Pitt-Rivers makes a connection between current preoccupations in anthropology and anxieties about a European decline into barbarism: 'The great world-shattering changes of the past decade, the War, the Russian Revolution, the Treaty of Versailles…have led [anthropologists] to question for the first time many of the previously unchallenged assumptions implicit in their own civilization'.[20]

Pitt-Rivers' insight that anthropology was a mirror for Europeans' anxieties about themselves strongly influenced the thinking of A. P. Elkin, the foundation Professor of Anthropology at the University of Sydney.[21] In *Society, the Individual and Change, with Special Reference to War and Other Present-Day Problems* (1940), Elkin poses the question: how can a democratic society successfully engage in total war with a fascist state without itself becoming fascist, without reverting to the primitive?

> Civilized people are confronted with a dilemma. We would fain outgrow the weaknesses and also the reputed savagery of primitive peoples and regard ourselves as different from, and superior to, them. But at times we indulge in behaviour which is apparently as savage as that of any Solomon Islander or West African…Such is modern warfare in which all the ingenious inventions and refinements of modern mechanical and chemical science are employed to strike terror in and to destroy whole populations…Must we not, therefore, explain or excuse our savagery by attributing it to a resurgence of a fighting instinct inherent in human nature, primitive and civilized, an instinct, indeed, which is too powerful to be curbed by civilization?[22]

In fascism, then, Elkin thought that he was confronting an efflorescence of the primitive within European civilisation. His understanding of this threat was grounded in a crude cultural relativism and European anxiety about primitivism. Accordingly, he asks, what would happen if an Englishman were placed in a different culture, such as that of Nazi Germany, or of a tribe of head-hunters on the

Sepik River? Would there be a racial or cultural disposition to remain 'English', or would he lapse into barbarism? What if white Australia were to engage in total war with Nazi Germany or Japan? Would it evolve, of necessity, into a fascist state? Elkin's own racism is evident in his equation of Nazi Germany with a tribe of head-hunters, which he uses as a signifier of the most depraved form of human society. It is remarkable how closely these speculations about transculturation resemble the literary conventions of the captivity narrative, in which an individual representative of 'civilisation' is immersed in another, more 'primitive', culture. What we find in Idriess's captivity narratives, then, is a kind of fictional experiment that allows him to test out many of the ideas which anthropologists between the wars, like Pitt-Rivers and Elkin, explored either through fieldwork or through anthropological theory.

Under the Act

These concerns with racial degeneration and the threat of fascism suggest some of the preoccupations white Australian readers pro-jected onto the borrowed rituals of traditional Melanesian society. But in turning to the other cultural context in which captivity nar-ratives operate, we need also to ask: what was life like on the Torres Strait Islands during the period Idriess did his fieldwork? We need to ask what the consequences are for our analysis of modernity when we seek to confer agency on its others, the not-modern.[23]

All of the texts I have examined to this point are instruments of plagiarism — they carry off Islander materials into a network of textuality that reinvests this 'borrowed' material with European meanings. More recent ethnography, however, attempts to make white texts answerable to Islander voices, recorded either through the techniques of oral history or through Islander life writing. An example is the innovative ethnography *Stars of Tagai* (1993) by La Trobe University sociologist Nonie Sharp. Sharp offers a history of cultural contact in Torres Strait that weaves together the written record of white history with Islander oral history. The tissue of quo-tations from which her text is woven allows Islander voices to speak out against the network of colonial textuality. In Sharp's account of the 1930s, images of incarceration recur, but in Islanders' accounts it is they, not the white men and women, who are the captives.

In the years between the wars, Islander society was shaped over-whelmingly by the Queensland Aborigines Protection Acts. The purpose of the first Act of 1897 was to protect Islanders from blackbirding, but, as anthropologist Jeremy Beckett notes, 'The official Protectors were soon armed with draconian powers to control the movement and residence of Aborigines'.[24] The period of Idriess's fieldwork belongs to an especially paternalistic phase of this administration. At this time, the powers formerly delegated to the *mamus* or 'chief' on each island were transferred to the government teacher, who was appointed by and subject to the Aboriginals (Protector's) Department. The teacher had extraordinary powers over many aspects of Islanders' personal lives, including the right to make deductions from their wages, to impose a curfew on their night-time activities, and to prohibit their fraternising with members of the opposite sex. A delegation of Islanders told the Deputy Chief Protector in 1936, 'We are in a closed box and wait for the lid to be taken off'.[25] Islanders were defined, literally, as 'inmates' under the Act. Other inmates so defined were those of the Diamantina Hospital for Chronic Diseases, the Inebriate Institution, and the Home for Epileptics.[26] As Nonie Sharp observes, 'Mateship is for equals…Inmateship is the obverse side of mateship…You cannot be mates with those you suppose to be your inferiors.'[27]

One of Nonie Sharp's Islander informants, Au Bala, was born on Mer on 29 August 1912. In 1898 his grandfather wrote fifty-nine pages in English on myths, customs and classificatory systems for members of the Cambridge expedition. Au Bala's testimony is a counter to that act of textual kidnapping. Recalling his schooling in the 1930s, he said, 'The Superintendents in some Islands were just like little tin gods. Mrs Zahel was teaching over the other side at Badu. The way she spoke to me made me think that she was a little god.'[28] Mrs Zahel was the subject of an article published in *Walkabout* in 1938, titled 'Badu Island, Torres Straits: where a woman is Superintendent'.[29] Ironically, the article casts her in the role of a modern-day captive or castaway, a Barbara Thompson, nobly enduring her 'life of isolation' on the island as part of the white man's burden. Another of Sharp's informants, Nau Mabaig, recalls Mrs Zahel's regime on Badu:

> Mrs Zahel was very strict with us…She wanted we to go out and come back with her permission. She noted us. One person went out from here to visit the woman who loves him at St Paul's Mission, but he forgot to get a permit. And when the police caught him, they stood him before the court and fine certain money from him for going without a permit. We don't like her but Government still wants her to stay. She was their right-hand man.[30]

These accounts of Islanders' experiences as inmates under the Act suggest that Idriess's books and other widely read accounts of Torres Strait have not only elided Islander testimony, but have actually worked to invert the truth about race relations in Queensland, turning 'inmates' into captors and their superintendents into 'captives'. And in performing this reversal, in presenting the Islanders as savages, they not only erase the real conditions of their existence, but actively work to justify contemporary government policies of paternalistic regulation.

Drums of Mer *(1996)*

In this chapter, I have sketched a network of colonial textuality which, for a period of 100 years, has carried off Islander materials, borrowing them for other uses that reflect the preoccupations of white Australian readers. I began exploring this network with Raymond Blanco's 1996 production *Drums of Mer*, and I want now to return to it by way of conclusion. One of the reasons that Blanco chose to begin his production with ceremonial decapitation is that it enabled him to contest colonial discourse as espoused by Elkin at one of its most vulnerable points: its unstable obsession with head-hunting as a marker of the primitive. Blanco's quotation of Idriess's account of the dance of death can therefore be understood as an attempt to reclaim stolen goods, a textual equivalent to the current practice of returning items of material culture stored in museums, such as Ken Colbung's efforts during 1997 to have the head of the Aboriginal warrior Yagan returned to Australia from Liverpool. Blanco was taking back an account of a ceremonial practice taken by Idriess, who in turn took it from Haddon, who in turn took it from the transcripts of his Islander informants. His objective was to counter the desacralisation of ritual that is a consequence of its entry into the realm of textuality. Blanco's use of Idriess's text to recapture indigenous meanings is really rather remarkable, suggesting not only his own courage in the face of Idriess Enterprises, but also something surprising about Idriess's text — that despite its emphasis on the negative meaning of captivity as a kind of enslavement, it also retained a latent sense of its other meaning as fascination and enchantment. For as Idriess's biographer attests, in the late 1920s he was indeed 'captivated by the islands of the Torres Strait, especially Mer, and had no real desire to return to the mainland'.[31]

Blanco's reading of Idriess, then, is only partly a reading *against* Idriess, for it is also a reading that uses Idriess's own fascination with native spirituality for positive purposes. In reading colonial texts, I believe it is a mistake only to read *against* them, denouncing their racism and misogyny from the high moral ground of the present. Blanco's daring theft from Idriess Enterprises shows that we can also read *with* such texts, or at least read them strategically and selectively. We can recover from them something of that other sense of 'captivity' as fascination, wonder and enchantment. For in addition to their racism, one also finds in Idriess's books about Melanesia a sense of wonder that *might have been* the basis of reconciliation. As Stephen Greenblatt argues in *Marvellous Possessions*, there are two paths that lead out from the sense of 'wonder' we experience in encountering other cultures: one path leads to denial and estrangement, so that 'you make the other become an alien object, a thing, that you can destroy or incorporate at will'; the second path leads us to a recognition of 'the hidden links between radically opposed ways of being and hence to some form of acceptance of the other in the self and the self in the other. The movement is from radical alterity — you have nothing in common with the other — to a self-recognition that is also a mode of self-estrangement: you *are* the other and the other is you.'[32]

Chapter 7

Lines of fright: fear, perception, and the 'seen' of cannibalism in Charles Wilkes's *Narrative* and Herman Melville's *Typee*

Paul Lyons

Ignorance is the parent of fear — Herman Melville, *Moby-Dick*

The innocent eye sees nothing. We see what, in one way or another, we are disposed to see — Ernst Gombrich

I. Fear and perception in nineteenth-century American Pacific narrative

IT SEEMS self-evident that fear — its generation, its repression, its negotiation — informs all perception, and most clearly that involved with early intercultural contact. Fear acts through and upon what Michael Taussig describes as 'the nervous system', a sociosymbolic order made sensate within both individuals and the body politic.[1] Fear stimulates, immobilises, activates aggressive defences; it renders the boundaries of order palpable and permeable, subsides and intensifies in reaction to the perceived threat of the 'other' it both frames and is, in turn, reconstituted by. In part, because of the given nature of these conditions, along with the customised specificity and frightening theoretical abstractness of fear and perception as categories, the relations between fear and perception are rarely analysed in discussions of crucial episodes in the formation of American Pacific orientalism and its archive.

These scenes, which generally rely on 'eyewitness' accounts, reveal not only psychodynamics that feed mutually confirming lexicons or inflationary systems of citation, but also senses in which the communication of fear contributes to the making of history. As Greg Dening demonstrates, Pacific encounters are 'compounded histories' made in the transactions between various players, whose actions and reactions, and perceptions and misperceptions of each other's poetics, are co-creative.[2] The more fear saturates the scene of contact, the more dramatic becomes the performative qualities of action, including a range of mimicries and staged deterrences. Fear does not simply inform perception in these scenes. In fact, neither fear nor perception can be taken as anterior to the other. Rather, an economy of fear of the kind which operates around the discourse of cannibalism is itself transactive. Rather than leaving it static, fear alters and transforms the field of perception.[3] This generates histories that, Dening argues, 'change the environment in which others will act' because they 'will have to respond in some way to the history that has been made'.[4] History made in an economy of fear feeds itself, forming 'fright-lines' that circulate through cultural representations and into material practice. As Gananath Obeyesekere demonstrates in a reading connecting nursery rhymes to the 'seen' of cannibalism, 'where there is fantasy there could be slippage into reality and from there into human institutions'.[5] In the sense that these institutions are jointly made, a semiotics of fear comes into play, deployable and connected to relations of power. In a reading of Cabaza de Vaca's experience among Amerindians, Rolena Adorno argues that, 'Fear of the other was a weapon employed on both sides, the native American and the European. Both groups created, managed, and manipulated it, depending on who had the upper hand.'[6]

For Freud, fear depends 'on the state of a person's knowledge and on his sense of power vis-a-vis the external world', and this knowledge may in fact be the 'expression of a general hysteria which has become a heritage'.[7] Post-Freudian accounts of fear likewise stress its accumulative nature. Julia Kristeva, who uses 'abjection' to name ejective fear mechanisms, asks if abjection is a revolt within being that sustains the horrors that civilisations and individuals need to 'seize on in order to build themselves up and function?'. Abjection is 'a massive and sudden emergence of uncanniness'; on the border of existence the 'abject and abjection' act as 'safeguards' and 'primers' of culture. Abjection both fascinates and repels the subject.

Kristeva emphasises the ambiguity of the phobic object, citing its 'indexing value', its quality of 'pointing to something else, to some non-thing, to something unknowable'.⁸ Fear, then, haunts the interstices between preconception and experience, drawing force from insinuations of obscure agency which may be hallucinatory. Conventional distinctions between reasonable caution and neurotic anxiety rest on whether there is a basis for the fear, which must be determined retroactively. Hence, the satisfaction of witness. If the not-knowing produces shudders and a kind of spell, then reality or eyewitness dispels fear by making it nameable.

This assumes that witness can be dissociated from forces that structure perception, a formulation whose ambiguities are suggested in Ishmael's first sighting of Ahab in Melville's *Moby-Dick*: 'foreboding shivers ran over me. Reality outran apprehension. Captain Ahab stood upon the deck.'⁹ When Ahab appears, apprehension is overrun by something claiming the status of the 'real'. The 'seen' overrides fear, which is legitimated by Ahab's aspect. At the same time, for apprehension to be outrun suggests a space temporarily beyond the real(m) of understanding and raises the question of whether Ishmael's perception of Ahab is part of a chain of apprehensions. Perception here stills fear only long enough to preserve and perpetuate it. The instance, if held as representative, reinstitutes fear effects.

The dynamics sketched above are most tellingly in play in the discourses about cannibalism that form a baseline to American perceptions of Pacific Islanders. This chapter juxtaposes the 'seen' of cannibalism in two founding texts of American Pacific orientalism: Charles Wilkes's *Narrative* and Herman Melville's *Typee*. In these texts, as in American Pacific texts in general, cannibalism is the master trope for the 'pinchpoint' of the nervous system, and for that space in which the perceiver is held by the desire to know or not know in a certain way. The scene of witnessing cannibalism literalises the trope, converting it into history. However, the styles of representing the 'seen' of cannibalism in each text suggest divergent conceptions of mimesis, of representing history, as fundamental to the simultaneous development of American Pacific orientalism and its critique.

Charles Wilkes's five-volume *Narrative* (1845) of the U.S. South Seas Expedition can be taken as representative of state knowledge (and the state of knowledges) about the Pacific in antebellum America. It is self-consciously a historic and nationalistic mission, begun with anxiety about American reliance on European science. It is intensely concerned with the impression it is intent on making upon both Europeans and Pacific Islanders. Wilkes emphasises on

the title page of the *Narrative*, 'Nothing has been used in its preparation that is not STRICTLY AMERICAN'.[10] *Typee*, Herman
Melville's quasi-autobiographical 'peep at Polynesian life', is widely
taken to inaugurate both a touristic, escapist tradition of literary
perceptions of the Pacific and a subversive, anti-imperialist tradition.
Melville's text is perhaps best read, ultimately, in Greg Dening's
words, not as 'history or autobiography but [as] significant narrative'
that speaks resonantly to the deep and violent poetics of a young
American's experiences among the *enata* (men) of Taipivai.[11]

In both these narratives cannibalism figures as a crucial semiotic
operator, as sign of the abject quality in the other against which the
nervous system revolts. Throughout the *Narrative*, Wilkes identifies
natives as either cannibals or not (or no longer) cannibals. The line
is drawn across Wilkes's map of the Pacific — a dotted arc along
which is written, 'The Natives East of this line were supposed to be
Cannibals'.[12] Wilkes and his officers express a Crusoe-like abjection
about cannibalism, consonant with the outrage at alleged cannibali-
sations of crews that circulated in the popular imagination and onto
the floors of Congress. In the face of cannibalism, scientific objec-
tivity breaks down into disgust. For Horatio Hale, philologist-eth-
nologist on the voyage, cannibalism is a racial category and a direct
index of 'evil qualities' with 'roots deep' in Fijian 'moral organiza-
tion'. For Fred Stuart, a clerk on the expedition, cannibal stories are
believable on phrenological grounds: 'We have too strong proof that
these people are Cannibals to believe otherwise. Just from what we
have seen and heard & secondly from the phrenological develop-
ments of their heads — which in itself would condemn them.'[13]

In Wilkes, the loathing bound up with believing Fijians to be
avid cannibals augments a fear and crisis environment in which Fiji
— its reefs regarded as the natural equivalent to human dangers —
becomes a synonym for danger. 'The least degree of confidence
reposed in the natives', Wilkes writes, 'was attended with the greatest risk...So treacherous a people were not to be trusted under any
circumstances.'[14] At the same time, Wilkes always argues the vital
importance of not showing fear and distrust: in his *Autobiography* he
asserts that 'difficulties arising with the Savages may be imputed to
the apprehensions of the whites showing signs of mistrust which the
savages are quick to perceive and take advantage of...In dealing
with the savage all fear should be carefully concealed.'[15] Such an
outlook — distrustful and determined not to show it — leads both
to deterrence and the displacement of fear by creating fear in the
other, and to a resentment of what causes fear and necessitates its

concealment. Deterrence forecloses perception and feeds an ontology that originates in and desires revulsion.

For Melville, cannibalism is a hackneyed theme, madly blown out of proportion, irresponsibly deployed as a justification for pre-emptive violence, and productive of blockages within perception.[16] Cannibal fantasies structure and delimit what the 'I' witnesses, and how it processes information, and prevents contact that might lead to understanding. In *Typee* he notes how:

> ...a fear of the natives, founded on a recollection of the dreadful fate which many white men have received at their hands, has deterred their crews from intermixing with the population sufficiently to gain any insight into their peculiar customs and manners.[17]

Fear generated through 'recollection' literally prevents whites from finding out if there is any basis for their fear. At the same time, Melville feels the attractions, revulsions and odd comforts of 'cannibalism' as corporeal 'fright site' or nerve cluster for what William Arens calls 'cultural boundary construction and maintenance', including anxieties about race, masculinity and sexuality.[18]

The staged 'seen' of cannibalism in *Typee* both mimics and enacts the psychosocial forces of perception involved in scenes of witness like those found in Wilkes. Among the poetic and productive achievements of Melville's text is the apprehension, registered intuitively, somatically, and through mimicking citation, that from the moment of encounter *a priori* discourses about self and other may be productively unsettled. In effect, the whole idea of organic cultures can only be maintained from outside. The archive is shown to be a congerie of theatrical performances that have lost their context while purporting to uphold a naive mimetic realism.

Against such static notions of archive, *Typee* makes conceivable a history-making in which western classifications create much of what is handed down as native practice: 'Those whom we denominate "savages" are made to deserve the title'.[19] The scenes that shock westerners may not represent ritual aspects of native mythic order, or metonymy for such order; or they may be reactivist indigenous theatre done as a counter-discourse, for amusement or simply for profit, as with the generic Pacific Islander Queequeg's selling of heads that Melville equates with his own concessions to the market in *Moby-Dick*. In the moments where he points to such performative contexts, and through his attempt to see through the myth of cannibalism, Melville begins in *Typee* to find a new and vital role for fear in the construction of cannibalism.

II. Surveying Fiji: Wilkes's and America's Pacific archive

Wilkes's sailing orders included rigorous requirements for record-keeping:

> It being highly important that no journal of this voyage, either partial or complete, should be published, without the authority and under the supervision of the government, at whose expense this Expedition is undertaken, you will, before you reach the waters of the United States, require from every person under your command, the surrender of all journals, memorandums, remarks, writings, drawings, sketches, and paintings, as well as all specimens of every kind, collected or prepared during your absence.[20]

In this spirit Wilkes issued a general order that 'All the officers of the Exploring Expedition' submit a journal to him every week, a duty to be considered 'as paramount to all others'. The journals were to be 'as full and complete as possible' in recording 'any information in regard to the manners, habits, or customs of natives'. What was to be noted was 'public information' and explicitly not 'private affairs', which Wilkes deemed 'sacred'. The journals and specimens would form 'a mass of evidence for the use of the government on our return';[21] in fact, they would serve multiple reference uses (commercial, scientific, artistic, religious, academic, military). The official history would be drawn in as circumspect a spirit as possible, as the narrative equivalent of the surveying that was among the expedition's primary functions. Vis-a-vis native peoples, Wilkes was not a discoverer but a surveyor, not an original observor but a certifier of 'knowledges'. Every textual position would be ascertained by multiple reckonings and reinforced, if possible, by visual proof (drawings or specimens tied to narrative events). In the process, the sanctity of the private experience of each journal keeper would be protected, at the same time that the fallibility of individual subjectivity would be minimised. In theory, the *Narrative* would be at once depersonalised and centralised; its authority would arise from not being, in a conventional sense, authored. Under these conditions — sanctioned by antebellum institutions — it would be expected that the *Narrative* would be as unsensational and positivistic a 'Pacific' document as America was then capable of producing.

That the five-volume *Narrative* fails to approach dispassionate ethno-history is in part attributable to Charles Wilkes, whose overbearing, self-vindicating character is stamped on every page, even where Wilkes can be seen largely as a collator.[22] Beyond this, there were perceptual problems inherent in the surveyor's model of textual production. This model works best where the object is stationary, but it is disastrous for producing intercultural understanding, especially where it records practices around which fears circulate, and where collecting constitutes unrecognised intervention. In cross-cultural contact, as suggested, perception tends to move in alliance with desires that inform preconceptions.

But the *Narrative*'s problems illustrate far more than the pathologies of Wilkes or his men, or even of the mechanisms within antebellum American institutions that block the processing of Pacific knowledges. Such a reading might concentrate on the public occasion of the narrative's telling, the senses in which, in Dening's words, audience and actors, or readers and writers, 'enter into the conspiracy of their own illusions'.[23] Rather, what is ultimately at issue is the idea of perceiving cultures as discrete and 'other' and the senses in which not acknowledging fear at play in such a perception induces conformity to preconception, which often discharges itself as outrage. The surveying method denies the dialectic between preconception and perception through its belief in fixable, empirical knowledge, after which the real can be cloned into history. These issues, which Melville fronts in places and intuits in others in *Typee*, are evaded in Wilkes's narrative, where fear is extravagantly disavowed as part of a semiotic in which not showing fear is a sign and instrument of power.

III. Evidence and performance: the 'seen' of cannibalism in Wilkes

O what ridiculous resolution men take when possessed with fear! It deprives them of the use of those means which reason offers for their relief
— Defoe, *Robinson Crusoe*

In Wilkes's narrative, as in those of other 'strangers' in the Pacific, cultural exchange invariably takes place within structures established by material exchange. As Nicholas Thomas has detailed, 'The American-Fijian encounter entailed both gift exchange and direct barter' that took a variety of forms.[24] Wilkes and his men entered a scene in which Fijians, who often had dealt extensively with sandalwood and bêche-de-mer traders, missionaries, and whalers, were unevenly familiar with Euro-American trading practices. The journal writers repeatedly evaluate Fijians in terms of how craftily they bargain. Wilkes had an abundance of advice, coming from the differently motivated accounts of beachcombers (Whippy, O'Connell), traders (Eagleston, Vanderford) and missionaries (Calvert, Cargill), on how to negotiate with Fijians, and for him it all added up to anxiety and the need for strict control of the conditions of barter. In recalling events leading up to a tragic conflict, he writes: 'I felt great anxiety for the safety of our parties in the boats, and issued the foregoing orders very particularly, in order to avoid all misapprehension'.[25]

Wilkes assembled the *Narrative* retrospectively, after having faced a highly publicised court martial that resulted in a public reprimand. It is hard not to see underscoring his avowedly scrupulous desire to 'avoid all misapprehension' as a means of preparing the reader for what the *Narrative* calls 'the affair at Malolo', without telling events out of sequence. The Malolo massacre was triggered when several 'strangers', desperate for supplies, went ashore. Another boat held a native hostage. When the hostage leapt overboard, and a shot was fired over his head, the natives attacked those on shore. In the skirmish, Lieutenant Underwood and Wilkes's nephew, Wilkes Henry, were killed. The loss of two popular officers activated a pent-up hostility toward the Fijians, and nearly all the journals record the anger with which the crew prepared to retaliate on the following day. Several journals describe Wilkes as weeping or fainting at the sight of his dead nephew, the only child of his widowed sister. Before describing the military operation, which included the massacre of more than eighty Fijians and the destruction of towns, canoes, breadfruit trees, and yam and hog reserves, Wilkes emphasises the attempts he made to keep the bodies of his officers from being exhumed and cannibalised.[26] Wilkes seizes on this notion that 'the grave might not be held sacred from their hellish appetites', imagining 'condor-eyed savages' watching from the highest peaks for signs of the burial site.[27] After Wilkes has described the Malolo massacre he again congratulates himself on 'the promptitude with which the bodies were saved from ministering to the cannibal appetites of the murderers'.[28]

Given the centrality of cannibalism to Wilkes's whole attitude toward Fijians, it is noteworthy that the single episode providing eyewitness evidence of the practice gets only a page in the *Narrative*. On the one hand, it is as if the sketchy rendition of this structurally crucial scene confesses the instability of the evidence, or of narrative as a medium of witness. What has been 'seen' seems to resist narration or a fullness of contextualisation in which it might become comprehensible. On the other hand, the *Narrative* takes cannibalism so much for granted that it is as if the event can simply be regarded as an instance of something never in question. The confirmation fulfils the crew's perceptual desires. There is even a suggestion that the 'seen' was used in a motivational capacity, because in several journals it is recalled as taking place before the attack on Malolo: Simeon Stearns, for instance, who was not aboard the *Peacock*, recounts the 'seen' directly before the description of the attack.

Although Wilkes himself did not witness Fijian cannibalism, members of the *Peacock* clearly did see something that dispelled any doubts about it. Charles Pickering conventionally prefaces his account by stating that he had previously doubted cannibalism:

> We had hitherto been so well treated by the Natives, had found them always so obliging, and so 'timid'; that many of us began to think they had been maligned. Some even doubted whether they were really *Cannibals*; and the question had been seriously discussed at the Wardroom table the previous evening…though we had been nearly two months on these islands, no one could say he had actually witnessed the fact, or name a person of credit who had.[29]

Wilkes, drawing on the reports of Pickering, Emmons and others, narrates the 'seen' as follows:

> On the 2nd of July the Peacock sailed from Muthuata [and]…they anchored in Naloa Bay…A fleet of canoes came off to the ship the next morning, from which they learned [that] Tui Mbua's party had killed three of the people of the opposite party…One human body had already been brought over and just feasted upon. Shortly afterwards a canoe came alongside, bringing the skull yet warm from the fire, much scorched, and marked with the teeth of those who had eaten it. The brain had been roasted and taken out, as well as the eyes and teeth. Another canoe came alongside with some roasted flesh in it.
>
> While Mr Spieden and others were agreeing with the natives for the purchase of the skull for a fathom of cloth, a native stood near him holding something in his right hand, which he soon applied to his mouth, and began to eat. To their utter astonishment they discovered it to be the eye of the dead man, which the native had plucked from the skull a few moments before. So

revolting and unexpected a sight produced a feeling of sickness in many; this ocular proof of their cannibal propensities fully satisfied them. The native was eating it, and exclaiming at the same time, 'Vinaka, vinaka' (good, good). Another was seen eating the last of the flesh from the thighbone. This was witnessed by several of the officers and men, who all testify to the same facts.

Previous to this occurrence, no one in the squadron could say that he had been an eye-witness to cannibalism, though few doubted its practice, but the above transaction placed it beyond all doubt, and we have now the very skull which was bought from those who were picking and eating it, among our collections.[30]

The scene may be taken as representative of instabilities in the poetics of 'witness'. Something has been seen, but it is unclear what this act of seeing has to teach us about Fijian 'cannibalism'. Rather, the scene suggests that witness may be in multiple senses participatory, not because fears and preconceptions are mixed up in recountings, but because what is seen happens within a regime of fear and within the context of a 'transaction', or a theatre of barter to which both parties bring knowledges and in which both fulfil desires to some degree unintelligible to the other. Furthermore, it is evident, from the ways the journals alternately echo each other, that what was witnessed was discussed before being recorded, so that each entry involves a measure of collaboration. The cliché that 'Western commodities exercised an irresistible magnetism' is clearly reversible here, as the Americans are eager to possess an artefact that, perhaps unconsciously, acts as a souvenir protecting a collective image of Fijians.[31] The skull becomes a prop, valuable for the narrative (or flesh) attached to it. In the sense that the expedition produces a narrative America wants to tell itself vis-a-vis Pacific enterprises, the skull, whether exhibited in museums or analysed by phrenologists, could be held up to authenticate that soliloquy.

One might begin, in reviewing Wilkes's account, by noting a number of unanswered questions raised by the phrase 'shortly afterwards'. Wilkes is unclear about the nature of the communication between the first fleet of canoes and the canoes that subsequently arrive; he also fails to mention whether or not anyone on board the *Peacock* responded to the report of the cannibalised body with a request for reliquaries. In Pickering's account, it is clear that this took place: 'We were anchored off the village on the island visited by us, and someone learning that there was a feast on shore, desired evidences of the fact'.[32] The Fijians, then, do not simply paddle up to the *Peacock* with a skull, on the chance that it will be of interest, but come for barter, with a sense of what can be gained in return. They know from experience or from the phrasing of the request that the strangers are eager to purchase a skull, just as the purser, Mr Spieden, knows the natives value cloth, if not why they value it. More specifically, the natives know that the skull is valuable in connection with the strangers obsessive interest in cannibalism. In this sense it seems hardly coincidental that 'while' Spieden is negotiating, the native begins to nibble on the eye, as if to say: 'Feast your eyes on this'.

It is worth noting that the details found in this 'seen' of cannibalism in Wilkes do not accord with anthropological records or theories about Fijian cannibalism, whether of the Peggy Sanday variety, in which cannibalism relates to 'a people's orientation to their physical and moral worlds', or in the details circulated by contemporary sources.[33] The missionary Thomas Williams pointed out that it was 'somewhat remarkable that the only instance of cannibalism in Fiji witnessed by any gentleman of the United States Exploring Expedition, was the eating of a human eye — a thing which those who have seen many bodies eaten never witnessed, the head, as has been stated already, being always thrown away'.[34] Similarly, after an assertion — based largely on missionary accounts — that cannibalism is practised to a frightful degree in Fiji, Sir Edward Belcher reports: 'I am told they threw one or more of the heads (which they do not eat) into the missionary's compound'.[35]

One might also note that what members of Wilkes's crew saw does echo famous 'confirmation' scenes in James Cook, Joseph Banks, and others. The crucial episode of confirmation in Cook involves a parallel 'seen' of witness: 'I now saw the mangled head or rather the remains of it for the under jaw, lip &c were wanting…a piece of flesh had been boiled and eat by one of the Natives in the presence of most of the officers'.[36] As Michael Hayes has argued, the skull is a conventional signifier of cannibalism: 'When Joseph Banks wants proof that the bone he buys from a group of Maoris is from a human body (and thus proves cannibalism) he asks for them to "Bring [the skulls] and we shall then be convinced that they are men"'.[37] The officers of the *Peacock* would have been familiar with the tradition, established by Banks, of buying Maori and Australian skulls. Likewise, if the eating of the eyeball was not generally the custom in Fiji, it is in several 'seens' in Tahiti and Hawai'i, as when Pomare is seen to eat (or simulate eating) the left eye of a human sacrifice.[38] It is conceivable, given the strangers' obsession with cannibalism and the fluency of several Fijians in European languages, that Fijians knew these stories.

There is, in any event, a decidedly literary quality to Wilkes's whole description of the 'seen' of cannibalism, with lurid phrases like 'yet warm from the fire' and 'picking and eating' seemingly used for effect and joined to odd 'eye' imagery.[39] The (un)fortuitously named Mr Spieden gets 'ocular proof' by seeing a native nibbling on a human eyeball. The reference to *Othello* tellingly backfires, because of course Othello's 'ocular proof', although it temporarily eases a mind that 'misgives' him, is manipulated to literalise erroneously his worst fears and lead him to homicide; Othello fears and desires the proof of what he fears.

Like many details in the scene, that of the Fijian punctuating his nibbling in front of strangers with exclamations of delectation seems at once staged and hard to stage imaginatively. In Wilkes's account it does not add up: the crew cannot first be vague about the 'something' held in the native's hand and then know that 'it' has just been plucked from the skull, especially because, when first mentioned, the skull is already without eyeballs. George Foster Emmons writes that 'one of the natives was seen chewing an eye which was procured from him & preserved by [*sic*] of our scientific gentlemen'.[40] In Simeon Stearns's second-hand account, the native has in fact snatched the eyeball out of the skull as a kind of afterthought: 'on observing he had left one of the eyes in the head he snatched it back gouged out the eye swallowed it smacked his lips and returned the now completely picked skull. Some of this flesh is now aboard the ship preserved in spirits.'[41] In these accounts, the eyeball moves back and forth across the deck, before winding up — if not swallowed — preserved as no. 29 in Titian Ramsay Peale's catalogue of items for the Smithsonian (no. 30 was Vendovi's skull).[42]

One might question whether the whole sequence, in which the native 'begins' to eat an eyeball before members of the crew, who exhibit nausea and astonishment, and then agrees to have this eye purchased, could be nothing other than a command performance, a native enacting his cannibal self in the eye of the beholder. These natives are not chiefs, and their 'king', who subsequently comes on board to spend the night, claims no knowledge of the story they told prior to 'proof' being sent for, a fact which the strangers dismiss at once as Fijian lying.

However, there is no hint of ambivalence about any of the details in Wilkes's account, and subsequent commentators distort the scene further. For instance, William Stanton's thorough account of the expedition describes the 'seen' as follows:

What doubts remained were dispelled one day early in July when a native scrambled onto the *Vincennes*' quarterdeck munching on a human head from which he casually plucked an eye 'and Eat it, smacking his lips at the same time, with the greatest possible relish'.

It is curious that a historian as meticulous as Stanton would get details wrong, quote a lurid account, and add his own literary touches.[43] For instance, in Wilkes's narrative, it was with crew members of the *Peacock* that the 'transaction' took place. It seems that, where cannibalism is concerned, the transactional nature of witness is liable to be overlooked, and the conversion of a subjective moment of witnessing into a so-called objective historical 'truth' is accepted without qualification. Whatever the officers of the *Peacock* saw, they partly created, and what they communicated was absorbed into the archive, in which Wilkes continued to play a prominent role. The history made that morning was constructed of the conjunction of Fijian strategies of response to foreign incursion and the European need to satisfy its preconception of the primitive as cannibal — a fetishised other — an abject figure that both attracts and repels.

IV. The 'cite' of cannibalism in Typee

Espied by some...blundering discovery vessel from afar...the whale's unharming corpse, with trembling fingers is set down in the log — shoals, rocks, and breakers hereabout; beware! And for years afterwards, perhaps, ships shun the place — Melville, Moby-Dick

Melville saw the kind of archive created by Wilkes's *Narrative*, with its etchings of cannibal pots[44] and stories of feasts involving hundreds of bodies, credulously recounted from beachcombers and missionaries, as a false survey, underwriting what Brian Massumi calls a 'media scare campaign' or 'organised fear trade'.[45] In *Typee*, Melville wrote:

The fact is, that there is a vast deal of unintentional humbuggery in some of the accounts we have from scientific men...These learned tourists generally obtain the greater part of their information from the retired old South Sea rovers, who have domesticated themselves among the barbarous tribes of the Pacific.[46]

Like so much of the archive on cannibalism in the Pacific that filtered through whalers, traders, missionaries and beachcombers —

Illustration 1: *Bilin Bilin*, photograph, N.D. Courtesy John Oxley Library, Brisbane. Reproduced with permission from Ysola Best, Yugambeh Museum, Language and Heritage Research Centre, Beenleigh, Queensland.

Illustration 2: William Strutt, *Richmond Paddock — Black Troopers Quarters Melbourne*, 1851, pencil & wash, 10.2 x 15.3 cm, courtesy Dixson Galleries, State Library of New South Wales.

Charles Never

Illustration 3: William Strutt, *Portrait of Charles Never*, 1851, pencil drawing, courtesy La Trobe Collection, State Library of Victoria.

Illustration 4: William Strutt, *Black Troopers Escorting a Prisoner from Ballarat to Melbourne, 1851*, pencil and wash drawing, courtesy La Trobe Collection, State Library of Victoria.

Illustration 5: Cover of *Headhunters of the Coral Sea*, artist Walter Stackpool, by Ion L. Idriess, 1940, Angus and Robertson, Sydney, courtesy HarperCollins.

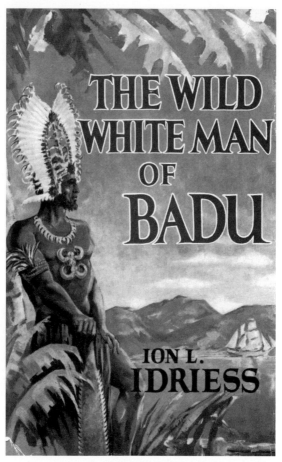

Illustration 6: Cover of *The Wild White Man of Badu,* by Ion L. Idriess, 1950, Angus and Robertson, Sydney, courtesy HarperCollins.

Illustration 7:
Postcard of Cataract Gorge, Launceston, 1910. Courtesy La Trobe Picture Collection, State Library of Victoria.

Illustration 8: Handkerchiefs distributed by the 1846 expedition led by James Warman and Christian De Villiers to locate the White Woman of Gippsland. These were illustrated and bore a message in English and Gaelic; it was widely believed the white captive was of Scottish origin. From the White Woman of Gippsland Collection, MS 10720, Box 286/6, Australian Manuscripts Collection, State Library of Victoria.

Illustration 9: Filipino nationals on display, still from Marlon Fuentes, *Bontoc Eulogy*, 1996.

Illustration 10: Marlon Fuentes searching for the remains of his grandfather Marcod, still from *Bontoc Eulogy*, 1996.

Illustration 11: Esther and John Truett at the Fair in the closing sequence of Vincente Minnelli's *Meet Me In St Louis*, 1944, courtesy Film Stills Archive, The Museum Of Modern Art, New York.

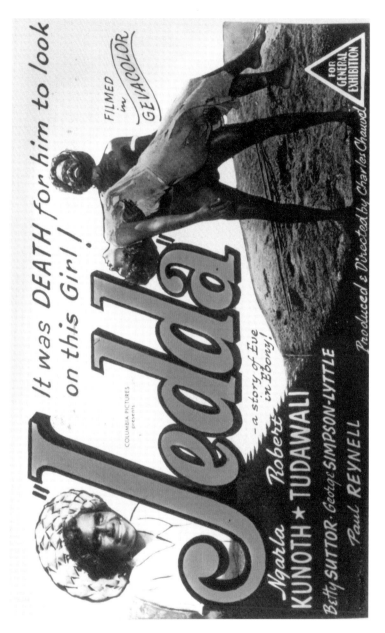

Illustration 12: Poster from Charles Chauvel's *Jedda*, 1955. Courtesy Susanne Carlsson and the H. C. McIntyre Trust, *c/–* Curtis Brown (Aust) Pty Ltd., Sydney, ScreenSound Australia.

Illustration 13: Jedda and Joe share a happy moment at the homestead. Courtesy Susanne Carlsson and the H.C. McIntyre Trust c/-Curtis Brown (Aust) Pty Ltd., Sydney, ScreenSound Australia.

Illustration 14: An idyllic episode in Marbuk and Jedda's journey to the distant lands of his people'. Courtesy Susanne Carlsson and the H.C. McIntyre Trust c/- Curtis Brown (Aust) Pty Ltd., Sydney, ScreenSound Australia.

and was absorbed into novels, paintings and exhibitions — Wilkes's *Narrative* reinforced both American fears and expansionist desires. Furthermore, it challenged 'beachcombers' like Melville to achieve a more elastic vision in and through his Pacific encounters.[47]

In a relatively carefree moment in Taipivai, Tommo asks, 'Are these the ferocious savages, the blood-thirsty cannibals of whom I have heard such frightful tales!'[48] The answer, of course, is yes: the cannibals he posits are directly out of the 'frightful tales' circulating from juvenile literature through scientific discovery narratives and back. Despite Melville's claim in the preface to speak the 'unvarnished truth' (a nod to Mungo Park's claim to tell 'a plain, unvarnished tale'), and though *Typee* everywhere insists, however apologetically, on the reality of cannibalism as practice, Melville probably never had an eyewitness account of Marquesan cannibalism in which he could place confidence. As Elizabeth Melville pointed out in 1901, more than fifty years after the fact, 'Mr. Melville would not have been willing to call his old Typee entertainers "man-devouring", as he has stated that whatever might have been his suspicions, he never had evidence that it was the custom of the tribe'.[49]

The cannibalism in *Typee*, then, is imagined, tropic and tellingly citational; from first to last it represents a troubled and troublesome performance, with its conventional single and delayed scene of witness seeming to fulfil a generic requirement. From the moment of approach to Taipivai, where Melville references Crusoe's panicky discovery of the footprint — 'Robinson Crusoe could not have been more startled at the footprint in the sand than we were at this unwelcome discovery'[50] — Melville acknowledges that he is following well-worn textual footsteps, both to confess their seductive imaginative hold and to show where they lead. Crusoe builds elaborate defences because of his 'apprehensions on the account of a man's foot' and refers to 'the life of anxiety, fear, and care which I had lived ever since I had seen the print of a foot in the sand'. In the penultimate 'seen' in *Typee*, Melville again recalls *Crusoe*, as if to acknowledge that Defoe's manner of using clusters of words to signify fear and panic has exercised a powerful influence on the whole phantasmal discourse of cannibalism.[51]

Melville's mode of citation involves a range of mimicking modes that attempt to 'incite' from within. Through his inventory of the various prior descriptions of cannibalism, Melville suggests the pressures citation places on sight, and the regulation of fear. In *Typee* he addresses the fetishised, performative nature of the discourses of cannibalism and the difficulty of achieving distantiation from such a heritage of fear. In many accounts, as suggested, the 'seen' of cannibalism appears obligatory, or staged in response to market demands. In *Typee* this is certainly at play, but the pressures are admitted and commented on at the same time that they are enacted, generating a staging place by which the whole scenario of cannibalism becomes allegorised.[52]

Typee is full of minor, nervous parodies that place all mention of cannibalism in conspicuous scare quotes. In Taussig's words, 'parody is where mimesis exposes construction'.[53] The accounts from which Melville draws differ in style and conclusion, and he is more concerned to mimic a sequence of styles than to create coherent narrative; parody itself confesses that mimicry works in and through languages that perform for the reader or that mimic the reader's presumed attitudes. When Melville uses phrases like 'inveterate gormandizers of human flesh'[54] he parodies authors like George von Langsdorff, who wrote, 'Incredible as it may appear, there have been people who feed upon human flesh merely on account of its delicacy, and as the height of *gourmandise*'.[55] It is easy for him to scoff at those who credit such fictions and believe that 'there are people so depraved that they would infinitely prefer a single mouthful of material humanity to a good dinner of roast beef'.[56]

At another level are a series of references to patterns of perception that have become formalised. For his 'seen' of cannibalism, Melville draws most directly upon David Porter's *Journal*. Like Porter, he professes the difficulty of connecting his preconceived notions about the Taipis as cannibals to the kindness they show him: Porter cannot 'reconcile [cannibalism] with the generosity and benevolence which were the leading traits of their character...There must have been some misconception.'[57] Then there is the conventional suggestion of information withheld, of things the Taipi do not want him to see, which immediately steps up the suspicion of cannibalism and a desire both to witness and to 'be spared the horror of witnessing'.[58] When Porter, 'desirous of clearing up...a fact so nearly concerned with the character of a whole people', comes across Taipis attending to slain bodies, the Taipis are 'thrown into the utmost confusion; the dead bodies were in an instant snatched from the place where they lay, and hurried to a distance among the bushes'. Porter recalls how his 'blood recoiled with horror at the spectacle I was on the point of witnessing' and how he 'told them that I was apprehensive that they intended to eat them'.[59]

Charles Stewart also describes a scene in which the Taipis seem to be concealing something from him. His guide, who has been carrying him on his back, as Kory-Kory will carry Tommo, 'manifest[s] some uneasiness, and [says], "let us return"…On asking why? The only answer I could get…from the guide was "*kakino!*" "*It is bad!*" as he hastened me forward, in evident apprehension till we came in sight of the ship…I have not yet learned the cause of anxiety expressed by my conductor, or the manifest ill will exhibited by many met on our return.'[60] What Porter finally saw, rather than cannibalism, was a mortuary rite, in which 'skulls are carefully perserved and hung up in their houses'.[61] This is what Tommo first glimpses when he solves the mystery of packages that the Taipi consider taboo for him: 'Several times I had asked Kory-Kory to show me their contents; but my servitor, who in almost every other particular had acceded to my wishes, always refused to gratify me in this'. One day when he returns unexpectedly his arrival seems 'to throw the inmates of the house into the greatest confusion…The evident alarm the savages betrayed filled me with forebodings of evil, and with an uncontrollable desire to penetrate the secret so jealously guarded'.[62] Forcing his way into the house, Tommo catches 'a glimpse of three human heads',[63] which are immediately taken as evidence for cannibalism: 'Was the same doom reserved for me…to be devoured, and my head to be preserved as a fearful memento of the event? My imagination ran riot in these horrid speculations'[64] — a paroxysm of fear echoing Crusoe's claim that 'terrible thoughts racked my imagination'.[65] After a Taipi battle, he is convinced that 'the savages were about to celebrate some hideous rite in connection with their peculiar customs, and at which they were determined I should not be present'.[66] The next day this anticipation is satisfied. Although the chiefs try to block his viewing of the remains of their 'inhuman feast', screaming 'taboo', Tommo catches a glimpse: 'The slight glimpse sufficed; my eyes fell upon the disordered members of a human skeleton, the bones still fresh with moisture, and with particles of flesh clinging from them here and there!'[67] The language echoes Crusoe, who saw 'great pieces of flesh left here and there, half-eaten, mangled and scorched',[68] and discovery scenes in Coulter and Cook.[69]

In heaping up his 'seen' of witness with references to Porter (who was never convinced of cannibalism but who led the first imperialistic American action in the Pacific), Crusoe, who vomits before cannibal remains, and other 'explorers', Melville suggests how the nineteenth-century discourse of cannibalism has absorbed imaginative and scientific texts into a genre of cannibalistic narratives imbued with fear.

Performing fear in Taipivai

For if the enemy is us, analysis, however necessary, is not enough to found a practice of resistance. Fear, under conditions of complicity, can be neither analyzed nor opposed without at the same time being enacted — Brian Massumi, *The Politics of Everyday Fear*

At several points in *Typee*, Melville refers to Tommo's having been 'consumed' by 'fearful apprehensions'.[70] The edgy puns literalise a link between cannibalism, fear, and the difficulty of Tommo sustaining the direct, sensuous insight into Taipi culture that his experience intermittently affords him. Tommo's apprehension (understanding) is shown to have been coterminous with his apprehension (anticipated misfortune) and ability to apprehend (capture in words) the *enata* of Taipivai; rather, his own perceptual faculties are apprehended (captured and held) and are thus 'fearful', in that they are suspiciously static in maintaining stereotypes of fear. To be consumed in this sense is to be (pre)occupied by and within semiotic grids of fear. 'Knowledge' and fear are repeatedly spliced together in the term apprehension, and these apprehensions are represented as obsessive and consumptive, the mind eating away at its own resources. Melville strains to contain these fears within puns, but his genial humour — the triumph of distance over fear — only pickles the memory of panic, signalling ways in which past apprehensions continue to haunt his imagination:

> In looking back to this period, and calling to remembrance the numberless proofs of kindness and respect which I received from the natives of the valley, I can scarcely understand how it was that, in the midst of so many consolatory circumstances, my mind should still have been consumed by the most dismal forebodings, and have remained prey to the profoundest melancholy. It is true that…kind and respectful as they were to me, [they] were…nothing better than a set of cannibals.[71]

These lines admit a gap between Taipi hospitality and Tommo's experience, showing Tommo's gaze to be consumed by conceptions projected into the future and read onto the present. Although Tommo maintains that he 'cannot call to mind [his experience] without shuddering',[72] Melville's assessment of the dynamic is retrospective, written at a distance from which he can stage even 'unmanageable terrors'[73] and the fact that, three years after his 'deliverance', he scarcely understands what consumed his mind.

This is to suggest that in *Typee* Melville performs, inside out, the problem of the relationship of fear to the sensuous perception of Taipivai *enata* by Euro-Americans, one of these fears being precisely that of his own threatened cultural conversion or assimilation. In doing so he works through the 'archive' on the Pacific as it is in the process of being shaped and deployed against Pacific Islanders, granting cannibalism its status as master trope while intuiting ways in which his apprehensions of indigenous metaphors must engage the revolt that is taking place within his inherited language, body and mind. For all his warmth toward the Taipis, for all the exuberance he enjoys when his fears abate, the interface with alien manners does shock his nervous system. However, although he admits to scarce understanding of his earlier visceral responses, Melville's style condenses and parodies the phantasmal dynamic writ large in the emerging archive on cannibalism, exemplified in the observations of Wilkes and his men.

Melville demonstrates, with a nervous retrospective humour, that nothing could have wholly allayed Tommo's fears; the greater the kindness shown him, the more a side of him would suspect the Taipis. Tommo is 'too familiar with the fickle disposition of savages' not to want to escape 'that fearful death which, under all these smiling appearances might yet menace'.[74] This 'guaranteeing the identity of [the cannibal] through all counterfactual situations' is, in Slavoj Zizek's words, 'the *retroactive effect of naming itself*. It is the name itself, the signifier, which supports the identity of the object'.[75] This is especially so in Taipivai, since, as Melville writes of the Taipis, erroneously following Porter (who follows Columbus's mistranslation of a tribal name into a practice), 'the word "Typee" in the Marquesan dialect signifies a lover of human flesh'.[76] Thus, echoing Stewart (their 'very name seemed to be a watchword of terror'[77]), Tommo admits, 'the very name of Typee struck a panic into my heart'.[78] 'You see how dangerous they are?' the discourse claims. 'It is difficult to recognize their real nature. They hide it behind the mask of everyday appearance — and it is exactly this hiding of one's real nature, this duplicity, that is the basic feature' of the cannibal nature.[79]

In other words, the network of illusions that make up an ideology really holds the perceiver when phenomena that seem to contradict it wind up confirming it. A cannibal is one who is 'stigmatized with the signifier' of a cannibal: 'All the phantasmic richness of the traits supposed to characterize [cannibals] is here to conceal the fact that [cannibals] are not like that…not the empirical reality "but" a purely structural function'.[80] The behaviour of posited cannibals thus matters not at all; every generous action steps up suspicions of hidden motives that feed what Tommo recognizes as an 'uncontrollable desire to penetrate the secret so generously guarded',[81] and that begs the question, 'What does this bloody cannibal really want?' If the cannibal feeds you, he may be fattening you for his feast. 'For what do you suppose the devils have been feeding us up in this kind of style', Toby, Tommo's companion, says, 'unless it were for something that you are too much frightened to talk about?'[82] Not surprisingly, Tommo wonders why, after a battle in which a Happar has been killed, the Taipis do not 'bring away materials for the cannibal entertainment which [he has] heard usually terminated every engagement?' 'After all', Tommo concludes, 'I was much inclined to believe that such shocking festivals must occur very rarely among the islanders, if, indeed, they ever *take* place'.[83]

Tonally, the passage enacts a perverse mixture of disappointment and relief. Tommo confesses 'a sense of regret at having hideous anticipations disappointed'.[84] His 'morbid curiosity'[85] battles a wish to 'be spared the horror of witnessing', in the process producing the longed-for phantasms and despised, grammatical shudders. His tenses slip. He says he 'was inclined' to believe cannibalism never took place, and thus should write *took*, but instead he writes *take*, intruding the retrospective narrator's perspective. This narrator should not doubt whether such events *take* place, since a few pages earlier he has used the future tense to prepare the reader for his eyewitness account:

> Although the assurances which the Typees had often given me, that they never eat human flesh, had not convinced me that such was the case, having been so long a time in the valley without witnessing anything which indicated the existence of the practice, I began to hope that it was an event of very rare occurrence, and that I should be spared the horror of witnessing it during my stay among them; but, alas! These hopes *were* soon to be destroyed.[86]

In short, Melville has already 'seen' yet he withholds the 'ocular proof', inserting a muddled and seemingly self-serving account of the problem of trusting anything but eyewitness, like his own. 'In all our accounts of cannibal tribes', Melville writes:

> ...we have seldom received the testimony of an eye-witness to the revolting practice. The horrible conclusion has almost always been derived either from the second-hand evidence of Europeans, or else from the admissions of the savages themselves,

after they have in some degree become civilized. The Polynesians are aware of the detestation in which Europeans hold this custom, and therefore invariably deny its existence, and, with the craft peculiar to savages, endeavor to conceal every trace of it.[87]

The passage, which cannot simply be taken as irony toward Tommo, performs the twisted logic of a whole discursive field. Natives who confess cannibalism are not only influenced by European contact but have to some degree renounced prior ways by becoming civilised. Unregenerate natives are posited as craftily anxious about offending European taste, an ability to conceal 'every trace of it' characterising their craft. In effect, in the absence of witness by a stranger, native statements are assessed on the basis of the auditor's desires and convictions. And, as Melville asserts between exclamations of disgust ('revolting', 'horrible'), the 'fact' is that he cannot point to proof of cannibalism, beyond that of his own eyes, that could not be suspected of hidden motives.

The avoidance of speculation about confessions and denials, or even about the reasons for his own 'captivity', reveal an ignorance based on fear. Tommo repeatedly recognises that 'the terror of the name [Typee] had preserved them from attack'[88] and stresses that the Taipi dwell on the 'cannibal propensities' of the Happars of cannibalism, in ways that they are 'perfectly aware could not fail to alarm' him.[89] But Tommo fails to pursue possible complexities of native theatricality — the splendid mimicry of Kory-Kory seizing 'the fleshy part' of Tommo's 'arm in his teeth' in describing Happar behaviour — or the possibilities of feigned denials and confessions. Maybe accusing others or hiding practices offensive to strangers proves useful in seeking influence with strangers who might later aid in intertribal conflict. Maybe the Taipi hold Tommo as a potential translator and negotiator, as beachcombers often were, or because they hope to barter him to ship captains for muskets, cash, or other desired items, as happens in several places in *Typee*. Tommo moralises 'upon the disadvantage of having a bad name',[90] but maybe the *enata* encourage the strangers to read denials as confessions, since being thought to be a cannibal is an efficacious deterrent in a moment of invasion.

What Melville apparently realised in performing such fear and confusion in *Typee* is the power of the nervous system to stay tantalisingly, in Taussig's words, 'a jump ahead'.[91] In *Typee*, Melville senses the futility of maintaining the violence of American Pacific orientalism of which he was a part. The placement of the 'seen' of cannibalism in *Typee* functions, conspicuously, to justify the book's subsequent single act of onstage violence: Tommo's own piercing of Mow-Mow's throat (or organ of speech) with the boathook. To confess the impossibility of coming clean, to perform fear and the violent denial of native speech, as Melville does, transforms fear in ways that almost redeem the text.[92]

V. Coda: the critique of American/Pacific narrative, and beyond

Walk through fear. Fear is a door — Denis Johnson, *Fiskadaro*

For the extremest top of love, is Fear and Wonder — Melville, *Pierre*

In Melville's imagination, scenes like that of Wilkes in Malolo typ-ify the fear-driven violence, based on an imperialist ontology, of the American errand. The flip-side of this destructive nationalist telos, touristic attraction and nostalgia, could seem, to the weary Melville giving lectures on the 'South Seas' for his supper, like the future of the Pacific. This sort of binary logic is disturbingly at play in *Typee* in patterns which, at the syntactic and narrative levels, juxtapose apprehension and its relief, as in 'From this apprehension, however, I was quickly relieved'.[93]

The oscillation between the spectre of cannibalistic fantasies that create 'frightful anticipations of evil',[94] and fantasies of Fayaway, who represents 'a perfect freedom from care and anxiety'[95] and 'tranquilizing influences of beautiful scenery',[96] has a clearly touris-tic economy. The binary, reinforcing Taipivai as a place free from the need to work, feeds the perception of the Pacific Islands as antidotes to the cares of civilisation and reproduces Fayaways, from the paint-ings of John LaFarge to tourist posters.[97] Yet there is, in *Typee*, a recognition of the limitations of conceiving fear through such bina-ries, as present or absent in degrees. Melville identifies blockages within this structuring regime of a fear which leads only to a form of anaesthesia, thus losing, for the individual, the chance for a sen-suous engagement with the world. In the act of apprehending trau-mas to his nervous system, caused by alternate signifying codes in Taipivai, Melville recognises that fear might be a magical door to places beyond an ironic, interior critique of the semiotic grids in which he was originally inscribed.

Michael Taussig describes senses in and through which a kind of mimesis impresses the world of the referent into the seams of sentences, whose mode of signification or making significance is thereby enhanced. For Taussig, 'The wonder of mimesis lies in the copy, drawing on the character and power of the original, to the point whereby the representation may even assume that character and that power. In an older language, this is "sympathetic magic".'[98] During the composition of *Moby-Dick*, Melville wrote of 'ontological heroics',[99] which might here be understood as the attempt to achieve forms of mimesis that refuse the language games and ontology of the imperial project by granting a sense of wonder and transformative power to that which is other to one's system. This involves allowing the fearfulness of the represented a contiguity with the processes of representation themselves. Elsewhere, in a review of Hawthorne's stories, Melville speaks of the capacity of art to make 'short, quick probings at the very axis of reality' and to catch truth through 'cunning glimpses' and in 'snatches',[100] a Benjaminian vision that becomes fundamental to his outlook, which moves from concerns with cultural difference and the meaning of civilisation toward a perspective from which the otherness of humans from any signifying code could be remarked.[101]

Melville approaches expression of this perceptual openness in *Typee* in moments where his language admits the fresh energies of Taipivai. 'In my altered frame of mind', Melville recalls, 'every object that presented itself to my notice in the valley struck me in a new light'.[102] Alex Calder considers such moments as central to a 'beachcomber style', expressed through mimicries and cross-cultural metaphors. For Calder, 'Melville has a style of not knowing, and it is a style in which things can be said' about the inadequacies of various models of perceiving culture.[103] Melville's critique of colonialism might be located, initially, in this undermining of the rhetorical separation of cultures.

One significant tension in *Typee*, then, is between two kinds of fear that correspond with two kinds of mimesis (or ways of relating [to] the world). The two are only provisionally separable, as the first kind of mimesis anchors the second, which is in turn repetitively recalled to the first's ethnologising procedures. The first mimesis is a fear-driven proto-anthropology that emphasises difference — a kind of history making that locks perception (or initiates a reproducing chain of perceptions) into forms of segregation. It claims to clone the world of the other into language without that language itself registering change. As Dening puts it, 'mimesis that clones the world...changes nothing'; admitting play, on the other hand, 'suggests that things might be otherwise'.[104] The second form of mimesis, a fear-accessed mode of representation, finds in flashes of similarity or relation a vision that estranges formalised notions of culture. It holds within it the sense of awe — fear linked to wonder — for the world as other. In the mystical strain of his thinking, Melville emphasises the awe-filled moment as an unsustainable but crucial state in which to glimpse a widening syntax of being. It is significant for students of cultural history in the Pacific that the first steps toward this apprehension were taken in *Typee*, in Melville's uneven enactment of what the encounter with the Taipis enabled him to realise.

Part III:
Captive White Bodies
& the Colonial Imaginary
in Terra Australis

Chapter 8

Captivating fictions: Younâh!: A Tasmanian Aboriginal Romance of the Cataract Gorge

Susan K. Martin

IN AUGUST 1893 the Launceston meeting of the Tasmanian Amateur Gardener's Association heard a paper presented by Mr Thomas Carr on 'The Wild Flowers of Tasmania'. The *Tasmanian Mail* reported him as 'giving an outline of the characteristics of the different sort of native flora, and before concluding he strongly urged upon the Committee of the City and Suburban Improvement Association the cultivation of native flora at the Cataract Gorge and Park. He said it would not only be ornamental, but would have an educational influence on the rising generation...'[1]

In the nineteenth century, white Tasmanians of reasonable means could sit down on a Sunday and read the *Tasmanian Mail: a weekly journal of politics, literature, science, agriculture, news and notes for Tasmania*, a publication from the *Hobart Mercury* office.[2] Soon to take up Mr Carr's call to 'plant natives' in Cataract Gorge, though not quite in the way that he meant, was Mrs W. I. Thrower, whose short novel *Younâh!: A Tasmanian Aboriginal Romance of the Cataract Gorge* was serialised in the journal, with the first instalment appearing on 14 October, 1893 before its publication as a separate volume in 1894. Mrs Thrower planted not indigenous plants, but indigenous people, in the Gorge of her fiction. My comparison here is not intended to be flippant or disrespectful, but to point out the ways in which the notions behind Mr Carr's paper and Mrs Thrower's novel were extremely similar, and similarly bizarre.

This chapter was produced at a pivotal moment of intense debate about Aboriginal native title in Australia, in an atmosphere of racist paranoia, white nationalist discourse, and anxiety about Aboriginal and non-Aboriginal land ownership. Rather than resorting to some apolitical and safely distant past, I seek in this paper to uncover the ways in which Australian cultural products of the late nineteenth century reveal and produce the founding concepts which have led to exactly this state of affairs in the late twentieth century.

In the 1890s Cataract Gorge was a well-established and much-visited tourist spot for Launceston and Tasmanian residents as well as interstate and overseas visitors, as it is today (see Illustration 7). Initially it was visited for its untouched picturesque beauty: a set of rapids, and two deep pools, the first and second basins, embedded in a gorge on the South Esk River, at the edge of Launceston. By the 1890s, as is clear from Mr Carr's paper, the picturesqueness had been enhanced by considerable planting of European species and some clearing, as well as the erection of various built structures, including the 'Crusoe Hut'. Its accessibility had been facilitated by the erection of a raised walkway along the north side. In early 1893 work commenced on a hydro-electric generating plant upstream from the Gorge.[3] Clearly there was almost no sense in which Cataract Gorge remained a pristine site when Mrs Thrower wrote her novel *Younâh!*

Younâh!

The novel, however, is set in, or produces, a pristine moment, in a kind of pre-lapsarian world at the very beginning of white encroachment onto Aboriginal land in Tasmania.[4] It recounts the kidnap of a three-year-old white girl, Keitha St Clair, by a group of local Aborigines, the Pialummas. Keitha is taken in retaliation for depredation and the theft of women by local white settlers. There is some suggestion that Keitha may be sacrificed to avenge the loss of the young women, but the chief's son, Eumarrah, becomes the child's protector. She is renamed Younâh, and brought up amongst the Pialummas, though there are distinctive differences in the way she is treated. Eumarrah believes she may be useful as an intermediary between themselves and the whites in the future.[5] However, after years of unlikely peace, with the group spending summers at Cataract Gorge and winters on the coast west of the mouth of the Tamar, white encroachment again threatens.

At this point Eumarrah's mother decides they should kill Younâh, but Eumarrah conceals her and her best friend, Natone, from the group. Before he can retrieve them, they are discovered by a couple of English squires, Colin and Jack, out exploring in the antipodean wilds. Younâh's whiteness is instantly recognised. She and Natone, who gets little choice in the matter, return with the men to 'civilisation'. Younâh is identified by the coral necklace that she still wears as Keitha, lost daughter, and now heiress, of the St Clairs. Younâh rapidly and miraculously acquires language, manners and class in a few months in Australia, before she is sent home to her family for the completion of her education.

After a few years she is engaged to her 'rescuer' Jack Ormond. Jack and Keitha, as she is now again called, take their honeymoon trip to Tasmania so that Younâh/Keitha can repay Eumarrah for all his kindness. But the so-called Black Wars have been perpetrated in her absence, and she finds Eumarrah dying of consumption on Flinders Island with the remaining Tasmanian Aborigines. The novel closes with Eumarrah and his people remembered only through the tales Keitha tells her enthralled children.

Younâh! is clearly a rather obscure text to which to devote such attention — its *Tasmanian Mail* serialisation and its paperback publication combined can have reached only a limited audience. Mrs Thrower does not appear to have published any other fiction. The novel is important because it is a fiction about Tasmanian Aboriginal people at a time when the white population regarded them as 'extinct', and more particularly because the Aborigines depicted are not just anonymous plot elements.[6] A large part of the narrative is taken up with a version, however fanciful, of Tasmanian first peoples' daily life and culture. *Younâh!* is also distinct because it is one of relatively few captivity narratives published in nineteenth-century Australia, and because it is a novel with a local setting, by a local woman and published only locally, at a time when much Australian long fiction, women's and men's, was still being published in Britain. There are a number of other singular features about *Younâh!* which I will discuss later.

Australian captivity fictions

Despite its distinctness, I want to consider *Younâh!* as representative, even emblematic, of a number of the effects and uses of similar, better-known, fictions published in Australia around the same time, and as symptomatic of the production of race relations in the alleged decade of Australian nationalism. That it is part of some wider discourse becomes evident when you look at the serial immediately preceding *Younâh!* in the *Tasmanian Mail*: Rosa Praed's *Outlaw and Lawmaker*. This novel also contains a brief captivity scene, in which the desired heroine Elsie is lured from a picnic and exploring party, with the complicity of Aboriginal workers, into a concealed hideaway strongly associated with the local Aborigines. Praed's novel uses the captivity and associated events to negotiate similar anxieties about race, sexuality, nation and the environment.

Many of the few other existent nineteenth-century Australian *fictional* captivity narratives, or narratives which contain a captivity episode, are more or less contemporary with *Younâh!* I am excepting here what might be called 'reverse' captivity narratives — fictions which contain the implicit or explicit kidnap of Aboriginal characters by Europeans, though *Younâh!* belongs in this group also. The European-victim narratives — which include Rosa Praed's *Fugitive Anne* (1902) and *Outlaw and Lawmaker* (1893), Ernest Favenc's *The Secret of the Australian Desert* (1895), and various short stories and tales inspired by the White Woman of Gippsland — work in similar ways and have some very similar elements.[7]

These fictions produced representations of indigenous people which worked to a greater or lesser extent to displace actual Aboriginal people, not just to the degree in which any representation displaces or replaces that which it ostensibly represents or encapsulates, but through the violent rewriting of the, or an, indigenous people/person. Clearly in Australia any version of the 'white captured by Aborigines' narrative works to obscure the facts and history of the common and systematic abduction and rape of Aboriginal women by white men, and the abduction of Aboriginal children by white men and women. Intimately connected to this obfuscation of atrocities are the moves these fictions made to produce and perform a romantic history of place for the non-Aboriginal population. They might also be seen to partake of and duplicate the discourses of the growing industry of tourism, in order to map the country as unfamiliar, exotic and unexplored *and* as familiar, picturesque, historically inscribed, owned and available.

Younâh! *as captivity narrative*

If the term is taken in its strictest sense, neither *Younâh!* nor the other novels I have mentioned are captivity narratives. They are fictional and make no specific claims to the sort of authenticity found in the North American Indian captivity narratives which give rise to the term. Nor do they draw on a broad Australian historical record and cultural tradition around actual captivities of settler or invader peoples by indigenous peoples, though obviously there are actual tales and myths in Australia which inform them — Eliza

Fraser, the White Woman of Gippsland stories, the story of William Buckley and others.[8] I am using the term 'captivity narrative' in this chapter partly to register the circulation of particular understandings of captivity or cohabitation with indigenous people which are informed directly or indirectly by the ideologies and forms of North American captivity narratives and their offshoots.

The Australian fictions, including *Younâh!*, can be seen in relation to the North American narratives in a number of ways. The Australian fictional narratives, like many of their North American counterparts, are obviously concerned with notions of race: racial identification, nineteenth-century hierarchies of racial development, and especially intense anxieties about miscegenation and sexual contact between indigenous men and European women. The Australian fictions likewise negotiate anxieties and desires circulating around the environment, ideas of wilderness and possession of the country through the captivity narrative.[9]

The unsettling familiarity of woman with wilderness, common to American captivity narratives and described by Annette Kolodny in her discussion of the 'Panther Captivity', is matched in *Younâh!*, and doubled. Younâh's bush skills and closeness to indigeneity are mapped on her body ('the natural fairness of her skin had deepened into an almost brunette like tint, by reason of continued exposure to the open air…')[10] *and* through her proximity to her Aboriginal companion Natone. Despite this, femininity and class are clearly legible after years in the supposed wilderness. Jack comments confidently:

> If she had parents in this wilderness they could be none other than runaway convicts. This girl belongs to a better type of race than is generally found among that class. I am of the opinion that she has been lost, or it may be that she was stolen from her home by some of the tribes…[11]

Such figures enact that unsettling association of women with nature, with the physical and earthy, and of white women with indigeneity, even as they are being used to rehearse and dispel that fear. The woman's recuperation is into a 'civilisation', which for her consists of both a libidinal economy and a mercantile one. The female prize of the wilderness is both beautiful and (soon to be) well endowed with cash. It is tempting to see this unsettling vision of a feminised wilderness/wilderness-woman converted into attractive domestic lucrative property.[12]

There is a limit to general comparisons between 'captivity narratives', however. In *The Indian Captivity Narrative 1550–1900*,

Kathryn Derounian-Stodola and James Levernier read one of the Eliza Fraser narratives unproblematically as an extension of the North American captivity narrative's westward trajectory across the Pacific. In a consistently U.S.-centric, if somewhat bizarre, geographical slippage they read the narrative as set not in Australia, but New Guinea.[13] Quite clearly there are obvious and distinct differences between North American captivity narratives and Australian narratives of captivity, even Eliza Fraser's, and certainly later captivity fictions. Various cultural practices of capture in Native American societies have been documented, and the numbers taken in the eighteenth and nineteenth centuries are relatively substantial. Most of the North American narratives, whether they claim or feign truth or fiction, are in the first person. The nineteenth and very early twentieth-century Australian fictions are not. North American captivity narratives date from the seventeenth to the twentieth centuries, but what might be called the key texts of the genre — narratives like Mary Rowlandson's — are mostly considerably earlier than the Australian stories. Such a slippage should alert us to the distinct cultural, historical and geographic differences between North American captivity narratives and Australian narratives of captivity.[14]

Derounian-Stodola and Levernier acknowledge what might be called the shifting use-value of North American captivity stories, but they seem to adhere to a notion that such stories' 'archetypal patterns' are more important to their surviving popularity than their 'cultural significances' (quoting Van Der Beets). In contradiction to such a stance, Chris Healy argues in *From the Ruins of Colonialism* that Eliza Fraser does not stand at the centre of a stable narrative but is rather a multiple figure, an 'event under description',[15] a name used and useful in various forms of cultural work, including attempts to stabilise the impossibly unstable categories of race and gender which circulate in captivity narratives. Though the Fraser narratives are a separate case from the later fictions, Healy's argument is relevant because it highlights the geographical and cultural specificity, and the distinct historical and cultural circulations, of such tales. While the European colonial context of captivity narratives makes likely some commonality of narrative form and narrative anxiety, this should not be taken to override the specificity of moment, use and circulation, to the extent that Eliza Fraser becomes some vague Pacific extension of a North American form and archetype.[16]

The Australian narratives I have mentioned are late nineteenth-century manifestations, emerging from, and encoding, fundamentally different historical situations and indigenous/non-indigenous relations. They work, as I said earlier, to fundamentally displace the 'real' Aboriginal population by positing more or less fictional versions of indigenous societies.[17] These stories, as Robert Dixon points out in his discussion of Lemurian romances, are implicated in fin-de-siècle anxieties about gender, sexuality and the 'New Woman'.[18] They also work as travelogues, as part of the developing genre of tourist texts and scenic guides — to produce the landscape as scene of history and adventure. To consider these aspects of the texts it is necessary to address their particularity.

Younâh! *and negotiations of race*

The opening of the narrative of *Younâh!* is interesting, though not unique, in its shifting and unstable emplacement of traditional binary opposites.[19] Chapter Two begins with a lengthy argument for the connection between land and Aboriginal people, through occupation, tradition, intimate familiarity and sacred association:

> For generation after generation had the ancestors of Warnee owned all the mountains and valleys of Pialumma; there were the vast forests wherein to track down, and catch the timid kangaroo and wallaby,[20] the brightly plumaged birds belonged to them alone, and for whom else did the agile opossum surrender at once its life and the furry covering of its body!...
>
> How well they knew each giant of the forest, remembered every streamlet as it dashed impetuously over its brown and rocky bed ere it mingled its clear waters with those of some deeper, calmer stream! Familiar to them, not alone from the associations of a lifetime spent amid these wilds, but by reason of the legends which tradition had preserved to the tribe, were every steep, tree-crowned summit, each ferny moss-carpeted glade.
>
> And no less dear than familiar were all their well-known haunts...
> Amid the depths of the sombre forest reposed the relics of many a brave, and reverently moved the tribe as they passed by the spots made hallowed to them by the presence of their dead. For so great an awe possessed the Tasmanians of those days, when death severed their family ties, that the name of a departed one was never again mentioned among them, nor any reference made to him. Nevertheless his memory lingered with the relatives and friends as something too sacred to be touched upon.
>
> Household gods, such as civilisation prizes, they had not, it is true, for the great vault of heaven was their canopy, the soft, springy turf their carpet. They needed not tables, chairs, nor couches; and

yet they possessed one element which they treasured with jealous care, for although the household was to them unknown — the household fire was theirs.

Certain members of the tribe had the care of this…Individual families possessed, when they were in settled quarters, their own household fires…The dismay and anger which filled the breasts of Warnee and his savages may easily be gauged by the feelings which might be expected to animate those of a peaceful settlement of civilised beings were a horde of barbarians suddenly to descend into their midst, assume to themselves the right of possession and treat as trespassers the original owners.

Such had been the bitter experience of the Pialumma tribe, as one settler after another marked off and occupied selections of the hunting grounds which had belonged to them and their ancestors for countless ages. Week after week they found the area within which they were permitted to remain unmolested growing more circumscribed, until at length, driven by hunger and the impossibility of obtaining in their old haunts the game which had been their chief means of subsistence, they sought and found among the flocks of the settlers upon their own grounds that food without which they could not exist.

It is important to read this against the background of the claimed extinction of Tasmanian Aboriginal people at the time of writing, which enables a level of sympathy and elegiac rhetoric always liable to be more vexed in the face of an existing indigenous population. Nevertheless in the wider context of Australian relations with mainland Aboriginal peoples, its tone is interesting. The narrative makes a strong claim for rightful ownership through traditional usage, knowledge and occupation, association and religious significance,[21] and against the founding notions of what is now known as *terra nullius* — the idea that the land was not morally occupied because inhabited by 'barbarians'.[22] Thrower describes a domestic society — a society with household arrangements not absent because they dwell in the bush, but present in that very environment, and symbolised by and centred on the fire as household emblem. The domestification of the landscape is not uncommon in nineteenth-century Australian women's fiction — which frequently represents the natural environment in non-threatening terms through a kind of imaginative extension or opening out of the internal domestic sphere into the garden and surrounding bush. This is reiterated, and also inverted here — the bush *is* the household, and fire is not an uncontrollable element, but a clear sign of domesticity, and therefore civilisation. It renders the bush a domestic site.

This is of course enhanced by the complete reversal of common understandings of the processes of settlement, and a common trope of early fictions and settler accounts, in which the domestic hearth of a 'peaceful settlement of civilised beings' is rudely disrupted by a 'horde of barbarians'. In Thrower's version Warnee's 'tribe' are the peaceful beings, at this moment, and throughout this chapter, and the white settlers become 'hordes of barbarians', with no respect for the domestic, peaceful civilisation depicted.

Clearly this is not a stable representation. While the novel opens with, and for a while continues, this sympathetic portrayal of an imaginary Aboriginal settlement in the Cataract Gorge, to some extent establishing point of view and sympathy with the Aboriginal people, it inevitably reverses this picture. The opening chapter of the novel describes an idyllic scene of Aboriginal life, and then records the arrival of Eumarrah with the white female child.[23] The second chapter chronicles the abduction of 'young maidens' of the tribe, one of them Eumarrah's sister. The question is whether the initial trope of black man with abducted white girl (however represented) militates against the subsequent logic and justifications of the action in the ensuing narrative. Thrower's shifting narration fundamentally confuses the distinctions between barbarians and civilised.[24]

Younâh! *and Tasmanian Aboriginal culture*

An internal subjective view of tribal life, even a fabricated one, might be seen as a quite radical reorientation of understandings of black/white relations in Australian fiction, even if, as in this case, that representation is 'retrospective'. Nevertheless, as argued, this narrative displaces the original and still extant population by installing a more palatable and exotic indigenous society, and one which is used to negotiate a European relationship to the environment. Clearly this is more profoundly evident in novels like *Fugitive Anne* or *Secrets of the Australian Desert* where an entirely 'other' population is 'discovered' in Australia, but *Younâh!* colludes in this particularly as it works to deny and erase the fact of the continuing existence of the Tasmanian Aborigines.

The sources for Thrower's fiction are not clear. Some of her material presumably came from local folklore; Thrower appears to have spent some of her early life in Campbell Town, south of Launceston. Thrower was probably not alive for the genocidal period of martial law in Tasmania known as the 'Black Wars' from 1828–1832,[25] but her life span would overlap with those of the community on Flinders Island[26] and at Oyster Cove. She almost certainly would have read in the *Tasmanian Mercury* in 1876 of the death of Truganini, who was pronounced the last 'full-blood' Tasmanian Aborigine, and of the theft of her body.[27] Truganini was neither the last 'full-blood' Tasmanian Aborigine to die, nor did her death mark the end of the Tasmanian Aborigines, but the white Tasmanian community largely used her as a marker of Aboriginal pastness.[28]

Many of the features of Thrower's representation seem completely spurious, but in fact the novel does have a complicated relation to knowledges about the Aboriginal groups around Launceston — the North Midlands groups. Apart from her suggestion that the people were initially driven out of Ben Lomond, the land occupied by the 'Pialummas' in their seasonal migrations maps vaguely onto what is known of the movements of the Panninher people of the North Midlands.[29] Certainly Thrower's representation is anachronistic, and in the whites' favour — suggesting as it does that peaceful occupation of Cataract Gorge would have been possible up until the late 1820s and the Black Line, when in fact the North Midlands people 'suffered European invasion from the end of 1804'.[30] Thrower's flights of fancy are in fact enabled by the early dispossession and disruption in this area, which resulted in a dearth of information about the pre-invasion boundaries and culture of these people,[31] and therefore provided a palimpsest for the inscription of Thrower's noble savages.

In 1893 Thrower would have had various histories of Tasmania and studies of the Tasmanian Aborigines available to her as source material.[32] Thrower may well have known the real Umarrah's name from her Campbell Town relatives. Other names in the novel appear to come from Aboriginal Protector G. A. Robinson's, (or some other's) list of survivors on Flinders Island. While the character Eumarrah coincides in age, place and authority with the historic Umarrah, the other names seem to have been chosen more overtly for some effect of authenticity unconnected to historical accuracy or respect for persons. Younâh was the name of a child also known as Nancy who died as a young woman sometime between 1847 and 1851. Her father was a white sealer.[33] Considering the importance of names for the Tasmanian Aboriginal people, as noted by Thrower in Chapter Two, her theft of these names is insensitive. They do, however, work to further fracture the narrative — marking the romantic text of the found heiress with the names of dispossessed and prematurely dead female children, and raising the spectre of miscegenation in the name of Younâh when the text works so hard to obviate and obscure any such possibility, with her sparkling and unmistakable whiteness and middle classness, with her instant removal from the Aborigines to permanent European female chaperonage as soon as she reaches puberty.

The use of Eumarrah, and possibly the character called Manalargaua, or Manalagana, seems to have been more self-conscious on Thrower's part. In the novel, Eumarrah is Younâh's friend and protector, the chief's son. The only raid he is depicted as being involved in is the one in which Younâh is kidnapped, where the hut is burnt, but no blood is shed. The historical figure Umarrah was an extremely well-known guerilla fighter in the North Midlands area. G. A. Robinson spent some time in pursuit of Umarrah's band in 1830 and 1831. Umarrah had led raids against European settlements, had been jailed for all of 1829, had assisted Robinson in his attempts to collect together the Aborigines of the settled districts, but had escaped and returned to the North Midlands where he joined in raids on settlers around the Tamar and the North Esk Rivers in which settlers and shepherds were speared, and some killed.[34] Robinson repeatedly lied to the warrior Mannalargenna to convince him to assist in the capture of Umarrah's band — promising him that if they ceased their raids, 'they would be allowed to remain in their respective districts' and to hunt.[35] Robinson made similar unfounded promises to Umarrah when he was located.[36] Umarrah died on Flinders Island of influenza in March 1835.[37] Robinson, as Superintendent, used his death in his program of cultural disruption, insisting that he be buried rather than cremated in the traditional manner.[38]

In *Younâh!* Eumarrah dies of consumption shortly after Younâh/Keitha visits him at Flinders Island, where she and husband Jack enjoy the 'hospitality of the Superintendent's house'.[39] Eumarrah dies in Christian resignation. No further mention is made of the other Aborigines, except that many are also dying from consumption.

This section of the novel, like the rest of it, is fractured by contradictory impulses. The novel continues clearly to represent dispossession as dispossession, though the line has softened somewhat. In fact, Keitha's intended reward for Eumarrah closely resembles Robinson's false promises to Umarrah and Mannalargenna. When asked what she would like to do for Eumarrah she tells her father 'Oh! I would buy for him the old hunting grounds of his race, and give them to him, so that neither black nor white men could ever take them from him again!'.[40]

The novel converts Eumarrah from a freedom fighter to an 'Uncle Tom' figure. His gentleness and the representations of the Pialumma's culture to some extent dispute understandings of the Tasmanian Aborigines as mindlessly violent and without culture, but the use of *parts* of the history of Umarrah, while excluding the history of his sustained resistance, his imprisonment, and the role of Robinson, who is not named in the novel, erases political history in favour of personal stories. On a personal level, with Eumarrah dying and the Governor forbidding Aboriginal return to the Tasmanian mainland, Keitha's well-meaning scheme is pointless. This use of the personal erases the political fact of genocidal policies and the failure or refusal to address the situation of the Flinders Island community. The English 'squirearchy' are exonerated from any connection to such policies through ignorance: 'When Jack Ormond and his wife reached Hobart Town...they learned for the first time that all the survivors of that race, to whom the land had formerly belonged, had been banished from it by the stronger one which had ousted them'.[41] The honeymoon of the English propertied classes in Tasmania takes place across the territory and via the deathbeds of the Tasmanian Aborigines, with no irony intended. It is only a further irony here that Younâh and Keitha have disappeared into the unnamed wife of Jack Ormond.[42]

Younâh! *as tour guide*

Another notable aspect of the passage from Chapter Two (quoted above) is the extent to which this fiction makes an argument for the discursive production of landscape, and the ways in which narratives of place forge connections and signify ownership:

> Familiar to them, not alone from the associations of a lifetime spent amid these wilds, but by reason of the legends which tradition had preserved to the tribe, were every steep, tree-crowned summit, each ferny moss-carpeted glade.[43]

This is mobilised to demonstrate Aboriginal connection to the land, but ultimately the story of *Younâh!* functions in place of the tales described. Thus this story, as one which inserts the white settler into the landscape and traditions of Aboriginal land, becomes also a story of right and habitation — producing the scene as the space of white experience, white narrative and white history. The telling and retelling of the history of Younâh's capture and rescue within the tale contribute to this, but the narrative itself enacts it.

Part of the way it does this is through selling Cataract Gorge to Tasmanians as a tourist site of uniqueness and naturalness, peopling it with colourful indigenes at the (same) moment it erases those occupants and turns it back into wilderness but occupiable space — space which had been *both* occupied *and* untouched. It buys into the rhetoric of barbarism used 100 years earlier to occupy the land in the first place — that it is physically but not morally occupied 'wasteland', wild and available first for the settlement described and second for the specular occupation encouraged.

Its familiarity is repeatedly pointed out in the story, usually in contexts which highlight the historical separation which enable the romance and (perhaps) deny responsibility for the emptiness produced. For instance, when Eumarrah withdraws for a conference with his father and mother, Warnee and Makooi, they retreat to a private area in the Gorge. The narrator locates it specifically as an unexplored site, at the same time as mourning the 'vandalism' that has befallen it:

> As 'Mossy Dell' it still exists for modern explorers, although the hand of the vandal, who rejoices in destruction, has shorn it of its pristine beauty, and neither clematis, woodbine, nor other beauteous climber of the woodlands clothes it as with a veil to conceal its cool, inmost recesses.[44]

Colin and Jack are proto-tourists for the later nineteenth-century Cataract Gorge. As tourists, they are not responsible for the dispossession disapproved by the narrative, even while tourism is implicated in this through its interconnectedness with the entire process and economy of settlement and development, as well as the vandalism mentioned earlier. Colin and Jack's trip to Australia is a sequel or alternative to the Grand Tour. They are landed gentlemen in search of the new:

> [they]...left England behind them in a spirit of adventurous longing for 'something new under the sun' — something new to them at least, for they had used up all the resources of travel and exploration which Europe could present to them at the period of which I write, when the facilities for moving from one country to another were by no means so numerous or so convenient as

they are in these Cook-tourist days. The great invention of steam was as yet in its infancy, and did not extend to foreign countries so that a Continental tour was an event in the lifetime of the few who were fortunate, while a trip to the Antipodes was equivalent to a sentence of exile. For there were no 'ocean greyhounds' in those remote days...[so travel was a serious matter to those who went by necessity]...But Jack Ormond and his friend were not impelled by such motives as these, as fortune had smiled upon them from the time at which they had commenced life's journey.

They were the eldest sons and heirs of wealthy Englishmen, whose large estates in Sussex adjoined...they had spent a considerable time abroad when their education was completed, had gone through a London season together, and emerged thence heart-whole.[45]

They follow Jack's sister to Australia, because, 'You see, old fellow, there is not much European ground that we have left untrodden. We have explored a goodly part of Asia, been to Egypt, and would have been certain to make for America next. We can go there some other time...'[46]

As Dona Brown points out in relation to America: 'Tourism offered tourists satisfaction through acquisition (...the acquisition of experiences) emotional fulfilment through spending money. Throughout the nineteenth-century the product that tourism offered most consistently was some form of antidote to industrial capitalism [but]...far from opposing that order, tourism was an integral part of it'.[47]

Jack and Keitha's wedding tour is similarly composed of ownership and sentimental inscription:

The settlement, which had consisted but of a few straggling, small houses when Jack had visited Launceston before, had increased to very respectable dimensions, and there was even an hotel at which fair accommodation was to be obtained. [They hired a boat and went] up the Gorge as far as they could be rowed; then they scrambled across rocks and through shrubs and dense undergrowth afterwards, until they reached the spot where they two had first met.

Keitha sends Jack into the cave to retrieve the skeleton of her little pet albino kangaroo, which she proposes to keep as a 'relic of a faithful, although dumb friend'.[48]

The touristic acts of visiting romantic spots and collecting souvenirs are the same here, it is just that such forms of tourism as ways of owning and knowing the landscape are more clearly connected to their implications and sources through the grim echo in this passage of the thieving and keeping of Tasmanian Aboriginal remains by 'scientific' whites and collectors in Australia.[49] There might be a further level of cultural appropriation at work also: according to Ryan, the Tasmanian Aborigines sometimes kept the bones of their dead as 'relics'.[50]

For Tasmania, more intensively than for other colonies in the 1890s, tourism was becoming a potentially vital industry. The Van Diemen's Land Bank collapsed in August 1891[51] and prefaced a major economic depression in the colony, by some accounts more severe than that on the mainland.[52] Thrower's publication might have been partly motivated by financial need — a little pocket-money for her or necessary funds for the family.

Either way Thrower appears to have had a strong interest in promoting the Cataract Gorge and environs as a specular site — a destination for local tourists, but more importantly for those further afield. Thrower Street, in Launceston, runs parallel to Basin Road, the road leading down to the south side of the Gorge. The land belonged to William Ignatius Thrower, husband of Mrs W. I. Thrower.[53] For whatever purpose the land adjoining the Basin might have been used, the other property owned by the Throwers in Launceston would clearly have benefited from any touristic side effects of Mrs Thrower's romantic fictional exercise. It was Thrower's Court House Hotel.[54]

It is seldom that fiction so clearly displays its use-value — the hotel with 'fair accommodation' may be the Thrower's own. It is surely not just the case that Thrower's novel is trash fiction or glorified advertising, but rather that the bare bones and implied use of national fictions is a little more evident in this as a raw product. Captivity narratives, romance fictions and Lemurian novels open up and make the country available in a new way. The trope of the white lost, stolen captive who disappears in the landscape is used in a project of inserting the figure of the white into the landscape. Younâh is kept with the intention of making her into an intercessor for the Aboriginal people, but of course in her textual use she becomes an intercessor between the white reader/Tasmanian/Australian and the native landscape. In this configuration it is not just the represented Aborigines who displace the original Tasmanians and their descendants' rights, but the native landscape.

Thomas Carr's call for the planting of natives in Cataract Gorge seems to have been part of a popular movement to reauthenticate the environment, to restore what had been lost and make it available for the specular pleasure of those inheriting that loss. Mrs Thrower installs in the Gorge a dispossessed and fantasised indigenous population, who are replaced only to be dispossessed again in the space of the novel. The novel inevitably has to reiterate their doom to legitimate the colonial adventure it is proposing, yet it has to reinvoke them to make it adventurous. Such a project inevitably disintegrates under the pressure of its own contradictory discourses. Unlike introduced plants, white settlers have entirely refused any notion of sharing or co-existence, much as in the present day the Howard government seems incapable of comprehending, explaining or tolerating the notion that pastoral leases can co-exist with native title on mainland Australia or that the stolen generations are historical fact. Thrower's indigenous plantings are ghosts whose removal forms the romance of her tale and the attraction of her vacated site, but her placement of them reveals a different sort of haunting.

Chapter 9

'Cabin'd, cribb'd and confin'd': the White Woman of Gipps Land and Bungalene

Julie E. Carr

THIS CHAPTER examines the frontier legend of the White Woman of Gipps Land (later 'Gippsland'),[1] allegedly held captive by Aborigines, and the 1846–7 expeditions to rescue her. The legend emerged in 1840, circulated in the early colonial period of the Port Phillip District (now Victoria), and to this day continues to resurface in local histories and literary and creative works. Whether any such woman existed is questionable. However, for a transplanted European culture seeking to establish and perpetuate its own myths and practices of dominance, the legend served numerous ends. In particular, the White Woman story mediated contestation for the control of Gippsland, facilitating and justifying the dispossession of the Kurnai peoples of the region.[2] In its variant forms the legend has functioned as founding myth and authorising agent for selective versions of colonial history.[3] The story also reflected and reproduced the colonists' anxieties about contact with the racial 'other' and about civilisation at risk in remote unsettled zones.

Helen Tiffen has examined the discursive functions of textuality, arguing that 'European texts captured those worlds, "reading" their alterity assimilatively in terms of their own cognitive codes. Explorers' journals, drama, fiction, historical accounts, "mapping" enabled conquest and colonisation and the capture and/or vilification of alterity.'[4] In this respect, representations of Aboriginality in the White Woman stories have mediated contact between colonists, government authorities and indigenous peoples in ways which have buttressed European cultural, political and administrative dominance. However, when read critically, colonial texts also reveal counter-hegemonic elements. The black subject in colonial discourse — as Homi Bhabha has noted — is ambivalently constituted in a 'repertoire of conflictual positions'.[5] By examining key documents relating to the 1846–47 searches for the White Woman, this chapter teases out ambivalences and contradictions in a rescue project premised on binary definitions which pitted 'civilised' European *liberators* of the White Woman against her 'savage' Aboriginal *captors*.

The documents which I examine include newspaper accounts, official government correspondence, reports of a foray after the White Woman in mid-1846 by government officers stationed in Gippsland, and the journals of two rescue expeditions: the first (October 1846–January 1847) organised and funded by the citizens of Melbourne, the second (March–June 1847) authorised by Charles La Trobe, Superintendent of the Port Phillip District. Before turning to the documents, a brief summary of the story's emergence will place the expeditions in context.

The White Woman of Gippsland (as she came to be known) first came to public attention in late 1840. At this time Gippsland was (for Europeans) a remote and largely unexplored, but potentially lucrative, frontier zone. Pioneering Gipps Land squatter, Angus McMillan, described in the *Sydney Herald* of 28 December 1840 how his exploration party, having disturbed an Aboriginal encampment, found bloodstained items of European clothing, household articles, a bible, English and Scottish newspapers, and the body of a child enclosed in kangaroo skin bags. McMillan surmised that the child was of European parents, as parts of its skin were 'perfectly white', and that 'a dreadful massacre of Europeans, men, women and children, ha[d] been perpetrated by the aborigines in the immediate vicinity of the spot'. He concluded that 'the unfortunate female', whom he glimpsed being driven on at spear point by the fleeing Aborigines, was 'a European — a captive of these ruthless savages'.[6]

Although rumours of a white female captive revived periodically over the next few years, it was not until mid-1846 that the story became big 'news' in Melbourne. This followed a reported sighting by a white officer of the Native Police Corps stationed in Gippsland of 'a white woman with two half caste children, in company with a large body of the Aborigines'. A young Aboriginal boy, Jacka-wadden, was also alleged to have attested that the woman was with his tribe.[7] Reports of messages carved on trees in a remote part of Gippsland further fuelled speculation. From mid-August 1846 the White Woman's imagined plight, promoted and politicised in the Port Phillip newspapers, served to propagate representations of Gippsland Aborigines as demonic, subhuman brutes. 'Humanitas', a pseudonymous correspondent in the *Port Phillip Herald*, urged readers to 'rescue this defenceless female from the grasp of the harpies of hell...Port Phillipians!', he exhorted, 'come forward and do what you can for this poor woman, and God will reward you'.[8] A public meeting at Melbourne's Royal Hotel on 2 September resolved to appoint an expedition committee to raise funds and organise a rescue expedition.[9] George Cavenagh, editor of the *Port Phillip Herald* and chairman of the expedition committee, took a central role in heroising the expeditioners and imbuing the venture with a higher moral purpose:

> ...it is a consolation to know that the Melbourne public and the Executive are at length actively engaged in the sacred cause of suffering humanity, for the success of which the asperations [*sic*] of the community are fervently poured forth to Providence...[10]

In undertaking this 'sacred duty', those meeting — a Christian, middle-class coterie — positioned themselves in opposition to the government which they claimed had failed to act. On 20 October 1846 the expedition, led by Christian de Villiers, former head of the Port Phillip Native Police, embarked with the 'generous assistance of a most benevolent public...and with God's blessing'.[11]

The expeditioners arrived in Gippsland as heroic adventurers embarking on a noble quest on behalf of the citizens of Melbourne. Initially they met with little opposition from Gippsland settlers, although the interference of outsiders into local affairs must have been resented.[12] As the expedition progressed, however, the political realities which confronted the expeditioners necessitated a re-evaluation of what they saw as the ambit of their role. De Villiers and second-in-command of the expedition, James Warman, were to pen searing exposés of systematic and widespread violence against Gippsland Aborigines (termed 'Worrigals') by settlers and Native Police under the command of government officers. Warman wrote of the 'great many skulls and human bones' at a place named Golgotha, near Lake Victoria and Lake Reeve, which were, he said, the 'remains of Worrigals who had been shot...' The squatters, Warman wrote:

> ...think no more of shooting them [than] they do of eating their dinners, and from what we can learn, some fearful slaughters have

taken place…the 'Worrigals' are most anxious to be on good terms
with the white fellows; but that is not what is wanted by some of
the squatters, nothing more nor less than their extermination…[13]

Warman and De Villiers' allegations caused a furore when published in the *Port Phillip Herald* in February 1847, as the unsuccessful expedition straggled back to Melbourne. Outraged Gippsland
squatters refuted the charges and launched counter-accusations
against De Villiers of incompetence and misappropriation of expedition funds. These recriminations, played out in the pages of the
Melbourne press, momentarily destabilised colonialist assumptions
on which not only the rescue project but settlement itself was
predicated.

Superintendent La Trobe, although sceptical, bowed to public
pressure and despatched a second expedition on 4 March 1847,
under the command of Sergeant Windridge of the Native Police.[14]
This expedition, which I shall discuss shortly, details the capture
and incarceration of tribal 'chief' Bungelene, his wives and children. The fate of these Aboriginal captives provides a tragic and
unintendedly ironic counterpart to the putative captivity of the
White Woman. Together with Bungelene, the key figure who fea-
tured in, and was essential to, the White Woman saga was the
abducted Aboriginal child, Jacka-wadden.[15] The latter's alleged
attestation to the White Woman's existence was cited as authenti-
cation of the story's veracity. Both de Villiers' and Windridge's parties took Jacka-wadden with them as informant, interpreter and
diplomat. Jacka-wadden's capture was described in an official
report made in March 1846 by John Paine, storekeeper on squatter Lachlan Macalister's station.

> The aboriginal native, Jacka-wadden, (about seven or eight years
> of age,) has been living with me for six months; he is a native
> of Gipps' Land, of the Lake tribe; he was taken by Mr.
> Wilkinson, a settler, while driving the blacks who were spear-
> ing cattle off his run on Lake Wellington. I heard that Mr.
> Wilkinson put him out of the boat in which he was placed, but
> he insisted on remaining with Mr. Wilkinson and his party; and
> this native boy told me that he wanted to stop with the whites,
> and planted himself in the boat. He came up to Mr. Macalister's
> from Mr. Raymond's with Mr. Macalister's cart, with his own
> free will, and he has been living with me ever since. He is
> beginning to speak English and understands everything that is
> said to him.[16]

Marie Fels considers that Jacka-wadden was 'an emissary, either sent in or permitted to stay with Europeans...to gather information from the centre of European administration'.[17] Paine's defensive explanation of how the boy came to be living with him suggests, however, his sensitivity to potential charges that Jacka-wadden had been abducted and/or was being held against his will. Wilkinson's act of 'taking' a very young Aboriginal child from his people, a practice commonly employed by settlers, is elided in an expansive explanation of the boy's alleged complicitness in his own abduction.

Paine's assertion that Jacka-wadden 'is beginning to speak English and understands everything that is said to him' is offered as validation for Paine's version of events and justification for the child's continued retention. The underlying assumption, presumably shared by those who read the report, is that Jacka-wadden was better off at the station, where he was learning the English language and ways, than with his own people. The primary purpose of Paine's report was to record information allegedly provided to him by Jacka-wadden, namely that among his tribe there was a white woman whom he had never seen but that he had been in the habit of playing with the elder of her two children. According to Paine, Jacka-wadden informed him that his mother and others of his tribe had told him:

> ...that this white woman came from a big canoe, called by him Bunga Bunga; that there were also many white men, described by him to have been ship-wrecked, and that they swam on shore; that they kept the white gin and sent the white men away. The eldest half-caste child is said by him to be about five or six years old, and to bear a resemblance to two half-caste children at present on the station, one of which is about six years old.

Paine's comparison of the 'half-caste' children at the station with Jacka-wadden's tribal playmates is not pursued to the more likely conclusion — that all were fathered by white men. Instead, evidence of sexual relations between white men and Aboriginal women is inverted to confirm a white woman's 'captivity' by, and sexual relations with, men of Jacka-wadden's tribe. His inclusion of the Aboriginal term 'Bunga Bunga' works to authenticate the story as Jacka-wadden's, and to de-emphasise Paine's role as mediator and interpreter. However, Jacka-wadden's tender age and limited English, and the cultural and political contingencies of his situation, as well as his contact with neighbouring squatter Angus McMillan, with whom the White Woman rumours originated, provide cause for scepticism about information on the White Woman attributed to Jacka-wadden.

Despite Jacka-wadden's reluctance, due to his fear that he would be shot, he was 'prevailed upon' to accompany a party led by Sergeants Walsh and Windridge, of the Native Police. During May and June 1846, several months before the publicly funded expedition left Melbourne, this party — which was ostensibly organised to locate Jacka-wadden's father with a view to negotiating the White Woman's release — pursued, captured and harassed Worrigals over a distance of some 100 miles.

In his official report of this foray,[18] Sergeant Windridge described how the party fell in with a few Aboriginal camps, and took 'one of the native men — and old man with grey hair — [who] said the white woman had gone into the Mountains with a wild black named Bunjeleena, whom Jacka-wadden says is a man of some consideration with his tribe — but not chief'. This was the first mention of the second key Aboriginal figure — Bunjeleena (or Bungelene) — who was to be cast as the 'villain' of the piece. Once in circulation, the unsubstantiated charge that Bungelene was the White Woman's captor was repeated endlessly. The implications of this are taken up later in the chapter.

Windridge also placed on the official record the first report of cannibalism — again 'authenticated' by Jacka-wadden — as a component of the White Woman story:

> At the camp…we found portions of a body of a black woman, being cooked at the several fires, and some pieces from the thighs and other parts of the body, put away in some bark. The blacks were eating the flesh, and the man, through Jacka-wadden, told me that it was his gin that had died, and acknowledged having partaken of it. Jacka-wadden said it was not uncommon for the men to kill their gins and eat them.

In addition to providing implicit endorsement for the settler practice of removing Aborigines, including children like Jacka-wadden, from their tribes, purportedly to 'Christianise' or 'civilise' them, the charge of cannibalism was also used to incite public outrage over the White Woman.[19] The *Herald*, citing Windridge's report, claimed that the Gippsland tribes were 'not only cannibals but the actual devourers of the remains of the deceased gins, whose corpses instead of honouring with the rights of interment, they commit to the process of an aboriginal baking, and feast on the roasted flesh. This is a sickening but truthful fact!'[20]

The politics of racial difference embedded in such representations produces moral and cultural distinctions between the 'civilised' reader and 'demonic' Kurnai, while pandering to the reader's prurient interest in 'savage' customs.[21] The White Woman, as the imagined mute witness to, possible partaker in, or potential future victim of, a cannibal barbecue, acts as a site for the articulation of anxiety about Aboriginal sexual appetite and about 'civilisation' being swallowed up by 'savagery'.

As Peter Hulme and W. Arens,[22] amongst others (see also Gananath Obeyesekere and Paul Lyons in this volume), have argued, the ubiquitous charge of cannibalism invoked in colonialist texts reflects as much the fears, assumptions and political intent of European explorers and colonisers as what they actually encountered. Such textual representations produce and sustain categories of race which aid and justify the colonialist project.

In forwarding Windridge's report to La Trobe, Commissioner Tyers, the senior government officer in Gippsland, speculated further: '...The prevalence of this horrible custom [cannibalism] may possibly account for the refusal of the natives who have been brought in by the police, to return to their tribes'.[23] Tyers did not elaborate on why 'natives' had been brought in by police, or on what basis, or for how long or under what conditions they were held. The spectre of cannibalism served in the report to deflect attention from such questions and from other explanations as to why Aborigines might choose to remain at the station, such as their loss of access to traditional food sources as settlers took over tribal lands, fear of settler violence, or political expediency.

Similarly, while white men, including Warman, could be incensed about the White Woman's imagined sexual enslavement by Bungelene, sexual relations between white men and Aboriginal females (women and children) do not attract their censure. Warman's published journal of the expedition[24] alludes to the circulation of Aboriginal females in the sexual economy of post-settlement Gippsland as an inevitable component of frontier life:

> ...the lubras were all young and good featured; one of them named Mary, had been stopping for several weeks at Mr. Cunningham's; she gave a very good account of the white woman, and stated she was with a man named Bungelene, in the direction of the head of the Mitchell...[25]
> ...At 11 a.m. landed the three Worrigal women on the island 'Powel Powel', on account of some alledged [sic] misunderstand-

ing between our blacks and those belonging to the Native Police, the latter claiming them on account of priority of right, as it appears those were part of the lubras that were taken by Mr. Walsh, and had been staying at the police station for some time. They did not wish to leave us…[26]

…[the Worrigals] have a custom of showing their good will to the parties by offering their lubras and females, even of the most tender years; for chastity among them is a thing very little cared for, they behaving to mere infants in a most brutal manner. There seems to be a great disparity in the sexes, not being half as many females as males[27]

Warman does not say whether his own party accepted the 'good-will' offers made to them of 'lubras and females'. Neither does he speculate on the cause/s of 'the great disparity in the sexes'. Presumably some females, like Mary, were at squatters' stations, either of their own volition or otherwise.[28] Warman's comments both highlight and elide the double standards and contradictions in the expedition project.

While the expeditioners might have been convinced of the woman's 'plight', there are indications that neither the settlers nor the government officers in Gippsland believed in the White Woman's existence. The *Port Phillip Gazette*'s 'own Correspondent', writing on 10 May 1847 from Tarraville in Gipps Land described the reports as 'a clever hoax'.[29] The *Port Phillip Patriot* reported on 7 April 1847 that 'Captain Dana, and the government party who proceeded to Gipps Land in search of the white woman…have returned to town after having convinced themselves that their sympathies and those of the public have been enlisted in behalf of an imaginary being' and that the affair 'appears to have originated in a joke upon the part of a few waggish settlers in the district, with a view to test the gullibility of the "Herald"…' The article continued: 'Mr. Tyers, we understand, has become heartily tired of the undertaking, from a conviction…that the white woman, respecting whom so much has been said and written, is an "invisible girl", a mere creature of the imagination, or perhaps a feminine Bunyip'.[30]

Tyers, nevertheless, in his letter to Superintendent La Trobe three weeks later blamed the 'bad faith of that chief', Bungelene, for the failure of attempts to recover the woman. On the pretext of Bungelene's deception, and ostensibly 'to be no longer duped by this wily Black', Tyers advised that he had 'thought it advisable to try the effect of a compulsory detention of [Bungelene] and his family, intimating that concession to our demands is the surest means of recovering his freedom'.[31]

Bungelene had eluded the government forays during 1846, and De Villiers' party, but was captured by the second expedition (led by Sergeant Windridge) and brought to Tyers' headquarters at Eagle Point on 10 April 1847. Tyers reported to La Trobe that '[j]udging from the deference and respect the Gippsland Blacks pay him, there is no doubt Bungelene is a man of no small consideration among them, — probably their chief. This may account for the want of success hitherto attending the search after him...'[32] While the title 'chief' may be inaccurate in terms of tribal structures, it reflects Bungelene's influence and status with his people. Bungelene's capture and detention would have demoralised his people. The aim of his captivity might have been primarily to break Worrigal resistance to white settlement.[33]

Tyers estimated in 1846 that between 800 and 1,000 'wild blacks' (Worrigals) were in Gippsland.[34] They outnumbered the European population and were, Tyers said, 'very destructive to the stock of the settlers, killing perhaps on the average not less than 150 head of cattle annually'. Tyers conceded to a select committee some years later that 'at least fifty [Worrigals] were killed by the Native Police and other Aborigines attached to the parties in search of a white woman.'[35] They were led by white officers.

When Bungelene's 'compulsory detention' did not produce the White Woman, Tyers had an official document drawn up — a 'memorandum of agreement' — to which Bungelene was induced to put his mark:

> Memorandum of agreement entered into this day between Charles J. Tyers, Esq., on the part of Her Majesty's Government, and Bungelene, Chief of the Gipps Land Tribes:–
>
> I, Bungelene, promise to deliver to Charles J. Tyers the white female residing with the Gipps Land blacks, provided a party of whites and Western Port blacks proceed with me to the mountains at as early a day as may be convenient, for the purpose of obtaining her from my brothers. I also agree to leave my two wives and two children with the said Charles J. Tyers, as hostages for the fulfilment of my promise. And I, Charles J. Tyers, promise, on the part of Her Majesty's Government, to give Bungelene one boat, with oars, a tent, four blankets, a guernsey frock, some fish-hooks and a fishing-line, and a tomahawk for the said Bungelene's own use, and six blankets, two tomahawks, three guernsey frocks,

and other articles between three or four men of the said
Bungelene's tribes who may be instrumental in the recovery of
the said white female, conditioned that the said Bungelene fulfil
his part of the agreement.

BUNGELENE X his mark.

Witness — S. WINDRIDGE.
CHARLES J. TYERS.

Witnesses to the agreement —
S. WINDRIDGE.
WILLIAM PETERS
DONALD McLEOD.
RICHARD HARTNETT.
Done at Eagle Point, Gipps Land,
this seventeenth day of May,
one thousand eight hundred and forty-seven.[36]

There was little precedent for such a document in early colonial history in Port Phillip and its legality must have been questionable. One comparable document was the agreement — subsequently disallowed by Governor Bourke and the Colonial Secretary
in London — which John Batman, on behalf of the Port Phillip
Association of Van Diemen's Land, had attempted in 1835 to effect
with Port Phillip Aborigines of the Dutigallar tribe.[37]

At the time Bungelene affixed his 'mark' to the agreement he
had been held in custody at Eagle Point, closely guarded, for over a
month.[38] No formal charges against him had been made. His command of English was minimal. He was not literate. Nevertheless, he
was required to enter into a formal agreement, couched in 'legal'
terminology. In a private communication to La Trobe, Tyers stated
that Bungelene 'seem[ed] thoroughly to understand the nature of
the agreement, and that it is equally binding on both parties...'
Neither La Trobe nor Governor FitzRoy, to whom Tyers' correspondence was duly forwarded, questioned this assertion, or objected to the undertaking.[39]

The idea for an agreement with Bungelene was foreshadowed
in February 1847 in a letter to the editor of the *Port Phillip Gazette*
— notably in relation to the deportation of the remnant tribes from
Van Diemen's Land. In suggesting how the forthcoming (second)
White Woman expedition should be conducted, the anonymous
correspondent — 'A Fellow Colonist' — recommended:

...sending forth a competent leader, in company only with some two or three blacks as guides, interpreters, and negotiators. It was in this way, and this way only, that Chief Protector Robinson succeeded in bringing the hostile tribes of V. D. Land into Hobart town, and causing them to enter into a treaty of deportation to Flinders Island, [after] Military, Police, and posse comitatus of the colony, had failed in coercing them to the same end.[40]

As contracted in the agreement, Bungalene accompanied the expeditioners on a fourteen-day trek through the mountains in search of the White Woman. As with De Villiers' expedition, much importance was attached to circumstantial 'evidence' of the woman's existence encountered along the way. On 25 May the party made its fire 'on the spot where [Bungelene] pointed out as been [sic] the Identical spot where the [White Woman] Slept'; five days later the party stopped at one of Bungelene's camps, 'where he pointed out to us the Mia Mia which the White woman Lay in when with him' and, on 29 May, the party came upon 'the remains of three Mia Mias where we found a Log of wood which the boy said was used to tiy to the White womans Legs the Grass was still on the log' [sic].[41]

On 31 May, after ten days out in bitterly cold and difficult conditions, and with still no sign of the White Woman, the expeditioners 'upbraided [Bungelene] for his duplicity' and threatened to 'shoot him for Leading us astray'. On 8 June, four days after their return to Eagle Point, the expedition journal records:

> ...the old man is very uneasey...we have been telling him that the White people are Comming from Melbourne to Shoot the blacks on the Islands and in the Mountains and that we are to bring him to Melbourne there to be hanged all which he believes which makes him rather Down hearted and frightened while out with us in the Mountains he asked [Jacka-wadden] if we would alow him to bring his Lubra to Melbourne with him that shews that he has No Great Intention of Giving up the woman'. [sic]

On 12 June the expedition party started for Melbourne, taking with them '...Bungelene, two lubras, and two picaninnies'.[42] They were duly handed over to Captain Dana, Commandant of the Native Police headquarters at Narre Narre Warren, some twenty miles east of Melbourne, on 28 June. Mr Thomas, Assistant Protector of Aborigines at Western Port, was to testify in 1861 to the Central Board appointed to watch over the interests of

Aborigines in the Colony of Victoria, that while at Narre Narre Warren, Bungelene 'was brutally chained to a gum tree for many days and nights', until Thomas 'brought the matter officially under the notice of the Government'.[43]

Although the purpose and legality of Bungelene's detention at Narre Narre Warren was never adequately established, none of the government officers appears to have been willing or able to make a decision to release him. Tyers[44] passed responsibility to La Trobe, who in turn sought instructions from Governor FitzRoy. La Trobe admitted to FitzRoy:

> It is true that Bungelene cannot be detained by legal forms, and I am very doubtful whether any good can be expected to result from his detention; but it is also true that as far as his own acts and supposed admissions can be received in proof, he may justly be charged with holding a European female as his Captive, as it may be presumed, against her will…[45]

FitzRoy, however, declined involvement: '…your Honor must exercise your own discretion with respect to the detention of Bungelene, and his Wives'.[46]

The *Gazette* had speculated on 3 July that this 'lady-killer', would be 'immediately turned adrift, as there is no charge against him'. However, although La Trobe and G. A. Robinson, Chief Protector of Aborigines, both of whom visited Bungelene at Narre Narre Warren, remained sceptical about the White Woman rumours,[47] Bungelene was to remain there in custody for a further fifteen months until his death on 21 November 1848.[48] In the interim, one of his wives had died. The surviving wife and her two young sons were subsequently removed to the Merri Merri Creek Mission Station.[49] La Trobe had authorised Bungelene's return to Gippsland in January 1848, some ten months before his death.[50] Why this did not occur is unclear.

A pretext for La Trobe to suspend the case had presented itself with the unsubstantiated report in early November 1847 of the discovery at Jemmy's Point (Gippsland) of the remains of a white female and child. The newspapers took this opportunity to relinquish a story which had probably outworn its newsworthiness. The report of the woman's death relieved the citizens of Melbourne of the need to undertake any further efforts to rescue her and the *Herald*'s eulogy provided an appropriate sense of closure:

> Death though regarded as a mishap by others, must have descended as a blessing upon this poor woman, who has undergone a trial

far more harrowing and terrible than even Death's worst moments. She is now no more — and it is a melancholy gratification that the public suspense has been at length relieved, by her discovery even in death.[51]

However, the story did not die. The 'idea of a young, lovely, and accomplished female, being "cribbed, cabined and confined" [*sic*] in the Harem of one of the petty chiefs of a barbarous tribe of the wretched aborigines of New Holland' — as the *Port Phillip Gazette* put it — was to spawn the legend which continues to this day.[52]

Over the past 160 years, since McMillan's account first appeared, a plethora of textual material (newspaper reports, expedition journals, parliamentary papers, official documents, historical analyses, poetry, fictional accounts and academic writings) has produced and reproduced the legend for successive generations.[53] This body of material attests to the story's function at various historical moments within colonial and post-colonial discourses of power relations. Each revival of the story reinvokes the 'captive' White Woman and her Aboriginal 'captor', in an endlessly rehearsed originary moment in Gippsland post-settlement history.

Chapter 10
Material culture and the 'signs' of captive white women
Kate Darian-Smith

IN 1840 white settlers in the rugged Gippsland (called 'Gipps Land' at the time) region of eastern Victoria reputedly located items of European origin in a camp abruptly abandoned by local Kurnai people. A detailed inventory of these objects was printed in a letter written by Angus McMillan — Scottish immigrant, and one of the 'founders' of modern Gippsland — in the *Sydney Herald*. Upon entering the camp, McMillan and his companions 'discovered':

> ...several check-shirts, cord and moleskin trousers, all besmeared with human blood; one German frock; two pea-jackets, new brown Macintosh cloak also stained with blood, several pieces of women's wearing apparel, namely, prints and merinos; a large lock of brown hair, evidently that of an European woman; one child's white frock, with brown velvet band, five hand towels of which one was marked R. Jamieson No. 12, one blue silk purse, silver tassels and slides, containing seven shillings and sixpence British money, one women's thimble, two large parcels of silk sewing thread, various colours, 10 new English blankets perfectly clean, shoe-makers' awls, bees' wax, blacksmith's pincers and cold chisel, one bridle bit, which had been recently used, as the grass was quite fresh on it, the tube of a thermometer, broken looking glass, bottles of all descriptions, two of which had castor oil in them, one sealskin cap, one musket and some shot, one broad tomahawk, some London, Glasgow and Aberdeen newspapers, printed in 1837 and 1838. One pewter two-gallon measure, one ditto handbasin, one large tin camp kettle, two children's copy books, one bible printed in Edinburgh, June 1838, one set of National Loan Fund regulations, respecting policies of life insurance, and blank forms of medical men's certificate for effecting the same...[1]

This list, quoted here in full, accounted for two-thirds of the letter. Despite the implausibility of such a find (for there is no explanation as to how a European family came to be travelling in such dense and remote bush) McMillan was presenting a carefully orchestrated 'showcase' or display of ordinary, domestic objects. Individually, each object had a limited meaning. But when placed together, as a collection, these items appeared to be the material remnants of a god-fearing, provident, respectable and literate family, implicitly of Scottish extraction, taking up land in the new colony. Missing from this collection of material culture was, of course, the family itself. The displacement and disarray of the objects represented far more than an assault on the trappings of European civilisation; their very *presence* in an Aboriginal camp spoke of the *absence* of European bodies. McMillan certainly had 'no doubt' he was witnessing the aftermath of a dreadful massacre of Europeans by the Kurnai — a view supported by the claim that some clothing was soiled with possible human blood, the subsequent identification of a dead white child in the camp, and the glimpse of a white woman being driven away by Aboriginal men.[2]

It was no accident that the first published account of Australia's most fully documented female 'captive' — known simply as the White Woman of Gippsland — drew so strongly upon the cultural meanings ascribed to both European and Aboriginal culture in mounting its case against the 'barbarity' of the Kurnai. The white settlers moving their stock into Gippsland from the late 1830s were met with violent resistance. The Kurnai killed cattle and white shepherds; the Europeans retaliated with a series of violent massacres.[3] But Angus McMillan and his fellow settlers also waged an ideological war against the Kurnai, and in doing so drew upon both their 'European vision' and deeply held imperial memories of the western conquest of non-European peoples in colonial theatres.[4] One facet of this discourse of conquest was the articulation of stereotypes of the 'native' as degenerative and uncivilised, morally and spiritually bereft, and with a material culture that was neither technologically nor artistically advanced.

On imperial frontiers, objects played a fundamental role in the economic and social dynamics of cross-cultural interactions. From the late fifteenth century, cheaply produced trade goods, like mirrors, beads and blankets — and later, bibles and guns — were instrumental in the project of European expansion into 'new worlds' and the subordination of indigenous peoples and the acquisition of their lands and resources. By the time that the British annexed Australia, they accepted that the technologies of production and the material culture of a people were emblematic of that people's 'civilisation', taking little account of the adaptation and inventiveness with which Aborigines embraced European goods. As Ian Donaldson and Tamsin Donaldson point out, Europeans 'examined the Aborigines with a gaze that was at once comparative and classificatory'.[5] White, Christian, industrial capitalism represented the pinnacle of techno-logical, social and moral advancement. In contrast stood the 'prim-itive' anatomical structure, 'mentality' and material culture of Aboriginal people, a view that was to be supported by a rapidly expanding body of scientific and anthropological 'evidence' during the nineteenth century.

The push for progress, and the popular circulation of theories of social Darwinism by the second half of the nineteenth century, served to define further the evolution of a society through the pro-duction and the consumption of its material culture — how objects were made, used and valued. Social evolutionists argued that Aborigines were, in the words of Augustus Lane-Fox Pitt-Rivers, 'living representatives of our common ancestors'. The material cul-ture of Aboriginal people thus stood, according to Pitt-Rivers, in the same relation to that of prehistoric Europe.[6] Pitt-Rivers, who saw artefacts as being the physical manifestation of human ideas, employed a typology at his famous ethnographic museum at Oxford that classified Aboriginal weaponry and other objects as the lowest on the scale of all human societies. In an Australian example, the anthropological displays under the direction of Baldwin Spencer at the National Museum of Victoria deployed material cul-ture to emphasise the cultural simplicity and stagnation of Aboriginal society.[7] The wholesale collection and commercial exchange of ethnographic objects, so prevalent during the period of 'high imperialism', and the systems of hierarchical classification and exhibition of these non-western artefacts and their peoples in inter-national exhibitions, museums and other public and institutional sites, illustrated in very explicit terms the ways that European dis-course evaluated cultures through things.

Given this broad context, it is not surprising that objects, of both European and Aboriginal origin, took on a significance within the White Woman of Gippsland narrative as material and ideological symbols of the culturally transgressive captivity experience. McMillan's report, with its elaborate collection of objects, was re-published in the *Port Phillip Patriot and Morning Advertiser* in 1841.[8] In 1843 the *Port Phillip Herald* published an anonymous letter which told of the recovery of European goods, including clothes and a prayer book, from an Aboriginal camp, 'evidence' that suggested that it was possible that the Kurnai had captured a white person of indeterminate sex.[9] By the mid 1840s there was no question that the gender of the elusive captive was female, and this marked a significant shift in the discursive and cultural power of the captivity narrative.

The words 'white' and 'woman' were a powerful combination in the colonial imagination. They fused together multifarious racial, gendered and sexual ideologies, constituting women as both symbols of European civilisation and chattels of patriarchal capitalism. As cultural symbol and as property, the colonial white woman was constructed as the object of indigenous or primitive sexual desire. Apprehensions about the racial and sexual threat to the status of white womanhood were echoed and amplified around the imperial world, and in Australia, as elsewhere, they rose to a pitch when localised friction between colonisers and colonised became intense — as they were in Gippsland in the 1840s.[10] Furthermore, while material culture was a measure of a people's level of advancement, so too was a people's treatment of its women.[11] If Aborigines treated their women as drudges, as was commonly believed, what would be the fate of a white woman in Aboriginal society? This question, combined with the possibilities of cross-racial bodily and sexual intimacy, fanned the European hysteria that surrounded the White Women of Gippsland phenomenon of the 1840s.

Several expedition parties funded by either the colonial government or private subscription embarked from Melbourne. They tracked the movements of the White Woman through a trail of signs and objects: a scrap of European cloth, a crocheted grass bag of such intricacy that it was said it could only have been made by feminine, white hands. In the numerous letters and poems that were printed in the Melbourne newspapers, and in the private correspondence and expedition journals of those aiming to rescue her, the White Woman's 'piteous plight' was consistently described in terms of the absence of European goods and technology in Aboriginal society. Her life was one of cold and dirt, as she was without permanent shelter, soap and, most importantly, European clothes. Her material and mental comfort, as well as her person, were seen to be subjected to unspeakable indignities.

In turn, the expeditions scattered their own artefacts throughout Gippsland. Handkerchiefs (see Illustration 8) and mirrors were distributed bearing instructions in English and Gaelic for the White Woman: '...Be particularly on the lookout every dawn of morning, for it is then that the party is in hopes of rescuing you. The white settlement is towards the setting sun.'[12] There were attempts to exchange trade goods with local Aborigines for the return of the White Woman, and when this failed an Aboriginal 'chief', Bungelene, and his wife and children, were held as hostages until she was brought forward. Then, in late 1847, McMillan presided over the hasty inquest of the body of a European woman and her 'half-caste child' found at Jemmy's Point in Gippsland. The White Woman was thus officially laid to rest. By this stage, most of Gippsland had been claimed by settlers, indigenous resistance had been generally squashed, and large numbers of Aborigines had died as a result of the spread of diseases and frontier violence.

But if no flesh-and-blood White Woman was ever recovered (or indeed, ever existed), a material representation of her was eventually located. In 1847 some of the Kurnai handed over a wooden ship's figurehead. This was said to be in the form of Britannia, a particularly potent symbol of imperial power and white womanhood. There were reports from the Crowns Land Commissioner, Charles Tyers, that the Aborigines worshipped the wooden figure as an idol, 'forming the centre around which they danced their most solo coroborees'. The figurehead, when it was eventually recovered, was disappointingly small and battered but nonetheless it was transported back to Melbourne for public display as both a curiosity and a trophy.[13]

The copious documents that have been written about the White Woman of Gippsland, both as historic event (or phenomenon) and as a representation of that event, without exception integrate objects into their narratives. So in varied newspaper reports and editorials, parliamentary papers, expedition journals, memoirs and autobiographical jottings, and literary and fictionalised accounts, objects are mentioned over and over. But three broad overlapping and interconnected modes are employed in this cultural task of expressing social, racial and sexual differences through material culture. First, there is the sensational nature of such descriptions as that in McMillan's 1840 catalogue of goods found at the empty Kurnai camp. In such an instance it is the spatial displacement of objects from their original social context and utilitarian function that is both obvious and significant. Here, it is the juxtaposition, which would have been striking to settler society, between the goods of 'civilisation' and their location in the 'primitive' camp of the Kurnai: what use were such things as books or coins or even tools and textiles to a society that was, according to prevalent European views of Aborigines, unable to understand the economic, social and technological functions of these objects? Nonetheless, it was assumed that the Kurnai coveted, and thus collected, European objects. Indeed, the 'precious' European objects were only 'discovered' because, according to McMillan's narrative, the Aborigines fled their camp in haste and fear at the sight of a party of mounted Europeans — with no time to hide the evidence of their 'barbarous' crimes against a god-fearing European family.

Second, there is the ethnographic record of Aboriginal material culture and customs. Such collection of knowledges were essential to the imperial project to take possession of the land and its indigenous peoples. The two surviving journals from the rescue expeditions for the White Woman are filled with detailed descriptions of the land and its possibilities for pastoral use, as well as containing information about the culture and activities of the Kurnai. The *Port Phillip Herald* published the journal and letter of James Warman, who led the privately funded search party. Warman, who was appalled at the evidence he found that settlers and members of the official expedition had massacred the Kurnai in retaliation, provided sympathetic accounts of the Kurnai, including ethnographic descriptions of their material culture. Nonetheless, the public circulation of his observations that the Kurnai were weakened by disease and were retreating from their lands did little to challenge the view that the Kurnai were a primitive people, and may have even lured intending settlers to the promise of the Gippsland region.

Third, there is the commemorative function of objects as a reminder and physical link to histories and places. The exhibition of the wooden figurehead in Melbourne provides one contemporary example of this commemorative impulse. As memories of the White Woman narrative were passed down from generation to generation in Gippsland, so too was local knowledge about the location of pivotal events in her story; the spot where the White Woman carved a heart on the ground, or where she was first seen. Associated with this collective remembering of the pioneer life in 'old Gippsland' was the passing on of valued objects, such as the handkerchiefs urging the White Woman westwards. Local histories and memoirs, which recall and commemorate the White Woman story, are, in their own right, memory objects which may be collected and valued as the conveyers of a particular 'truth' about pioneer society.

Domesticating the body

Through these modes, the cultural meanings and functional role of European objects, always contrasted with the 'primitivism' of indigenous material culture, frame the White Woman of Gippsland incident. That many of the objects were domestic and the captive a European woman — not a man — helped stir the righteous anger of the colonialists and to fuel their desire for revenge. Other historical and fictional captivity tales involving European women in Australia are equally fulsome in references to objects and their social, performative and bodily functions. Soap, in particular, emerges as a signifier of white civilisation. The maintenance of personal hygiene was an act that was at once private, domesticated and sexually charged. One of the hardships the White Woman supposedly faced during her time with Aboriginal people was that she was forced to live in a state of filth. The notion of cleanliness operates here in both a literal and metaphorical sense: the White Woman's person was polluted through her association with the Kurnai.

Anne McClintock has traced the shift, in the nineteenth century, from 'scientific racism' as exemplified in ethnographical, anthropological medical and travel writings, to 'commodity racism'.[14] This commodity racism, she argues, was inherent in Victorian forms of advertising, photography and exhibition, fusing together narratives of imperial progress and capitalism into a mass-produced consumer spectacle. The centrality of the cult of domesticity to the imperial project can be seen in Victorian advertising campaigns for a range of cleaning products, including soap; in one famous advertisement, the use of Pears soap literally whitens the body (but not the face) of a black child, as if magically erasing the racial degeneration of blackness.[15] An extraordinary reworking of this message can be seen in the 1896 photographic tableau of the little-known Australian photographer Thomas Cleary. Entitled 'Divorced' or 'Disowned', the photograph shows an Aboriginal mother explaining the skin colour of her fair-skinned child to her Aboriginal husband by pointing to Pears soap. The image presents an elaborate and cross-textual joke to its audience — Cleary publicly displayed his creative work in several Victorian country towns — by mocking Aboriginal responses to European technology.[16] Within this broader colonial context, it is not surprising that in nineteenth-century captivity narratives the domestic ritual of washing the body with soap functioned to mark the literal re-entry of a white 'captive' into European society and also, at a symbolic and psychological level, signalled the cleansing of the polluted and sexually degraded body of the female captive.

On 16 October 1849, the private journal of Oswald W. Brierly, official artist on the survey vessel H. M. S. *Rattlesnake* recorded the 'rescue' of Barbara Crawford Thompson at Evans Bay, on the eastern tip of Australia's Cape York Peninsula.[17] According to Brierly, '...a young woman very much browned by the sun' had been brought by 'the Blacks' down to the beach.[18] The men of the *Rattlesnake*, who were busily bleaching the ship's laundry, were initially blind to Thompson's own whiteness. Her skin was darkly tanned, scarred from burns down one side of her face and body. It was only after she spoke some words of English, in a thick Scottish brogue, that they were alerted to her race.[19] Their stunned recognition was quickly followed by their transformation of a hitherto anonymous 'native' woman into the young white woman, Barbara Thompson. The now *white* nakedness of her body was washed and hastily covered by shirts plucked from the washing pile. Her hair was combed. She was given a plate and cutlery to eat from the communal pot, a gesture not extended to her indigenous companions. A little later, where she was spatially relocated from the beach to the *Rattlesnake*, Barbara Thompson was served meat and apple pie with a cup of tea.[20]

At the time of her reinstatement into European society, Barbara Thompson was aged twenty-one. She had emigrated with her family from Aberdeen to Sydney, from where, in 1844, aged sixteen, she eloped with William Thompson to Moreton Bay. The Thompsons refitted a small cutter to salvage goods from a shipwreck in Torres Strait. The trip was a disaster: the crew argued, the wreck proved elusive, two seamen died, and rations became short. In a sudden summer squall, the vessel was smashed on a coral reef. William Thompson and the remaining sailors drowned, while Barbara Thompson clung to the cutter until she was saved by a turtling party of mainland Aborigines and Kaurareg from Muralag (Prince of Wales) Island. She was integrated into Kaurareg society until her adopted brother, Tomagugu, a leading mainland Aborigine, took her to her 'own people' at Evans Bay.[21]

Although no portrait of her has survived, Thompson was described as follows by John MacGillivray, the *Rattlesnake*'s zoologist, on the day of her reinstatement into white society: 'Though not pretty, [she] has a soft, feminine and very pleasing expression'.[22] T. H. Huxley, the ship's assistant surgeon, recorded in his diary that when 'appropriately dressed' — that is, when her nakedness was covered — that Thompson would be 'not bad looking'.[23] In Brierly's expedition journal, his detailed description of her reconnection with the daily objects that marked out European civilisation — cutlery, proper bedding, furniture, European food — served to emphasise the dislocation of her 'captive' existence. Her material reincorporation into white society was accompanied by her spiritual awakening. Brierly likened Barbara Thompson's 'curious manner', and inability to 'collect her ideas', to that of one surfacing from 'a deep sleep'. She spoke in starts, with long pauses, and her face bore a 'dreaming vacant expression'. In white company she grew suddenly 'ashamed' of her nakedness.[24] She was given cloth and needles and was soon at work making 'proper' feminine clothes.

Within an existing network of (male) trade between the two parties, the crew of the *Rattlesnake* formalised Thompson's bodily return by presenting Tomagugu and his companions with knives, axes, biscuit and tobacco. Distressed at her departure, the Kaurareg sent their own commodities — roasted turtle eggs, grass for weaving baskets — and visited her by canoe. But on the white space of the ship's deck the mutual affection between Thompson and the Kaurareg could not be expressed, as it had been on the beach, through the physical intimacies of bodily contact. Brierly, who had an ethnographic interest in the culture of the peoples of Cape York and the Torres Strait, was fascinated by these cross-cultural exchanges. During the return voyage to Sydney, Brierly carefully interviewed Thompson at great length about the material culture of the Kaurareg; his journal constructs (or captures) the lives of the Kaurareg through the objects that were used every day and on ceremonial occasions. Tales and trails of material culture, both European and indigenous, are woven through Brierly's account of Thompson's years with the Kaurareg.

Mary Watson: remembering the frontier

In 1881, on the far northern coast of Queensland, Aborigines attacked a remote fishing station at Lizard Island, in the Great Barrier Reef.[25] The station was operated by Captain Robert Watson, who at the time was absent searching for new fishing grounds for his bêche-de-mer operations. His young wife, Mary, their four-month-old son, Ferrier, and two Chinese servants, Ah Leong and Ah Sam, remained at Lizard Island, tending to the domestic chores of the garden and homestead. On 29 August local

Aborigines arrived on Lizard Island and Ah Leong was speared and killed. The next day, Mary Watson noted in her *Letts Australasian Diary and Almanac* that: 'Natives down at the beach at 7 p.m. Fired off the rifle and revolver and they went away.'[26] But the Aborigines remained, blocking access to the fresh water supply. So Mary Watson prepared to flee Lizard Island with her son and the remaining Chinese servant, Ah Sam, who was speared in several places, but was still alive. She packed a revolver and collection of 'survival' goods: 'clothes, a saw, a hammer, her watch, jewellery, money (£2 and some silver coins was all she had), umbrella, bonnet, pillow, food — including tins of sardines, bread, goat's and condensed milk, a new exercise book, a new sharp pencil'.[27] The remaining fresh water was poured into canvas bags.

Mary Watson, Ah Sam and the baby fled Lizard Island in a four-foot-square iron tank used for boiling bêche-de-mer, with the large wooden stirring paddles serving as oars. Her diary records that she was hoping to land on a nearby island, where she would be able to wave down a passing vessel.[28] On 7 September she wrote:

> Made for an island four or five miles from the one spoken of yesterday. Ashore, but could not find any water. Cooked some rice and clam-fish. Moderate S.E. breeze. Stayed here all night. Saw a steamer heading north. Hoisted Ferrier's pink and white wrap but did not answer us.[29]

Three days later, the fresh water ran out. Ah Sam left the iron tank and disappeared into the bush. Mary Watson entered her last diary entry on 11 September: '…Self not feeling at all well. Have not seen boat of any description. No water. Near dead with thirst.'

Mary Watson and her child, still in the iron tank, were not discovered until 16 January 1882 by the first officer of a passing vessel. The tank was almost full with fresh water, in the wake of monsoonal rains. In a camphorwood box was Mary Watson's diary, protected from the elements and providing details of her last few days. The skeletal remains of Ah Sam were located nearby. Robert Watson, who had been searching for his wife and child for some months, assisted by the colonial police and harbour authorities, identified the bodies.

In late January 1882 Mary Watson's funeral was held in the busy port of Cooktown, and was then the largest public event ever held in North Queensland. The funeral procession was led by a band and the fire brigade, and included groups of school children, the Good Templars, and 'European mourners'; a wagonette carrying the body of Ah Sam, and 'Chinese residents' followed at a discreet distance.[30] The motto 'All for one' was attached to the funeral wreath, referring to the collective consciousness of the North Queensland community. Four years later, with funds raised by public subscription, a memorial with a large white marble column and a drinking fountain was erected in the main street of Cooktown to honour Mary Watson. Inscribed on the memorial was the last stanza of a poem by 'A. F', printed in the *Bulletin*[31]:

> Five fearful days beneath the scorching glare,
> Her babe she nursed,
> God knows the pangs that woman had to bear,
> Whose last sad entry showed a mother's care,
> 'Then — nearly dead with thirst'.

Although this inscription highlighted Mary Watson's role as a pioneer heroine and a dedicated mother, her tragic fate was seen to be preferable to 'nameless horrors' far worse — captivity and rape by the Aborigines.[32] For while Mary Watson's story is not, in the conventional sense, a captivity narrative, it nonetheless drew upon the same fear of interracial bodily violence and contact in recounting the realities of frontier life. Violent reprisals against the local Aborigines were justified not by Mary Watson's death alone, but by the suggestion of what her fate might have been as a white 'captive'. Like the White Woman episode forty years earlier, the idea that a white woman — as a signifier of refinement and delicacy — could be captured by the primitive Aborigine provided settlers with additional moral ammunition in their war for land.

The imposing presence of the Cooktown memorial provided an object lesson for settlers in North Queensland. But the public display of other artefacts further commemorated Mary Watson's history. Just after her funeral, in February 1882, Robert Watson donated the iron tank and wooden paddles to the Queensland Museum.[33] This was an unlikely addition to the museum's collections. In the 1880s the board of trustees of the Queensland Museum, which was founded by the Queensland Philosophical Society in 1862, was busy pressing the colonial government for funds to enable the acquisition of technological items 'of public interest', including mining implements, raw and manufactured food and clothing, building materials and other artefacts so these '...be sufficiently represented to assist in the rise and progress of colonial industries'.[34] In line with other colonial collecting institutions, the priorities of the Queensland Museum were clearly to expand its zoological, geological and ethnographic holdings, rather than open a historical branch.[35] Indeed, the main historical items held by it were primarily from archaeological sites in the Middle East or were described as Asian curiosities; the Queensland Museum, in common with other colonial collecting institutions in Australia, had little interest in local items. So, in this context, Robert Watson's donation was an anomaly. One can only speculate as to why he was motivated to place the bêche-de-mer tank in the museum, other than to preserve this object, and with it Mary Watson's history — her suffering as a woman and as the mother of a small baby — for posterity. A photograph taken in 1922 shows the iron tank and oars, accompanied by a small photo of Mary Watson, displayed on the verandah of the Queensland Museum at its Gregory Terrace site.[36] In 1959, when the museum staged its first major historical exhibits for the state's centenary celebrations, the Mary Watson objects were included. By the 1960s the tank and other items were incorporated into the expanding historical section of the museum, where they 'told the graphic story of her last few days'.[37] The tank is now on loan to the Museum of Tropical Queensland in Townsville, where its meaning is shaped by the other objects that surround it in a broad exhibition of local 'tropical heritage'.

In nineteenth-century historical narratives of captivity, such as those of the White Woman of Gippsland, or Barbara Thompson, or of near-captivity as in the Mary Watson story, European and Aboriginal objects become representative within settler discourse of the social and cultural values of 'civilisation'. The displacement of European bodies, especially those of women, and of European material culture from their broad social context had immense cultural and discursive power in reinforcing white ideologies of racial superiority, fanning fears about interracial sex, and shaping the ways that settlers responded to, recorded and commemorated incidents of white female captivity on bloodily contested frontiers. But the histories of objects do not end with the 'rescue' of these white women. Colonial museums and local historians sought to collect, and often publicly display, material culture believed to be associated with white captivity experiences; such objects were thus to acquire a new function and a place in social memory as the commemorative markers of capture, bearing the sexualised and racialised violence of past Australian frontiers into the present.

Part IV:
Film, Desire &
the Colonised Body

Chapter 11

Captivity, melancholia and diaspora in Marlon Fuentes' *Bontoc Eulogy*: revisiting *Meet Me In St Louis*

Jeanette Hoorn

Mrs Anna Smith: 'There's never been anything like it in the whole world.'
Rose Smith: 'We don't have to come here in a train or stay in a hotel —
it's right here — right in our own home town.'
Esther Smith: 'I can't believe it — right here where we live, right here in
St Louis.'

Meet Me In St Louis, Vincente Minnelli, MGM 1944.

MARLON FUENTES' documentary film *Bontoc Eulogy* (1995) traces the film-maker's quest to find his grandfather Marcod, who disappeared in America early this century, after he was taken from the Philippines to St Louis. Displayed as an ethnographic object in the famous Louisiana Purchase Exposition of 1904 (St Louis World Fair), Marcod, a Filipino Igorot, never returned. Mixing original documentary footage from the fair with fictional and biographical sequences about his life in America, Fuentes uses the strategies of what Mary Louise Pratt has called auto-ethnography.[1] He positions himself as both a colonised subject and a diasporic intellectual. By turning around the premises of ethnography, Fuentes provides himself with an appropriate position from which he is able to take a tool of western imperialism, namely ethnographic film-making, and do what Gayatri Spivak thought impossible, namely represent his own alterity.[2]

The film uses a combination of original footage from the fair and from late nineteenth-century Filipino history and staged re-enactments. These are combined with fiction sequences and location shots of Fuentes searching for his grandfather's remains in the storage spaces of various museums and of the film-maker contemplating his life in such quintessentially American locations as a sport's stadium. He examines the endowment of these histories from a post-colonial perspective, for himself, his family and for the Philippine nation itself.[3]

Fuentes presents these histories through the trope of melancholia — the major device adopted by the narrative to theorise his experience of personal and national loss. In so doing, Fuentes doubly interrogates traditional and mainstream cultural tropes. While working in a documentary style, he takes up and re-works the *modus operandi* of conventional popular films such as *Out of Africa* and *Indochine,* in which colonising subjects express the pain of loss of empire through a melancholic state.

Bontoc Eulogy is a story about captivity — a reverse captivity narrative — in which the director traces the journeying of Marcod from his home in Luzon in the Philippines to the United States.[4] In 1904 Marcod and more than 1,000 Filipino men and women were transported from their homeland to be put on display in a recreated village at the St Louis World Fair. While most of the Filipinos who went to St Louis were returned, a large number of Igorots remained in America because of their great popularity with fair-goers. Many were signed up by fair promoters to perform at other sites in America and, as a result, never returned home (see Illustration 9). The display of the Igorots, and the failure of the authorities to return them home, was the subject of sustained protest, both in the Philippines and in America, at the time.[5]

At this, one of the largest exhibitions in the world's history, America's premier position as an industrialised western nation was on show. In addition the organisers sought to provide, by means of contrast, a remarkable number of displays of peoples, thought of as representing the 'primitive' past and the various stages of Darwinian evolution. As part of the show's interest in representing diversity and in demonstrating what was seen as the West's leadership in the unfolding of human history, a very large number of people, representing a range of nationalities, were selected from their homelands and taken to St Louis. As well as the inside of an American factory or 'the greatest corn exhibit ever made,' fair-goers could see Central African Pygmies, Patagonian 'giants', Japanese Ainu or chief Geronimo himself.[6]

The largest and most impressive installation was the one euphemistically described as the Philippine Reservation. The Philippines had, of course, become America's most recent colonial possession. The installation spread over forty acres to accommodate separate exhibits for the range of Filipino ethnicities drawn from the 7,000 islands of the archipelago, and included Moros, Negritos, Bagobos, Igorots and Visayans.[7] These are all named and described in *Bontoc Eulogy*'s ethnographic footage.

The most popular of the Filipino nationals among the fairgoers were the Igorots, of whom Marcod was a member. Igorots were of particular interest because they were thought to consume dog meat. They were also reputed to be headhunters. There are a number of sequences in Fuentes' film in which Igorots are seen killing and skinning dogs and eating their meat. As well, a number of dances which involve the use of fake human heads are included, together with footage showing the crowds who watched these displays. Unlike the majority of Filipinos, the Igorots were unchristianised and therefore a convenient advertisement for what could be presented as a fertile field for American missionary imperialism.[8] Christopher Vaughan, in his essay on the Filipino installation, notes:

> Introduced corporeally to Americans under the auspices of the nascent field of anthropology, the animists from the remote mountains of Northern Luzon quickly achieved prominence far out of proportion of their minority status, drawing huge crowds to see the scantily clad 'dog-eaters' in the flesh. The Igorots' exotic rituals and reputation as fearsome headhunters fed a ravenous public hunger for cultural difference affirming American's sense of remove from the spectre of 'savagery'.[9]

The underlying ideals of exhibitions like St Louis were also reflected in novels of the period such as H. G. Wells' *The Time Machine,* in which a scientist builds a contraption that allows him to travel through time encountering along the way a plethora of strange and exotic creatures and plants. Like the great exhibitions, Wells' novel fetishises evolution and progress, producing for the reader a range of primitive and modern phenomena read against each other in order to critique the 'progressiveness' of the West. Wells has his scientist exclaiming, 'Conceive the tale of London which a negro, fresh from Central Africa, would take back to his tribe! What would he know of railway companies, of social movements, of telephone and telegraph wires, of the Parcels Delivery Company, and postal orders and the like.'[10] The contemporary theme parks which have emerged all over the western world might be thought of as a rough comparison, in spirit at least, to the human circuses of the great world exhibitions. The difference of ethnicity is parodied by actors who masquerade as 'authentic' members of exotic cultures. Coco Fusco's contemporary performance pieces, in which she dresses in a range of exotic costume and has herself locked in a cage and placed on view to visitors of national museums, comments on the ethnographic gaze, scandalising the practice of placing human beings on display.[11]

Bontoc Eulogy deals with Fuentes' search for his grandfather, which begins following Fuentes' own college education in the United States. The film briefly traces his education in America, his subsequent marriage and his settling down in California. The subject of the narrative clearly is to be not only Marcod's fate but the story of the grandson, of Marlon himself, and his own grim endowment as a displaced person in America. From the first moments, the mood of the film is melancholic. This is achieved through the deployment of a narrative of loss and through a range of visual and sound strategies. For example, Fuentes adopts a tone of sadness in his voice-over narration, which gives way to pensive and lilting music interrupted at various points by the cheerful mechanical tones of a popular song of the period, 'Meet me in St Louis, Louis, Meet me at the Fair'. This produces a distinctly melancholic mood for the viewer as the tragic story is gradually revealed though Fuentes' monologue, pronounced in flat tones, as he contemplates both his grandfather's fate, as well as his own past and his future. In the cycles devoted to describing the colonial history of the Philippines, the camera pans in a leisurely fashion across fertile and beautiful country frequently shot through remnants of colonial architecture — picturesque arches and doorways which open onto village life. This slow camera painfully produces the substance of Marlon's loss.

The power of the film lies in the way in which Fuentes inverts the positions of both the ethnographic subject and the melancholic commentator, reading, as he does so, the history of colonialism through his own family's stories and through, in particular, the body of his grandfather Marcod. By employing the voice-over, and by using ethnographic footage, Fuentes destabilises both the ethnographic gaze and the ideals of the melancholic subject, recounting first the fate of one grandfather, who died in the fighting between the Spanish colonial government and the invading Americans, and then the fate of Marcod, his other grandfather, who left his homeland for St Louis and never returned.

As Fuentes surveys his own life away from his homeland, he positions himself as both a casualty of colonialism and as a displaced person living in the culture of the West. Fuentes speaks of living in two worlds, referring to: 'the sites and sounds of my new life and the flickering after images of the place I once called home'.[12] It is as though Fuentes carries the pain of the fate of both his grandfathers in the form of a generational and national suffering which is kept alive through his own predicament. This suffering is invoked in an almost exaggerated fashion by the use of footage about flagellation — ethnographic footage in which young men are seen scourging themselves and others — which is played at the very moment when Fuentes recalls the pain of his separation from his homeland.

In his discussion of the difference between mourning and melancholia, Sigmund Freud argues that:

> Mourning is regularly the reaction to the loss of a loved person, or to the loss of some abstraction which has taken place of one, such as one's country, liberty, an ideal and so on. In some people the same influences produce melancholia instead of mourning and we consequently suspect them of a pathological disposition.[13]

The symptoms of this melancholic disposition, Freud concludes, include profoundly painful dejection and loss of interest in the outside world, and culminates in 'a delusional expectation of punishment'.[14] Whereas the subject who mourns overcomes his loss, the melancholic refuses to relinquish his or her grief.

Further into his discussion, Freud reads the state of melancholia in the context of guilt which subjects may feel in relationship to the death of a parent (as a result of earlier hostile impulses against the parent). According to Freud, the state of melancholia itself may be interpreted as an attempt by the subject to punish him or herself over the death of a parental figure. The notion of punishment as central to the melancholic's experience is relevant to our understanding of Fuentes' presentation of himself as a melancholic subject in *Bontoc Eulogy*. Freud's theory of the causes of melancholia, namely an inability to overcome loss or to handle the feelings of guilt which may attend these feelings, helps to account for the film's images of flagellation and its fetishisation of the narrator's melancholic voice-over. Fuentes bears the pain of the deaths of his grandfathers, and, in a symbolic way, the loss or death of his country. In locating the substance of mourning and melancholia around loss, Freud's particular naming of the loss of one's country as a primary example of one of the causes of melancholia is therefore of particular interest in relationship to the arguments I have presented here.

The use of the panning camera with the voice-over of the film's protagonist in *Bontoc Eulogy* can be compared to similar strategies in a number of recent films about colonialism. In such well-known

Oscar-winning films as *Out of Africa* and *Indochine*, for example — films in which the protagonist is looking back upon a time spent in a former colony of a European empire now past or disintegrating — the use of melancholic references generated through a slow camera and voice-over is easy to identify. Who can forget Meryl Streep as the deeply melancholic Karen Blixen contemplating her lost life in Kenya in the opening scenes of *Out of Africa*? With the camera panning across a magnificent savanna landscape, Streep carefully articulates her lines in imitation of an upper-class Danish woman of the period speaking English with the thrice slowly and tenderly repeated phrase 'I once had a farrrrrm in Arrfricaaa'.

The last lines of the film, spoken rhythmically and following the story of Blixen's failed attempts at growing coffee in Kenya, her disastrous marriage and tragic love affair ends this hymn of loss:

> If I know a Song of Africa, of the giraffe and the African new moon lying on her back, of the ploughs in the fields and the sweaty faces of the coffee pickers, does Africa know a song of me?
>
> Will the air over the plain quiver with a colour that I have had on, or will the children invent a game in which my name is, or the full moon throw a shadow over the gravel of the drive that was like me
>
> Or will the eagles of Ngong Hills look out for me?

In *Indochine*, Catherine Deneuve's evocative performance as the colonialist French planter in mid-century Saigon looking back from Europe, with her adopted grandson, at her destroyed life in Indochina, relies upon a melancholic undertow for effect which is largely conveyed through Deneuve's own voice-over narration. As in *Out of Africa*, there is much slow camera work, this time around the plantation and the extraordinary villa owned by the French planter family, as well as arresting views of Ha Long Bay during the scenes involving the escape of the two lovers. While both films are imbued with a melancholic mood, Régis Wargnier's film has a great deal more bite, from a post-colonial point of view, than does Sydney Pollack's *Out of Africa*. While we feel that it is Africa which has defeated Blixen, it is clear from the closing scenes of *Indochine* — when her Vietnamese daughter refuses to return home and tells her mother that 'her' Indo-China no longer exists — that it is the forces of anti-colonialism which have thrown Eliane Devries out of Vietnam. It is a very bitter melancholia that overtakes Madame Devries, an enormous Swiss flag flapping behind her, as she sits with her grandson on a boat on Lake Geneva witnessing the formal withdrawal of France from Vietnam and the participation of her daughter in the ceremonies.

Other films which deal in some way with Europeans returning to colonial sites or fetishising the colonial expatriate experience through loss expressed through a melancholic or nostalgic mood cover a range of styles, and include Marguerite Duras' *India Song,* Claire Dennis's *Chocolat* and Michael Radford's *White Mischief.* Fuentes, as I argue above, consciously takes the position commonly occupied by the European colonialist, that of the melancholic, and appropriates it for his own political purposes.

It is relevant to my argument that all of the above films which I have selected as dealing particularly with colonialism through the trope of melancholia are about loss of country, in these cases, with adopted countries, countries which have been colonised by the film's protagonists who are almost always female. These 'daughters' are filled with melancholia at the loss of their adopted 'mother' countries. They seem to experience their separation as keenly as if they were losing their own mothers. In Blixen's poem to Africa, it is precisely the country itself which she mourns. In her soliloquy, Blixen seeks to implicate herself, to paint herself into the landscape in a clearly narcissistic way. She hopes that Africa will throw back an image in which she can see herself reflected as though her ego, her sense of self, is threatened as a result of her separation from it. 'Will the air over the plain quiver with a colour that I have had on?' asks Blixen. (Will) 'the full moon throw a shadow over the gravel of the drive that was like me?' Freud also linked the uncanny to the loss of the original birthplace, the womb of the mother. It is as if the loss of the adopted mother country gives rise to an acute melancholia which is imbued with a sense of the uncanny place — the colonised country as an uncanny double of the absent or lost mother.

Another film which we can compare with *Bontoc Eulogy* in this regard is *The Scent of Green Papaya,* the work of Tran Anh Hung, a Vietnamese film-maker living in France, about life in a well-to-do Vietnamese merchant's house during the last years of French colonialism. Adopting the melancholic mood of the colonialist film, this text looks, as much as anything else, at the impact of modernism and modernity on a traditional ruling-class Vietnamese family. Yet it is the passing of a grander, perhaps more elegant, lifestyle under colonial rule which is also mourned here. Tran Anh Hung in *The Scent of Green Papaya* and Marlon Fuentes in *Bontoc Eulogy* invoke the sites and, in the case of *Green Papaya,* the smells and sounds of home in a way which produces a melancholic mood. The sound of the green papaya being prepared for the evening meal, the chorus of crickets at dawn and dusk are powerfully evoked to represent Vietnam itself. As the director puts it:

> The scent of green papaya is a personal childhood memory. Everyone (in Vietnam) knew the gestures associated with the preparation of the papaya and, since the houses weren't sound-proofed, you often heard it being prepared in the house next door. You knew the sound because the papaya is hollow and when you hit it (with a knife) it makes a very characteristic noise. The papaya was really a part of everyday Vietnamese life.[15]

The sounds which signify Vietnam under colonial rule are, in the second half of the film, challenged by a new set, the discordant notes of modernist tunes played by the new young master on the piano, and the intrusive roar of war planes. These represent the collapse of the old colonial order and the ushering in of the new Vietnam. Like *The Scent of Green Papaya*, but unlike the mainstream films about colonialism referred to above, *Bontoc Eulogy* is a text which is written from the point of view of an expatriate colonial subject who considers the impact of colonialism on his country rather than that of a former member — albeit a female member — of the white colonial elite looking back on a grand era now vanished. The film is about what Fuentes, and by extension members of the Philippine nation, have lost as the result of the colonialist histories of their country from three centuries of Spanish occupation to the late nineteenth-century defeat of the Spanish by the Americans and their subsequent control of the Philippines. A lengthy cycle is given over to original footage in which Filipino nationals are seen to defend their country, at the behest of their Spanish overlords, against the invading American forces.

In his film, Fuentes produces his own subjectivity as emerging directly from the histories of colonialism in the Philippines. The film suggests that this is as a result of the incursions of foreigners into his homeland and that he finds himself a displaced person, a person without a country.[16] In doing so, he appears to have — at least from a post-colonial point of view — as much, if not considerably more, moral weight behind him than the coffee or rubber planter who mourns a former colonial possession, albeit a much loved one.

As discussed, all of the films about loss of empire referred to above are read through the eyes of female colonists. In these films it as almost as though the West has sought to distance itself from the colonial project by gendering it as feminine. In some of them, such as *Out of Africa*, the female protagonist is represented as ill, in this case as infected by a sexually transmitted disease. This may be a strategy which ultimately, as Laura Kipnis has argued, 'redeems the male experience of colonialism by coding colonialism as female'. Kipnis argues that the filmic spectacle of texts such as *Out of Africa* disavows the colonial project by displacing its scandal onto the female — representing colonialism in retrospect as a female enter- prise, and a diseased one at that.[17] I would argue there is more at stake in these representations — that loss of the motherland is linked irrevocably to the loss of the actual mother. Fuentes' posi- tioning of himself as a masculine protagonist produces a third level of inversion. It is as though he is able to authenticate his position by invoking his masculinity in this feminised context of melancholia.

As well as reading the state of melancholia as a trope which Fuentes invokes as a means by which to read the trajectory of loss with which his film is concerned, the story of Marcod and his cap- tivity becomes a focus through which Marlon recovers his past. It is through his recounting of the story of Marcod's absence, his search for his grandfather's remains, the eventual fetishisation of Marcod's absence/disappearance, and the pain of his own story, that Marlon finds his own identity. In order to explain his obsession with the past, Marlon quotes a Filipino proverb: 'He who does not look back from whence he came from will never reach his destination'.[18] The film — its documentary footage, the poetic recreations through which Fuentes recalls and tells the story of his life — through the threefold inversion, becomes the means through which Fuentes transcends his own loss of identity.

At the beginning, Fuentes talks about his experience of being a Filipino in America — of the imperative to lose cultural identity, to wear, as he calls it, 'a cloak of silence which makes us invisible, except to each other'. As the narrative unfolds, it recreates the story of Marcod's journey from the jungles, his life as an object of curios- ity — for the audiences that daily attended the St Louis World Fair to look at examples of 'the most primitive forms of humanity'. The film also tells of Marcod's probable violent end in a ferris wheel accident and explores the possibility of his remains being those of one of the many Igorots whose bones are still held in American ethnographic collections (see Illustration 10). But in the end the search for Marcod is fruitless: hard evidence of his grandfather's fate proves out of reach and Marlon is left in a state of mourning which he is unable to transcend.

The film offers a way in which Fuentes can give substance to his sense of loss. Through the story of his grandfather's captivity and his own captivity as a diasporic Filipino, Fuentes himself finds a kind of melancholy release. it is a release from loss of identity which nevertheless confines him in the painful pleasures of melancholia — in which, as the film ends, Fuentes seems destined to linger, a prisoner of the fate of his ancestors and kinsmen who were the real subjects of the St Louis World Fair. Just as we see Marlon creating his identity through his search as a melancholic diasporic subject, we also see, in the original footage which makes up *Bontoc Eulogy*, Marcod's captors, the American people at the St Louis World Fair, strolling among the Filipino people, subjecting them to their voyeuristic, colonising gaze, and in so doing creating their own identity as so-called civilised, modern, progressive Americans.

One final comparison can fruitfully be drawn between *Bontoc Eulogy* and Hollywood cinema. There are a number of unexpected parallels between *Bontoc Eulogy* and the classic Hollywood narrative, Vincente Minnelli's *Meet Me In St Louis* of 1944. These parallels reflect the fact that both films deal with the World Fair and that both are about the family. More particularly, I want to suggest that these two films can be read as an odd couple, or as inversions of each other. With hindsight, *Bontoc Eulogy* opens up new ways of looking at Minnelli's much-loved musical.

Meet Me In St Louis is a family melodrama, a boy-meets-girl story, in which the fair is referred to but never actually depicted. Even in the last scene, when the family attend the fairgrounds and Judy Garland marvels, 'I can't believe it, (it's) right here where we live, right here in St Louis', we don't see the fair itself — even in the final frames which are set in the grounds, there is no reverse shot in which the audience is invited to see what is actually on display (see Illustration 11). Instead we are given a glimpse of the excited bustling crowd of sightseers framed against classically proportioned buildings and classical statuary which suggest the architectural and intellectual achievements of the western world. Clearly if we did have shots of the various exhibits and the people on display, Minnelli's musical would have ended on a very different note. The delightful cries of the family would have sounded hollow.

Bontoc Eulogy is very painfully about who was displayed and who was looked at, and about the endowment of colonialism for one Filipino family living in the late twentieth century in the United States. *Meet Me In St Louis*, which nostalgically revisits the late-Victorian family while at the same time clearly locating itself within a 1940s sensibility, looks back with nostalgia to small-town, pre-modern city life while at the same time clearly embracing modernity.

While the subject of the fair itself is clearly avoided in *Meet Me In St Louis* — that of the display of the nations of the world, of primitive people against the modern inventions of the West — the subject of the colonised 'other' is indirectly referred to at various stages of the film. These references constitute a kind of repressed thematic or motif that runs through the narrative. For instance, there are the camera shots of the plaster statue of a black man wearing a turban, a highly orientalised piece, of the kind which were immensely popular with middle-class Americans in the 1940s and can today be still bought in antique shops in the Opera district in Paris, and no doubt in America itself. The statue has pride of place, located centrally in the living room close to where the stairs ascend, and is a focus against which many of the most romantic and dramatic moments of the film are played out. One such scene is that of the jungle song — 'Under the Bamboo Tree' — in which Tootie (Margaret O'Brien), the youngest child of the family, and Esther (Judy Garland), the eldest, do their jungle dance. Here, romance amongst 'primitives' is the subject of humour as the sisters regale the audience with a Vaudeville-style dance replete with canes and straw boaters as they sing the following song:

> Down in the jungles lived a maid,
> of royal blood though dusky shade,
> a marked impression once she made,
> upon a Zulu, the Madabulu
> and every morning he would be,
> down underneath the bamboo tree,
> awaitin' there his love to see and then to her he'd sing,
> to her he'd sing.
> If you like-a-me like I like-a you and we like-a both the same,
> I like-a say this very day I like-a change your name,
> cause I love-a you and love-a you true and if you-a love-a me,
> one live as two, two live as one, under the bamboo tree.

The film's use of this 'native' backdrop occurs immediately before the first episode in the courtship of Esther and John Truett and enables Tootie and Esther to sing of love as a 'primitive' passion in a manner which would not otherwise be possible in a respectable late-Victorian family. There is also another reference to the exotic/erotic in relationship to song and dance. In the opening scenes of the film, Tootie and Grandpa sequentially sing lines from the popular song of the period 'Meet me in St Louis, Louis, Meet me at the Fair' — the lines of which include 'We will dance the Hoochy Koochy, you will be my Tootsie Wootsie'. The term Hoochy Koochy came into usage in the 1890s. It originated with the craze for what is described by the Oxford Dictionary as 'the new negro dances', which became all the rage following their popularity at the Chicago Exhibition of 1893.[19] While Grandpa sings the song, he, in an unrestrained way, appears to dance the Hoochy Koochy, and while he is singing and dancing, he tries on a number of exotic-looking hats, settling finally on a fez. As a somewhat elderly and slightly senile character, Grandpa is permitted to act out these fantasies. Similarly, as a child, Tootie can speak about taboo or forbidden subjects with greater freedom than permitted the adults. It is Tootie who, in the penultimate scene, destroys the ice sculptures of a ghostly white family made earlier in the garden. Enraged by her father's decision to move the household to New York, taking them away from their heritage and their roots, Tootie smashes the family of ice, creating a macabre graveyard. Like Marlon, she rails against the thought of losing her heritage, but fortunately for her the imaginary world of the family musical can offer a happy solution.

Tootie herself is, during the course of the narrative, caught up in a number of childish games to do with imaginary devils who form a black underside to the 'grown ups' culture. She, as the naughty child, is continually silenced by everyone else. For instance, in the final sequence Tootie rushes in to meet the family gathered at the fair, saying: 'Papa we saw the flood. Big waves came up and flooded the whole city and when the water went back it was full of dead bodies — all muddy and horrible'.[20] As usual, no one pays Tootie any attention. With hindsight we could argue that the 'dead bodies' — at one level — represent the bodies of the indigenous peoples, such as Marlon's grandfather, who were put on display and sacrificed to the commerce of the fair.

In the end, the outcome of *Meet Me In St Louis* is an affirmation of American life, of small-town American values, of the modern family ruled over by the benevolent patriarch who has the interests of the family at heart and who is seen to be progressive by the film. But the unnamed, undetermined casualty of these values is another nation, another family, another father who are the victims of American modernity and progress. *Meet Me In St Louis* can look back with nostalgia rather than melancholia, because it's not mourning a loss — what is past is perceived as something better. For

Marlon Fuentes, on the other hand, there is no happy past or optimistic future to contemplate. He cannot look back with nostalgia but rather is overtaken with his melancholia, which by the end of the film has become a strategy for remembering and for fetishising his loss and the loss of his people.

While Freud may be right in recognising melancholia as ultimately a kind of illness which captures its subjects, rendering them powerless to act, except within the trope of the sad subject, Fuentes turns his condition into a weapon.[21] He turns it into the means through which he can draw attention to the story of his life, the means through which his grandfather can gain an identity outside of the one of human-animal, placed on display for the fair-goer, an example of what natural selection failed to select. Instead, Fuentes produces a critique of the monsters who looked, who sought to deprive his grandfather of his humanity and, in the end, of his life. Fuentes succeeds in naming his pain.

Chapter 12

Breeding out the black: *Jedda* and the stolen generations in Australia

Barbara Creed

What nonsense! You're no more like them than night is to day... The best walkabout for you is to come to Darwin with me next year. I have other plans for you, Jedda. I want you to go on living like a white girl, like my own daughter — Sarah McMann, *Jedda*

They took us around to a room and shaved our hair off... They gave you your clothes and stamped a number on them... They never called you by your name; they called you by your number — John's Story[1]

JEDDA HOLDS an unrivalled place in the history of Australian cinema. Considered at the time to be the first truly 'Australian' film, *Jedda* was a trailblazer for a number of reasons: it was the first film in which the two main stars were Aborigines; for the most part it examined racial issues (considered at the time 'box office poison'); it was filmed on location in central and northern Australia; it was Australia's first colour film; the first Australian film to be invited to the Cannes Film Festival, where it received high praise; and it was made by one of Australia's greatest directors, Charles Chauvel, in association with his partner Elsa Chauvel. From the beginning, *Jedda* was promoted as the film that 'only Australia could give the world', 'a really BIG Australian picture', a film whose significance 'restored confidence in a vision of a permanent local film production industry' (see Illustration 12).[2]

Jedda had its premiere in the Star Theatre, Darwin, on 3 January 1955. One Darwin reviewer stated that *Jedda* 'will probably prove to be the best advertisement Australia has had, since the discovery of the platypus'. 'With its fine interpretation of the Territory, its people and its scenery', he concluded, 'it cannot fail as an Australian film'.[3] Reviewers praised the film for its 'superb acting', 'breathtaking scenery', a script 'full of action', and its power to move the audience to tears — even the 'toughest territorians' brought out their handkerchiefs.[4] Hardly any reviews, however, commented on the film's central theme of assimilation and the predicament of the Aboriginal people living under the paternalistic control of a dominant white culture. *Jedda* was viewed at the time as a film which would promote an image of 'Australianness' — of an Australian identity based on the exotic rugged splendor of the Centre and on the wild beauty of its indigenous people.

Until now, critical articles have concentrated on the film's 'bold' intentions and 'radical, but not necessarily progressive' approach to questions of assimilation; its 'elegant' and 'triumphant' mix of scenes of 'scenic grandeur', 'ethnographic realism' — through its choice of untrained Aboriginal actors — and its sophisticated stylistic use of the conventions of Hollywood melodrama.[5] The film has been praised for making central an issue of great importance to Aboriginal — rather than white — culture, the violation of laws about correct 'skin' relationships. Robert Tudawali's performance as Marbuk, the male lead, has been praised as strong and 'dignified' — a far cry from the stereotype of the Aborigine. 'No rages, no downcast eyes, no sullenness, no drunken swagger', writes Colin Johnson.[6] Marbuk is proudly savage, seen as a 'fascinating sexual object' by the Aboriginal women in the film.

Charles and Elsa Chauvel's stated intention in making *Jedda* was to tell an authentic Australian story. They began looking for locations and casting early in 1952 and spent a year travelling through the Northern Territory collecting stories — finally they decided to merge the story of Namaluk,[7] a legendary outlaw, also the subject of Ion L. Idriess's 1948 novel *Nemarluk King of the Wilds*, with the stories they had gathered concerning lonely, childless white women who 'adopted' Aboriginal babies, raising them as their own.[8] *Jedda* tells the story of an Aboriginal baby from the Pintari whose own mother died in childbirth. The film's opening voice-over belongs to Joe, the narrator, who tells us that Jedda was 'born in the dust of the cattle tracks'. Bulu, her father, wonders if 'one of the lubras will take it'. None of the women come forward to look after the baby; Felix, the 'boss drover', and Bulu take the baby to Mungalla, the nearby buffalo station owned by their boss, Doug McMann. Felix says that 'Mrs McMann is *one* woman who understands these people'. The question as to whether one of the other 'lubras' will look after the infant is not raised again.

Baby Jedda is, at first, reluctantly taken in by Sarah McMann

(Betty Sutor), wife of Doug McMann (George Simpson-Lyttle), who is away droving. She is a stern, moralistic woman who runs her household with the assistance of a group of Aboriginal women referred to as 'station blacks'. Grieving and embittered over the recent death of her own baby, Sarah McMann at first rejects the motherless black child. When one of the women offers the baby to her she screams: 'Take it away!' At first the Aboriginal women look after the baby, naming her Jedda, meaning 'Little Wild Goose' before Sarah McMann takes over. Conferring on baby Jedda (Margaret Dingle) all the benefits of white culture that would have been the birthright of her own daughter, Sarah begins her project of civilising Jedda.

The first half of the narrative deals with Jedda's childhood and her development into a beautiful young woman. Sarah McMann clearly loves Jedda, who is torn between her love of and loyalty to Sarah and her desire to be with her own people. Interspersed with scenes of Jedda's development are a number of key episodes in which Sarah and her husband argue heatedly about whether or not Jedda, a 'full-blood' Aborigine, can be successfully assimilated into white culture. When Jedda, fascinated by a new arrival at the buffalo station — a proud, handsome tribal Aborigine named Marbuk — runs away with him in the dark of night it seems that Doug McMann is right: a wild Aborigine cannot be assimilated, and will always return to her or his own people.

In my view, it is now impossible to discuss *Jedda* without reference to the stolen generations. This chapter argues that, behind the heated discussions about assimilation which take place between Sarah and Doug McMann, lies another narrative, one which is submerged, camouflaged by the deliberate staging of debates about assimilation between the McManns who represent opposing views. Sarah supports assimilation, arguing that it is the duty of white Australians to take Aborigines into their homes, to 'civilise' them, to prevent the Aborigines 'slipping back'; Doug argues that, for the 'full-blood' Aborigine, full assimilation is impossible, that 'these people' will always respond to the 'call of the wild' which courses through their blood. This 'silent' narrative, repressed by the very staged debates between Sarah and Doug, concerns Jedda's origins and arrival at the homestead. She is, in effect, one of the children of the stolen generations. Her tale of 'captivity', represented in the film not as captivity but as a tale of Jedda's good fortune, occupies the first half of the narrative, where the drama is played out in and around the McMann homestead. With the arrival of Marbuk, the question of assimilation — and the related but unspoken issue of Jedda's origins as a stolen child — is dropped and replaced by a classic captivity narrative in which spectator interest is displaced away from assimilation and onto the outlaw couple and their flight into the desert.

The Chauvels conceived of *Jedda* as a story of 'Pygmalion in ebony'.[9] The reference to the Greek myth, which inspired George Bernard Shaw's 1912 play of the same name, refers to the idea of bringing into creation from some inferior source a woman of great beauty and accomplishments. In his play, Shaw transforms a poor London girl into a fashionable society lady who is a perfect but lifeless statue — she lacks the zest of the cockney girl. The reference to *Pygmalion* in *Jedda* is in the 'miraculous' transformation of a motherless full-blood Aboriginal girl into an attractive young woman who, in all respects — 'except for the colour of her skin', the script informs us — might be 'a white girl'. The aim of the government policy which gave rise to the stolen generations was to achieve such a transformation but on a much larger scale; the intention was to 'whiten' the Aboriginal race through the adoption, intermarriage and education — specifically of 'half-caste' Aborigines. Like the contrasts implied by the words of a popular song, 'Ebony and Ivory', 'Pygmalion in Ebony' suggests that Jedda's skin colour is black in the extreme — the opposite not of 'white' but of 'ivory'. Jedda is a full-blood Aborigine. Hence the task facing Jedda's adoptive white mother, the film speculates, will prove difficult, if not impossible.

Felix's earlier comment that 'Mrs McMann is *one* woman who understands these people', is not borne out by her relationship with Jedda. Ignoring her expressed desire to be with her own people, Sarah dresses Jedda in clean, dainty clothes, teaches her the principles of Christian living, educates her and, when Jedda grows older, teaches her classical music on the piano. Joe tells us that Jedda never 'learnt the language of her tribe or to chant the Pintari' songs. Instead, we see Jedda playing a classical piece of music — Mozart's Sonata in C. Sarah tells Jedda she wants her to be 'like my own daughter'. But Jedda prefers to make animal tracks in the dough during cooking lessons, rather than learn the alphabet. Chauvel emphasises Sarah's rigorous attempts at assimilation, even showing the frustrated Sarah snatching the little girl away from her playmates — whom she calls 'dirty black pickanninies'. The battle between Sarah and Jedda continues as Jedda grows into a beautiful young woman — played by Rosalie Kunoth (given the stage name Ngarla for the film).

The search for an Aboriginal actor to play the role of Jedda took two years and spread out over 20,000 miles. Chauvel was looking for a young Aborigine who felt free enough from 'tribal taboos' to act on film. 'The search went on for months', he said in interview. 'It became disheartening because we were trying to make women, who had been hopelessly suppressed for thousands of years "emote" freely before the cameras.'[10] Eventually they found Ngarla Kunoth, whom he described as 'a girl free of tribal restrictions, yet a genuine Aborigine; a girl of the Arunta tribe, beautiful, intelligent and a born actress'. Ironically Ngarla Kunoth — like Jedda herself — was brought up within the white community, a member of the stolen generations. The promotion booklet, *Eve in Ebony…the Story of Jedda*, states that: 'When still young enough to be taught, Ngarla was taken to St Mary's Hostel at Alice Springs, where she was raised in the ways of the white people'.[11] Presumably, the young actor had experienced in reality the role — her difficult journey from one culture into another — that she was to play in the film. Four years before starring in Jedda, Ngarla knew only her own language; she spoke no English.

The script refers to Sarah's domestication of her young charge as 'the taming of Jedda'; it became a crusade for Sarah McMann, 'a fanatical "Pygmalion" like crusade'. There is also reference to the 'miracle' of Jedda's transformation. Except for the colour of her skin, the film insists that she is white in every other respect. Due to proper nutrition 'her figure is round and well-shaped. Her feet are reasonably small and well-shaped. She wears her pretty pink frock with a natural grace. Her black hair shines like curled satin…' The most significant comment perhaps refers to Jedda's voice. 'Even the voice of the girl is that of a white girl — or perhaps better — for she has as vocal background the deep well modulated notes of the Aborigine.'[12] Jedda's beauty, her Pygmalion-like transformation, has been achieved precisely because of the intersection of white and black, the creation of Jedda as a primitive/civilised exotic other. Jedda is the Pygmalion beauty who arises from the intermarriage of two cultures in which the white bridegroom fashions his subaltern bride after his own repressed desires. It does not matter that in this instance the 'bridegroom' is a woman, the adoptive mother; colonial imperialism speaks through both sexes.

Jedda is meant to 'marry' Joe, the film's narrator who tells us in the opening sequence that he is 'the half-caste son of an Afghan teamster and an Australian Aborigine woman' (see Illustration 13). Joe is played by a British actor, Paul Reynell, whose skin has been darkened for the role. Like Jedda, Joe also appears to have been 'adopted' by the McManns. 'I was reared by a white woman and her husband who educated me and made me their head stockman.' No further mention is made of his Aboriginal mother or Afghani father — the reason for his adoption is never explained, which has the effect of suggesting that, like Jedda, he was effectively abandoned by his people. Joe delivers his narration in BBC documentary style — sounding more educated than the McManns themselves. Unlike Jedda, Joe has been successfully assimilated and indeed is essentially Doug McMann's surrogate son; Sarah McMann may have been his surrogate mother but there is no suggestion that the 'white woman' — as he describes her — has ever had any kind of intimate or familial relationship with him. Jedda appears to go along with the plan that she will marry Joe, until the day when Marbuk arrives at the station.

Joe's presence in the film is essential to Chauvel's plan — to include in *Jedda* representatives from a range of positions within Aboriginal society since colonisation. Jedda is a full-blood Pintari who has been brought up from birth by a white family and as such has no real knowledge of her own culture; Joe is a half-caste Aborigine who has been successfully assimilated, living primarily within white culture; Marbuk is a wild, tribal Aborigine who clearly holds white law in contempt and has no intention of forsaking his own society and culture. According to Stuart Cunningham, what happens in the film is: 'a systematic staging of conflicting positions that reflects a desire on Chauvel's part to document a full range of Aboriginal cultural spaces as outlined in the research document 'The Tribal Natives and the Reserves'.[13]

Never at home in her adoptive culture, Jedda is immediately attracted to Marbuk, who wears only a red loincloth, his beautifully muscled body on display for all to see. Notorious for absconding with the women belonging to other Aboriginal tribes, Marbuk holds a powerful attraction for the Aboriginal women at the station and for Jedda. Nita, one of the young women, tells Jedda that Marbuk has the power to 'sing a girl to his campfire even against her will'. Determined to make their film as authentic as possible, the Chauvels undertook anthropological research into the details of Western Desert culture and customs, as well as studying official government policies of the period. Nita's reference to the power of Marbuk's singing refers to the practice of 'love magic', that when a man sings to a woman she will be unable to resist him. One night, during a men's ceremony, Marbuk 'sings' Jedda out into the darkness where, mesmerised, she secretly feasts her eyes on Marbuk's body as he dances erotically in the moonlight. Later that night he steals Jedda away from Mungalla and takes her to join his own people on their distant tribal lands (see Illustration 14). Repelled by, yet attracted to, her abductor, Jedda's response is ambiguous, and throughout their long and dangerous journey together Jedda both struggles against her fate while remaining in thrall to Marbuk's physical beauty and allure.

The script is very clear about the sexual attraction Marbuk holds for Jedda, and — if anything — gives Jedda more agency than does the film in her response to Marbuk. In the script, Marbuck does not force Jedda to flee with him; rather, he stands before the fire — 'a great ebony figure' — and as he moves towards Jedda; the film cuts and takes us back to the camp where we see Jedda's empty bunk and hear Sarah McMann calling in vain for her daughter. His chanting, which drew Jedda out into the night, is described as 'passionate and compelling, seductive and promising'. Jedda is drawn from her tent 'as if compelled by some force'. There are more references to their sexual encounters during the journey to Marbuk's people. In one episode, he 'takes a handful of her wet dress in his hands and tears it from her'. This attraction is clear but in the film Jedda is also depicted as experiencing ambivalent feelings for Marbuk, resisting him at several key moments. Vijay Mishra, in his discussion of Aboriginalism in relation to orientalism, points out that the 'real strength' of Chauvel's film is that 'he avoids the total inevitability of genetic forces and leaves a certain space open within which Jedda may respond to Marbuk'.[14]

When the couple reach their destination, Marbuk's people refuse to allow them to stay. Marbuk has broken the fundamental taboo on marriages between men and women of the 'wrong skin'. The male tribal elders point the bone and sing Marbuk to death while the women beat Jedda mercilessly. The couple flee alone into the desert. Gradually Marbuk — under the curse of the elders — loses his grip on sanity and takes Jedda with him over a precipice. The couple fall to their deaths below while Joe, who has finally found them, watches helplessly. His voice-over narration, in which he mourns the loss of his beloved, concludes the film. Jedda's fall over the cliff can be read in several ways — a physical fall, a moral fall, and a 'falling back' into the other, so-called 'primitive' culture — the fall which Sarah McMann so desperately tried to prevent.

Jedda lends itself to a number of different, even opposing, interpretations, which is one reason why the film is so powerful. First, it could be argued that the violent death of the couple — both full-blood Aborigines — signifies symbolically the impossibility of assimilation programs. Unsuccessfully assimilated, Jedda cannot continue to repress her desire to be with her own people; she runs away with Marbuk only to discover she has broken a taboo on 'wrong skinned' relationships. Having broken both white law and black law, Marbuk is doomed from the start but his punishment, madness and death is brought about by the violation of his own people's law — a problematic narrative device. As Marcia Langton argues: 'Jedda rewrites Australian history so that the black rebel against white colonial rule is a rebel against the laws of his own society. Marbuk a 'wild' Aboriginal man, is condemned to death, not by the white coloniser, but by his own elders. It is Chauvel's inversion of truth on the black/white frontier, as if none of the brutality, murder and land clearances occurred.'[15] Unable to feel sexual attraction for the mild-mannered Joe, Jedda is drawn to the side of a man who embodies the wildness and passion for which she yearns; Jedda's tragedy is that, brought up in a white world, she doesn't know about tribal law which decrees that she and Marbuk are of the wrong skin. Such a tragic outcome, the film appears to argue, would never have befallen Jedda if Mrs McMann had listened to her husband and not attempted to assimilate Jedda. Cultures, this position asserts, should respect each other's differences — not try to destroy difference and assimilate the 'other'.

A second interpretation (and this is not necessarily in opposition to the others) is that Marbuk himself is a doomed figure. Like Jedda and Joe he is a victim of the effects of colonisation. Living away from his own people, working for white colonial bosses, he is neither a station black nor a tribal black. Marbuk is a liminal figure who takes pleasure in stealing Aborginal women from stations. His actions are clearly provocative. The anxiety of colonial culture about the theft of white women by indigenes is well documented (see the chapters in this book by Carr and Darian-Smith); however the theft of female station blacks brought up according to the conventions of white culture is a different but related issue. In stealing Jedda, the adopted 'daughter' of the station owner, the daughter who is white in every respect bar the colour of her skin, he strikes at the heart of white society. It could be argued — although this was not part of the Chauvels' intentions — that Marbuk is a freedom fighter (more akin to Idriess' depiction of Nemarluk) who steals stolen women back. Jedda's 'whitening' is evident in the way she talks to the Aboriginal women at the station: 'How is the pickaninny today?' she asks of one of her people. Girls of her own age fall silent when she passes by as if she were the white mistress. To some degree, Marbuk's actions fuels the colonial fantasy of 'black rape of white womanhood' — a fantasy historically used to justify reprisals on local indigenous people — as happened in Gippsland with the supposed abduction by aborigines of a white woman and her child (see the chapters by Carr and Darian-Smith). In this context, Marbuk's abduction of Jedda, despite the fact she is also black, follows the conventional pattern of the classic captivity narrative in which the captive is a white woman. Joe and the police set out to capture Marbuk and bring him to justice.

Jedda's journey with Marbuk into the interior is clearly intended to bring about the de-whitening of Jedda, who, in response, is effectively initiated back into the black nation. The film's title for its American release, *Jedda, The Uncivilised*, draws attention to this dynamic. Like a shamanistic guide, Marbuk takes Jedda on a journey of rebirth in which she learns the ways of her people: her civilised garb is torn and ruined; she learns to travel barefoot and sleep under the stars as she yearned to do from childhood; she eats snake; she experiences the dangers of living in the bush and near crocodile-ridden swamps; she has her first sexual experience in the wild. From the first moment Jedda sets eyes on Marbuk, she is 'enscorcelled',[16] unable to resist his call. The tragedy is that the couple — who do appear to be in thrall to each other, must die. Like Romeo and Juliet, Marbuk and Jedda have broken the customary marriage laws and must suffer the punishment. To complicate the tragedy further, Marbuk is driven insane by his act. Thus *Jedda*, in which the black male captures a 'whitened' black woman, is not a classic captivity narrative; Jedda is not rescued by Joe and re-civilised, as happens in films such as *The Searchers*. Having broken both white and black laws and contravened so many cultural codes, the couple must die. Further, Marbuk's construction as a 'criminal' serves to hide white criminality.

Finally, it could be argued through Jedda's terrible fall — taken to her death over the precipice by a man who is insane and of whom she is now terrified — the film creates in the spectator such a profound sense of loss that it is difficult not to feel that Jedda would have been much wiser to have stayed with Joe, the assimilated, 'civilised' Aborigine and not run away with Marbuk, the tribal 'primitive' outlaw. Marbuk's defiant laugh at the end, as he takes Jedda with him over the precipice, even suggests he is perversely delighted that she will die with him. If Jedda had followed Sarah McMann's wishes, she would be not have had to endure such a terrible ordeal, and fall to her death. The decision to represent Marbuk as a proud commanding figure yet also irresponsible and brutal only serves — it could be argued — to reinforce the film's pro-assimilationist discourse.

It is difficult to settle definitively for any one of the above interpretations, although I believe the film's emotional tone, at the end, encourages us to support assimilation. If Jedda had listened to her mother's voice, the film implies, she would, in the end, have been spared a shocking and brutal fate. In his final voice-over, Joe raises the question directly, stating that Jedda — a full-blood Aborigine — was too 'mystic and removed' to traverse the difficult path of assimilation in 'one short lifetime'. Assimilation works — but only for those like Joe who have already been 'whitened':

> Was it our right to expect that Jedda one of a race so mystic and so removed should be of us in one short lifetime? The Pintaris whisper that the soul of Jedda now flies the lonely plains and mountain crags with the wild geese. And that she is happy with the great Mother of the World in the Dreaming time of Tomorrow.

Most critical writings on the film concentrate partly on Jedda's personal tragedy as a victim caught between two cultures and partly on Jedda's flight into the unknown with Marbuk. The issue of the stolen generations has not been raised. In order to address this, it is necessary to consider the way in which the film draws on three related strategies in order — consciously or otherwise — to cover over or render invisible the fact that Jedda is, in essence, one of these children. These devices are: the staged debates between Sarah and Doug about assimilation; the presence of Joe, the half-caste, as the film's narrator; and the ideological function of the film's double captivity narrative. I am not arguing that *Jedda* is a consciously racist work, although the representation of the black women at the station is completely stereotyped. They are represented as were American blacks in Hollywood films, 'as docile, giggling, backward servants'.[17] In general the film's intention appears to be to present the plight of the Aboriginal people from a sympathetic white liberal perspective, but in so doing it draws upon narrative strategies that enforce racist values, ultimately constructing *Jedda* as a deeply contradictory, troubling text.

The stolen generations

In 1951 assimilation was established as an official policy of the Commonwealth government. Chauvel himself — according to his wife Elsa — believed cultural assimilation could be achieved through intermarriage,[18] which was of course the aim of assimilation. His daughter, Susanne Chauvel Carlsson, stated that *Jedda* was a 'simple plea for empathy on behalf of the Australian Aborigines, for whom he had a sincere respect'; he believed that they should not be 'catapulted into a framework of a conventional white society, for which they were not prepared'.[19] The 'stolen generations' refers to the practice by which Aboriginal and Torres Strait Islander Children were forcibly, or by other means, taken from their families and adopted by white families and other bodies. In her introduction to a collection of stories by the stolen children, published in 1998, Carmel Bird states the aim of the policy as:

> a long-term government plan to assimilate Indigenous people into the dominant white community by removing children from their families at as young an age as possible, preferably at birth, cutting them off from their own place, language and customs, and thereby somehow bleaching aboriginality from Australian society. This attempt at assimilation was nothing but a policy of systematic genocide, an attempt to wipe out a race of people.[20]

The stolen children, almost always 'half-castes', were taken from their families, 'by compulsion, duress or undue influence'.[21] They were the victims of a white society that tolerated shocking cruelties towards the indigenous owners of the land. They were either placed in government/welfare institutions or adopted by white European families in the hope they would lose their blackness. Henry Reynolds has described the consequences of the policy designed to 'breed out colour' as tragic, leading to worse acts of racism:

> For all their talk about 'civilising' and 'saving' and 'uplifting' the Indigenous people, white Australia could not accept Aborigines as equals even when they had grown up in European society and had received a western education. The caste barrier was impenetrable. Those who had most reason to assume they could become part of settler society were more rather than less likely to become objects of derision and abuse.[22]

Lorna Cubillo,[23] a child of the stolen generations, has drawn attention to the importance of skin colour in her account of how she was taken from her people. She was sitting with her grandmother by a campfire when two horsemen appeared. In order to try and save her from forced removal, her grandmother blackened her face with ash in order to give her the appearance of a full blood. The horsemen were in search of children whose skin was lighter, whose 'blackness' could be more easily bred out. Fred Schepisi's *The Chant of Jimmie Blacksmith* (1978), based on Thomas Keneally's novel, emphasises the problem of colour. Jimmie, also a stolen child, is brought up by a mission superintendant and his wife, who urge him to marry a white girl so that his children will be 'quarter caste'. If his grandchildren carry on this process then eventually the black will be bred out altogether.

Although not physically separated from her people, Jedda is essentially one of those children. Orphaned at birth, baby Jedda's future looks bleak. Although Sarah McMann, reluctantly at first, takes Jedda in, she does so without ever considering an alternative, that is, of returning Jedda to her own people. Given that Jedda is a full-blood Pintari baby, Sarah's decision to 'adopt' her and turn her into a station black without even considering the possibility of returning her to her people is cruel. Although the film reinforces the myth that assimilation was not a form of captivity, the baby is a captive. Assimilation is the answer. As we watch the opening scenes we are encouraged to think that the motherless baby is indeed lucky to be taken in by Sarah McMann and given the benefits of white culture.

Jedda was in production from early 1952 until its release in 1955. Not only was assimilation adopted by the Australian government during this period, the West was experiencing the social and political consequences of centuries of imperial rule, slavery and colonial empire-building. The year of *Jedda's* release, 1955, was also the year in which blacks in Montgomery, Alabama, boycotted segregated city buses. A year later, Martin Luther King emerged as the leader of black rights in the U.S.A. Four years later, in 1960, the Sharpeville massacres occurred in South Africa. During this period of international racial dissent and warfare, Australia lauded the virtues of an assimilation policy whose aim was not to bring about a properly functioning interracial society but to eliminate or render invisible the existence of indigenous people in Australia. Attitudes of white Australians to racial issues were clearly divided. There were debates in the media in the 1950s about a range of topics affecting Aborigines — in particular debates about practices of apartheid by local councils, country churches and hospitals in Queensland. An angry letter to the *Bulletin* expressed outrage at the fact that no 'full-blood aborigine is a citizen of the Commonwealth, although he may have worked for the white-man all of his life and paid taxes'. 'How many people in Australia know', the writer continued, 'that aborigine artist Albert Namatjira, who pays 500 pounds a year in taxes, is not technically a citizen of Australia, has no federal vote and is not entitled to any Commonwealth social services?'[24]

A nursing sister expressed outrage that at the Cairns hospital 'sick animals are treated with more loving kindness than many a black man in the north'.[25] However, reports of white Australian families 'adopting' Aboriginal children met only with praise. Although the individual families involved had the 'best intentions', the system itself was based on shocking cruelty and disregard for human rights.

Stories of adoption were regularly reported in the newspapers. One of the best-known cases of adoption was that undertaken by the Deutscher family. The *Sydney Morning Herald* ran an article under the heading: 'Family To Bring Up Native Girls'. It read: 'A Melbourne couple plan to bring up 3 Aboriginal girls, on a footing of equality with their own children, in their 15–room mansion at East Brighton'. The article states that the girls (Doris, Christine and Faye), who came from the Croker Island Methodist mission 180 miles from Darwin, knew little about their own parents. Mr Deutscher said he believed it was possible 'to integrate Aborigines into white families and should be encouraged'. What pleased him most, however, was the way his own children, Lorraine and Trevor, 'have accepted them'.[26]

The following day the *Sydney Morning Herald* editorial praised the effort of the Deutscher family. 'This lesson in assimilation has a double value — first, in setting a fine community example…and second, in providing evidence over the years on the capacity of Aboriginal children to develop in the environment of a comfortable white household'. The editorial referred to the slowness of assimilation policies and the problem of the growing segregation of Aborigines even in churches. It concluded with a statement about 'Aborigines as victims of white man's neglect'.[27] This patronising sentiment was expressed more directly in a letter to the editor of the *Bulletin* which stated: the degree to which Aboriginal people of 'settled areas are deficient in hygiene or moral conduct is also the extent of our failure as their protectors and mentors'.[28]

Indigenous children placed in institutions were subject to shocking cruelties. In comparison the Deutscher story reads like a fairy tale. Carmel Bird's collection of stories makes this tragically evident. In 'John's Story' the narrator describes his first encounter with his so-called protectors:

> First of all they took you in through these iron gates and took our little ports off us. Stick it in the fire with your little bible inside. They took us around to a room and shaved our hair off…They

gave you your clothes and stamped a number on them…They never called you by your name; they called you by your number. That number was stamped on everything.[29]

The intention of the authorities appears to have been to adopt methods akin to those used in prisons and detention camps to rob the children of all sense of their birthright, true identity and racial pride.

Assimilation and the threat of devolution

Jedda's life might appear to have been idyllic but nonetheless she suffered the pain of being cut off from her immediate family, her people and her culture. 'It is our duty', says Sarah, 'to bring them closer to our way of living'. 'No I'm not going to let the child slip back'. 'It is my duty to try'. Sarah is, of course, motivated also by the loss of her own daughter, but Doug fails to understand the extent to which his wife has displaced her loss onto Jedda, who is assigned the task of making good the mother's pain, of taking the place of the dead white child.

One of the film's most powerful motifs is that of the mother-daughter relationship, which Chauvel powerfully imbues with the classic psychoanalytic motifs (loss, displacement, sacrifice) of the Hollywood woman's film such as *Mildred Pierce* and *Imitation of Life*.[30] Doug argues that Sarah will only change Jedda on 'the surface', that Sarah won't be able to wipe out Jedda's 'tribal instincts and desires'. 'They don't tame', he states with conviction. Doug believes that it is essential to let Jedda join the yearly walkabout so that she can breathe again, 'regain her tribal status'. Doug appears to have a deep understanding of racial difference but, in the end, he still believes in the superiority of his own culture. He seems to see walkabout as an interlude in the annual routine of the station blacks; he does not suggest that Jedda should — if she wishes — return to her people.

The argument between the McManns about assimilation has the effect of highlighting the assimilationist debate while downplaying the much more basic question as to whether or not the McManns had the right to effectively 'adopt' baby Jedda in the first place. The film does not even raise this issue at all.

In one of the film's most moving scenes — one which clearly acknowledges the influence of the Hollywood melodrama — Jedda expresses her frustration at the piano. Playing a classical piece, Jedda stares at the Aboriginal instruments artificially arranged on the wall;

gradually the sounds of the didgeridoo, accompanied by chanting, drown out the classical chords and the distressed girl throws herself over the keyboard, thumping the keys in an attempt to block out the music of her own people. At first she begins by playing from a modernist piece (modernist music was, of course, associated with primitivism) and ends up banging out tuneless chords which merge with the sounds of tribal music. The so-called primitive artefacts on the wall unexpectedly offer up a different meaning: much prized by modernists who fetishised everything related to the idea of 'negri-tude',[31] which was seen as decadent and hence seductive, they signi-fy the impossible situation in which Jedda is trapped. She belongs both to her people and to the times in which she lives. She is the sub-ject of her destiny and the object of the voyeuristic and fetishistic gaze of a modernised western culture largely unable to understand its own desires and repressions in relation to the colonised other.

In the end, not even the tulle curtains, vases, grand piano and other insignia of respectability that Sarah has arranged in the order-ly living room can suppress Jedda's hunger for experience. Jedda longs to shed the trappings of white domesticity and proper femi-ninity, to go on the yearly walkabout and to understand the wild-ness that tugs at her heart. But Sarah forbids her keep company with 'those naked monkeys'. When Sarah asks her what she will do on walkabout, Jedda replies, with a clear suggestion of irony in her voice, that she will 'do what all the other monkeys do'. 'The best walkabout for you is to come to Darwin with me next year', says the uncomprehending Sarah.

Sarah's fear of Jedda's 'slipping back' refers to a widely held racist belief that the non-white races were interstitial, that is, easily able to bridge the gap between species, in this case, between human and non-human, human and animal. In his book on turn-of-the-century art and stereotypes of women, Bram Dijkstra discusses the popularity of the theory of devolution, that is, the belief that — drawing on Darwin's notion of reversion — that just as races evolved, they could also devolve, particularly the 'lower' races, as well as homosexuals, women and children.[32] Dijkstra examines a series of very popular paintings of the period, paintings belonging to the 'Nymphs and Satyr' genre, in which a woman is shown cavorting in the forests with a wild half/human, half/animal crea-ture. Dijkstra points out that frequently the satyr was given either Semitic or Negroid features — the idea being that woman, in dan-ger of devolving, consorted with the 'bestial Jew' and the 'bestial black'. Hence it was the duty of the male, the patriarch of the family, to rule over lesser beings such as women, children and blacks. Such a view was demonstrable in the circus exhibitions of indigenous people which were held as recently as the 1920s and 1930s. In her discussion of early captivity films, Rhona Berenstein refers to the case of 'Clicko', a South African man toured as a circus exhibit and described in the publicity 'as near like the ape as he is like the human'.[33] Sarah views the Aboriginal people as aligned to the animal world, referring to them as the 'naked monkeys' of the bush. She fears that if Jedda comes into close contact with her people she will also run naked, live in the dirt, and regress to an animal state.

Significantly, it is woman who signifies the possibility of devolution: it is her body that represents the unnameable, the abject, the threat of devolution, of crossing the boundary between civilised and uncivilised. Jedda is no exception. Her attraction to Marbuk is represented in the film not only as a desire to be with her own people but also as a woman's supposedly innate desire for the sexually primitive male. It is woman who responds to the call of the wild — to the possibility of a return to a primitive world given over to savage rites of sexual pleasure. Hollywood has explored this theme in many films about female captivity which include: the white slave films such as *The Sheik* and *Harem* in which western girls are kidnapped by dashing Arabian sheiks; the warlord films in which white women are captured by Asian warlords or bandits, as in *Shanghai Express* and *The Bitter Tea of General Yen*; the jungle captivity films of the 1930s in which a white woman was taken captive by a black African 'beast'; and the American frontier captivity tales in which a white woman is taken captive by American Indians, as in *The Searchers*.

In *Jedda* we see a double captivity at work: Jedda as a child of the stolen generations, is the subject of a reverse captivity narrative. The reverse captivity narrative occurs in those instances in which an indigenous woman (and sometimes a man) is taken captive by a dominant Caucasian culture. These have not historically been seen as classic captivity tales. Rather, indigenous captives were viewed as 'lucky' to be taken in by the white culture and given the so-called benefits of European civilisation. Jedda is caught up in a reverse captivity in relation to the McManns, and a classic captivity in relation to Marbuk. It is my contention that the film utilises a double captivity structure, that of the reverse captivity and classic captivity narrative, in order initially to explore white Australian anxieties about assimilation and miscegenation and then to bury this exploration of racial relationships under the excitement generated by the more conventional story of classic captivity.

In the classic captivity narrative, the white female hostage functions as a signifier of cultural boundaries. Historically, in American frontier tales for instance, stories of a woman's capture by indigenous people would circulate amongst the dominant culture, enabling its subjects to mentally explore the unthinkable (particularly in terms of sexual desire), even deriving gratuitous pleasure from such ruminations, while in the end mentally redrawing and reinforcing the moral, sexual and cultural boundaries that separate their own culture from the alien one.[34] In *Jedda* the classical captivity narrative serves various key functions.

Because Jedda is black yet brought up as white the symbolic meaning of her capture is clear. Like the traditional heroine of these tales, she is in danger of losing her innocence and virginity to the eroticised wild male. He threatens her as a woman and the values of the adopted culture that she represents. But because she is of the same race as Marbuk, there is an added attraction for the viewer — the possibility that her passion, once set free, will match the wild expression of his desire. Like other captivity tales, *Jedda* encourages the white spectator to relate to the expression of primitive passion — forbidden in civilised culture except in the cultural imaginary (painting/film/literature). Primitive passion — or any form of passion — is something which has no place in the McMann household. Mrs McMann's baby has died; the land is dry; her husband is absent. The white baby is buried and — as if by magic — her place is taken in the crib by the black baby, the 'little monkey'. Jedda — the laughing black baby, the playful girl, the desirable young woman — brings life back to the McMann household. Jedda is a perfect figure to signify the possibility of crossing boundaries — she is female, black, yet brought up white. She offers to bring back fertility and passion to the land rendered barren by white settlement.

Throughout their journey back in time, Jedda's response to Marbuk, as in many filmic representations of captive women (*The Sheik*, *Uncivilised*, *The Bitter Tea of General Yen*), is deeply ambivalent. At times she is drawn to him; at other times hostile. Those moments of attraction occur when Marbuk performs an act that is coded as primitive or as in harmony with the time-honoured rituals and practices of his people — such as the dance before the fire, and his life-and-death battle with the crocodile. Through the symbolism of flames from the fire, Chauvel makes it clear that Jedda and Marbuk have sex. Some critics have referred to what took place as a 'rape' but my reading is that Jedda actively desires sex with Marbuk. Marbuk evokes or brings to light in Jedda desires which — according to the dominant white culture — are incompatible with progress and civilisation. In his attempt to define the uncanny, Freud argues that uncanny things or feelings are those which invoke a sense of doubling and which 'ought to have remained secret and hidden'.[35] The sexual encounter between Jedda and Marbuk in the cave evokes the uncanny in that the fire of their primitive passion points to its counterpart, the repression of passion demanded by the moral dictates of white civilisation.

Thus the film ultilises the classic captivity narrative for two reasons. Firstly, it does so to draw audience attention away from the issue of Jedda's original 'capture' by the dominant white culture. The tale of reverse captivity is displaced by the more narratively exciting, erotic story of classic captivity with its emphasis on sexuality and eroticism. Secondly, it gives voice to white anxieties about assimilation, particularly the fear of the superior sexual prowess of the black male. These anxieties are raised in the text, played out, and then buried. Sarah McMann is the one who argues in favour of assimilation. She believes that it is the duty of the dominant culture 'to bring them closer to our way of living'. She hopes Jedda will marry Joe, the half-caste surrogate son who is already much closer to white culture. Joe is perfect for Jedda. Joe looks like an Aborigine but he has been assimilated; he even speaks with an impeccable English accent. 'Jedda, I want to marry you', he says. 'I want to build a little house for you and me.' Jedda replies by saying she likes an open roof. 'But you can't see the stars through a roof', she protests. She likes it best when she can feel 'wild', and see the stars 'dancing a big corroboree'. Then she can go barefoot with 'not too much dress'.

From the moment she sets eyes on Marbuk, barefooted and semi-naked in his red loincloth, Jedda is doomed. In scene after scene, Chauvel's camera deliberately eroticises and fetishes Marbuk's body. As his name suggests, Marbuk signifies the animalistic, primitive wild male — the mythic figure of the classic captivity narrative. He is akin to the sheik, the warlord, the wild chieftain. The other women tell Jedda about the powers of his 'mating' and how he can lure a girl to his blanket, even against her will. Eventually, this is exactly what Marbuk does to Jedda.

The McManns' annual buffalo shoot is a major event; they set up a large camp in buffalo territory far from the homestead. The men shoot the beasts and prepare their hides while the women cook and run the camp. Far away from the white world of Mungalla, Jedda is at last able to sleep under the stars. Her proximity to the wild also makes Jedda more vulnerable to Marbuk. That night, on hearing Marbuk's song, Jedda steals away from the camp and spies on Marbuk as he sings and dances. At one point he wraps a large python around his skin in a gesture that is overtly sexual. Listening to Marbuk's throbbing hypnotic chant, Jedda falls asleep under the moon only to awake and find herself alone with Marbuk. Seizing his opportunity, Marbuk creates a diversion by setting fire to the horse corral and forcing Jedda to flee with him.

In the script the sequence of events which take place in the film were originally set out differently. As Jedda makes her way back to the camp, four Aboriginal women emerge from the night and beat her mercilessly: 'Black hands claw and beat her head and tear her hair...She has broken a tribal totem'. Hearing Jedda scream, Sarah wakes and goes to her. When she tells Jedda it was bad of her to watch a man's corroboree, Jedda explodes. 'How do I know what's bad and what's good. You never let me know — never let me go walkabout — never let me learn corroboree.' What follows is a scene of great emotional intensity played out between Sarah and Jedda. During the scene, in which mother and daughter open up their hearts to each other, Jedda tells Sarah that she feels torn between her two worlds. She is glad to have her 'pretty room' and 'clean dresses' but at night she yearns to be with her own people, 'to dance naked under the moon'. Jedda takes Sarah's hand, 'passionately pressing it against her face'. 'I'm so shamed for this Bardi — so shamed.' Sarah tells her that she need not feel ashamed for wanting to be with her people and that things will change.

It is a great pity that this scene was deleted from the final shooting script. Not only does it bring Jedda and Sarah together in a cathartic scene of emotional release, it also makes it clear that the film is sceptical of the assimilationist position — particularly the view that Aboriginal children should be taken away from their people and their culture. The deleted mother–daughter scene would have offered us a much more complex picture of the relationship between the two, as well as a different view of Sarah who, in the film, is finally represented in a much less sympathetic light. Had the scene been included Sarah would have been depicted as someone who is able to learn and change. Mother and daughter might have engaged in an exchange of looks, as equals, rather than Jedda being represented always as the object of Sarah's loving but imperial gaze.[36] The Chauvels, however, deleted the scene of reconciliation between mother and daughter and instead concentrated on Jedda's awakening sexual desires and her abduction by Marbuk. Meaghan Morris rightly points out that not until Tracey Moffat's *Night Cries* does Australian film explore the 'emotional dependency of the white mothers on their black daughters, as well as of the daughters on their mothers' — a dependency which we see 'more intensely in *Jedda* after seeing *Night Cries*'.[37] We also see this dependency after reading the excised scene.

Jedda belongs to that variant of the classic captivity narrative that explores the story of the 'renegade captive', that is, the female captive who might find that living with an alien culture could offer an appealing alternative and cease to see herself as white. Jedda of course is not 'white' by birth — but she is in the context of her upbringing and her cultural affiliations. Because Jedda is caught between cultures in this way, the film can show her in a sexual context with a black male, exploiting the erotic appeal of the scenario while, in the end, demonstrating the failure of the 50s vision of assimilation seemingly brought about by what Joe, as narrator, refers to as Jedda's 'native' mind. Without the scene of emotional reconciliation between Jedda and Sarah, the film appears to be arguing that if assimilation is to work then the Aboriginal subject must be completely cut off from his or her people — the rationale behind the policy which led to the tragedy of the stolen generations. Why has Joe been successfully assimilated? Perhaps, because unlike Jedda he is — in his own words — a 'half-caste', someone who has already been 'whitened'. Further, he is male. As a woman Jedda is more of a liminal figure and hence more susceptible to the erotic appeal of the other.

In the end, Jedda's fate proves Sarah McMann wrong and appears to endorse the position of Doug McMann, who adheres to an essentialist view of race. It is, however, difficult to attribute any one position to the film — its various discourses clash and compete, marking it as a deeply contradictory text. McMann believes that nothing that Sarah does will wipe out Jedda's 'tribal instincts and desires'. Even though, as the script tells us, 'except for the colour of her skin; Jedda might have been a white girl', she is, in her heart, one with her people. Jedda, born black and brought up as 'white', is unable to resist the call of sexual desire and the so-called 'primitive' pleasures of a tribal existence; in the end, she finally returns to the ways of her ancestors and rejects Joe, the assimilated Aborigine, for Marbuk and the 'call of the wild' which she also, in the end, appears to reject.

Race & the problem of voice

Like Jedda, Joe is also a liminal figure. Joe has been successfully assimilated but his 'character' is not convincing — primarily because Joe is played by a white actor whose voice is used in a such a way as to constantly undermine the film's realism. Not only do we hear Reynal speaking as if he is Joe, the half-caste, we also hear him delivering the film's documentary-like voice-over.

Reynall's voice is identical to so many male voices used during the 50s and 60s to narrate documentaries, with the ring of authority, as if by 'the voice of God'. Yet, when we see Joe and listen to him speak from within the diegesis, as a character, his voice is different — less formal and omniscient. The mismatch of Joe's two voices creates a troubling effect, reminding us that the actor playing Joe is a white actor pretending to be black. Another noticeable difference is that Joe the narrator refers to the indigenous people in the third person — as 'they' — while Joe the character in the film refers to them as his people. For instance when he comes across Jedda at the piano he invites her to ride with him to meet 'our people', yet in the opening sequence he refers to the Aboriginal race as 'a race so old', not as '*my* race, a race so old'. When describing Jedda's emotions he refers to the 'pull of her race' not the pull of *our* race. This disjuncture is most marked in the final sequence when Marbuk, driven mad by the curse of his tribe, drags Jedda with him over the precipice to their deaths. Joe rushes towards them, pleading with Marbuk to let Jedda go. 'She no good for you', he cries in broken sentences typical of a pidgin English, 'she wrong skin'. It could be argued that Joe is using broken English here in order to communicate with Marbuk, the tribal Aborigine, but the fact that Joe in other scenes dissociates himself from the Aboriginal people suggests otherwise. His voice speaks in many registers in order to reinforce the film's position on assimilation. Joe's desperate pleas are in vain. As he stumbles away from the cliff edge, a broken man, the camera pulls up and away, focusing on a flight of geese in the blue sky above. At the same time the voice of Joe the indigenous character is replaced by the voice of Joe the 'white' narrator. 'Was it our right to expect that Jedda, one of a race so mystic and so removed should be one of us in one short lifetime?' Suddenly, Joe is identifying himself as 'white', speaking to a white audience. Jedda is from a 'mystic' race, 'so removed' in time: he is 'one of us'.

Then, as often happens when a text cannot resolve its own ideological contradictions, the narrative moves into the time-honoured realm of myth: 'The Pintaris whisper that the soul of Jedda now flies the lonely plains and mountain crags with the wild geese and that she is happy with the Great Mother of the world in the dreaming time of tomorrow'. It is significant that Jedda's people, the Pintari, have not been mentioned in the entire narrative apart from the opening and closing scenes. Only in her death is Jedda returned to the Great Mother who presides over the Dreamtime.

Joe's conflicting voices have a specific ideological function. Joe's official, narrating voice serves to distance him from the actual Joe and to give him — in the role of narrator — a superimposed identity, that of a white man. Thus, when he speaks of his desire for Jedda, the effect is to suggest his desire is also white or civilised — he wants a cottage for two and a picket fence while Jedda dreams of the open night sky. Successfully assimilated, moving between two worlds, speaking in two voices, Joe signifies the possibility that Aboriginality may be bleached from Australian society and the indigenous subject will become 'one of us'. Those who falter along the way will be returned to their own mystic race in the myths of time.

In *Jedda,* woman signifies the 'other' of the 'other' — it is woman who moves between the civilised and primitive worlds, and whose body offers the possibility of the impossible union. This would appear to be the role of woman in many films dealing with captivity and race — to enter into the imaginary relationship with the other in order to reinforce the racist and sexist myths which empower and strengthen the dominant culture. Yet, in so doing these cinematic narratives not only place strain on the cinematic apparatus itself (in this instance, in terms of voice and realism) but also establish a contradictory relation with the spectator; in relation to the narrative they demonstrate the failure of taboo relationships while in terms of image they play to the voyeuristic desire of the spectator to embrace the taboo, that is, that relation which, according to Freud, 'leads back to what is known of old and long familiar' (the desire for the primitive other).

In *Jedda,* the narrative of reverse captivity, that is, the tale of Jedda as one of the stolen children, is not properly explored. Instead the reverse captivity tale, that of Jedda's captivity by the dominant white culture, is masked by the introduction of a classical captivity tale, that is, of Marbuk's abduction and seduction of Jedda. In turn, the film's sexist anxieties about woman, the figure that is passed between men, is masked by the narrative's exploration of race. Jedda is both a stolen child and a stolen woman — but in both contexts her captivity is subordinated to the imperative of upholding the myth of white superiority that the dominant culture seeks to maintain at any cost. There are moments, however, when Jedda's desperate plea that she should be free to be with her own people drowns out the paternalistic voice of assimilationist rhetoric. The tragedy is that Jedda's freedom can only be realised in the impossible image of the jedda birds flying high above the cliffs at one with the mythical Great Mother and the Dreamtime.

Chapter 13

Blame and shame: the hidden history of the comfort women of World War II

Freda Freiberg

I

IN THE nineteenth-century captivity narratives of North America, the Pacific and Australia, white men save white women from brown or black men, following thrilling encounters in exotic settings with primitive cultures. The captivity narratives of North-East Asian women are quite different. They generally dramatise the pathetic experiences of women who are abducted by slave traders, sold by their families or sell themselves to support their impoverished families, and are incarcerated in walled houses of prostitution, unable to escape except by suicide. These captive women have provided male artists, actors and writers with popular dramatic heroines. In fiction, drama, art and movies these captive women have been represented as beautiful and artful creatures, suffering victims and/or deceitful seducers of men. The male adventurer in search of thrilling encounters in exotic settings leaves behind his everyday world of family responsibilities and work commitments and goes off to the exciting other world (called the Floating World in early modern Japan) of the 'pleasure quarters', to be pampered, titillated and entertained with wine, women and song. But this journey does not involve overseas travel, for the bordello district is situated close to home, involving a short coach ride or boat trip up the river.

Between the late nineteenth century and World War I, Japanese brothels were established in South-East Asia, initially in Singapore and Manila, but later extending as far as northern Australia. The prostitutes, known as karayuki, in these overseas brothels, were recruited from destitute farming families in Kyushu, who sold them into captivity and lived off their earnings, but later disowned them. The captivity narrative of the karayuki, unlike those of the Floating World courtesans and prostitutes, came to be told by the surviving karayuki themselves, as a result of the efforts of a post-war Japanese feminist sociologist, who sought them out and recorded their memoirs in a book called *Sandakan No 8* (the address of a Japanese brothel in Borneo). Two films were produced as a result of her research: a tear-jerking dramatised fiction (starring veteran screen actress Tanaka Kinuyo as the old karayuki), and a tougher documentary, starring a real karayuki veteran, telling her story on camera in the actual locations of her ordeals.

The elaborate network of brothels set up all over North and South-East Asia and the Pacific to service Japanese military personnel during World War II required the forced labour of large numbers of non-Japanese women — Pacific Islanders, Chinese, Burmese, Philippinas, and Dutch women resident in Indonesia, but especially large numbers of Korean women. Their narratives of captivity, once again elicited by sympathetic feminist scholars, introduced a new element into the narrative text. In addition to the issues of gender and class, raised by the karayuki captivity narrative, the issues of Japanese imperialism and racism figure significantly. It appears that the staffing and working conditions of the military brothels were organised according to racist criteria. Japanese prostitutes were reserved for the officers; Korean women were required to service the sexual needs of large numbers of enlisted men in quick succession and in appalling conditions. In Indonesia, where there was a short supply of Japanese prostitutes, attractive young Dutch women were removed from internment camps and obliged to work as prostitutes in officers' clubs, where the workload was light and the surroundings attractive in comparison with most military brothels. Nevertheless, the eruptions of long-harboured bitterness and painful distress in the narratives of all surviving captives indicate the physical and emotional trauma of their experience, exacerbated by its unspeakability.

It is only in the past decade, as a result of the concerted efforts of Korean, Japanese and Philippine feminists, that former so-called comfort women (*ianfu* in Japanese, the euphemistic term for military prostitutes) from Korea, Indonesia, China and the Philippines have come forward to testify to their wartime experience of abduction, rape, incarceration and sexual abuse by Japanese military forces, and the consequent trauma, sterility and terrible shame.[1] For a long time the Japanese government refused to acknowledge the veracity of their claims, counterclaiming that rape and prostitution have accompanied wars throughout history, that the services of prostitutes in this war were provided through independent private operators, outside official military channels, and that the motives of the women claimants were suspect — smacking of financial greed and an insult to the reputation of honourable Japanese soldiers. For a long time, too, the former comfort women had little support from their own governments, who were busily courting Japanese capital and industrial investment and did not want to antagonise the Japanese government and hamper official relations. In the neo-colonial climate, Japan was the strongest economic power in Asia and it was not politic to risk upsetting the old boys in power there by reminding them of their wartime atrocities and seeming to support the fifty-year-old grudges of a bunch of old women.

In this situation, liberal and feminist documentary film-makers in several countries took up the issue and provided a forum for former comfort women to relate their experiences and express their grievances. An examination of these films raises important issues of representation as well as history.

II

In 1995 I was commissioned by the International Documentary Film Conference in Melbourne to research and write a paper on documentaries made about the comfort woman issue.[2] A Korean film on the issue had been invited to the Documentary Film Festival, along with its feminist director, Byun Young Joo, who had previously made a documentary about the Japanese sex tour industry on Cheju Do island in Korea. Prior to this assignment, I had viewed and written on two other films which raised the issue: *Senso Daughters*, a 1989 documentary on the experience of women during the Japanese occupation of New Guinea, made by Sekiguchi Noriko, a Japanese postgraduate researcher at the Australian National University; and *Ianfu*, a Philippine short film screened at the 1993 Melbourne International Film Festival. For the research paper, I also viewed *A Half Century of Homesickness*, a co-production between Shanghai and Korean television; the Australian documentary, *Fifty Years of Silence*, directed by Ned Lander, centring on the experience of Jan Ruff, an Adelaide grandmother who was removed from an internment camp in Java and, along with other young Dutch women, forced to work in a brothel for Japanese officers; and *The Murmuring*, Byun's documentary, which covers the memories and current activities of a group of former comfort women now living in a hostel in Seoul, as well as those of three Korean women who remained in China after their traumatic wartime experiences in Japanese brothels, and were interviewed in Hubei province in 1994.[3]

All of these films attempt to expose a suppressed history through evidence and testimonies. When Sekiguchi made her film, none of the former comfort women had yet come out publicly, so their testimonies are absent, but she provides telling and disturbing testimony from former doctors, nurses and local residents familiar with the conditions in military brothels, and archival evidence in the form of photographs and documents pertaining to military brothel regulations. The Korean interviewees in Byun's *The Murmuring* testify to the difficulties of their post-war lives: the shame of their former occupation; their reluctance to marry, because of their sterility; poverty, neglect and illness (including suicidal tendencies). Their social disadvantages — lack of education and family support in early life — hamper their social confidence and political effectivity. The most disturbing verbal testimony is provided by one of the Korean women who remained in China, when she tells Byun how she was forced to submit to surgery in a Japanese military hospital to enlarge her small vagina. 'Japanese perverts' is what she calls her oppressors. Archival photos of the brothels are also briefly shown, but the strongest visual evidence is reserved for the final shot of the film — the wrinkled, disfigured, battle-scarred body of one of the victims. This is bodily evidence of abuse, evidence written on the body.

A Half Century of Homesickness also includes archival photographs, as well as location shots of former comfort stations in Harbin and Shanghai. The Japanese units stationed in the Harbin area, where Li Tianying (the subject of the film) was raped, imprisoned and forced to practise prostitution, are identified by name. *Fifty Years of Silence* employs archival photographs, old newsreels and home movie footage of life before, during and after the Japanese invasion of Java, and life in the internment camps. Jan Ruff's testimony — regarding her selection for, and her traumatic experience of, the brothel, as well as her acts of resistance — is verified by supportive testimony from a nun, a fellow internee, and other former inmates of the brothel now resident in Holland. At a reunion in Holland, she displays a handkerchief autographed by all the girls in the Semarang brothel on 26 February 1944. There is also on-the-spot documentary footage of her testifying at the International

Public Hearing in Tokyo in December 1992, and excerpts from Japanese and Dutch television, and press coverage of her testimony.

The voice of an academic expert is occasionally audible in these films. Kako Senda, author of *Jugun Ianfu* (San-Ichi Shobo, Tokyo, 1978) is interviewed in *Senso Daughters*. Professor Yun, a leading feminist activist working on behalf of the former comfort women of Korea, gives short expositions of their shameful treatment and neglect in both *The Murmuring* and *A Half Century of Homesickness*.[4]

As well as exposing a hidden history, through traditional methods of expository documentary film (i.e. archival evidence; the testimony of former victims, witnesses and experts; and location footage), some of these films invite a strong emotional identification with the victims through the use of the devices of film fiction. *Fifty Years of Silence* and *Ianfu* employ dramatised re-enactments of the ordeals of their subjects, the former using the services of the Jakarta theatrical troupe, Teater Populer, to portray (subjectively) the fear aroused by the arrival of Japanese officers (shown largely from the waist down, with emphasis on their heavy boots and long swords), the latter employing a professional cast of actors for all its horrific flashbacks. Slow motion is used for dramatic effect (to heighten and prolong moods of fear and foreboding, or of pathos) in both *Fifty Years of Silence* and *A Half Century of Homesickness*. In all three cases, the issue is personalised and individualised as one woman's story.

The recourse to melodramatics in these three films underlines the role of the surviving comfort woman as victim. Melodramatic elements are present not just in the scenes of dramatic recreation, but in heightened performances, close-ups of suffering faces, dramatic music and editing. *Ianfu* recreates the ordeal of a Philippine comfort woman: as a series of brutal atrocities in flashback appear, the elderly Carmen watches a television newscast reporting the 'coming out' of a fellow Philippine former comfort woman. She finally acknowledges that she was herself one, but has lived under an alias because of the terrible stigma and the shame she experienced. She is shown to be the victim of both Japanese brutality and Philippine prejudice against the *ianfu* — which was exhibited in insults and social rejection. This film is actually a short fiction, with actors portraying the characters, and the drama given over-the-top melodramatic treatment, but the shame and blame are real enough.

In the documentaries, too, melodramatic elements are present to a greater or lesser extent. Most markedly they appear in the television documentary *A Half Century of Homesickness*, a co-production between Shanghai and Korean television stations telling the story of one Korean comfort woman who remained in China after the war, and was recently located by a young Korean postgraduate student. There are numerous close-ups of the agonised and distressed face of Li Tianying sobbing, moaning, throwing herself about and mopping her eyes. Slow motion is used to underline the pathos of separation (from homeland and family) and reunion (with adopted family and home) in airport scenes of departure and arrival at the end of the film. Li Tianying's story is largely presented as a family melodrama: her life is dramatised in terms of Confucian family relationships. She is devoted to her old Chinese husband; her adopted Chinese son is devoted to her; the Korean student (who discovers her in China, arranges for her to visit Korea and acts as her interpreter there) assumes the role of a good daughter; Li Tianying insists on paying respect at the grave of the old Chinese man who rescued her at war's end, like a filial daughter; the former comfort women in Seoul represent themselves as her sisters; she prostrates herself at the graves of her grandfather, father and brother in Korea; and she has emotional meetings and partings with her surviving family in Korea. There is also much emotional weight given to reconnecting with the motherland — through the soil (especially in family graveyard scenes), the donning of national costume, and, most pathetically, through the singing of old Korean folk songs.

Political, economic and cultural factors all contribute to the recourse to melodrama. The resumption of diplomatic relations between South Korea and China after forty years of ideologically charged rupture, and current courting of Korean capital investment in China, means that efforts must be made to stress goodwill and friendship between the people of South Korea and China. Since the subject of politics is fraught with divisive tensions, the forging of kinship and friendship through personal relations is safer and preferable. The television co-production stresses the love and efforts of the Chinese foster-father, husband and adopted son for the poor, sick and abandoned Korean comfort woman. It stresses the common Confucian heritage of China and Korea, especially the virtue of filial piety; the common love of motherland; and the common experience of suffering at the hands of the Japanese. The melodramatic mode is required in part to mask the operations of economically motivated Realpolitik.

But the emotional performance of the protagonist is also necessitated by bitterness and shame, as a result of the social and cultural stigmatisation of the fallen woman in traditional Korean society. George Hicks, in his account of the testimonies delivered at the

International Public Hearing in Tokyo, notes the 'emotionally charged' performances[5] of North Korean and Chinese women, which he found in some cases excessive but which are clearly required to be necessary expressions of suffering and victimisation by subjects suffering from a great weight of guilt for the transgression of social codes.

There is a strong tradition of melodrama in Chinese and Korean cinema — where typically woman is the archetypal victim figure and symbol of oppression. But not just in the East. Melodrama in the West too has been the medium of expression for the oppressed classes, certainly in the nineteenth-century theatre and the early cinema — both of which catered to proletarian audiences. Western scholars on Victorian melodrama have noted that melodrama always sided with the powerless,[6] its basic energy was proletarian,[7] and it was the echo of the historically voiceless.[8]

A common trope of both Victorian stage melodrama and silent cinema melodrama was the unjust betrayal of a pure young lady, who is seduced (or raped) and abandoned, oppressed and victimised. There are elements of this scenario in Jan Ruff's narrative and performance, which stress her former desire to be a nun, her purity, her devotion to God, her desperate fight against her fate, not giving in but being overpowered by a physically superior force, a brutal power against which she was defenceless. Despite the superior 'dignity' accorded to her performance by some commentators[9] — produced by an amalgamation of class and cultural characteristics (erect posture, good grooming, carefully prepared and well-modulated speech, repressed emotion) — the dramatic effect of her self-presentation relies on its melodramatic base, betrayed innocence, just as do the presentations of the Korean, Chinese and Philippine women.

However, the former comfort women are not just represented as victims. In two of these films they are represented also as committed political activists. *The Murmuring* shows the tired and ailing old comfort women in Seoul tirelessly dragging themselves off to weekly demonstrations outside the Japanese embassy in Seoul, rain or shine, winter and summer; giving testimonies before commissions and hearings in Korea and Japan; and asserting claims for recognition by and restitution from the Japanese government. Jan Ruff is also shown giving public testimony, inspiring fellow Dutch women to come out publicly, supporting the Korean women, quoting scripture to endorse her political stance ('a time to be silent, and a time to speak'), and delivering a message of peace at a Japanese war memorial, which caused her Japanese interpreter to break down. The other former comfort women in Holland make explicit connections between their experience and the experience of women in Bosnia, and talk of their experience of forced prostitution as a 'war crime'. These former victims have become highly politicised.

Clearly, documenting the story of the comfort women has been a project driven by mixed motives and a variety of agendas. It can too easily fall into the category of Japan-bashing — as if militarism, misogyny and racism were specifically and exclusively Japanese diseases. The documentary films which I have discussed here are feminist initiatives in that they seek to uncover and expose areas of experience largely ignored by historians — to put women back into the story of history. Through employing the techniques of conventional documentary films — use of archival documents, interviews, on-location footage shot at the sites of past atrocities and recent political activism — some of these films also encourage sympathetic identification with former comfort women. This is achieved through the devices of melodrama — music, emotive performances, highlighting of subjective feelings in dramatic and traumatic predicaments through re-enactment, and artful use of camera and editing techniques. These films seem to say that the conventional detachment of the traditional documentary film cannot contain, convey or express the explosive mixture of pain and anger experienced by the comfort women.

Endnotes

Foreword

1. Gananath Obeyesekere, 'Cannibal Feasts in Nineteenth-Century Fiji: seamen's yarns and the ethnographic imagination', in *Cannibalism and the Colonial World*, Francis Barker, Peter Hulme, and Margaret Iversen (eds), Cambridge University Press, Cambridge, 1998, pp.63–86. The first of the sequence was "British Cannibals": Contemplation of an event in the death and resurrection of James Cook, explorer', *Critical Inquiry*, 18 (1992), pp.630–54.
2. *Critical Inquiry*, 18 (1992), pp.630–54. See below, p.256, footnote 10.
3. See below, p.247, footnote 1.
4. J. W. Davidson, *Peter Dillon of Vanikoro: chevalier of the south seas*, ed. O. H. K. Spate, Oxford University Press, Melbourne, 1975, p.13.
5. Anderson eventually got the skull to Banks, who passed it to his friend, Johann Blumenbach, in Göttingen, who used it as to represent the entirety of the 'American race': see Turnbull, 'Enlightenment Anthropology and the Ancestral Remains of Australian Aboriginal People', in *Voyages and Beaches: Pacific Encounters, 1769–1840*, Alex Calder, Jonathan Lamb, and Bridget Orr (eds), University of Hawai'i Press, Honolulu, 1999, pp.202–25.
6. See below, p.258, footnote 20, and p. 267, footnote 16.

Introduction

1. We are grateful to Mr Harry Persaud, Curator Library Collections, Department of Ethnography, the British Museum, for providing this information.

Chapter 1: Paul Turnbull — 'Rare work amongst the professors': the capture of indigenous skulls within phrenological knowledge in early colonial Australia

1. *Sydney Gazette*, 7 April 1829.
2. *Australian*, 10 October 1827.
3. Neil Gunson (ed.), *The Australian Reminiscences and Papers of Lancelot*

Threlkeld, 2 vols, Australian Institute for Aboriginal and Torres Strait Islander Studies (AITSIS), Canberra, 1974, vol.1, p.49.

4. Eve Mumewa Fesl, for example, has claimed that thousands were killed specifically for phrenological study, *Conned!*, University of Queensland Press, Brisbane, 1993, p.30.

5. Roger Cooter, *The Cultural Meanings of Popular Science*, Cambridge University Press, Cambridge, 1984.

6. George Mackenzie, a leading figure in the Edinburgh Phrenological Society, was optimistic about the capacity of indigenous Australians to be incorporated within settler society. See his *Illustrations of Phrenology*, Constable & Co., Edinburgh, 1820, pp.236–7. The skull of the Noongar warrior Yagan was similarly interpreted as suggesting that indigenous people were capable of 'moral education', Paul Turnbull, '"Outlawed Subjects": the Procurement and Scientific Uses of Australian Aboriginal Heads', ca. 1803–1835', *Studies in the Eighteenth Century*, vol.22, no.1, 1998, pp.156–71.

7. Berry Papers, Mitchell Library, MSS 315/46, ff. 247–8.

8. On the history of the pre-1832 body trade, see Ruth Richardson, *Death, Dissection and the Destitute*, Routledge and Kegan Paul, London, 1988.

9. Alexander Berry, *Reminiscences*, Angus and Robertson, Sydney, 1912, p.2.

10. William Rimmer, *Portrait of the Royal Hobart*, Royal Hobart Hospital, Hobart, 1981, pp.5–6.

11. An Irishman originally convicted in County Monaghan for stealing several pairs of shoes, Pearce, due to his rebelliousness during assigned service, earned a secondary punishment at the infamous Macquarie Harbour on Tasmania's bleak and isolated west coast. It was from the harbour that Pearce and several other convicts escaped, and on his recapture confessed to having helped kill and eat several of his fellow escapees. Perceived as deranged, he was returned to the Macquarie settlement, from where with one other convict he again escaped. This time he was recaptured with human flesh in his pocket, and was able to lead his captors to the remains of his companion. Some time after his execution and dissection, Henry Crockett gave the skull to a colleague, William Cobb Hurry, who in turn eventually presented the skull to Samuel George Morton, America's leading mid-nineteenth-century investigator of the relations between cranial form and personality. See Dan Sprod, *Alexander Pearce of Macquarie Harbour*, Cat & Fiddle Press, Hobart, 1977, pp.123–9.

12. *Tasmanian*, 12 January 1825.

13. Berry Papers, Mitchell Library, Ms 315/46, f.9.

14. Royal College of Surgeons of England, Library, Ms 275.g.9.

15. Christ Church College, Visitations of Dr Lee's Anatomy School, 1796–1860, 23 October 1821.

16. Michael Hoare, 'Science and Scientific Associations in Eastern Australia 1820–1890', Ph.D. Thesis, Australian National University, 1974.

17. Anon., 'Review of Field's Geographical Memoirs', *South-Asian Register*, 1828, p.161.

18. John Mulvaney, 'The Australian Aborigines, 1606–1929: Opinion and Fieldwork, Parts 1 and 2', in J.J. Eddy and F.B. Smith (eds), *Historical Studies: Selected Articles*, Melbourne University Press, Melbourne, 1967, pp.16–17.

19. Robert Reece, *Aborigines and Colonists: Aborigines and Colonial Society in New South Wales in the 1830s and 1840s*, Sydney University Press, Sydney, 1974, pp.87–9.

20. Paul Turnbull, 'Enlightenment Anthropology and the Bodily Remains of Indigenous Australian Peoples', in Alex Calder, et. al. (eds), *Voyages and Beaches: Pacific Encounters, 1769–1840*, University of Hawaii Press, Honolulu, 1999, pp.202–25.

21. 'On the Aborigines...', *Geographical Memoirs*, pp.228–9.

22. Joan Evans, *A History of the Society of Antiquaries*, Society of Antiquaries, Oxford, 1956, p.158.

23. John Gascoigne, *Joseph Banks and the English Enlightenment: Useful Knowledge and Polite Culture*, Cambridge University Press, Cambridge, 1994, pp.136–7.

24. Gascoigne, *Joseph Banks*, pp.124–5.

25. Evans, *Society of Antiquaries*, p.202.

26. Evans, *Society of Antiquaries*, p.153.

27. Richard Colt Hoare, *The Ancient History of Wiltshire*, 2 vols, William Miller, London, 1810–1821, vol.1, p.81.

28. Evans, *Society of Antiquaries*, p.203.

29. Hoare, *Ancient Wiltshire*, vol.1, pp.239–40.

30. Hoare, *Ancient Wiltshire*, vol.1, p.184.

31. Hoare, *Ancient Wiltshire*, vol.1, p.20.

32. John Oxley, *Journals of Two expeditions into the Interior of New South Wales...in the Years 1817–18...* John Murray, London, 1820, p.111.

33. Oxley, *Journals*, p.140.

34. Oxley, *Journals*, p.139.

35. Alan Cunningham Diary, microfilm 6034, New South Wales State Archives.

36. As I suggest in 'Outlawed Subjects', pp.156–71, and a forthcoming study of indigenous resistance to grave desecration.

Chapter 2: Chris Healy — Chained to their signs: remembering breastplates

1. Michael Taussig, *Mimesis and Alterity: A Particular History of the Senses*, Routledge, New York, 1993, p.237.

2. Perhaps the most famous of such photographs is 'Native Prisoners in Chains' by Frances Birtles, which appeared in *The Lone Hand*, 1 March 1911.

3. See *ADB* and M. H. Ellis, *Lachlan Macquarie: his life, adventures and times*, Sydney, Angus & Robertson, 1973.

4. Tania Cleary, *Poignant Regalia – 19th Century Aboriginal Breastplates and Images*, The Historic Houses Trust of New South Wales, Sydney, 1993,

p.7: 'The breastplates included in the exhibition reveal the following divisions: 15.2% Chiefs, 57.7% Kings, 4.3% Queens, 3.8% Royal Couples, 2.2% Royalty, 5.4% Rewards, 4.8% In Recognition of Service and 6.5% Unspecified Recognition. These groupings would be broadly representative of the entire range of extant breastplates'. The other major account of breastplates is Jakelin Troy, *King Plates: a history of Aboriginal gorgets*, Aboriginal Studies Press, Canberra, 1993.

5.   Cleary, *Poignant Regalia*, p.7.

6.   Cleary, p.11.

7.   Cleary, p.14.

8.   Cleary, p.17.

9.   Carl Lumholtz, *Among Cannibals: an account of four years travels in Australia, and of camp life with the Aborigines of Queensland*, London, John Murray, 1889, p.363 quoted in Troy, p.24.

10. Cleary, p.11.

1.   Cleary, p.11. Jimmie Barker makes in a similar point about 'inappropriate Kings' not being respected by Aboriginal people in his biography, *The Two Worlds of Jimmie Baker: the Life of an Australian Aboriginal 1900–1972*, cited in Troy, pp.41–42, where she also argues that changing Aboriginal responses to breastplates is a reflection of changing Aboriginal social relationships under pressure from colonialism.

11. I've borrowed this sense of indigenous people in an 'open-air museum' from the following passage: 'This flattening of cross-cultural sensory experience into visual diagrams and atemporal spatial metaphors exported the parlor to the field site and transformed the latter into an open-air museum'. C. Nadi Seremetakis, 'The Memory of the Senses: historical perception, commensal exchange, and modernity', in Lucien Taylor, ed., *Visualising Theory: Selected Essays from V.A.R. 1990–1994*, Routledge, New York, 1994. Troy, p.80, also notes the rarity of photographs of Aboriginal people wearing breastplates.

12. Cleary, p.44.

13. Cleary, p.37.

14. Cleary, p.35.

15. See Letter of E. Reid to E. Milne 13 October 1911, which reads in part, 'she [Hopping Molly] died some five or six years later and was buried on the sea shore…Some years afterward…I was informed that there were some human bones on the beach, and upon investigation, I found the skeleton of "Hopping Molly"…the identification rested upon the old residents of the place, who upon being shown the thigh and shin bone…declared it to be the leg of Hopping Molly, the knee joint having become completely ossified, which caused her to hop, and from which she derived her name…This was one of the best curios I ever saw…I finally decided to give it to [Dr Forbes who very much coveted the same]…a matter I have very much regretted ever since, as I should have never separated it from the plate [that of 'Billy Kelly King of Broadwater' the husband of 'Hopping Molly']' (Cleary, p.76). See Troy, pp.45–50, for a discussion of the role on Edmund Milne as a collector.

16. Cleary, p.15.

17. Cleary, p.17. Troy, p.39, also notes that '[Jimmie] Barker inherited a gorget from a man who had been like a father to him and it became a treasured relic'.

18. 'British disdain for the indigenous people has been well enough recorded as has been their utter inability to come to terms with a society that did not conform to their own. Their creation and distribution of "king plates" is a prime example. In Aboriginal society there were not kings, queens or chiefs — laws were made by a consensus reached by a council of tribal elders, who, unlike today's society, could not buy their way into the decision-making process. Membership was attained by virtue of acquired wisdom, experience and community respect...The king plates were an attempt to legitimise the procedure whereby regal status could be bestowed by the British but became, instead, degraded symbols of colonialism, engendered from the values of the conqueror and inflicted upon those whom they oppressed and whose "kingdom" they were in the process of stealing. The driving motive of the colonisers was to appropriate the land from its indigenous owners and establish themselves on it, but the lifestyle, culture and indeed the very presence of Aboriginal people directly conflicted this goal' (Paul Behrendt in Cleary, p.19).

19. Cleary, p.107.

20. Cleary's contention is that these 'badges of distinction' were 'an attempt at social control and domination', p.9.

21. Ellis, *Lachlan Macquarie*, p.355, quoted in Cleary.

22. Cleary, p.9.

23. *National Times*, 7 March 1981.

24. *Milton and Ulladulla Times*, 6 February 1906. See also National Museum of Australia, Breastplates File, 35/310 f.165. 'The breastplate was presented to Coomee by Edmund O Milne in 1909. He has first become acquainted with "Coomee" about 1868 when a boy attending school at Ulladulla. In those days it was stated by her that she remembered her grandmother speaking of "the first time the white birds came by", an allusion to the sailing ships of Captain Cook or the First Fleet.' See also the discussion in Troy, pp.35–8 and p.82.

25. Frederick McCarthy, 'Breast-plates: the Blackfellows' reward', *The Australian Museum Magazine*, 10, p.327.

26. Alex McAndrew, *Memoirs of Mollymook, Milton and Ulladulla*, Epping, NSW, A. McAndrew, 1990, p.30.

27. The only sense in which the inscription might be regarded as a fact would be the sense in which Coomee might have been regarded as the last 'full-blood', to use the contemporary expression. Whether Milne or anyone else actually believed that is of no consequence to my argument that the plate performs the conclusion of a seemingly successful genocide.

28. National Museum of Australia: 1985.59.374 (A-ON-93).

Chapter 3: Yves Le Fur — How can one be Oceanian? The display of Polynesian 'cannibals' in France

First I would like to thank Jeanette Hoorn, who gave me the chance to be here, as well as Marie Claire Bataille, Roger Boulay, Isabelle Guy, Sylviana Jacquemin and the director of the Gisborne museum for their precious information, and Amiria Salmond for her invaluable assistance in the writing of this chapter.

1. Baron Godefroy Van Swieten, quoted in Patrick O'Reilly and Raoul Teissier, *Tahitiens*, Repertoire Biographique de la Polynésie Francaise. Société des Océanistes, no.36, Paris, (1962) 1975, p.16.
2. Amanda Beresford, 'Omai' in *Terra Australis*, Art Gallery of New South Wales, Sydney, 1988, p.147.
3. H. Geust (1992) quoted by J. Fleming, 'The Renaissance tattoo' in *Res*, Spring 1997, pp.34–52.
4. Alfred Gell, *Wrapping in Images: tattooing in Polynesia*, Clarendon Press, Oxford, 1993, p.208.
5. Joseph Kabris, *Précis historique et véritable du séjour de Jh. Kabris, natif de Bordeaux, dans les îles de Mendoca, situées dans l'Ocean Pacifique*, circa 1817, Paris, Dentu, (15p); Rouen, F. Mari (15p); Paris, Herhan (13p); with a poem of two pages by M. C.: 'Le départ de Joseph Kabris de l'ille de Nou — Kaiva', Geneva, Luc Sestie (14p).
6. Ibid., p.15.
7. Picot Mallet, hand-written notation in the book.
8. Aimé Leroy and A. Dineaus, *Les hommes et les choses du Nord de la France*, Valenciennes, 1829, p.132.
9. Aimé Leroy and A. Dineaus, *Les hommes*, p.133.
10. J. Fleming, 'The Renaissance tattoo', p.50.
11. A. Leroy and A. Dineaus, p.132.
12. *Barnet Burns exploits. Life on the east coast a century ago Tattooed from head to foot An extraordinary story* in Times Jubilee Handbook, 1927, p.21.
13. *Barnet Burns exploits*, p.21.
14. Jean-Pierre Velot, 'L'exposition coloniale, Paris, 1931', in *Mwà Véé*, no.13, Nouméa, 1996, p.8.
15. Letter reproduced in the *Bulletin du Commerce* of the 7 November 1931, in J-P Velot, p.10.
16. J-P Velot, p.16.
17. J-P Velot, p.20.
18. J-P Velot, p.21.

Chapter 4: Mary Mackay — Captors or captives? The Australian Native Mounted Police

1. The word 'black' has had a chequered history, in and out of favour. I use it here as it was used in the nineteenth century, to distinguish the indigenous race from white settler society.
2. For a discussion of the 'statement' see Mary Mackay, 'Foucault's statement and paradigm change in 19th-century Australia', *Foucault: the*

legacy, Clare O'Farrell, (ed.), Queensland University Press, Brisbane, 1997, pp.180–89.

3. Homi K. Bhabha, 'The Other Question: Stereotype, Discrimination and the Discourse of Colonialism', *The Location of Culture*, Routledge, London and New York, 1994, p.70.

4. Several authors have tackled the formidable task of researching and writing histories of the various corps. See Barry Bridges, 'The Native Police Corps, Port Phillip district and Victoria 1837–1853', JRAHS, vol. 57, pt. 2, June 1971, pp.113–42; Marie Hansen Fels, *Good Men and True: The Aboriginal Police of the Port Phillip District 1837–1853*, Melbourne University Press, Melbourne, 1988.

5. For detailed accounts of conflicts, depredations, etc. see Bain Attwood, *The Making of the Aborigines*, Sydney, 1989 and Henry Reynolds, *With the White People: the crucial role of Aborigines in the exploration and development of Australia*, Penguin, Ringwood, 1990. I mention this among several publications by Reynolds because it includes a chapter on the native police.

6. Reynolds, *With the White People*, p.47.

7. James Backhouse, *A Narrative of a Visit to the Australian Colonies*, London, 1843, 502. Cited Barry Bridges, 'The Native Police Corps, Port Phillip district and Victoria 1837–1853', p.115.

8. For a detailed account and analysis of the various early attempts to form organised corps, see Bridges, pp.113–142.

9. Bridges, p.114.

10. Bhabha, 'The Other Question', p.67.

11. Hayden White, 'The forms of Wildness: Archaeology of an Idea', *Tropics of discourse: Essays in Cultural Criticism*, Johns Hopkins University Press, Baltimore, 1978, pp.150–182.

12. Hayden White, 'The forms of Wildness: Archaeology of an Idea', p.162.

13. Albert Memmi, *The Coloniser and the Colonised*, Beacon Press, Boston, 1965, pp.54–55.

14. Michel Foucault, 'Nietzsche, Genealogy, History', in Donald F. Bouchard, (ed.) *Language, Counter-Memory, Practice: Selected Essays and Interviews* by Michel Foucault, trans. Donald F. Bouchard and Sherry Simon, Cornell University Press, Ithaca, p.148. See also M. Foucault, *Discipline and Punish*, trans. Alan Sheridan, Pantheon, New York, 1977.

15. Thomas Baines, *Meeting with Hostile Natives*, Victoria River, 1855, oil on canvas.

16. Abdul R. JanMohamed, 'The Economy of Manichean allegory' in Bill Ashcroft, Gareth Griffiths, Helen Tiffin, (eds), *The Post-colonial Studies Reader*, Routledge, London and New York, 1995, p.20. The Manichean allegory operates as a series of binaries, e.g. good/evil, white/black etc.

17. See Candice Bruce and Anita Callaway, 'Dancing in the Dark', *Journal of the Art Association of Australia*, vol. ix, 1991, pp 79–104.

18. Frantz Fanon, *Black Skin, White Masks*, Grove Press, New York, 1967, pp.108–110.

19. Bhabha, 'The Other Question', p.78.
20. Bhabha, 'The Other Question', pp.74–75.
21. Thomas Browne, *Woman with dilly bag, water-carrier and fishing line*, watercolour c.1817, Mitchell Library, Sydney.
22. Apparently Sir Joseph Banks returned from his voyage with Captain Cook wearing a small tattoo but this was viewed as an eccentric gesture of the aristocracy.
23. Bain Attwood, *The Making of the Aborigines*, Allen and Unwin, Sydney, 1989. See in particular chapter 5, 'White Man's Laws' pp.104–134.
24. Port Jackson Painter, *Colebee*, watercolour, c. 1800. See also Peter Turbet, *The Aborigines of the Sydney District before 1788*, Kangaroo Press, 1989. See chapter 8, 'Death and its consequences' pp.82–91.
25. JanMohamed, 'The Economy of Manichean allegory', pp.18–24.
26. Henry Reynolds, *With the White People*, Penguin Books, Ringwood, Australia, 1990, pp.41–84.
27. Henry Reynolds, *With the White People*.
28. William Strutt, watercolours reproduced in Album, *Victoria the Golden*, the original held by the State Parliamentary Library, Melbourne. Reproductions of the Album in Fisher Library, the University of Sydney and elsewhere.
29. *White on Black: the Australian Aborigine portrayed in art*, Macmillan, North Sydney, 1974, p.49.
30. Fels, *Good Men and True*, page X.
31. Bhabha, 'Of Mimicry and Man: The ambivalence of colonial discourse', in *The Location of Culture*, p.88.
32. Bhabha, 'Of Mimicry and Man: The ambivalence of colonial discourse', p.90.
33. L.J. Blake, 'The Gold Escorts', *The Victorian Historical Magazine*, vol. 41, no. l, Feb. 1970, pp.244–264. Blake refers to Henry and William Dana as organisers of the native police participation, p.247.
34. Not the bible in this case but the learning process based in the English language.
35. Bhabha, 'Signs taken for wonders: Questions of ambivalence and authority under a tree outside Delhi, May 1817', in *The Location of Culture*, p.106.
36. Michael Taussig, *Mimesis and Alterity- A particular History of the Senses*, Routledge New York, 1993, p. 255.
37. Michel Foucault, *Discipline and Punish*, trans. Alan Sheridan, Pantheon, New York, 1977, p.36.
38. Frederick Walker, to the Colonial Secretary, Sydney, 17 December, 1849, vol.1, 1850 Copy Letters, Walker, Middle District, NSW Archives.
39. Ibid., pp. 126–7.
40. Frederick Walker, Copy of letter no. 2 from the Commandant of Native Police, Middle District to the Colonial Secretary, 31 December 1849, NSW Archives.
41. J. O'Sullivan, *Mounted Police of Victoria and Tasmania: a history of heroism and duty since 1837*, Rigby, Adelaide, 1980, p.7.

42. William Strutt, *Australian Journal*.
43. Fels, *Good Men and True*, pp.95, 220.
44. Edward Snell, pp.121–125 .
45. Jean Tregenza, Entry in Joan Kerr (ed.), *Dictionary of Australian Artists*, Sydney 1991, p.141.

Chapter 5: Gananath Obeyesekere — Narratives of the self: Chevalier Peter Dillon's Fijian cannibal adventures

I am deeply grateful to the National Library of Australia for a Harold White Fellowship in 1997 which permitted me to collect the material that went into this paper, and for Graeme Powell and other members of the Library staff whose courtesy and helpfulness made my stay a success. The first draft of this paper was written during my tenure as a Fellow at the Department of Fine Arts in the University of Melbourne. I thank my friends Jeanette Hoorn and Barbara Creed for making this possible, and my colleague Larry Rosen for his critical look at the manuscript and editorial help.
1.   La Perouse's expedition was meant to be a French response to Cook's exploration of the Pacific and its loss meant a great to French pride. Several attempts were made to find the wrecks of the two ships, including a famous expedition led by D'Entrecasteaux in 1792. For an account of this voyage see Frank Horner, *Looking for La Perouse: D'Entrecasteaux in Australia and the Pacific 1792–1793*, Melbourne University Press, Carlton South, 1995; see also M. Labillardiere, *Voyage in Search of La Perouse Performed by Order of the Constituent Assembly during the years 1791, 1792, 1793, and 1794*, volumes 1 and 2, John Stockdale, London, 1800.
2.   Peter Dillon, *Narrative and Successful Result of a Voyage in the South Seas Performed by Order of the Government of British India to Ascertain the Actual Fate of La Perouse's Expedition, interspersed with accounts of the Religion, Manners, Customs, and Cannibal Practices of the South Sea Islands*, volumes 1 and 2, Hurst, Chance and Co., London, 1829.
3.   Peter Hulme, *Colonial Encounters: Europe and the Native Carribean 1492–1797*, Methuen, London, 1986; Frank Lestringant, *Cannibals: The Discovery and Representation of the Cannibal from Columbus to Jules Verne*, University of California Press, Berkeley, 1997. Unfortunately, Lestringant, while providing considerable evidence for the invented nature of cannibalism, generally as a discourse on otherness, also continues to believe somewhat naively on the reality of anthropophagy in some of the cannibal narratives he recounts.
4.   References to Dillon's ego-ideal, 'the immortal Cook', is found in his *La Perouse's Expedition*, pp.xx and xxxi of the preface.
5.   J.W. Davidson, *Peter Dillon of Vanikoro, Chevalier of the South Seas*, edited by O.H.A. Spate, Oxford University Press, Melbourne, 1975. I am utterly indebted to Davidson's pioneering biography of Dillon without which my own work on Dillon would be much the poorer.
6.   Dillon, *La Perouse's Expedition*, p.29.

7.   Many of these Europeans were survivors of the American brig *Eliza* that carried 40,000 Spanish dollars and was wrecked in the Fijian coast. Survivors, deserters and beachcombers alike were anxious to collect as much of the scattered loot.

8.   This, and the following account dealing with the collection of bêche-de-mer is not in Dillon's *La Perouse's Expedition* but Davidson gets them from other sources, particular Dillon's deposition, which I will discuss later.

9.   This is Davidson's own inference though Dillon himself does not mention it anywhere and Davidson does not cite other sources either.

10.   I am a bit puzzled why Davidson on p.32 of *Peter Dillon* imagines that Robson had no trade goods when he has just arrived after a trading trip.

11.   Davidson, *Peter Dillon*, p.32.

12.   Davidson, *Peter Dillon*, p.33.

13.   Here and elsewhere I am only using Davidson's account. Unfortunately, this is not all very clear. Davidson is trying to reconcile several versions of Dillon's adventures: his shipboard version, the version in the *Sydney Gazette* of 23 October 1813, and his sworn Deposition of 6 November 1813. All three accounts refer to the same load of sandalwood but give different versions of it. Davidson tries to reconcile these versions which in fact refer to the same episode and are not easily reconcilable.

14.   Davidson, *Peter Dillon*, p.34.

15.   Davidson, *Peter Dillon*, pp.35–36. These are Davidson's words, not Dillon's; as Davidson recognises, there is no way one can clearly identify the place from Dillon's own vague description.

16.   Davidson, *Peter Dillon*, p.37; Dillon, *La Perouse's Expedition*, p.18.

17.   Davidson, *Peter Dillon*, p.38; Dillon, *La Perouse's Expedition*, p.18.

18.   Dillon, *La Perouse's Expedition*, p.20.

19.   Davidson, *Peter Dillon*, p.38.

20.   Davidson, *Peter Dillon*, p.39; Dillon, *La Perouse's Expedition*, p.22.

21.   'Cannibal Feasts in Nineteenth Century Fiji: Seaman's yarns and the ethnographic imagination' in Margaret Iverson, Peter Hulme, Francis Barker, (eds), *Cannibalism and the Colonial World*, Cambridge University Press, Cambridge, 1998, pp.63–86. Throughout my discussion I will often refer to Fijians as natives, as indeed Melville does throughout his text. The term does have derogative connotations when used in some contexts. In my own writings I speak of myself as a native and, for the sake of plain English, have followed Melville's use of the term in some parts of my text. Sometimes I have also used the term ironically.

22.   Dillon, *La Perouse's Expedition*, p.6.

23.   Dillon, *La Perouse's Expedition*, p.6.

24.   I have some doubts whether the dressing of the corpses by a priest comes from Fijian cannibalism; it might be based on another model, a European model of the quartering of criminals and traitors, though

it is not identical with that model. In Dillon's narrative the quarters are halved again and the body is cut into eight portions with the trunk separated. The presence of a priest, the parts wrapped in plantain leaves and cooked with the taro root in earth ovens gives the authentic native touch. I am not suggesting that Dillon invented this account de novo; more likely it was a version of cannibal corpse-dressing circulating among Europeans residents in Fiji and elsewhere in the South Seas.

25. Dillon, *La Perouse's Expedition*, p.9.
26. Dillon, *La Perouse's Expedition*, pp.11–12.
27. Davidson, *Peter Dillon* p. 36; Dillon, *La Perouse's Expedition*, p.14.
28. Dillon, *La Perouse's Expedition*, p.18.
29. Dillon, *La Perouse's Expedition*, pp.18–19.
30. Dillon, *La Perouse's Expedition*, pp.19–20.
31. Dillon, *La Perouse's Expedition*, p.24.
32. Davidson, *Peter Dillon*, p.17.
33. Davidson, *Peter Dillon*, p.17.
34. Peter Dillon, 'Extract of three Letters addressed to the Right Honorable LORD JOHN RUSSELL, Secretary of State for the Colonies, by the Chevalier Dillon, on the subject of Colonizing New Zealand, A.D. 1840'. London, ?1840, copy in Davidson collection, National Library Australia (NLA).
35. See also p.12 of *Peter Dillon*: 'Peter Dillon arrived as a seaman; but he was a man of unusual qualities of intellect and imagination, of courage and perseverance...In later life as a writer and companion of scientists and scholars in London and Paris, he joined that body of men — including his hero, Cook, and the impressionable Commerson — who had sought to explain the Pacific to the European world'.
36. *Sydney Gazette*, 23 October 1813; 'The Deposition of Peter Dillon' *Historical Records of Australia*, 1, pp.103–107.
37. *Sydney Gazette*, my italics.
38. Peter Dillon's deposition, p.106.
39. Peter Dillon's deposition, p.106.
40. Dillon, *La Perouse's Expedition*, p.14.
41. *Calcutta Government Gazette*, May 8, 1828, reprinted as appendix in Peter Dillon, *La Perouse's Expedition*, p.433.
42. Dillon has a further addendum not found in the *Calcutta Gazette*, though the unsuspecting reader would not have noticed it. Once again this addendum brings the *Calcutta Gazette* of 8 May 1828 in line with the La Perouse account: 'All the persons whom we have already mentioned as living among the natives of Bough [Bau] lost their lives in the melancholy contest, as did also Mr. Norman and Mr. Cox, officers; Hugh Evans seaman; and a Lascar named Jonno, belonging to the vessel; in all fourteen persons. The same day (the 7th) they left the dreadful place, and kept company as far as the New Hebrides, where they and the (the *Hunter* and *Elizabeth*) parted, the 22d ult'. (p.433).

43. Dillon, *La Perouse's Expedition*, p.27, my italics.
44. Dillon, *La Perouse's Expedition*, p.80.
45. Dillon, *La Perouse's Expedition*, p.81.
46. Dillon, *La Perouse's Expedition*, p.81.
47. Davidson, *Peter Dillon*, p.131.
48. George Bayly, *Journal of Voyages to Various Parts of the World written by Geo Bayly for the Amusement of such of his friends as feel themselves disposed to read it*, 1831, typescript in NLA among Davidson's papers, p. 67 (55) from original in the Hocken Library, University of Otago, Dunedin.
49. Dillon, *La Perouse's Expedition*, p.81, Dillon's italics.
50. Dillon, p.82.
51. Dillon, p.83.
52. Dillon, p.84.
53. Dillon, p.85.
54. Dillon, pp.89–91.
55. Dillon, p.93.
56. Dillon, p.93.
57. Dillon, p.94.
58. Dillon, p.94.
59. Dillon, pp.94–95.
60. Dillon, p.96.
61. Dillon, p.96.
62. Davidson, *Peter Dillon*, p.156.
63. This letter is printed as an appendix to Dillon's *La Perouse's Expedition*, p.411.
64. Dillon, p.411.
65. Dillon, p.97.
66. Dillon, p.98.
67. Dillon, p.100.
68. Dillon, p.100.
69. Dillon, p.101.
70. Dillon, p.101.
71. Dillon, p.114.
72. Dillon, p.114.
73. Dillon, p.116.
74. Dillon, p.117.
75. Davidson, *Peter Dillon*, p.138.
76. Davidson, p.144.
77. Davidson, p.14.
78. George Bayly, *Journal of Voyages*, p.50.
79. See Davidson, *Peter Dillon*, pp.97–98, for details. Bayly in *Journal of Voyages* has vivid accounts of Dillon cheating the crew of the *St Patrick* for their rightful wages when they were discharged in Calcutta. Fearing their anger, Dillon made his servant and Bayly pay the crew while he feigned illness and took to bed. Some of the men, says Bayly, threatened to seek him there but abandoned the idea 'knowing that Captain D never laid down without loaded pistols and

blunderbuss' (p.63). Bayly himself was cheated of '20 days pay' (p.64).

80. Bayly, *Journal of Voyages*, p.63 (50).
81. Davidson manuscripts at NLA, # 5101, box 10, file entitled 'Dillon comments'. Norah's (Honore Forster) italics. Norah's reference to the Bengali servant is derived from Bayly, *Sea-Life Sixty Years Ago. A record of adventures which led up to the discovery of the relics of the long-missing expedition commanded by the Comte de la Perouse*, Kegan Paul, Trench & Co, London, 1885. In it Bayly says that the Bengali servant was a 'stupid and careless fellow'. 'In a man of the Captain's irascible temperament they produced an almost daily fit of exasperation, vented on the unfortunate steward in cruel beatings and floggings with the cat-o'-nine-tails' (p.88). Bayly refers in detail to one such occasion: 'The poor wretch was seized up to the hammock-rail by the wrists, and his feet were made fast to a capstan-bar. The north-country man took his station, "cat" in hand, and ran his fingers through the cords to keep them clear. At a sign from the captain, he performed the duty of a boatswain's mate, by giving the poor old man a dozen lashes. Writhing in agony, he shrieked out in vain for mercy. There was not a shadow of pity expressed in the countenances of his tormentors (they said he was only a black fellow), and he was cast adrift after the execution, with his blood streaming from his wounds inflicted by this horrible instrument of torture, and (as the log book stated) "returned to duty".' The poor steward was discharged in Valparaiso on 13 May, (p.89).
82. Davidson, *Peter Dillon*, p.138.
83. Davidson, p.149.
84. Davidson, p.13.
85. Davidson, p.14.
86. Davidson, pp.13–14.
87. This is Dillon's second son, born 6 November 1821 and named Napolean according to the birth certificate, a copy of which is available among Davidson's documents. Interestingly he was also known as Joseph Napolean.
88. Davidson, p.266.
89. Davidson, p.289.
90. Bayly writes about his meeting Dillon in 1836 in *Journal of Voyages*, vol. 2. p.331: 'I had not long been in Sydney when I received a visit from my old Commander the Chevalier Peter Dillon: He had been appointed French Consul for the South Sea Islands and had lately arrived from England...'
91. Davidson, *Peter Dillon*, p.277.
92. Davidson, p.277. This imposture was very effective and navigators like Bayly believed in the reality of his consular rank.
93. Letter to the Duke of Bedford, 4 August 1841, Colonial Office 209/13, copy in the Davidson manuscripts in NLA, # 5105, box 10.
94. Davidson, *Peter Dillon*, p.311.
95. For the power of this fantasy see Otto Rank, 'Myth of the Birth of

the Hero' in *Myth of the Birth of the Hero*, Philip Freund (ed.), Random House, New York, 1959, p.65.

96. The date is probably a typological error and not a lapse of memory on Dillon's part.

97. Dillon, *La Perouse's Expedition*, p.13.

98. Dillon, *La Perouse's Expedition*, pp.156–57.

99. Dillon to the Duke of Bedford, Davidson Manuscripts, NLA, 5105, Box 10.

100. Gananath Obeyesekere, *The Work of Culture: Symbolic Transformation in Psychoanalysis and Anthropology*, University of Chicago Press, Chicago, 1990.

101. I still have the fantasy that Wijedasa's disappearance is a story invented by him in order to hide from the security forces and that one day he will appear at my doorstep not as phantasm but as Wijedasa in flesh and blood.

102. George Bayly in *Sea-Life* says that the 'marvellous escape of Dillon and Buchert was described to me circumstantially by both of them independently, and their accounts agree in every particular' (p.viii). Davidson takes this statement to show that the events that Dillon describes in the La Perouse account did take place. This is a mistaken inference. First, the Bayly and the La Perouse accounts are quite different in thrust and detail. Second, it is unlikely that Buchert confirms Dillon. Buchert could hardly speak English (and even Tikopian only imperfectly), according to Dillon (p.156). It is hard to believe that this native Prussian could retain the little English he knew as a sailor during his fifteen or so years in Tikopian self-exile. He might simply have assented to whatever questions Bayly put him. Third, knowing Dillon, it is not likely that Buchert would have the temerity to question his account.

103. My argument in this section is that the Bayly account was based on Dillon's own narration and it could only have been given during the trip from Valparaiso to Calcutta after picking up Buchert in Tikopia. Buchert's presence probably triggered Dillon's narrative imagination. Buchert would not contradict any of this, not only owing to his poor knowledge of English but also because he, like any subordinate, dared not contradict Dillon and face his explosive anger. The other possibility is that Bayly is retelling the story found in Dillon's own book; but there are incidents in Bayly's version that are not found in the La Perouse account. Bayly met Dillon twice in 'after years' but neither visit constituted a proper context for storytelling. The first visit was on 7 April 1828 when Bayly's vessel passed Dillon's as he was returning from the discovery of the French wrecks. He and Mrs Dillon invited Bayly on board but it a very brief visit. The other was between 12 October and 2 December 1836 in Sydney, according to Davidson's notation on a copy of Bayly's manuscript. Bayly says that because 'he had half starved me on the voyage from S. America to Calcutta I revenged myself by setting before him a variety of good

things and he took leave well pleased with his entertainment'. This too does not strike me as the proper context for storytelling. In any case Bayly tells us that Dillon used to regale them with stories on board ship, not during a dinner on land.

104. Bayly, *Sea-Life*, pp.9–10.
105. Bayly, pp.83–84.
106. Bayly, pp.11–12.
107. Bayly, p.12.
108. Bayly, p.12.
109. Bayly, p.14.
110. Bayly, p.15.
111. Bayly, p.16.
112. Bayly, p.16.
113. Bayly, p.17.
114. Bayly, Journal of Voyages p.37 [55]; this is elaborated in *Sea-Life*, p.17.
115. Bayly, p.18.
116. Bayly, p.19.
117. Bayly, p.19.
118. Bayly, p.20.
119. Bayly, pp.20–21.
120. Bayly, p.21.
121. Bayly, p.17.
122. Bayly, p.39 [55].
123. *Asiatic Journal*, vol. xxiv, 1827, pp.778–79.
124. (1) The Sydney paper says that the massacre occurred in 1826 when this is not the case, because it occurred in 1813. Though I have not been able to track down this particular Sydney paper the problem is easily resolved. Very likely Dillon gave an interview to the Sydney paper in 1826 and simply narrated the story and the newspaper reported it as if it were a recent event. (2) The *Asiatic Journal* says that according to this same Sydney paper 'the *Elizabeth* cutter, commanded by Capt. Dillon (whose name is familiar to our readers, as the discoverer of the traces of La Perouse, in the New Hebrides) visited the Feejees, in company with the *Hunter*' when it is clear that Dillon 'was an officer of the *Hunter* (not in command of the *Elizabeth* cutter.)' Dillon was first officer or commander of the cutter *after the Fijian adventure and when he was instructed by Robson to take the Buchert and the lascar with him*. However, it appears that Dillon is now inventing himself as the commander or first officer of the cutter from the very start, which is how Bayly also reports about him.
125. *Asiatic Journal*, p.779.
126. *Supplement to the Calcutta Government Gazette*, Thursday, 8 May 1828.
127. I *am* being facetious: needless to say, Dillon may simply have got the numbers of the dead all wrong; and in any case it is possible that the defenders of the Rock were those from the ship who did not die.
128. The La Perouse narrative also retains the number fourteen and lists their names of fourteen dead but, like the deposition, cannot account

for their deaths. However, there are six from the ship who died (not four) and eight (not ten) of the Bau residents. The two lascars in the Bau list are omitted and instead two seamen with Muslim names (Hassen and Mosdean) substituted.

129. Dillon, *La Perouse's Expedition*, vol. 1, p.32.

130. Bayly has two versions of this meeting. The first version is from *Journal of Voyages*, p.40 [57] and is close to Dillon's own and refers to their landing in Tikopia on 13 May 1826: 'He [Buchert] was tattooed all over the body and several marks on his face. He did not recognise Captain D. at first but after being reminded of some of the circumstances of the flight to the Feejees, he was overjoyed to see Captain D.' Bayly has another story in his later reminiscences in *Sea-Life*. Apparently Buchert recognised him but not immediately. Yet 'when Dillon held out his hand, and said, "Well, Buchert, my old comrade, how are you?" he started. That voice brought back the long past to his mind in an instant. He seized Peter's hand in a transport of joy, struggling to pour forth his delight in a mixture of German, French, English, Fijian and Tucopean...' p.150. I do not find this a reliable account and much prefer Dillon's own version and Bayly's first account.

131. Dillon, deposition, p.106.

132. Gananath Obeyesekere, 'Cannibal feasts in nineteenth century Fiji: seamen's yarns and the ethnographic imagination', in Barker, Hulme and Iverson, (eds), *Cannibalism and the Colonial World*, pp.63–86.

Chapter 6: Robert Dixon — Cannibalising indigenous texts: head hunting and fantasy in Ion L. Idriess's Coral Sea adventures

1. Aboriginal and Islander Dance Theatre, *Drums of Mer* (Program), Seymour Centre, Sydney, 1996.

2. Roland Barthes, 'The Death of the Author', in *Image Music Text*, Fontana, Glasgow, 1977, p.146.

3. Gananath Obeyesekere, '"British Cannibals": Contemplation of an Event in the Death and Resurrection of James Cook, Explorer', *Critical Inquiry*, 18, Summer 1992, p.641.

4. Steve Mullins, *Torres Strait: a history of colonial occupation and culture contact 1864–1897*, Central Queensland University Press, Rockhampton, Queensland, 1995, pp.14–15.

5. Marianna Torgovnick, *Gone Primitive: savage intellects, modern lives*, Chicago University Press, Chicago, 1990, p.148.

6. Mary Louise Pratt, 'Scratches on the Face of the Country; or What Mr. Barrow saw in the Land of the Bushmen', *Critical Inquiry*, 12.1, Autumn 1985, pp.119–43.

7. A. C. Haddon, *Reports of the Cambridge Anthropological Expedition to Torres Straits*, Volume V, [1904] Johnson Reprint Company, New York, 1971, p.v.

8. James Clifford, *The Predicament of Culture: Twentieth-Century*

Ethnography, Literature, and Art, Harvard University Press, Cambridge Massachusetts, 1988, p.21ff.

9. A. C. Haddon, *Reports*, p.2.

10. A. C. Haddon, p.34.

11. Foreword by William MacFarlane in Ion L. Idriess, *Drums of Mer*, Angus and Robertson, Sydney 1933, p.v.

12. Author's Note by Ion L. Idriess in *Drums of Mer*, pp.ix-x.

13. Beverley Eley, *Ion Idriess*, ETT Imprint, Sydney, 1995, pp.151,168,188.

14. Cited in Eley, *Ion Idriess*, p.310.

15. Elizabeth Edwards (ed.), *Anthropology and Photography 1860–1920*, Yale University Press, New Haven and London, 1992, p.13.

16. Ion L. Idriess, *Drums of Mer*, p.11.

17. Ion L. Idriess, p.12.

18. Marianna Torgovnick, *Gone Primitive*, p.151.

19. *Daily Telegraph Pictorial*, 12 November 1929, cited in Eley, *Ion Idriess*, p.75.

20. George Henry Lane-Fox Pitt-Rivers, *The Clash of Culture and the Contact of Races*, Routledge, London, 1927, p.xii.

21. Tigger Wise, *The Self-Made Anthropologist: a life of A. P. Elkin*, Allen and Unwin, Sydney, 1985, p.85.

22. A. P. Elkin, *Society, the Individual and Change with special reference to war and other present-day problems*, The Livingston Lectures, 1940, [No publisher], pp.74–5.

23. Terry Smith, 'Modernism, Modernity and Otherness', *Australian Journal of Art*, 13, 1996, p.158.

24. Jeremy Beckett, *Torres Strait Islanders: custom and colonialism*, Cambridge University Press, Cambridge and New York, 1987, p.46.

25. Cited in Nonie Sharp, *Stars of Tagai: the Torres Strait Islanders*, Aboriginal Studies Press, Canberra, 1993, p.181.

26. Sharp, *Stars of Tagai*, p.273.

27. Sharp, pp. 146–7.

28. Cited in Sharp, p.83.

29. Violet A. Roche, 'Badu Island, Torres Straits: where a woman is Superintendent', *Walkabout,* 4.9, 1 July 1938, pp.20–21.

30. Cited in Roche, 'Badu Island, Torres Straits: where a woman is Superintendent', p.142.

31. Eley, *Ion Idriess*, p.115.

32. Stephen Greenblatt, *Marvelous Possessions: the wonder of the New World*, Clarendon Press, Oxford, 1991, p.135.

Chapter 7: Paul Lyons — Lines of fright: fear, perception, and the 'seen' of cannibalism in Charles Wilkes's *Narrative* and Herman Melville's *Typee*

1. Michael Taussig, *Mimesis and Alterity: A Particular History of the Senses*, Routledge, New York, 1993.

2. Dening, *Performances*, Chicago University Press, Chicago, 1996, p.45.
3. On the philosophical complexities of 'perception', see Maurice Merleau-Ponty, *The Primacy of Perception and Other Essays*, James M. Edie (ed.), Northwestern University Press, Evanston, 1964. As Merleau-Ponty observes:

   > The things we see somehow manifest something that transcends both the features disclosed by vision and the consciousness of the one who sees. What there is then are not things first identical with themselves, which would then offer themselves to the seer, nor is there a seer who is first empty and who, afterward, would open himself to them — but something to which we could not be closer than by palpitating it with our look, things we could not dream of seeing 'all naked' because the gaze itself envelops them, clothes them with its own flesh. (Maurice Merleau-Ponty, *The Visible and the Invisible*, Claude Lefort (ed.) trans. Alphonso Lingus, Northwestern, Evanston, 1968, p.131).

4. Greg Dening, *Performances*, p.144.
5. Gananath Obeyesekere, '"British Cannibals": contemplation of an event in the death and resurrection of James Cook, explorer', *Critical Inquiry,* 18, Summer 1992, p.630 n.1. My essay follows Obeyesekere's thesis on the shift from cannibalism as symbolic structure (perhaps involving cannibalistic acts) to a conspicuous anthropophagy and extends to the American context his idea that 'inquiries produced a *new* discourse on cannibalism' that must be located in specific historical contexts of 'power, domination, and terror' (p.644). In the nineteenth century, as Obeyesekere argues, 'cannibalistic discourse [became] a weapon employed by all parties' (p.646); as the discourse around cannibalism 'evolves it begins to affect the practice' (p.650).
6. Rolena Adorno, 'The Negotiation of Fear in Cabeza de Vaca's Nalufragos', in *New World Encounters*, Stephen Greenblatt (ed.), University of California Press, Berkeley, 1993, p.52.
7. Sigmund Freud, 'Anxiety', in *Introductory Lectures on Psycho-Analysis*, ed. and trans. James Strachey, Norton, New York, 1989, pp.489, 492.
8. Julia Kristeva, *Powers of Horror: an essay on abjection*, trans. Leon S. Roudiez, Columbia University Press, New York, 1982, pp.210,2,42.
9. Herman Melville, *Moby-Dick, or The Whale*, Harrison Hayford, Hershel Parker, and G. Thomas Tanselle (eds.), Northwestern University Press/Newberry Library, Evanston, 1998, p.45.
10. Charles Wilkes, *Narrative of the United States Exploring Expedition*, 5 vols. Lea and Blanchard, Philadelphia, 1845. Melville echoes this passage in the prophecy in *Moby-Dick* that the doomed Pequod's materials 'could only be American'. David Jaffe considers Wilkes as a model for Captain Ahab, in *The Stormy Petrel and the Whale: some origins of Moby-Dick,* Port City Press, Baltimore, 1976. Concern with appearances before natives, expresses the desire to exhibit 'moral advancement'. Several American ships forbade officers to go ashore 'without appropriate uniform' or to

allow chiefs aboard without proper dress (leading to a scene Melville parodies in *Typee: a peep at Polynesian life*, Harrison Hayford, Hershel Parker, and G. Thomas Tanselle (eds), Northwestern University Press/Newberry Library, Evanston, 1968, pp.7–8. See the General Orders cited in Charles Stewart, *A Visit to the South Seas, in the U. S. Ship Vincennes, During the Years 1829 and 1830,* John P. Haven, New York, 1831, vol.1, pp.214–15; Wilkes ordered his men to shave their 'mustachios', an excess ridiculed in the press (see *Narrative*, vol.1, p.416).

11. Greg Dening, *Islands and Beaches*, University of Hawai'i Press, Honolulu, 1980, p.148. Dening characteristically distinguishes between what 'actually happened' and what 'significantly happened' (*Performances,* p.140).

12. Wilkes, *Narrative*, vol.1, p.306.

13. Horatio Hale, *United States Exploring Expedition: ethnology and philology*, Lea and Blanchard, New York, 1846, p.37; Fred Stuart, *Journal on Board U. S. S. Peacock* (National Archives, Washington, D.C., Roll 20), entry for 8 May 1840. Hale writes, 'The Polynesians may, without injustice, be called a race of cannibals' (p.37) and concludes, tautologically, that cannibalism would not 'exist among any but a sanguinary people' (p.15). Likewise, the missionary William Armstrong refers to Marquesans as 'a race of cannibals' in a letter to Charles Anderson, quoted in Herbert, *Marquesan Encounters*, p.63.

14. Wilkes, *Narrative*, vol.3, p.53.

15. Charles Wilkes, *Autobiography of Rear Admiral Charles Wilkes, U.S. Navy, 1798–1877*, William James Morgan, David B. Tyler, Joyce L. Leonhart and Mary F. Loughlin (eds), Naval History Division, Department of the Navy, Washington, D.C., 1978, p.457. Wilkes always emphasises visual economies of fear: not showing fear, noting the degree of fear natives display, and so on.

16. Cannibalism functions in several ways in Melville's work. Although at times Melville develops symbolic uses of cannibalism, this reading focuses on his concern in *Typee* with a cannibalism literalised by readers. Elsewhere, Melville's texts admit the difficulty of separating tropic uses of cannibalism — in which everything that lives and grows does so by consumption of something else — and the use of cannibalism to designate human eaters of human flesh (in antebellum America this 'cannibalism' functions as a ethnic signifier). There is certainly a sense in which the eventual embrace of the head-selling 'cannibal' Queequeg in *Moby-Dick* gets beyond the ignorant fear that first paralysed his powers of inquiry, and thus revises the semiotic system that necessitated the rejection of cannibals in *Typee*.

17. Melville, *Typee*, p.6.

18. William Arens, *The Man-Eating Myth: anthropology and anthropophagy*, Oxford University Press, New York, 1979, p.145. Caleb Crane in 'Homosexuality in Melville's Novels' *American Literature* 66, no. 1, 1994, pp.25–53, argues that in Melville's works one unspeakable subject (homosexuality) may be imaginatively conflated with another

taboo but discussable (because displaceable) subject — cannibalism. Following Eve Sedgewick, Crane compares the anxiety in the face of cannibalism to 'homosexual panic': 'The writer is attracted to something repulsive; he is not in control of his own actions' (p.32).

19. Melville, *Typee*, p.26.
20. Wilkes, *Narrative*, vol.1, p.366.
21. Wilkes, *Narrative*, vol.1, pp.367–68.
22. Nathaniel Hawthorne applied for the position of expedition historian, and James Fenimore Cooper and Washington Irving were considered. On the composition of the *Narrative* and its reception, see William Stanton, *The Great United States Exploring Expedition of 1838–1842*, University of California Press, Berkeley, 1975, pp.305–15. Stanton notes that, given the degree to which he draws on the journals submitted by his officers, Wilkes might best be considered a compiler (p.308). In addition to Wilkes's volumes, the expedition produced twenty-three volumes of 'scientific' information, including volumes on philology and ethnology.
23. Dening, *Performances*, p.105.
24. Nicholas Thomas, *Entangled Objects: Exchange, Material Culture, and Colonialism in the Pacific*, Harvard University Press, Cambridge, 1991, p.113. In David A. Chappell's *Double Ghosts: Oceanian voyagers on Euroamerican ships*, M. E. Sharpe, Armonk, N.Y., 1997, there are numerous references to the rapidity with which Pacific Islanders 'learned to drive a hard bargain'. 'As early as 1565', Chappell writes, 'the Chamorros of Guam used sign language to barter baskets of provisions for Spanish iron. But the bottoms of their baskets of food were filled with sand and stones' (p.9).
25. Wilkes, *Narrative*, vol.3, p.53.
26. Wilkes's versions of the Malolo incident are recorded in his *Autobiography*, pp.469–72, and in the *Narrative*, vol.3 pp.265–316. Several charges in the *Records of the Proceedings in the Case of Lt Chas Wilkes* (National Archives, Washington, D.C., rolls 26 and 27) involve cruelty to natives. The words 'ruled out' are scrawled over these; Wilkes was exonerated of wrongdoing against natives. In a bizarre twist, Wilkes was charged with leaving the survivors in Malolo 'exposed to the murderous hate and anthropophagian appetites of their cannibal enemies' (roll 26).
27. Wilkes, *Narrative*, vol.3, p.265.
28. Wilkes, *Narrative*, vol.3, p.285. Several journals stress the care taken to avoid exhumation, so it is likely that this was discussed on deck. The notion of exhumation for cannibal purposes may come from David Cargill, who reported the practice to Wilkes, who could not doubt information from 'such respectable authority' (vol.3, p.158). See *The Diaries and Correspondence of David Cargill, 1832–1843*, Albert J. Schutz (ed.), Australian National University Press, Canberra, 1977, p.39.
29. Charles Pickering's *Journal*, entry for 3 July 1840, quoted in Jessie

Poesch, *Titian Ramsay Peale, 1799–1885, and His Journals of the Wilkes Expedition*, American Philosophical Society Memoirs, Philadelphia, 1961, p.84. This evenhandedness often comes after witnessing, as a retroactive installation of empiricist consciousness. Most of the journals refer to cannibalism all along as established fact. Silas Holmes claims that 'in the northern islands, human flesh is a regular article of food and nearly all the officers of the other vessels have seen them cooking and eating it'. See *Journal Kept by Silas Holmes, Assistant Surgeon during a Cruise in the U. S. Ship Peacock and Brigs Porpoise and Oregon, 1838–1839–1840–1841–1842: Exploring Expedition*, 3 vols, Western Americana Collection, Beinecke Library, Yale University, vol.2, p.23. George Foster Emmons writes that the incident on the *Peacock* 'is *one* of many instances that has come to our knowledge while among these islds clearly establishing the fact that these people are *cannibals*, a matter that has been disputed by some & disbelieved by many who have not had a personal opportunity of knowing any better', in *Journal Kept while attached to the S.S.S. & Exploring Expedition, in the U. S. Sloop of War Peacock*, Western Americana Collection, Beinecke Library, Yale University, entry for 3 July 1840.

30. Wilkes, *Narrative*, vol.3, p.234.
31. Thomas, *Entangled Objects*, p.94.
32. Qtd. Jessie Poesch, *Titian Ramsay Peale*, p.84.
33. Peggy Sanday, *Divine Hunger: Cannibalism as a Cultural System*, Cambridge University Press, Cambridge, 1986, p.x. Obeyesekere challenges some of Sanday's evidence in 'Cannibal Feasts in Nineteenth-Century Fiji: Seamen's Yarns and the Ethnographic Imagination', in *Consuming Others: 'cannibalism' in the 1990s*, Peter Hulme and Margaret Iverson (eds) (forthcoming).
34. Thomas Williams and James Calvert, *Fiji and the Fijians*, George Stringer Rowe (ed.), Appleton, New York, 1859, p.167. Williams quotes 'the favorite wife of Tuikilakila' as saying the head is 'the portion for the priests of religion' (p.166). Williams' observation is copied (unattributed) by a later missionary, Basil Thompson, in *The Fijians: A Study of the Decay of Custom*, 1908; Dawson of Pall Mall, London, 1968: 'It is strange that the only act of cannibalism seen by any member of the United States Exploring Expedition in 1840 was the eating of an eye — a part of the body which was nearly always thrown away' (p.102). Thompson's assertion that cannibalism was at first unconfirmed but later ascertained suggests an increase in conspicuous anthropophagy as a result of the Euro-American presence.
35. Edward Belcher, *Narrative of a Voyage around the World*, Henry Colburn, London, 1843, vol.2, p.56. Belcher has this from Cargill, who recounts the episode in *The Diaries*: 'The head had been thrown into our garden during the night, with the intention no doubt of annoying us and shocking our feelings. The victims of war were brought from Verata, & were killed by the Bau people. 260 human beings were killed & brought away by victors to be roasted and eaten' (p.159). The

skull is clearly part of a discourse of terror and insult, a point which perhaps lies behind the comment Williams recounts, cited in the previous note.

36. James Cook, *The Voyage of the 'Resolution' and 'Adventure' 1772–1775*, vol.2 of *The Journals of Captain Cook of His Voyages of Discovery*, J. C. Beaglehole (ed.), Hakluyt Society, Cambridge, 1961, p.292. Obeyesekere discusses this passage in 'British Cannibals', p.637.

37. Michael Hayes, 'Consuming Cannibalism: The Body in Australia's Pacific Archive', (unpublished manuscript). On Banks' role in procuring skeletal remains, see Paul Turnbull, 'Enlightenment Anthropology and the Ancestral Remains of Australian Aboriginal People', in *Voyagers and Beaches: Europe and the Pacific, 1769–1840*, Alex Calder, Jonathan Lamb, and Bridget Orr (eds), University of Hawai'i Press, Honolulu (1999). See their introduction for an exemplary discussion of the challenge of finding 'a mode of ethnographizing European voyages on the one hand, and of reciting local histories in their own terms, without falling foul of the very categories which make the reversal necessary in the first place'.

38. In *The Man-Eating Myth*, Arens uses the example of traditional insults involving cannibalism to argue that the fact that many cultures, including western ones, have conventional phrases or stories relating to cannibalism, does not prove ritual cannibalism. In this case, however, there does seem to be abundant evidence of ritual eyeball consumption. See for instance the chapter 'Killing the Cannibal King' in Dennis Kawaharada, *Storied Landscapes: Hawaiian literature & place* (Noio, Honolulu, 1999), which cites David Malo, *Hawaiian Antiquities* (Bishop Museum, Honolulu, 1951), pp.152, 174–5. See also Dening's account of Pomare (in *Performances*, p.41) and Obeyesekere ('British Cannibalism') on how, in Tahiti and Hawai'i, sacrifice is often associated with 'a chief symbolically accepting the eye of the sacrificial victim' (p.653). Kawaharada argues that, outside of such instances as ritual eyeball consumption, cannibalism is condemned within Hawaiian legend and history as contrary to Hawaiian values.

39. Wilkes draws on George Foster Emmons, *Journal Kept while attached to the S.S.S. & Exploring Expedition, in the U.S. Sloop of War Peacock*, 3 vols (Western Americana Collection, Beinecke Library, Yale): 'Some natives…came alongside and produced the skull of one out of 3 prisoners which they reported they had lately taken — killed — baked & devoured — this skull was yet warm from the fire, had a little flesh left upon it, & bore the prints of teeth' (entry for 3 July, 1840).

40. George Foster Emmons, *Journal*. Entry for 3 July 1840.

41. Simeon Stearns, *Journal on Board U. S. S. 'Vincennes' of the So-called 'Wilkes Exploring Expedition' to the South Pacific 8/13/39–5/9/40* (in the New York Public Library, Rare Book Room), entry for 30 July.

42. The label for item no. 29 reads: 'Cranium of a Fiji who was killed, with others by a neighboring tribe, and portions of their cooked bodies taken on board the U.S. Ship *Peacock* for sale, at Naloa bay, Island

of Vanu-levu, July 3rd, 1840'. Quoted in Poesch, who notes, 'Vendovi's skull is still carefully stored among the ethnological collections of the Smithsonian Institution' (*Titian Ramsay Peele*, p.84). Vendori was a Fijian chief who was captured, taken to America, and died while there.

43. Stanton, *Exploring Expedition*, 203, quotes John W. W. Dyes, *Journal of John W. W. Dyes Aboard the Vincennes* (National Archives, Washington, D.C., Roll 11); the entry for 3 July 1840 concludes, 'The smell the smell I never shall forget it it inough to make a man blood run cold to think of sutch cannibalism these people treated it as...if they had been eating pastrey'. Stanton is not the target here; rather, as Arens puts it, if the idea of avid cannibalism is 'commonly accepted without adequate documentation, then the reason for this state of affairs is an even more intriguing problem' (p.9). Much Melville criticism adopts a highly uncritical attitude toward 'evidence' of Marquesan cannibalism. For instance, Peter Shaw, in *Recovering American Literature* (Ivan R. Dee, Chicago, 1994), states: 'As Melville's discovery scene indicates, cannibalism was not limited to the ingestion of the enemy's virtue. One learns from anthropology, furthermore, that the Typeeans ate children as well as adults, their own tribesmen as well as enemies (and hapless strangers found on the beach). Furthermore, human flesh was eaten not only in ritual but was also part of the Typeean diet...It was practiced by women and children as well as men' (p.165). For a review of accounts of Marquesan cannibalism, see Dening, *Islands and Beaches*, pp.247–49, especially his critique of Ralph Linton's ethnography of the Marquesas, on which many Melville critics have depended for 'scientific' evidence (pp.270–83). The most convincing witness of cannibalism in the Marquesas, found in *The Marquesan Journal of Edward Robarts, 1797–1824*, Greg Dening (ed.) (Australian National University Press, Canberra, 1974), p.116, suggests that cannibalism during Robarts' prolonged stay was rare and idiosyncratic.

44. Wilkes, *Narrative*, vol.3, p.105.

45. Brian Massumi, 'Everywhere You Want to Be: Introduction to Fear', in *The Politics of Everyday Fear*, Brian Massumi (ed.), University of Minnesota Press, Minneapolis, 1995, p.4.

46. Melville, *Typee*, p.170.

47. In *Typee*, recounting western atrocities in the Pacific, including Porter's massacre in Taipivai, Melville refers to the Wilkes expedition, whose orders included punishing those responsible for the alleged massacre of the crew of the *Charles Doggett*: '[We] equip armed vessels to traverse thousands of miles of ocean in order to execute summary punishment upon the offenders. On arriving...they burn, slaughter, and destroy, according to the tenor of written instructions' (*Typee*, p.27). In the 'South Seas', Melville refers to ships opening 'their batteries in indiscriminate massacre...splattering the torn bamboo huts with blood and brains of women and children' (Herman Melville, 'South Seas', in *The Piazza Tales, and Other Prose Pieces,*

1839–1860, Harrison Hayford, Alma A. MacDougall, G. Thomas Tanselle (eds) [Northwestern University Press/Newberry Library, Evanston, 1987], 415–16). Newspapers heard this as a reference to 'the destruction of Malolo by the U.S. Squadron in 1840' and objected to Melville's 'placing it in the light of an atrocity rather than a punishment'. The paper reminded its readers that 'murder after murder had been committed and passed unnoticed', that 'prevention of further evil was one avowed object of the Expedition', and that 'however severe the punishment might have been, the benefit is now being reaped' ('South Seas', p.768).

48. Melville, *Typee*, p.203.

49. Response to a request by Mary L. D. Ferris to correct her 'Melville' entry for the *Bulletin of the Society of American Authors*, quoted in Jay Leyda, *The Melville Log*, Harcourt, Brace, New York, 1951, vol.1 p.137.

50. Melville, *Typee*, p.44.

51. Daniel Defoe, *Robinson Crusoe*, Penguin, New York, 1985, pp.170, 200. One could argue (from word clusters, syntax) that *Crusoe* informs textual 'cannibalism', from the journals of Cook and Wilkes to the fiction known as 'literary Crusoeism'. Reviewers dubbed Melville 'the modern Crusoe' and 'the man who lived among cannibals'. The latter epithet in particular irked Melville, who feared going 'down to posterity [as] a "man who lived among the cannibals"'! (Herman Melville, *Correspondence*, Lynn Horth (ed.), Northwestern University Press/Newberry Library, Evanston, 1993, p.193). Charles Anderson, *Melville in the South Seas* (Dover, New York, 1966), pp.117–78, gives the fullest account of Melville's sources, concluding that Melville could have written *Typee* without having visited the Marquesas.

52. On *Typee* as Melville's anxious allegory of the market see John Evelev, '"Made in the Marquesas": tattooing and Melville's critique of the marketplace', *Arizona Quarterly*, 48. no.4, Winter 1992, pp.19–45. Evelev reads tattooing as a 'representation of representation: a place where Melville's attitudes about writing get expressed' (p.20).

53. Taussig, *Mimesis and Alterity*, p.68.

54. Melville, *Typee*, p.25.

55. George von Langsdorff, *Voyages and Travels in Various Parts of the World*, 1813; Da Capo Press, New York, 1968, vol.1, p.141.

56. Melville, *Typee*, p.205.

57. David Porter, *Journal of a Cruise Made to the Pacific Ocean*, 1815; Naval Institute Press, Annapolis, Md., 1986, p.323. Because Melville's claim in *Typee* that he did not 'meet with' Porter's journals (p.6) is contradicted by extensive echoings, critics speculate that Melville read Porter late in the composition process. Another possibility is that Melville had Porter secondhand from a source like Charles Hale's compilation. See Hale's *A Description of the Washington Islands: and in Particular the Island of Nukuhiva, the Principal of the Group: with Some*

Account of the Manners, Customs, &c., of the Inhabitants: with a Few Remarks upon the Other Islands of the Mendana Archipelago (Boston, 1845), which draws upon 'the work of Mr. Dalrymple, the Voyages of Forster, Vancouver, Langsdorff, Krusenstern, and Porter, and Various Other Sources' without always attributing these. Melville, then, is not always necessarily mimicking specific works, even those clearly echoed, but rather mimicking tropes in general circulation, that were reprinted in newspapers and compilations.

58. Melville, *Typee*, p.233.
59. Porter, *Journal of a Cruise Made to the Pacific Ocean*, p.335.
60. Stewart, *A Visit to the South Seas*, vol.1, pp.323–24.
61. Porter, *Journal of a Cruise Made to the Pacific Ocean*, pp.337–38.
62. The idea that packages conceal human remains is common to several narratives: for instance, the 'only evidence' for cannibalism that comes under Edmund Fanning's 'immediate observation' in forty years of sailing begins with a native who has 'some-thing wrapped up in some palm leaves' that he does not offer for barter: 'this was so unusual' that Fanning examines it and finds 'the same to be a piece of human flesh, baked'. See *Voyages around the World*, Gregg Press, Upper Saddle River, N. J., 1970, pp.212–13.
63. Melville, *Typee*, p.232.
64. Melville, *Typee*, p.233.
65. Daniel Defoe, *Robinson Crusoe*, p.163.
66. Melville, *Typee*, p.236.
67. Melville, *Typee*, p.238.
68. Daniel Defoe, *Robinson Crusoe*, p.210.
69. Cf. Cook, *The Voyage of the 'Endeavour' 1768–1771*, vol.1. of *The Journals of Captain James Cook on His Voyages of Discovery* (Hakluyt Society, Cambridge, 1967): 'There was not one of us that had the least doubt but what this people were Canabals but the finding this Bone with part of the sinews fresh upon it was a stronger proof than any we had yet met with' (p.169). John Coulter, whose sensationalised text Dening questions on a variety of factual grounds (*Islands*, p.147), typifies what might be called the revulsed glimpse of cannibalism: 'I must throw a veil over the feast of the following day, as I had only one look at the beginning of it, and left the arena sick to loathing: went off to the house, and did not leave it until this horrid scene was ended'. See *Adventures in the Pacific; with Observations on the Natural Production, Manners and Customs of the Natives of the Various Islands; Together with Remarks on Missionaries, British and Other Residents* (William Curry, Dublin, 1845), p.232.
70. Several critics note that in *Typee* there are two narrators: 'the author at the time' (p.2) — Tommo, held captive in Taipivai — and Melville, who escaped to tell the tale. 'Post-colonial' readings of *Typee* are often based on the gap between the experiencing sailor, imprisoned by pre-conceptions, and the mature, subversive writer. Thus, in distancing himself from Tommo's errors, and through analysing the sources of

Tommo's false consciousness, Melville turns antebellum discourses inside out. See John Samson, *White Lie: Melville's Narratives of Facts* (Cornell University Press, Ithaca, 1990): 'Between the facts in Typee and the narrative of *Typee*, Melville interposes the distancing process of perception and preconception' (p.24), and Walter T. Herbert, *Marquesan Encounters: Melville and the Meaning of Civilization* (Harvard University Press, Cambridge, 1980). My own reading, following Samuel Otter's sense that Melville cannot be purified by irony, suggests Melville's awareness that distantiation from an earlier self is messier and partial. See Otter, *Melville's Anatomies*, University of California Press, Berkeley (forthcoming).

71. Melville, *Typee*, p.118.
72. Melville, *Typee*, p.53.
73. Melville, *Typee*, p.170.
74. Melville, *Typee*, p.97.
75. Slavoj Zizek, *The Sublime Object of Ideology*, Verso, London, 1989, p.49. Melville echoes the order reported by Stewart: 'The natives of Nukuhiva [have] been so variously described…and their treatment of strangers represented as so fickle and uncertain, that I feel it a difficult task to determine in what light safely to regard them' (*Visit to the South Seas*, vol.1, p.214).
76. Melville, *Typee*, p.24.
77. Stewart, *A Visit to the South Seas*, vol.1, p.223.
78. Melville, *Typee*, p.51.
79. Zizek, *Sublime Object*, p.49.
80. Zizek, *Sublime Object*, p.99.
81. Melville, *Typee*, p.232.
82. Melville, *Typee*, p.94.
83. Melville, *Typee*, p.130, my emphasis.
84. Melville, *Typee*, p.128.
85. Melville, *Typee*, p.237.
86. Melville, *Typee*, p.233.
87. Melville, *Typee*, p.234.
88. Melville, *Typee*, p.138.
89. Melville, *Typee*, p.102.
90. Melville, *Typee*, p.129.
91. Michael Taussig, *The Nervous System*, p.2.
92. In *Foe* (Penguin Books, New York, 1987), J. M. Coetzee emphasises the degree to which 'cannibalism' as a signifier is at once phantasmal and based on a denial of indigenous voice (or on the indigenous refusal to voice): Coetzee's Crusoe argues, 'Friday has no command of words and therefore no defense against being reshaped day by day in conformity with the desires of others. I say he is a cannibal and he becomes a cannibal' (p.121).
93. Melville, *Typee*, p.89.
94. Melville, *Typee*, p.56.
95. Melville, *Typee*, p.86.

96. Melville, *Typee*, p.110.
97. Melville's non-acknowledgement of even the labour that goes into producing the food that he eats suggests both the symbolic Edenic refrain in *Typee* and a sense in which for Melville, here, work primarily means 'alienated labour' and the industrial world of exploitation. Melville's attitude toward natives posited as happily indolent is usefully juxtaposed with Willodeen Handy's acute awareness of native labour and skill and a related panic about how to repay generosity: Handy, that is, acknowledges the senses in which she 'simply wanted to give money' and avoid the permutations of debt. See *Forever the Land of Men: an account of a visit to the Marquesas Islands* (Dodd, Mead, New York, 1965), p.59. It might also be noted in this context that Melville's visit in July/August missed the labour-intensive time of harvesting and preserving in the Marquesas.
98. Taussig, *Mimesis and Alterity*, p.xiii.
99. Herman Melville, *Correspondence*, p.196.
100. Melville, 'Hawthorne and his Moses', in *The Piazza Tales and Other Prose Pieces, 1839–1860*, p.244.
101. One might in this sense characterise Melville's trajectory between *Typee* and *The Confidence Man* as a shift in emphasis from the probing of the otherness of others (ethnocentrism) to an (ultimately disabling) probing of the otherness of humanoids; the move from anthropology to ontology, however, is never detached from an anxious, often backsliding critique of American imperialism.
102. Melville, *Typee*, p.126.
103. Alex Calder, 'Melville's *Typee* and the Perception of Culture', Paper presented at MELUS Conference, Honolulu, March 1997.
104. Dening, *Performances*, p.113.

Chapter 8: Susan K. Martin — Captivating fictions: *Younah!: A Tasmanian Aboriginal Romance of the Cataract Gorge*

1. *The Tasmanian Mail*, vol.41, no. 841, August 26, 1893, p.29.
2. *The Tasmanian Mail* was available for sixpence until the astounding price cut in October 1893 when the price dropped to one penny.
3. John Reynolds, *Launceston: History of An Australian City*, Sth. Melbourne, Macmillan/Adult Education Board of Tasmania, Victoria, 1969, p.129.
4. This 'Exploratory' notion of the untouched is evident in James B Walker's 'The Discovery of Port Dalrymple' [William Collins] entered the Cataract Gorge. Grand as its towering rocks are now, the Gorge in its natural state, when clothed in with the wild beauty of its native bush, and full of wild fowl, must have been magnificent. William Collins says of it; 'The beauty of the scene is probably not surpassed in the world. The great waterfall, or cataract, is most likely one of the greatest sources of this beautiful river, every part of which abounds with swans, ducks and other kinds of wild fowl. On the

whole, I think the River Dalrymple possesses a number of local advantages requisite for a settlement' (James Backhouse Walker, *Early Tasmania: Papers Read Before the Royal Society of Tasmania During the Years 1888 to 1899*, T. J. Hughes, Tasmania, 1973, pp.110–111).

5. Mrs W. I. [Marian Teresa or Mary Theresa] Thrower, *Younâh! A Tasmanian Aboriginal Romance of the Cataract Gorge*, Hobart, The Mercury Office, 1894, p.13. Unless otherwise noted, all references are to this edition. The story was serialised in *The Tasmanian Mail* 1893–4.

6. Other novels which mention Tasmanian Aborigines include James Bonwick's *The Tasmanian Lily* (1873).

7. For discussion of the Captive White Woman tales, see Julie Carr, *The White Woman of Gipps Land*, Melbourne University Press, Carlton, (2001) forthcoming.

8. See Ian J. McNiven, Lynette Russell, Kay Schaffer (eds) *Constructions of Colonialism: Perspectives on Eliza Fraser's Shipwreck*, Leicester University Press, London and New York, 1998; Chris Healy *From the Ruins of Colonialism: History as Social Memory*, Cambridge University Press, Melbourne, 1997; in this volume Julie Carr's " 'Cabin'd, Cribb'd, and Confin'd': the White Woman of Gipps Land and Bungalene' and Kate Darian-Smith's 'Material Culture and the "Signs" of Captive White Women'.

9. It is possible that *Younâh!* was directly influenced by two 'real' Australian captivity tales. Thrower may have seen a version of the White Woman of Gippsland tale in the March 1893 'Austral Light'; and she may, like other Australian children, have encountered the Eliza Fraser story in *A Mother's Offering to Her Children* (1841). Eliza Fraser was 'captured' by local Aborigines after a shipwreck off the Queensland coast in 1836. She spent three months living with the Aborigines before her 'rescue'. Various accounts of her experience were published (see McNiven, Russell, Schaffer (eds) *Constructions of Colonialism*). *Younâh!* also reveals some intertextual echoes of (or coincidences with) North American narratives. The trajectory of the tale, for instance, is in some ways quite close to the famous 'Panther Captivity'. In this late eighteenth-century narrative two men on an expedition of hunting and exploration encounter a beautiful woman in the wilderness who has been living alone in a cave for nine years, after eloping with her lover, losing him in an Indian attack, and being captured by, and killing, a giant. They return her to her father, who dies remorsefully leaving her with his sizeable fortune (Derounian-Stodola, Kathryn Zabelle and James Arthur Levernier, *The Indian Captivity Narrative. 1550–1900*, Twayne, N.Y., 1993, pp.46–7; Annette Kolodny, *The Land Before Her: fantasy and experience of the American Frontiers, 1630–1860*, University of North Carolina Press, Chapel Hill, 1984, pp.57–62). 'We desired her to be under no uneasiness [says the narrator], told her we were travellers, that we came only to view the country but that in all our travels we had not met with any thing that had surprised us so much as her extraordinary appearance in a

place which we imagined totally unfrequented' (quoted in Derounian-Stodola, p.48). *Younâh!* reiterates this tale of the two innocent white male travellers who encounter and are moved by a female figure who stands in some midpoint — and therefore potentially mediating point — between the supposed civilised and the supposed savage, between culture and nature, between masculine explorer and feminine wilderness. As in the Panther captivity, the young gentlemen of *Younâh!* find their white girl in a cave, though not with a pet dog as in the Panther Captivity, but with a pet albino kangaroo which is killed by their dog.

10. *Younâh!*, p.42.
11. *Younâh!*, p.42.
12. In accordance with Annette Kolodny's desire to read the female as representative of the land-as-female.
13. Derounian-Stodola, Zabelle and Levernier, *The Indian Captivity Narrative*, p.32.
14. Various cultural practices of capture in Native American societies have been documented, and the numbers taken in the eighteenth and nineteenth centuries are relatively substantial. Most of the North American narratives, whether they claim or feign truth or fiction, are in the first person. The nineteenth and very early twentieth century Australian fictions are not. North American captivity narratives date from the seventeenth to the twentieth centuries, but what might be called the key texts of the genre — narratives like Mary Rowlandson's — are mostly considerably earlier than the Australian stories.
15. Healy, *From the Ruins of Colonialism*, p.165.
16. Bob Hodge and Vijay Mishra make clear the uses and dangers of such parallel readings of post-colonial societies in *Dark Side of the Dream: Australian literature and the postcolonial mind*, Allen & Unwin, Sydney, 1991. See especially the preface.
17. This ranges from the retrospective fiction of *Younâh!* to the entirely different populations in 'Lemurian' novels like *Fugitive Anne*, and Favenc's *Secrets of the Australian Desert*.
18. Robert Dixon, *Writing the Colonial Adventure: Race, Gender and Nation in Anglo-Australian Popular Fiction 1875–1914*, Cambridge University Press, Oakleigh, Melbourne, 1995, pp.82–99.
19. Hodge and Mishra (*Dark Side of the Dream*, p.480) argue that in relation to representations of Aborigines in Australian cultural production, 'The problem of legitimacy was contained within a structure of contradictions that was inherently unstable, held in place by a complex double regime of reading'. This ambivalence and fragmentation can also be read as inherent in women's writing of the period (Dixon, *Writing the Colonial Adventure*, p.95).
20. Lyndall Ryan notes that the North Midlands people occupied the area with 'the biggest Kangaroo hunting Grounds in the country…at Campbell Town and Norfolk Plains', Lyndall Ryan, *The Aboriginal*

Tasmanians, 2nd Edition, Allen & Unwin, St Leonards NSW, 1996, p.32. This suggests that the kangaroo-hunting might have been conducted on the plains rather than in the forest.

21. The language and proofs are echoed in post-Mabo definitions of traditional evidence: 'history, moral obligation, legend and mythology, religion, an organised society, personal assertion of descent, cultural artefacts and an explanation of their significance, customs, territory, the traditions of family ownership, its acquisitions, succession and divestiture…' B. A. Keon-Cohen, 'Some Problems of Proof: the Admissibility of Traditional Evidence' in *Mabo: a judicial revolution — the Aboriginal Land Rights decision and its impact on Australian Law,* M. A. Stephenson and Suri Ratnapala (eds), University Queensland Press, St Lucia, 1993, p.197. I am indebted to Simon McCart for this reference.

22. Harry Gibbs, Foreword, *Mabo…*, 1993.

23. The disappearance of Keitha St Hill may be based on true stories. In *Land Settlement in Early Tasmania: creating an Antipodean England* (Cambridge University Press, Cambridge, 1992) Sharon Morgan records the 'mysterious disappearance' of a child in the Lake River area in March 1829 (pp.48–9); J. E. Calder in *Some Account of the Wars, Extirpation, Habits, &c. of the Native Tribes of Tasmania* (Henn & Co, Hobart, 1875) — the book was also published as three papers in the *Australasian* (1872), the Tasmanian *Mercury* (1874) and the *Tasmanian Tribune* (1875) — gives an account of a woman with two daughters attacked at her hut, though the circumstances are otherwise quite different (p.12).

24. The use of the domestic hearth as indicator of civilisation is also a vexed one. While at various moments the Aboriginal society of the Pialummas is represented as a patriarchal one, organised along non-Aboriginal lines with a 'chief' and an hereditary male leadership, the connection to the domestic clearly feminises the society in familiar ways. Indigenous peoples are frequently negatively associated with the feminine in colonial texts. In this woman's text some of that necessarily adheres to the feminine domestic association, but it is clearly also a positive representation in some ways. It has been argued in relation to *Fugitive Anne* that the imagined indigenous community is used to enact the desired freedom of the female character(s) or women in general (Dixon, *Writing the Colonial Adventure,* pp.94–96) and certainly some of that is present in *Younâh!* on basic and complex levels. Genteel European female freedom is explored through projections onto and connections with subordinated peoples here, and the rights of each are implied through arguments for the rights of one. As in the case of the connection between the anti-slavery and female suffrage movements in America, explored by Karen Sanchez-Eppler in *Bodily Bonds,* ultimately the interests of the European women subordinated those of the oppressed, which are then incorporated into a discourse in favour of the white women.

25. Ryan, *The Aboriginal Tasmanians*, p.113.
26. Ryan, *The Aboriginal Tasmanians*, pp.195–204.
27. Ryan, *The Aboriginal Tasmanians*, pp.218–220.
28. Partly this is founded in the investment in racial purity discernible in *Younâh!*, which made it possible for John Reynolds in his 1969 history of Launceston to refer to 'the extinct Tasmanian aborigines' on one page, and a couple of pages later mention song recordings made by a 'half-caste lady Mrs Cochrane' in 1904 (Reynolds, *Launceston: History of An Australian City*, pp.5, 8).
29. Ryan, *The Aboriginal Tasmanians*, pp.29–32, 30, 31, Map 11, Map 12.
30. Ryan, *The Aboriginal Tasmanians*, p.31; Morgan, *Land Settlement in Early Tasmania*, p.10ff. By 1811 Governor Macquarie had personally selected and named the Norfolk Plains area as a site for settlers from Norfolk Island (Morgan, *Land Settlement in Early Tasmania*, pp.11–13). This area held the biggest kangaroo-hunting grounds in Tasmania, according to Ryan, and was common territory for the North Midlands people around whom Thrower's story supposedly revolves. Many of those whites granted land here had already been living on it for five years (Morgan, *Land Settlement in Early Tasmania*, p.15).
31. Ryan, *The Aboriginal Tasmanians*, p.31. The Black Line was a term used by Governor Arthur to describe the military operation begun on October 7, 1830. A line of military and civilian volunteers were to sweep the island, herding the Aborigines before them.
32. Both James Fenton's *The Jubilee History of Tasmania* (Wells & Leavitt, Melbourne, 1888) and his *Bush Life in Tasmania* (Hazell, Watson & Viney, London & Aylesbury, 1891) were available; Calder had been published in 1875, Bonwick, & H. The "Black Line" was a term invented by Governor Arthur to describe the military operation begun on 7 October 1830. A line of military and civilian volenteers were to sweep the island, herding the Aboriginies before them. Ling Roth's *The Aborigines of Tasmania* was published in 1890. It is possible she had seen some version of the 'Notes on the Aborigines of Tasmania...' and 'Some Notes on the Tribal Divisions of the Aborigines of Tasmania', presented by James Backhouse Walker to the Royal Society of Tasmania in the 1880s-90s. At least some of the cooking practices described, and a few words in the vocabulary list coincide — particularly some Aboriginal words, though she spells them differently: 'Myneh' and 'Nyneh' — I and thou or you, which Thrower uses twice in what on the surface appears to be an extremely dubious formation: 'mena loveta nena' (p.25) which she translates as 'I love you'. The 'Notes' mentions the historic figure Umarrah, who was 'chief' according to Backhouse, of the Stony (or Stoney) Creek group, the Tyerrernotepanner, of the Campbell Town area (Walker; Ryan, *The Aboriginal Tasmanians*, pp.16, 155; Sue Kee, *Midlands Aboriginal Archaeological Site Survey*, Occasional Paper No 26, Department of Parks, Wildlife and Heritage, Tasmania, Hobart, 1990, p.12). She might also have consulted James Bonwick's *The Last of the Tasmanians* (1870).

33. Ryan, *The Aboriginal Tasmanians*, Appendix 3. Pillah, the name of Younâh's female protector in the novel, was one of the names of a young girl who died in 1837 at the age of eleven. She was from the Pieman River area (Peternidic), on the north-east coast of Tasmania.

34. Ryan, *The Aboriginal Tasmanians*, p.155.

35. Plomley quoted in Ryan, *The Aboriginal Tasmanians*, p.154. A character, Manalargaua, falls in love with Younâh's older friend, Pillah, but a hostile tribe steals her and they are only reunited on Flinders Island. Mannalargenna was an important figure amongst the north-east people in the first twenty years of the nineteenth century. He was from the George Bay Area on the east coast, a different group altogether to the North Midlands people and the Norfolk plains sub-group. Mannalargenna and his group were involved with negotiations and trading with Bass Strait sealers (Ryan, *The Aboriginal Tasmanians*, pp.67–70). Mannalargenna was freed from Gun Carriage Island, where he had been imprisoned, to assist Robinson in his trip to the north-east, and in the capture of Umarrah. Mannalargenna died in December 1835.

36. Ryan, *The Aboriginal Tasmanians*, p.157.

37. Ryan, *The Aboriginal Tasmanians*, p.163.

38. Ryan, *The Aboriginal Tasmanians*, p.184.

39. Manalagana's name shifts across this page — Manalagau; and three instances of Manalagaua — so that the 'ana' ending is likely to be a typesetter slip — possibly affected by the unfamiliarity of the name, or the familiarity of Mannalargenna's.

40. *Younâh!*, p.60.

41. *Younâh!*, p.57.

42. Her father tells her that is impossible, but they might 'secure a portion of the old grounds and settle Eumarrah upon it, assuring to him such a yearly sum as would enable him to provide himself with all that was necessary to his well-being as long as he lives' (p. 57).

43. *Younâh!*, p.60.

44. The character who might be seen to disrupt this happy closure is Natone. From being Younâh's friend and equal when the two first encounter white Tasmanian society and are locked together in an outhouse for the night, Natone gradually descends the class scale as Younâh rises. While Younâh is immediately dressed in European clothing — a servant's dress, Natone is dressed up as the exotic indigene — 'Mrs Hargreaves had found a quantity of bright scarlet cotton twill' for Natone which she 'draped…artistically about her dusky form' (p.45). By the time they reach England Natone has become Younâh's servant. But on their return to Tasmania she does not rejoin her people and their implied fate, but returns to England: though, '…equally moved at her leave taking with her people….she no longer desired to dwell among them, or to share the life that was so different from the wild, free existence in which never a care beyond the present disturbed the serenity, in which her childhood's days had been passed' (p.61). Natone disappears out of the narrative at this

juncture — the unnarratable subaltern perhaps (Gayatri Spivak, 'Three Women's Texts and the Discourse of Imperialism', *Critical Inquiry*, 12, Autumn 1985, pp.243–261) but also the suggestion of the Tasmanian Aborigine alive and free — a figure who might be aligned to the surviving community of Tasmanian Aborigines, uncontained, though not unaffected, by such narratives.

45. *Younâh!*, pp.36–37.
46. *Younâh!*, p.37.
47. Dona Brown, *Inventing New England: regional tourism in the nineteenth century*, Smithsonian Institution Press, Washington & London, 1995, p.12.
48. *Younâh!*, p.60.
49. See for example Tom Griffiths, *Hunters and Collectors*, Cambridge University Press, Melbourne, 1996.
50. Ryan, *The Aboriginal Tasmanians*, p.184.
51. Reynolds, *Launceston: history of an Australian city*, p.133.
52. Reynolds, *Launceston: history of an Australian city*, p.135. Certainly the establishment of a number of charitable institutions in Launceston across the early 1890s — the District Nursing Association in 1893, the Evangelical Nursing Association in 1896; the Citizen's Relief Committee (Reynolds, *Launceston: History of An Australian City*, pp.137–138) — and even an Association that lent blankets to the poor over winter for a nominal fee (Reynolds, *Launceston: history of an Australian city*, p.136) indicate the level of distress. Less directly the drastic reduction in price of the *Tasmanian Mail* looks like a survival strategy in the face of reduced sales.
53. Thrower's maiden name is unclear because the citation differs in the two wedding announcements in the Hobart Mercury. She is listed in one as Marian Teresa and the other as Mary Theresa Kean. The wedding was on 3 December 1868 at St Michael's Church, Campbell Town, Tasmania — the Catholic Church. Kean is cited in the wedding announcement as daughter of the late Hugh Kean and is quite likely connected to Kean's brewery in Campbell Town.
54. This establishment was not mentioned in the list of the best hotels in Launceston compiled by Edward Braddon, the brother of the Sensation fiction novelist Mary Braddon.

Chapter 9: Julie Carr — 'Cabin'd, cribb'd and confin'd': The White Woman of Gipps Land and Bungalene

1. The Gippsland region comprises the south-eastern corner of mainland Australia, bounded on the east by the Pacific Ocean and the west by the Great Dividing Range. The 1840s lexical convention of 'Gipps Land' (or Gipps' Land) is retained where applicable, rather than the later 'Gippsland'.
2. The term Kurnai for the confederation of the five Gipps Land tribes was used by A. W. Howitt in his 1880 publication *Kamilaroi and*

Kurnai. Howitt designates the tribes Brataualung, Brayakaulung, Brabralung, Tatungalung and Krauatungalung.

3. Kate Darian-Smith has written of the centrality of the White Woman incident to a specific Gippsland history of white settlement and its place as 'one of the founding myths which constitute the collective memory of modern Gippsland, and through which the unique history and identity of the region have been expressed': Kate Darian-Smith, 'Capturing the White Woman of Gippsland: A Frontier Myth', in Kate Darian-Smith, Roslyn Poignant and Kay Schaffer (eds), *Captured Lives: Australian captivity narratives*, Menzies Centre for Australian Studies, University of London, London, 1993, pp.14–34.

4. Helen Tiffin, 'Post-Colonial Literatures and Counter-Discourse', *Kunapipi*, vol.9, no.3, 1987, p.97.

5. Homi Bhabha, 'The Other Question', *Screen*, vol.24, no.6, 1983, pp.18–36, p.29.

6. 'Supposed Outrage by the Blacks', *Sydney Morning Herald*, 28 December 1840.

7. 'White Woman Detained by the Blacks', *Port Phillip Patriot & Morning Advertiser*, 7 March 1846.

8. Letter to the Editor, from 'Humanitas', in 'Miss Lord', *Port Phillip Herald*, 20 August 1846.

9. 'The Whites and the Blacks', *Port Phillip Patriot & Morning Advertiser*, 3 September 1846; 'The Gipps Land Expedition' and 'White Woman Meeting', *Port Phillip Herald*, 3 September 1846; 'The Gipps Land Blacks — Public Meeting', *Argus*, 4 September 1846; and 'The Report of Two White women Being Detained by the Blacks', *Port Phillip Gazette*, 5 September 1846.

10. 'The White Woman at Gipps Land', *Port Phillip Herald*, 26 November, 1846.

11. 'The Gipps Land Expedition', *Port Phillip Patriot & Morning Advertiser*, 20 October 1846.

12. Christian De Villiers wrote from Port Albert that the settlers, 'so far from their being averse to our humane undertaking…have expressed their readiness to give me every assistance…and we leave the settlement with the best wishes for our success by all parties here'. De Villiers to George Cavenagh Esq., in 'Gipps Land Expedition', *Port Phillip Herald*, 19 November 1846.

13. Letter from James Warman, Glengary [*sic*] River, 5 January 1847, published under 'Gipps Land Expedition' in *Port Phillip Herald*, 21 January 1847 (extraordinary ed.), and *Port Phillip Patriot & Morning Advertiser*, 22 January 1847. De Villiers' letter was published under 'The White Woman' in *Port Phillip Herald*, 21 January 1847 (morning ed.) and *Port Phillip Patriot & Morning Advertiser*, 22 January 1847, and under 'Gipps Land Expedition', *Argus*, 26 January 1847.

14. 'The White Woman', *Port Phillip Herald*, 4 March 1847; 'Gipps Land Expedition', *Argus*, 9 March 1847; 'The Blacks', *Port Phillip Herald*, 11 March 1847.

15. There are numerous spelling variations, the principal ones being Tacka-wadden, Jacka-wadden and Jacky-warren.

16. Statement of John Paine, Storekeeper to Mr. Macalister. Declared before Commissioner C. J. Tyers at Boisdale 30 March 1846. Item No. 7 in the schedule of correspondence tabled in the Legislative Council by the Colonial Secretary on 21st October 1846. Typescript copy in La Trobe Collection, State Library of Victoria (SLV), MS 10065.

17. Marie Hansen Fels, *Good Men and True: the Aboriginal police of the Port Phillip District 1837–1853*, Melbourne University Press, Melbourne, 1988, p.182.

18. Sergeant Windridge, Border Police, to C. J. Tyers, 8 August 1846. Item No. 20 in the schedule of correspondence tabled in the Legislative Council by the Colonial Secretary on 21 October 1846. Typescript copy in La Trobe Collection, SLV, MS 10065.

19. See for example the letter from 'An Englishman', published under 'Gross Inhumanity in a Christian Government' in *Port Phillip Herald*, 10 September 1846 (reprinted from the *Sydney Morning Herald*). The letter was also cited briefly in the *Argus* of 8 September 1846 and, in more detail, in the *Port Phillip Gazette* of 9 September 1846.

20. 'The White Woman at Gipps Land', *Port Phillip Herald*, 26 November 1846.

21. William Westgarth in his book *Australia Felix,* published the following year, cited Windridge's report as evidence that Gipps Land Aborigines 'were in the habit of devouring the bodies of deceased gins or wives, which they roast or bake after their own fashion, and thus dispose of instead of burying'. William Westgarth, *Australia Felix: or A Historical and Descriptive Account of the Settlement of Port Phillip, New South Wales,* Oliver and Boyd, Edinburgh; Simpkin, Marshall & Co., London, 1848, pp.75–6.

22. Peter Hulme, *Colonial Encounters: Europe and the native Caribbean 1492–1797*, Methuen, London, 1986; W. Arens, *The Man-Eating Myth: anthropology and anthropophagy*, Oxford University Press, New York, 1979.

23. C. J. Tyers to C. J. La Trobe, 11 August 1846, 46/1322, Victorian Public Records Series (VPRS), Public Records Office, Melbourne (PRO) 19/P, unit 84.

24. Warman's journal was published in *Port Phillip Herald* under the heading 'Gipps Land Expedition', in three instalments: 23 February, 25 February and 2 March 1847.

25. Journal entry Monday 9th [November 1846], *Port Phillip Herald*, 23 February 1847.

26. Journal entry for Friday 20th [November 1846], *Port Phillip Herald*, 23 February 1847.

27. Journal entry for Thursday 3rd [December 1846], *Port Phillip Herald*, 25 February 1847.

28. The abduction of Aboriginal women by shepherds and settlers has

been cited as a principal cause of hostility between Aborigines and whites in virtually all newly settled regions throughout the colony, and the cause of some Europeans and many Aborigines being killed. See, for example, Chief Protector GA Robinson's comments in Ian D. Clark (ed.), *The Port Phillip Journals of George Augustus Robinson: 8 March-7 April 1842 and 18 March-29 April 1843*, Monash Publications in Geography No. 34, Melbourne, 1988, p.10; see also Henry Reynolds, *Frontier*, Allen & Unwin, North Sydney, 1987, p.62.

29. 'Gipps Land', *Port Phillip Gazette*, 19 May 1847.

30. 'The White Woman in Gipps Land', *Port Phillip Patriot & Morning Advertiser*, 7 April 1847.

31. C. J. Tyers to C. J. La Trobe, 26 April 1847, 47/789 VPRS, PRO 19/P, unit 91.

32. C. J. Tyers to C. J. La Trobe, 10 April 1847, 47/698, VPRS, PRO 19/P, unit 91.

33. Gippsland historian, Peter Gardner, argues this point. Peter Gardner, *Gippsland Massacres: The Destruction of the Kurnai Tribe 1800–1860*, second revised edition, Ngarak Press, Ensay, 1993, p.75. See also Peter Gardner, 'The Journals of de Villiers and Warman: the expedition to recover the captive white woman', the *Victorian Historical Journal*, vol. 50, 1979, p.96; Don Watson, 'Removing Another Race', ch.8 in *Caledonia Australis: Scottish highlanders on the frontier of Australia*, Collins, Sydney, 1984; Phillip Pepper & Tess De Araugo, 'The Hunt for the White Woman', ch.12 in *The Kurnai of Gippsland*, Hyland House Publishing Pty Ltd, South Yarra, 1985; and Bruce Elder, *Blood on the Wattle: Massacres and Maltreatment of Australian Aborigines since 1788*, Child and Associates Publishing Pty Ltd, Frenchs Forest, 1988, pp.93–97.

34. C. J. Tyers to C. J. La Trobe, 15 July 1844, 44/1367, VPRS, PRO 19/P, unit 61, reproduced in Thomas Francis Bride (ed.), *Letters from Victorian Pioneers*, William Heinemann Limited, Melbourne, 1898, p.233; C. J. Tyers to C. J. La Trobe, 'Report by the Commissioner Crown Lands, Gipps Land on the Aborigines in his District, dated 9th December, 1846'.

35. Cited in Fels, *Good Men and True*, p.177.

36. The memorandum of agreement as reproduced here was published in 'The White Woman', *Port Phillip Herald*, 15 July 1847. It has minor spelling and typographical variations from the version in the Official Correspondence.

37. A facsimile of the parchment conveyance of the document is reproduced in James Dawson, *Australian Aborigines: The Language and Customs of Several Tribes of Aborigines in the Western District of Victoria, Australia*, George Robertson, Melbourne, Sydney and Adelaide, 1881 [facs. ed. Australian Institute of Aboriginal Studies, Canberra, 1981], no page no. The 'case for opinion', negating the document's legality, transmitted by Mr Burge of London, is reproduced in Westgarth, *Australia Felix*, pp.393–97.

38. Three watches were appointed to provide twenty-four-hour surveillance of Bungelene after he absconded on 19 April. 'Journal kept by a member of the second expedition for the recovery of the white woman held captive by the Gipps Land blacks', 6 March 1847 to 25 June 1847 (hereafter Journal, second exped.), entry Monday 26th (April 1847).

39. C. J. La Trobe to Col. Sec., 9 June 1847, 47/590, VPRS, PRO 2142, reel 6, p.179.

40. Letter to the editor, from 'A Fellow Colonist', in 'The Captive White Woman', *Port Phillip Gazette*, 20 February 1847.

41. Journal, second exped.

42. 'The White Woman', *Port Phillip Herald*, 1 July 1847. The article included an account of the expeditioners' journey to the mountains.

43. Report of the Central Board appointed to watch over the interests of Aborigines in the Colony of Victoria', Parliamentary Paper No. 39 of 1861.

44. C. J. Tyers to C. J. La Trobe, 14 June 1847, 47/1189, VPRS, PRO 19/P, unit 93; see also H. P. Dana to C. J. La Trobe, 29 June 1847, 47/1186, VPRS, PRO 19/P, unit 93.

45. C. J. La Trobe to Col. Sec, 7 July 1847, 47/742, VPRS, PRO 2142, reel 6.

46. Col. Sec. to C. J. La Trobe, 19 July 1847, 47/375, VPRS, PRO 19/P, unit 89.

47. H. P. Dana to C. J. La Trobe, 12 July 1847, 47/1269 VPRS, PRO 19/P, unit 94; G. A. Robinson to C. J. La Trobe, 19 July 1847, 47/1354, VPRS, PRO 19/P, unit 94.

48. Extracts from the daybook of the Native Police Station, Narre Narre Warren, relating to the search for the white woman with the blacks and the detention of Bungelene, VPRS, PRO 5519, unit no. 1.

49. In 1861, one of the children, Thomas Bungelene, came under the care of the Central Board appointed to watch over the interests of Aborigines in the colony of Victoria. His brother had by this time died. The board considered that Thomas presented an opportunity 'of proving to the world that the Aborigines of Australia are degraded rather by their habits, than in consequence of the want of mental capacity' and sought to have him educated. The scheme was abandoned shortly afterwards and Thomas was transferred to the S. S. 'Victoria' to be taught the duties of a seaman'. Parliamentary Paper No. 39 of 1861.

50. H. P. Dana to C. J. La Trobe, 5 January 1848, 48/53, VPRS, PRO 19/P, unit 101; C. J. La Trobe to H. P. Dana, 14 January 1848, 48/37, VPRS, PRO 2142, reel 4.

51. 'Murder of the Captive "White Woman" at Gipps Land', *Port Phillip Herald*, 5 November 1847, (extraordinary ed).

52. 'The Gipps Land Expedition', *Port Phillip Gazette*, 10 July 1847.

53. See White Woman manuscript material, La Trobe Collection, SLV.

Chapter 10: Kate Darian-Smith — Material culture and the 'signs' of captive white women

An earlier version of some material in this chapter appeared in Joy Damousi and Katharine Ellinghaus (eds), *Citizenship, Women and Social Justice: papers presented at the 1998 International Federation for Research in Women's History Conference, Melbourne, 1998*, Department of History, University of Melbourne, 1999, pp. 71–8. I am especially grateful for the support that Jeanette Hoorn and Barbara Creed have shown as editors of this collection.

1. *Sydney Morning Herald*, 28 December 1840, quoted in Don Watson, *Caledonia Australis: Scottish highlanders on the frontier of Australia*, Collins, Sydney, 1984, pp.161–2.

2. See the chapter by Julie Carr in this book for a more detailed account of the origin of the White Woman of Gippsland narrative; see also Kate Darian-Smith, 'The White Woman of Gippsland: A Frontier Myth', in Kate Darian-Smith, Roslyn Poignant and Kay Schaffer (eds), *Captured Lives: Australian captivity narratives*, Menzies Centre for Australian Studies, University of London, London, 1993, pp.14–34.

3. See Watson, *Caledonia Australis*, pp.165–9.

4. See Stephen Greenblatt, *Marvelous Possessions: the wonder of the New World*, Oxford University Press, Oxford, 1991, and Bernard Smith, *European Vision and the South Pacific*, Oxford University Press, Melbourne, second edition, 1989.

5. Ian Donaldson and Tamsin Donaldson, 'First Sight', in Ian Donaldson and Tamsin Donaldson (eds.), *Seeing the First Australians*, Allen & Unwin, Sydney, 1985, p.17.

6. Pitt-Rivers, pronouncing in 1867, is quoted in John Mulvaney, 'The Darwinian Perspective', in Donaldson and Donaldson (eds.), *Seeing the First Australians*, p.69.

7. John Mulvaney, 'The Darwinian Perspective', p.70. These displays remained in place until after World War II.

8. *Port Phillip Patriot and Morning Advertiser*, 4 February 1841.

9. *Port Phillip Herald*, 14 November 1843. This letter also told of a large heart carved into the ground with a sharp instrument, citing this as evidence that a white captive was held by the Kurnai.

10. See various texts on this point, including Vron Ware, *Beyond the Pale: white women, racism and history*, Verso, London, 1992; Chilla Bulbeck, *Australian Women in Papua New Guinea: colonial passages 1920–1960*, Cambridge University Press, Melbourne, 1992; Helen Callaway, *Gender, Culture and Empire: European Women in colonial Nigeria*, Macmillan, London, 1987; Claudia Knapman, *White Women in Fiji 1835–1930: the ruin of Empire?*, Allen & Unwin, Sydney, 1986; for a more general discussion of the intersections between British imperialism and women's history see Clare Midgley (ed.), *Gender and Imperialism*, Manchester University Press, Manchester and New York, 1998.

11. Don Watson makes this point in relation to the English view of the Highland Scots and their subordination of women, and Highland immigrants like McMillan were to level similar charges against the Kurnai. Watson, *Caledonia Australis*, pp.7–9.

12. A photograph of the handkerchief bearing this message is held at the Centre for Gippsland Studies, Monash University, Churchill campus. I have not sighted a handkerchief itself, although I have been informed that such an object is held in a private collection.

13. See Melbourne *Argus*, 7 May 1847; and correspondence of Governor La Trobe to the Colonial Secretary, 9 June 1847, 47/590/PRO, Melbourne.

14. Anne McClintock, *Imperial Leather: race, gender and sexuality in the Imperial contest*, Routledge, London and New York, 1995.

15. For an impressively nuanced reading of this advertisement, see McClintock, *Imperial Leather*, pp. 210–4.

16. Cleary was also to photograph tableaus of white male and female captivity. See Karen Donnelly, 'The Discovery of a 19th Century Photographer — Thomas Cleary', *Olive Pink Society Bulletin*, vol.7 nos.1 and 2. 1995, pp.9–21.

17. For a discussion of the term 'rescue' in this context see Kate Darian-Smith, 'Rescuing Barbara Thompson and other white women: captivity narratives on Australian frontiers' in Kate Darian-Smith, Liz Gunner and Sarah Nuttall (eds), *Text, Theory, Space: land, literature and history in South Africa and Australia*, Routledge, London and New York, 1996, pp. 102–4.

18. Oswald Brierly, 16 October 1849, 'Journal of the H. M. S. Rattlesnake, Second Visit to Cape York, October-December 1849' in David R. Moore, *Islanders and Aborigines at Cape York: An ethnographic reconstruction based on the 1848–1850 'Rattlesnake' Journals of O. W. Brierly and information he obtained from Barbara Thompson*, Australian Institute of Aboriginal Studies Press, Canberra, 1979, pp.76–80.

19. Brierly, information obtained from Thompson in 'Journal', 7 November 1849, in Moore, *Islanders and Aborigines*, p.195.

20. Brierly, 16 October 1849, 'Journal', in Moore, *Islanders and Aborigines*, pp.76–80; Thompson's own account of her 'escape' was recorded by Brierly, 7 November 1849, 'Journal', in Moore, *Islanders and Aborigines*, pp.186–97; see also Moore's 'Introduction', pp.5–8.

21. Brierly, information obtained from Thompson, 17 October 1849, 'Journal', in Moore, *Islanders and Aborigines*, pp.142–4; Moore, 'Introduction', *Islanders and Aborigines*, pp.5–8.

22. MacGillivray wrote this in a letter to J. B. Jukes on 16 October 1849, quoted in Moore, 'Introduction', *Islanders and Aborigines*, p.7.

23. T. H. Huxley, *Diary of the voyage of the H. M. S. 'Rattlesnake': edited from the unpublished manuscript by Julian Huxley*, Chatto & Windus, London, 1935; quoted in Moore, 'Introduction', *Islanders and Aborigines*, pp.5–7.

24. Brierly, information obtained from Thompson, 7 November 1849, 'Journal', in Moore, *Islanders and Aborigines*, p.197.

25. Jillian Robertson, *Lizard Island: a reconstruction of the life of Mrs Watson*, Melbourne, Hutchinson, 1981; *Brisbane Courier*, 23 January 1882, pp.2, 3.
26. Mary Watson, Diary, Oxley Library, OM81 — 120.
27. Robertson, *Lizard Island*, p.141. All of these items, or their remains, were found with Watson's body. See also the sworn evidence of William Henry Scott, mate of the Kate Kearney, who found Watson's body, dated 24 January 1882; quoted in Robertson, *Lizard Island*, pp.164–6.
28. The group landed on No. 5, Howick Island, where their bodies were recovered months later.
29. Mary Watson, Diary.
30. *Cooktown Herald-Sun*, 28 January 1882.
31. 'A. F.', Dead With Thirst', the *Bulletin*, 4 February 1882, p.2.
32. See, for this suggestion, other stanzas in the 'Dead With Thirst' poem, *The Bulletin*, 4 February 1882, p.2; see also *Brisbane Courier*, 25 January 1882, p.3.
33. Information from Chris Lloyd, Assistant Curator (Technology), Social History Section, Queensland Museum, 26 August 1997.
34. Queensland Museum Board Minutes, Special Meeting, 17 October 1884, quoted in Patricia Mather (ed.), *A Time for a Museum: the history of the Queensland Museum, 1862–1986*, Queensland Museum, Brisbane, 1986, pp.225.
35. It should be noted that the Industrial and Technological Museum (later the Science Museum) was founded in Victoria in 1870, taking over the mining and agricultural collections from the National Museum; and the Museum of Applied Arts and Sciences was founded in Sydney in 1880.
36. Mather (ed.), *Time for a Museum*, p.223.
37. Mather (ed.), *Time for a Museum*, pp.86–87.

Chapter 11: Jeanette Hoorn — Captivity and melancholia in Marlon Fuentes' *Bontoc Eulogy*: revisiting *Meet Me In St Louis*

1. Mary Louise Pratt, *Imperial Eyes, Travel Writing and Transculturation*, Routledge, London, 1992, p.7.
2. Gayatri Spivak, 'Can the subaltern speak?', reprinted in *Marxist Interpretations of Culture*, Cary Nelson and Lawrence Grossberg (eds), Macmillan Education, Basingstoke, 1988 (1985), pp.271–313.
3. For a discussion of the uses of auto-ethnography in contemporary post-colonial queer film and video, see Jose Munoz 'The autoethnographic performance: reading Richard Fung's queer hybridity' in *Screen,* vol.36, no.2, Summer 1995, pp.83–99.
4. The term 'captivity narrative' appeared in American literature in the 1930s as a term to describe frontier stories involving the capturing and holding of white women by American 'Indians'. These stories have particular features including inter-racial elements, moral panic and a backward temporal dimension. There are many examples of

whites holding native peoples hostage which share the structure of the captivity narrative. I refer to these as reverse captivity narratives. See my article 'Captivity and Humanist Art History: The Case of Poedua', in *Third Text*, 42, 1988, pp.14–21.

5. Protests against the exhibition of Igorots in the Philippines were extensive; see Christopher A. Vaughan, 'Ogling Igorots: The Politics and Commerce of Exhibiting Cultural Otherness, 1898–1913', in Rosemary Garland Thompson (ed.) *Freakery: Cultural Spectacle of the Extraordinary Body*, New York University Press, New York, 1996, pp.219–233. The Anti-Imperialist League in America, entered into a correspondence with the Bureau of Insular affairs seeking the return of the Igorots; see Winslow, Erving, 'The Anti-Imperialist League and the Igorots'. Excerpt from 'Report of the Secretary', *Report of the Eighth Annual Meeting of the Anti-Imperialist League*, Anti-Imperialist League, Boston, 1906, http://www.boondocksnet.com/expos/wfe_ail_igorots.html. In Jim Zwick (ed.) *World's Fairs and Expositions: Defining America and the World, 1876–1916* http://www.boondocksnet.com/expos/ (11 November 1999).

6. Christopher A. Vaughan, 'Ogling Igorots: The Politics and Commerce of Exhibiting Cultural Otherness, 1898–1913', pp.219–233.

7. See Tom Gunning's article 'The world as object lesson: Cinema audiences, visual culture and the St Louis World Fair' in *Film History*, vol.6, no.4, 1994, pp.422–445.

8. Vaughan, 'Ogling Igorots: The Politics and Commerce of Exhibiting Cultural Otherness, 1898–1913', pp.219–233.

9. Vaughan, 'Ogling Igorots: The Politics and Commerce of Exhibiting Cultural Otherness, 1898–1913', p.219.

10. H. G. Wells, *The Time Machine,* New York, 1991, first published 1895. See discussion in Fatimah Tobing Rony, *The Third Eye: race, cinema and ethnographic spectable,* Duke University Press, 1996, pp.129–30.

11. See Coco Fusco's *English is Broken Here, Notes on Cultural Fusion in the Americas*, The New Press, New York City, 1995, p.51.

12. Marlon Fuentes, *Bontoc Eulogy,* 1994.

13. Sigmund Freud, 'Mourning and Melancholia', in *On Metapsychology, The Theory of Psychoanalysis*, The Pelican Freud Library, London, 1984, p.252.

14. Freud, 'Mourning and Melancholia', p.252.

15. Tranh Anh Hung, quoted in review of *The Scent of Green Papaya,* by James Berardinelli, 1994, The internet movie data base.

16. Freud, 'Mourning and Melancholia', p.248ff.

17. Laura Kipnis, 'The Phantom Twitchings of an Amputated Limb', *Wide Angle,* vol.11, no.4, 1989, pp.42–51.

18. Fuentes, *Bontoc Eulogy*.

19. *The Oxford English Dictionary* has Hoochy Koochy as 'a kind of erotic dance' and quotes the *Record Changer* (Fairfax Virginia) January 1945, 'The Chicago World Fair of 1893…gave the widest possible publicity to the new negro dances, the cakewalk, the pasamala, the

hoochie koochi, the bully dance and the bombershay', second ed. Clarendon Press: Oxford, New York, 1998, p.373.

20. Vincente Minnelli, *Meet Me In St Louis,* 1944.

21. Freud, 'Mourning and Melancholia', pp.251–268.

Chapter 12: Barbara Creed — Breeding out the black: *Jedda* and the stolen generations in Australia

The first draft of this chapter was first presented at The Captivity Narratives and the Body Symposium held at James Cook University, Townsville in September 1997.

1. Carmel Bird (ed.), 'Introduction', *The Stolen Generation: their stories,* Random House, Sydney, 1998, p.57.

2. Stuart Cunningham, *Featuring Australia: the cinema of Charles Chauvel,* Allen & Unwin, Sydney, 1991, p.106.

3. Bill Tuckey, 'Jedda and the Platypus', *Northern Territory News,* 6 January 1955, p.7.

4. 'Still More Praise for *Jedda*', *Northern Territory News,* 18 January 1955, p.18.

5. Cunningham, *Featuring Australia,* pp.160–162.

6. Colin Johnson (Mudrooroo) 'Chauvel and the Centring of the Aboriginal Male in Australian Film', *Australian Film in the 1950s,* (ed.) Tom O'Regan, *Continuum: an Australian journal of the media,* vol.1, no.1, 1987, p.48.

7. Ion L. Idriess, *Nemarluk King of the Wilds,* Angus & Robertson, Sydney, 1948. Idriess depicts Nemarluk as a fierce resistance fighter who was finally captured by constable Taz Fitzer and who died in Fanny Bay gaol of 'a broken heart' (p.221). There is no figure like Jedda in the novel. The Aboriginal outlaw is referred to as 'Namaluk' by Susanne Chauvel Carlsson in *Charles & Elsa Chauvel: movie pioneers,* University of Queensland Press, 1989, p.154. She also notes that one of the mounted policemen in the film, played by Constable Tas Fitzer, is the man 'who captured the original Namaluk'.

8. *Eve in Ebony...The Story of Jedda,* promotional booklet, Sydney, Columbia Pictures Pty Ltd, 1954, p.1, Northern Territory Library.

9. Charles and Elsa Chauvel, The script of *Jedda,* Mitchell Library, State Library of New South Wales. ML MSS 666/2. All references to the script are to this manuscript. Material from the script is illuminating because it reveals the Chauvel's intentions at the time, although of course their intentions may not be necessarily realised in the finished film. However, it is clear that their intention was to represent Jedda's transformation, her passage from one culture to another. Reference to the Pygmalion myth is particularly pertinent.

10. *Eve in Ebony...The Story of Jedda,* promotional booklet, Sydney, Columbia Pictures Pty Ltd, 1954, p.1, Northern Territory Library.

11. *Eve in Ebony...The Story of Jedda,* p.3.

12. Charles and Elsa Chauvel, The script of *Jedda,* Mitchell Library, State Library of New South Wales. ML MSS 666/2.

13. Cunningham, *Featuring Australia,* p.160.

14. Vijay Mishra, 'Aboriginal representations in Australian Texts', *Asian Cinema. Continuum: an Australian journal of the media,* (eds.) Brian

Shoesmith and Tom O'Reagan, vol.2, no.1, 1988/89, p.179.

15. Marcia Langton, *'Well, I heard it on the radio and I saw it on the television...'*: *An essay for the Australian Film Commission on the politics and aesthetics of filmmaking by and about Aboriginal people and things*, Australian Film Commission, North Sydney, 1993, pp.45–46.

16. An observation made by Marcia Langton during a discussion of *Jedda* at 'The Other Frontier Seminar Series' at the Institute of Postcolonial Studies, Melbourne University, August 2000.

17. Anne Hickling-Hudson, 'White Construction of Black Identity in Australian Films about Aborigines', *Literature/Film Quarterly*, vol.18, no.4, 1990, pp.263–274.

18. Cunningham, *Featuring Australia*, p.106.

19. Susannne Chauvel Carlsson in *Charles & Elsa Chauvel: movie pioneers*, University of Queensland Press, 1989, p156.

20. Bird, 'Introduction', p.1.

21. Bird, 'Introduction', p.3.

22. Henry Reynolds, Afterword, in Carmel Bird (ed.), *The Stolen Generation: their stories*, Random House, Sydney, 1998, pp.183–185.

23. Paul Toohey, 'Stolen Pair Await Landmark Judgement', the *Australian*, Friday 11 August 2000, p.4.

24. The *Bulletin*, 21 December 1955, p.35.

25. *Sydney Morning Herald*, March 1956.

26. *Sydney Morning Herald*, 29 May 1957.

27. *Sydney Morning Herald*, 30 May 1957.

28. The *Bulletin*, 21 December 1955, p.34.

29. Bird, p.57.

30. For an interesting discussion of these parallels, see Stuart Cunningham, *Featuring Australia: The cinema of Charles Chauvel*, Allen & Unwin, Sydney, 1991, pp.160–161.

31. Peter Conrad, *Modern Times, Modern Places: life & art in the 20th century*, Thames & Hudson, London, 1998.

32. Bram Dijkstra, *Idols of Perversity*, Oxford University Press, New York, 1986, Ch. 9.

33. Rhona J. Berenstein, 'White Skin, White Masks: race, gender, and monstrosity in jungle-Horror cinema', *Attack of the Leading Ladies*, Columbia University Press, New York, p.166.

34. Christopher Castiglia, *Bound and Determined: captivity, culture-crossing, and white womanhood from Mary Rowlandson to Patty Hearst*, University of Chicago Press, Chicago, 1989.

35. Sigmund Freud, 'The Uncanny', in *The Standard Edition of the Complete Psychological Works of Sigmund Freud*, 24 vols, trans. James Strachey, Hogarth, London, 1953–66, vol.17, pp.217–52.

36. For an important discussion of psychoanalysis and the racialised gaze see E. Ann Kaplan, *Looking for the Other Feminism, Film, and the Imperial Gaze*, Routledge, N.Y. and London, 1997.

37. Meaghan Morris, 'Beyond Assimilation: Aboriginality, Media History and Public Memory', *Aedon*, vol.4, no.1, November 1996, p.18.

Chapter 13: Freda Freiberg — Blame and shame: The hidden history of the comfort women of World War II

1. See George Hicks, *The Comfort Women: Sex Slaves of the Japanese Imperial Forces*, Allen & Unwin, Sydney, 1995; Jan Ruff O'Herne, *Fifty Years of Silence*, Editions Tom Thompson, 1994; Keith Howard (ed.), *True Stories of the Korean Comfort Women*, Cassell, London, 1995; Maria Rosa Henson, *Comfort Woman: Slave of Destiny*, Philippine Centre for Investigative Journalism, Manila, 1996.

2. The paper, entitled 'Rape, Race and Religion: Ways of Speaking about Enforced Military Prostitution in World War II', was published in *Metro*, no.104, December 1995, pp.20–25 inc.

3. *The Murmuring* (Korean title: *Nazn Moksori*), South Korea, 1995, 16 mm and VHS, 98 mins, directed and produced by Byun Young Joo for Docu Factory VISTA, in Korean with English subtitles; *Senso Daughters*, Australia, 1989, 16 mm and VHS, 55 mins, directed and scripted by Noriko Sekiguchi, distributed by Ronin Films, Canberra; *Ianfu*, Philippines, 1992, 35 mm, 13 mins, produced and directed by Antonio Vidal Aguilar, Katyan Films, Manila; *Fifty Years of Silence*, Australia, 1994, written by Jan Ruff O'Herne and Carole Sklan, directed by Ned Lander, 56 mins, VHS, distributed by Ronin Films, Canberra.

4. Two pioneering studies of the issue were published in Japan in the 1970s — Senda Kako's *Jugun Ianfu* (Military Comfort Women), San-Ichi Shobo, Tokyo, 1978; and Kim Il Myon's *Tenno no Guntai to Chosenjin Ianfu* (The Imperial Military Forces and Korean Comfort Women), San-Ichi Shobo, Tokyo, 1976. An annotated bibliography of Japanese documents and historical studies is provided in Hicks, *The Comfort Women*, pp.235–38. Recent academic publications in English, not listed in Hicks, include: Yuki Tanaka, *Rape and War: The Japanese Experience*, Japanese Studies Centre, Melbourne, 1995; Kazuko Watanabe, 'Militarism, Colonialism and the Trafficking of Women: "Comfort Women" forced into Sexual Labour for Japanese Soldiers', *Bulletin of Concerned Asian Scholars*, vol.26, no.4, Oct–Dec 1994, pp.3–17; Mikiyo Kano, 'The Problem with the "Comfort Woman Problem"', *Japan-Asia Quarterly Review*, vol.24, no.2, 1993; and Vera Mackie, 'Militarized Memories and Sexual Silences: writing about military prostitution in the Second World War', *Japanese Studies Bulletin*, vol.16, nos 2–3, 1996, pp.62–8.

5. Hicks, *The Comfort Women*, p.217.

6. See Martha Vicinus, 'Helpless and Unfriended: nineteenth century domestic melodrama', *New Literary History*, vol.13, no.1, Autumn 1981, p.130.

7. Michael Booth, *English Melodrama*, Herbert Jenkins, London, 1965, p.52.

8. David Grimstead, 'Melodrama as Echo of the historically Voiceless', in Tamara Hareven (ed.), *Anonymous American: explorations in nineteenth century social history*, Prentics Hall, New Jersey, 1971, p.80.

9. For example, Hicks, *The Comfort Women*, p.217.

List of Illustrations

Illustration 1: *Bilin Bilin*, photograph, N.D. Courtesy John Oxley Library, Brisbane. Reproduced with permission from Ysola Best, Yugambeh Museum, Language and Heritage Research Centre, Beenleigh, Queensland.

Illustration 2: William Strutt, *Richmond Paddock — Black Troopers Quarters Melbourne*, 1851, pencil & wash, 10.2 x 15.3 cm, courtesy Dixson Galleries, State Library of New South Wales.

Illustration 3: William Strutt, *Portrait of Charles Never*, 1851, pencil drawing, courtesy La Trobe Collection, State Library of Victoria.

Illustration 4: William Strutt, *Black Troopers Escorting a Prisoner from Ballarat to Melbourne, 1851*, pencil and wash drawing, courtesy La Trobe Collection, State Library of Victoria.

Illustration 5: Cover of *Headhunters of the Coral Sea*, artist Walter Stackpool, by Ion L. Idriess, 1940, Angus and Robertson, Sydney, courtesy HarperCollins.

Illustration 6: Cover of *The Wild White Man of Badu,* by Ion L. Idriess, 1950, Angus and Robertson, Sydney, courtesy HarperCollins.

Illustration 7: Postcard of Cataract Gorge, Launceston, 1910. Courtesy La Trobe Picture Collection, State Library of Victoria.

Illustration 8: Handkerchiefs distributed by the 1846 expedition led by James Warman and Christian De Villiers to locate the White Woman of Gippsland. These were illustrated and bore a message in English and Gaelic; it was widely believed the white captive was of Scottish origin. From the White Woman of Gippsland Collection, MS 10720, Box 286/6, Australian Manuscripts Collection, State Library of Victoria.

Illustration 9: Filipino nationals on display, still from Marlon Fuentes, *Bontoc Eulogy*, 1996.

Illustration 10: Marlon Fuentes searching for the remains of his grandfather Marcod, still from Marlon Fuentes, *Bontoc Eulogy*, 1996.

Illustration 11: Esther Smith and John Truett at the Fair in the closing sequence of Vincente Minnelli's *Meet Me In St Louis*, 1944, courtesy Film Stills Archive, The Museum Of Modern Art, New York.

Illustration 12: Poster from Charles Chauvel's *Jedda*, 1955. Courtesy Susanne Carlsson and the H. C. McIntyre Trust, c/- Curtis Brown (Aust) Pty Ltd., Sydney, ScreenSound Australia.

Notes on the contributors

The editors

BARBARA CREED is the author of *The Monstrous Feminine: film, feminism, psychoanalysis* (Routledge 1993). She has written on film and popular culture for a range of journals including *Screen, New Formations, Camera Obscura* and the *Journal of Postcolonial Studies*. She is Associate Professor and Head of the Cinema Studies program in the School of Fine Arts, Classical Studies and Archaeology at the University of Melbourne.

JEANETTE HOORN is the author of *The Lycett Album: Aboriginal life and scenery* (Australian National University Press, 1990) and the editor of *Strange Women: studies in art and gender* (Melbourne University Press, 1994) and has written on Australian art, film and popular culture in journals such as *Third Text, Photofile* and *Art and Australia*. She teaches in the Cinema Studies program in the School of Fine Arts, Classical Studies and Archaeology at the University of Melbourne.

Foreword

PETER HULME is Professor of Literature at the University of Essex. He is the author of *Colonial Encounters: Europe and the native Caribbean, 1492–1797* (Routledge 1986) and of *Remnants of Conquest: the island Caribs and their visitors, 1877–1998* (Oxford Universty Press, 2000). He has co-edited a number of books, including (with Francis Barker and Margaret Iversen) *Colonial Discourse/Postcolonial Theory* (Manchester University Press, 1994) and *Cannibalism and the Colonial World* (Cambridge University Press, 1998), and (with William H. Sherman) *'The Tempest' and its Travels* (Reaktion Books 2000).

Contributors

JULIE E. CARR is a graduate scholar working in Australian literature at La Trobe University, Melbourne. She is currently completing a book entitled *The White Woman of Gipps Land: In Pursuit of the Legend*, Melbourne University Press, Carlton, 2001.

KATE DARIAN-SMITH is Director of the Australian Centre at the University of Melbourne. She has written widely in the field of Australian colonial history and is the editor of a book, with Roslyn Poignant and Kay Schaffer, entitled *Captured Lives: Australian captivity narratives* (University of London 1993).

ROBERT DIXON is Professor of English at the University of Southern Queensland in Toowoomba. He has published widely in Australian literature, post-colonial studies and Australian art history. His book *Writing the Colonial Adventure* (Cambridge University Press 1995) has been described by Graeme Turner as 'a major contribution to Australian literary and cultural studies' and by Elizabeth Webby as 'a landmark book, an exemplary work'.

FREDA FREIBERG is a film historian, lecturer and critic specialising in Japanese and Australian cinema. She is the author of *Women in Mizoguchi's Films* (1981) and co-editor (with Annette Blonski and Barbara Creed) of *Don't Shoot Darling! Women's Independent Filmmaking in Australia* (1987). She is a contributor to *The Australian Screen* (1989), *World War 2, Film and History* (1996) and *The Oxford Guide to Film Studies* (1998).

CHRIS HEALY is a Senior Lecturer in Cultural Studies and the Convenor of the Interdepartmental Program in Cultural Studies at the University of Melbourne, where he has worked since 1992. His book, *From the Ruins of Colonialism: history as social memory* (Cambridge University Press, 1997) was short-listed for the 1988 Gleebooks Prize in the NSW Premier's Literary Awards. He has written widely on history, popular memory and contemporary culture.

YVES LE FUR is a Senior Curator of Oceanic art at the Musée National des Arts d'Afrique et d'Océanie, Paris. In 1989 he completed his Ph.D in the History of Art, at the Sorbonne in Paris. He has since published widely in the field of oceanic art and anthropology.

PAUL LYONS is Associate Professor of English at the University of Hawai'i-Manoa, where he specialises in American literatures. His contribution to this book is part of a manuscript in progress entitled 'Where Cannibalism has Been, Tourism Will Be'. He has published in the *Arizona Quarterly*, *Esq: a journal of the American renaissance* and *Boundary 2*.

Mary Mackay teaches in the Fine Arts program at the Power Institute, University of Sydney, and is a writer and commentator on Australian colonial art and heritage issues. She has published widely on nineteenth-century Australian art and is currently completing a book on discourses surrounding the sublime in Australian art and writing.

Susan K. Martin is Senior Lecturer in English at La Trobe University, Melbourne. She has published broadly in the field of colonial women's fiction and feminist cultural studies. She has also written in the area of colonial race relations and is currently writing a history of women's gardening in Australia.

Gananath Obeyesekere is Professor of Anthropology at Princeton University. He is the author of a number of prestigious books and articles on history, anthropology and psychoanalysis in the Pacific and in the Indian subcontinent. His most celebrated book, *The Apotheosis of Captain Cook: European Mythmaking in the Pacific* (Princeton University Press 1992) has received great attention worldwide in relation to the book's critique of humanist histories of the voyages of Captain Cook.

Paul Turnbull is Associate Professor of History in the School of Humanities at James Cook University. He is also a Senior Research Fellow of the Centre for Cross-Cultural Research at the Australian National University, where he is Director of the South Seas Digital Library Project. He has written widely on Enlightenment anthropology and the history of racial thought in nineteenth-century Australia.

Index